POLITICS
IN SOUTH AFRICA
FROM MANDELA
TO MBEKI

Tom Lodge

D0916092

DAVID PHILIP
CAPE TOWN

JAMES CURREY
OXFORD

For Guy, Kim & Carla

Published 2002 in southern Africa by
David Philip, an imprint of New Africa Books (Pty) Ltd
99 Garfield Road
Kenilworth, Cape Town

Published 2003 in the United States of America by
Indiana University Press
601 North Morton Street
Bloomington, Indiana 47404-3797

Published 2003 in the United Kingdom by
James Currey Ltd
73 Botley Road
Oxford OX2 0BS

ISBN 0-86486-505-8 (David Philip)
ISBN 0-253-21587-0 (Indiana University Press)
ISBN 0-85255-870-8 (James Currey)

British Library Cataloguing in Publication Data
Lodge, Tom
Politics in South Africa: from Mandela to Mbeki. – 2nd ed.
1. South Africa – Politics and government – 1994–
I. Title II. South African politics since 1994
320.9'68'09049

ISBN 0-85255-870-8

Library of Congress Cataloging in Publication Data available on request

Printed in South Africa by Creda Communications

CONTENTS

ACKNOWLEDGEMENTS

An earlier and much shorter version of this book appeared in 1999 under a different title. In revising this text for a second edition I have accumulated new debts. I am especially grateful to my colleague Philip Frankel for allowing me access to his research findings on local government. Brian Culross made copies for me of the ACNielsen reports on market research concerning the Truth and Reconciliation Commission. Wendy Orr provided useful insights into the Commission's operations. A number of officials and elected representatives from the Democratic Alliance were very helpful in replying to my questions about ward committees; they include Mike Moriarty, Malcolm Lennox, Lorraine Hatch and Mariana Seyffert. I am grateful to Ashley Green of the South African Civil Society Observer Coalition for permission to cite their reports on the 2000 local government elections. Funding from the Swedish International Development Agency supported the research on social capital cited in Chapter 10.

Tom Lodge

PROLOGUE

NELSON MANDELA: POLITICAL SAINT IN A NEW DEMOCRACY

Nelson Mandela's first biographer, Mary Benson, at the beginning of her book, poses this question: 'How is it that a man imprisoned for more than twenty-three years ... has become the embodiment of the struggle for liberation ... and is the vital symbol of a new society?'[1] Biography itself can supply only part of the answer. Usually the processes that lead to certain men or women becoming venerated in popular political culture extend well beyond the concerns that inform the analysis of a particular life. Even so, biography represents an obvious starting point in the investigation of iconographies. This is especially true in the case of Nelson Mandela, whose public life features so conspicuously the deliberate construction of emblematic attributes by himself and others.

To date, Mandela's own testimony supplies the most comprehensive biographical portrait of Nelson Mandela the man.[2] *Long Walk to Freedom* is not quite autobiography, though. Part of the text is based on a manuscript written in prison in 1977. The rest is assembled from interviews conducted in 1994 by an American journalist, Richard Stengel. Since its publication, an illustrated coffee-table edition as well as an abridged edition in basic English has appeared – pointers to the heterodox social character of Mandela's devotees. Notwithstanding the participation of his ghost writer, it is a safe assumption that the book's 800-odd pages are a faithful reflection of Mandela's own conception of his life and personality. In Stengel's words, they are a mirror 'of the proud and graceful persona Mr Mandela has crafted for himself'.[3]

Even so, Mandela's autobiography reveals a complicated man. 'Nurture, rather than nature, is the primary moulder of personality,' Mandela maintains. In his case, nurture included a childhood shaped by an inherited sense of destiny, 'groomed like my father before me, to counsel the rulers of the tribe'. Despite his father's death, as a boy Mandela 'defined [him]self' through him. Brought up under the guardianship of the Thembu regent, he acquired knowledge 'like all Xhosa children through observation, through imitation and emulation', developing 'notions of leadership' by watching the regent in his court. Here he found 'democracy in its purest form', a democracy in which 'everyone was heard, equal in their worth as citizens', in which meetings would continue until the attainment of consensus and in which 'majority rule was a foreign notion'. Only at the end of the meeting would the regent speak. 'As a leader,' Mandela claims at this point in his narrative, 'I have always followed the principles I first saw demonstrated by the regent at the great place.' 'A leader is like a shepherd', nudging and prodding his flock before him. Mandela's birth name is Rolihlahla – he was only named Nelson later, on his first day at mission school – and Rolihlahla means 'trouble-maker' or, more literally, 'one who pulls branches off a tree'. Mandela's relation-ship with 'tradition' is by no means straightforward.

Today, Mandela likes his friends and political associates to call him by his clan name, 'Madiba', a name signifying both the intimacy of kinship and the respect of ascribed status. The name has become popularised in the South African press. Certainly, he continues to be attracted to what he perceives to be traditional notions of leadership and community but, as his history demonstrates, in his later career he was to exercise a completely different style of leadership – one in which personal initiatives had to usurp the imperative for consensus.

'Sometimes one must go public with an idea to nudge a reluctant organisation in the direction you want it to go,' he observed with reference to his unauthorised public statement in 1961 that the days of non-violent struggle were over. Or, as he explains when discussing his decision to begin negotiations with the apartheid government from prison, 'there are times when a leader must move ahead of the flock.' And though it is not quoted in his autobiography, Mandela's famous remark at a later stage of negotiations on his faith in the 'ordinary democracy' of majority rule suggests that his understanding of African traditions supplies only one element, though an important one, in his political make-up.[4]

Traditions can be useful – Mandela's manipulation of custom suggests a shrewdly instrumental recognition of their role – but his narrative acknowledges that the past is another country. Upon his return to his Transkeian birthplace after his release from prison he finds a landscape littered with plastic bags and a community in which pride and self-worth 'seemed to have vanished'. His view of tradition is underlined in his discussion of his relationship with the new gener-ation of Black Consciousness activists who appeared on Robben Island from 1974; he acknowledges the danger of clinging to ideas which 'had become frozen in time'. Mandela's empathy with rebellious youth is a frequent theme in his public utterances. In an angry speech delivered to a group of about a thousand amakhosi [traditional leaders] and indunas in KwaZulu-Natal in 1996, Mandela reprimanded local chiefs who had encouraged political violence, warning them that 'they would be left behind by the real leaders emerging from the youth of the country'.[5] A few months before the 1994 general elections he created a furore by suggesting that the franchise should be extended to 14-year-olds, a proposal which his embarrassed ANC colleagues hurriedly repudiated.

The tensions between different facets of Mandela's personality remain un-resolved in his autobiography. They are evident in the different voices that tell his story. One voice is magisterial and statesmanlike, the voice that emphasises the central themes of racial reconciliation and man's essential goodness ('all men have a core of decency') which run through the text. Another voice is the less measured one that expresses the anguish of personal loss, experiences which are rendered most poignantly in the powerful recurrent image of a child putting on the clothing of his dead or absent father. This is a voice that can subvert the impersonal, heroic, collective political emotions with which he clothes his public self. Of the day of the presidential inauguration he remarks, 'I felt that day, as I have on so many others, that I was simply the sum of all those African patriots who had gone before me.' But as he concedes one page later, 'every man has twin obligations' and in serving his people he was prevented from fulfilling his roles as 'a son, a brother, a father and a husband'. The pain that arises from this recognition is generally controlled and suppressed in the book. Indeed, learning to control and conceal pain and its accompaniment, fear, is one of the defining qualities of manhood he learns as a child. Nowhere is this more evident than in the curious mixture of bureaucratic rationality and private tribute in his choice of words to announce his separation from his wife, 'Comrade Nomzamo'.

The public emotions to which Mandela professes are carefully managed. The political Mandela is at least in part the product of artifice. The third section of *Long Walk to Freedom* is entitled 'The birth of a freedom fighter', and its occasional deliberate use of the third person – 'it is important for a freedom fighter to remain in touch with his own roots' – is a significant indication of Mandela's own consciousness of inventing a public identity and acting out an heroic role. There are other kinds of acting, too. At several points in the narrative Mandela assumes disguises and false identities. Clothing, costume and style are indispensable components in the different personas Mandela assumes. This was particularly obvious in his choice of wearing a leopard skin kaross during his first appearance in court after his arrest in 1962. 'I had chosen traditional Xhosa dress to emphasise the symbolism that I was a black African walking into a white man's court … I felt myself to be the embodiment of African nationalism.'

Later, he refers to prison as 'a different and smaller arena' compared to the courtroom, 'an arena in which the only audience was ourselves and our oppressors'. This awareness of an audience and his belief in historical destiny are both indispensable accomplices in Mandela's own crafting of his exemplary life. The links between political leadership and theatrical performance are emphasised in a reference to his role as Creon in Sophocles' *Antigone*. Significantly, several commentaries have used the metaphors of masks and masking in their analysis of Mandela's personality.[6] Mandela himself used these to describe the way in which he concealed his anguished longing for his family in prison.[7]

Mandela has an ambivalent attitude to his heroic status, recognising the merits of the ANC personalising the cause in the campaign for his release, but often affecting disdain for 'the exaltation of the president, and denigration of other ANC leaders [which] constitutes praise which I do not accept'.[8] In his speech after his release, as he suggests in his autobiography, '[I] wanted first of all to tell the people that I was not a messiah, but an ordinary man who had become a leader because of extraordinary circumstances'. The address is carefully written in the idiom of the ANC's conventions of collective leadership,[9] preceded by a long series of salutes to its various constituencies and organisational 'formations'.[10]

However, the ANC's development during Mandela's political life allowed plenty of scope for the influence of strong prophetic personalities. When Mandela joined the African National Congress in 1942, the organisation had only recently emerged from a decade of torpor. Its small following was concentrated in three cities. From its foundation in 1912 its programme had only occasionally extended beyond an annual convention of African gentry and notables. With the exception of a few communists, most of its leadership had at best been amateur politicians. Mandela and his fellow ANC Youth Leaguers were the first substantial cohort of African middle-class professionals to make political activism the central focus of their lives – hence their extraordinarily rapid ascent within a movement whose following ballooned as a result. From his first hesitant association with the organisation shortly after his arrival in Johannesburg, in just ten years Mandela emerged as its second-ranking leader.

The ANC's switch to militant forms of mass protest in the 1950s coincided with the development of a popular press directed at African readers. From the time of his appointment as 'National Volunteer-in-chief' in the Defiance Campaign of 1952 – a civil disobedience programme which emphasised the sacrificial role of inspirational leadership – Mandela became one of South Africa's first black media personalities. In the decade of mobilisation politics that followed, ANC leaders became increasingly aware of the potentialities of newspaper celebrity.[11] Mandela himself tells how in the first months of 1961, while he was hiding from the police and undertaking preparations for a national strike, his 'outlaw existence caught the imagination of the press'. Journalists called him the 'Black Pimpernel' and he would foster 'the mythology ... by taking a pocketful of tickeys [threepenny coins] and phoning individual newspaper reporters from telephone boxes and relaying stories of what we were planning or the ineptitude of the police'. Some of the myths generated during this period have enjoyed a long currency. In her biography of Winnie Mandela, Nancy Harrison describes Mandela's dramatic appearance at the 'all-in conference' in Pietermaritzburg in March 1961 and reproduces the populist legend that he made his speech barefoot, as a man of the people. Unfortunately, the photograph taken of this occasion confirms that he was wearing well-polished shoes to match his characteristically elegant three-piece tweed suit.[12]

In the early 1960s there was a particular need for the ANC to develop an heroic pantheon of leaders. On the African continent its exiled representatives were encountering strong opposition from its offshoot rival, the Pan Africanist Congress, which had been rather more successful in assuming an 'authentic' African identity roughly comparable to the popular nationalist movements presided over by the charismatic and messianic leaders who were spearheading African decolonisation at that time. When the Free Mandela Committee was established at the time of Mandela's 1962 trial, its organisers distributed a lapel button bearing a portrait of the imprisoned leader wrapped in the West African toga then favoured by the continent's emergent rulers.

The ultimate success of such efforts to embody the ANC's cause in a saga of individual heroism probably exceeded all expectations among ANC strategists in the early 1960s. In the 27 years of his confinement, Nelson Mandela accumulated honorary degrees, freedoms of cities and awards from governments. In 1988 admirers in Holland alone swamped the South African prison service with some 170 000 letters and birthday cards.[13] In the same year, 250 000 people assembled in London's Hyde Park at the conclusion of the Free Mandela March to listen to some thirty minutes of readings from Mandela's correspondence with his wife.[14] His face appeared on postage stamps and official sculpture, and his deeds – mythical and real – were celebrated at rock concerts.

By the 1980s, Nelson Mandela could with justification claim to be 'the world's most famous political prisoner'.[15] Some of this fame arose from the popular attention which his own actions commanded. At the time of his well-publicised court appearances his story exemplified old-fashioned virtues: honour, courage and chivalry. The explanation of this extraordinary international celebrity status cannot, though, be confined to Mandela's actions or the ANC's own efforts to foster cults of charismatic leadership, important as they were. Such endeavours were given ample assistance by the peculiar moral appeal of South African liberation and its resonance in the international politics of anti-racism and decolonisation; the emergence of a transnational anti-apartheid 'new social movement'; Mandela's cultural adaptability as a modern folk hero; and the immortality conferred upon him by seclusion.

The internationalisation of the South African political conflict can clearly be attributed to the existence of a uniquely institutionalised system of racism in a relatively important and accessible country and in a world climate shaped by the post-war reaction against Nazism and colonialism. Anti-apartheid as a social movement drew its strength from the same forces that helped to engender a range of new political identities in mature industrial societies. But Mandela's personal qualities, which made him especially susceptible to international cult status, and the effects of his compelled isolation from everyday life deserve more extended commentary.

'I confess to being something of an anglophile,' Mandela tells us in his autobiography. The passage continues, 'When I thought of Western democracy and freedom, I thought of the British parliamentary system. In so many ways, the very model of the gentleman for me was an Englishman ... While I abhorred the notion of British imperialism, I never rejected the trappings of British style and manners.' On the eve of his departure from Johannesburg on a journey to address members of both Houses of Parliament at Westminster in 1993, he told journalists: 'I have not discarded the influence which Britain and British influence and culture exercised on us.'[16] As Richard Stengel has noticed, 'to him, the British audience is more important than either the American or the European'.[17] Relatively few third-world insurgencies managed to combine in their leaderships such an effective mixture of guerrilla glamour and reassuring metropolitan respectability.

Like many other ANC leaders of his generation, Mandela's Anglo-Methodist schooling and his liberal literary education equipped him with a familiarity with Anglo-American culture and a capacity, consciously or otherwise, to invoke its social codes. A particularly telling example of this attribute in his personality and life history is the tragic story of his second marriage. (Significantly, one of his first acts of rebellion as a young man had been to reject a customary union arranged by his guardian.) During his imprisonment, his beautiful and personable second wife, Winnie, played a substantial role in ensuring the durability of his political authority. Notwithstanding such gestures to African tradition as the payment of lobola, Nelson and Winnie Mandela's correspondence with each other employs the informal egalitarian idioms and expresses the sexual intimacies of modern Western domestic life. Mandela's very public subscription to an idyll of romantic love was a vital element in the narratives directed at Western audiences.[18] More generally, his role and that of the ANC as representatives of an industrialised urban community made them culturally intelligible, particularly in Europe and North America. Their credibility was supported by the appearance in the 1950s of an unusually talented generation of black South African writers who began to find a significant readership outside South Africa.[19]

Mandela's incarceration and the official ban in South Africa on the publication of his words and portraits, as well as the authorities' refusal to allow photographs showing him in prison, encouraged public narratives that were shaped by the words and images available from the struggle epic, which stretched from the Defiance Campaign to the Rivonia Trial. A few timeless and ageless texts and pictures, as Rob Nixon perceptively noted, kept 'circulating in a heraldic fashion perfect for the needs of an international political movement'.[20] The imprisonment and isolation from public view kept the narrative and the accompanying images pristine, investing them with the glamour of martyrdom but also reinforcing the apocalyptic possibility of a second coming. Sipho Sepamla, a poet of the 1980s activist generation, powerfully expresses this vision of an assertive, youthful Mandela striding his way out of prison, fist raised high in the straight-armed black power salute:

I need today oh so very badly
Nelson Mandela
Out of the prison gates
to walk broad-shouldered – among counsel
down Commissioner
up West Street
and lead us away from the shadow
of impotent word weavers
his clenched fist hoisted higher than hope
for all to see and follow.[21]

Government strategists told an American researcher at the beginning of the 1980s that they were aware that Mandela's removal from the political stage freed him from the requirement 'to make hard, human decisions'.[22] 'Mandela is not so much a political figure as a mythical one. For this reason,' opined Professor Willie Breytenbach, a key government adviser in the 1980s, 'I believe that if he should be released, the key problem would be surviving long enough to play any role at all.'[23] Credo Mutwa, a self-professed 'High Witchdoctor' and an authority on indigenous culture much favoured by the old South African authorities, predicted in 1986 that Mandela's release would replace a revered hero-saviour with 'a spent force like an arrow which has spent its passion'.[24]

Public opinion polling after the Soweto uprisings in 1976 consistently suggested that Mandela's personal following exceeded that of the ANC.[25] This is indicative of the extent to which the alluring enigmas created by his absence from active politics had helped to transform the guerrilla convict into a patriotic icon. When Chief Mangosuthu Buthelezi's differences with the ANC became public, he attempted to demonstrate his membership of a more legitimate patriotic community by publishing his private correspondence with Mandela.[26] And though freedom did not bring all the dividends his captors may have hoped for, it certainly detracted from the more millenarian dimensions of the myth.

During the protracted negotiations that followed Mandela's release in February 1990, some South African urban legends inverted the logic of the second coming to explain why freedom was taking so long to arrive. A young black truck driver informed Jeremy Cronin, a South African Communist Party (SACP) leader, that the real Nelson Mandela was killed in prison. 'Today's Mandela is a lookalike. He was trained for years by the Boers and finally presented to the public in 1990. The mission of this lookalike is to pretend to be against the system. But in reality he is working for it.'[27]

Mandela's captivity enhanced the omnibus appeal of his authority. Mandela biographies and hagiographies project quite different understandings of his personal greatness and its broader social meanings. Such projections have reflected differing imperatives of various constituencies within the broad movement he represented during his imprisonment as well as its changing ideological predispositions. They also testify to the ways in which his life has become emblematic for people quite separate from the ANC's community and even outside South Africa.

Mary Benson, Mandela's first biographer, was secretary to the Treason Trial Defence Fund in the 1950s and close to many of the events she describes. In 1963, by which time she was living in London, she wrote a richly textured popular history of the ANC. Her Mandela biography was first published in 1980 as a volume in the 'PanAf Great Lives' series.[28] A second, updated edition appeared in 1986.[29] Limited by its author's restricted access to sources, Benson's book concerns itself mainly with Mandela's political career, at least until his first meeting with Winnie. (Evelyn, his first wife, receives only the most perfunctory of references.) The opening chapter supplies a bare outline of Mandela's genealogy, childhood and education. For Benson, the important developments in the story begin after his arrival in Johannesburg. At this point, she believes, he had put his rural upbringing firmly behind him. His rejection of his guardian's plans for an arranged marriage reflected a deeper political impulse: 'By this time he had realised he was being prepared for chieftainship and he had made up his mind never to rule over an oppressed people.' 'My guardian was no democrat,' Mandela had told Mary Benson many years earlier when she interviewed him, 'he did not think it worthwhile to consult me about a wife.'

This view of Mandela as a rebel against tradition was widely shared. In 1988 *New Nation*, a weekly paper in Johannesburg edited by ANC sympathisers, referred to Mandela as 'by birth a Xhosa chief who at a young age resisted all tribal ties'.[30] Most of Benson's biography comprises a chronology of public events and references to Mandela's contribution to these. Its treatment is very general and its focus is mainly on the organisation, not the man. Long extracts from Mandela's polemical writings and his trial addresses occupy a large portion of Benson's text. They contribute to reinforcing a rather impersonal tribute with the accent on Mandela's identity as a modern liberal democratic politician. This is the identity that was accentuated in those public commemorations of Mandela that were directed at Europeans and North Americans. In one volume of 'literary homage', Jacques Derrida writes of Mandela as the ultimate apostle and interpreter of the rational legal traditions associated with the Western Enlightenment.[31]

A fuller version of Mandela's political testament, a collection of his speeches and writings, was published in London in 1965 in the Heinemann 'African Writers' series, edited by Ruth First, with an introduction by Oliver Tambo. In her foreword to the second edition in 1973, First compares the author to the then fashionable American black power heroes George Jackson, Soledad Brother and Angela Davis. A grainy photograph of Mandela visiting an Algerian military facility adds visual confirmation to First's presentation of the ANC's 'underground political commander' as the personification of 'revolutionary power'.[32] The 'light editing' of the original material included the excision of a passage describing the benefits the Freedom Charter – a programme of rights adopted by the ANC and its allies in 1955 – would bring to a nascent African bourgeoisie, from an article first published in 1956.

However, even without Ruth First's editorial tidying, Mandela's 1950s writings suggest a more intellectually radical figure than the pragmatic reformist projected in British and American analyses of the ANC's leadership. Mandela initially gained his political experience from his casual attendance at night schools organised by the SACP. Although he subsequently opposed communist influence within the ANC for a while, he retained an affinity with the ideas of the left. In a speech delivered to the ANC Youth League in 1951, he reminded his listeners never to forget 'the advance guard of American penetration … the infinitely more dangerous enemy sustaining all those with loans, capital and arms'. Given the growing affinity between 'English, Jewish and Afrikaner financial and industrial interests' it was quite likely that all these 'found the fascist policy of [South African prime minister] Malan suitable'. 'The possibility of a liberal capitalist democracy in South Africa is extremely nil.' South Africa was rapidly becoming 'an openly fascist state', the creation of 'monopoly capitalism gone mad'. Political opposition required the talents 'of a professional revolutionary'.

Certainly, such rhetoric incorporated many of the sentiments which were then normal in anti-colonialist or anti-imperialist discourses, but Mandela's deployment of them is strikingly logical and disciplined. His often reprinted articles, first published in the left-wing journal *Liberation*, are especially impressive with their carefully structured and conceptually systematic arguments. This is particularly evident in his well-known characterisation of the Freedom Charter as 'by no means a blueprint for a socialist state' but rather 'a programme for the unification of certain classes' engaged in 'a democratic struggle' of 'various classes and political groupings'. The language is remarkable as much for its cerebral dispassion as for its sociological sophistication.

During the 1980s both the exiled ANC and internal political groups that positioned themselves within the Congress camp looked forward to a post apartheid 'National Democracy' in which 'monopoly capital' would be displaced, a transitional stage that would proceed to become a fully socialised society.[33] In this context, fresh meaning was given to Mandela's life history. For example, after the National Union of Mineworkers had elected Mandela as its honorary life president, 'work was done to inform workers of Mandela's history and the struggles he waged as a mineworker in Crown Mines',[34] according to one of its spokespeople. While Mandela did stay at Crown Mines for a very short period after his arrival in Johannesburg, he managed to secure the relatively privileged post of compound policeman by deploying his extensive family connections, until word arrived from the regent's court in the Transkei that he should be sent home. According to Mandela in his autobiography, he helped trade unionists to mobilise mining compounds during the 1946 mineworkers' strike.

Fatima Meer's 'authorised' tribute to Nelson Mandela on the occasion of his seventieth birthday – initially its first South African edition was effusively sub-titled *Rolihlahla We Love You*[35] – reflects a rather different set of social priorities and political imperatives from the earlier depictions of a liberal democrat, revolutionary intellectual and working-class hero. Fatima Meer herself is a member of an important Indian political family within the Congress movement, and her book was written from the perspective of a social elite whose moral authority experienced growing challenge in the insurrectionary climate of the 1980s. This volume, according to Winnie Mandela,[36] who supplied a supportive preface, is the 'real family biography'.

This is true in two senses. Firstly, the portrayal is as much of Mandela the private man as it is about him as a public figure. It describes the unhappy course of his first marriage and is openly honest about Mandela's contribution to its breakdown ('Nelson was extremely attractive to women and he was easily attracted to them'). It takes as a central theme the preoccupations of its protagonist as a father and head of 'a large household of dependants'. Secondly, it also deals with family as lineage, succession, dynasty and inherited greatness. For this book is about a royal leader, the descendant of kings who 'ruled all the Aba Thembu at a time when the land belonged to them and they were free'. It is about a man who learnt his patrimonial history in 'silent veneration' at the feet of his elders and is inspired with a lifelong mission to recapture for all South Africans 'the *ubuntu* [humanity] of the African kings'. Without a father from the age of ten, he was brought up by 'a member of our clan' for whom 'according to our custom I was his child and his responsibility'.

His second, more successful marriage was to another representative of aristocratic lineage, to the daughter of a line of 'marauding chieftains'. Winnie's upbringing owed much to the influence of her grandmother, a reluctant convert to Christianity. From her, she learnt 'things that my mother had taken care to see I'd never learn'. 'She took me into the ways of our ancestors, she put the skins and beads that had been hers when she was a young girl on me and taught me to sing and dance. I learnt to milk cows and to ride horses and to cook mealie porridge, mealie with meat, mealie with vegetables, and I learnt to make *umphokoqo* the way Makhulu made it.'

In Fatima Meer's book, it is this world that defines the Mandelas' moral centre. For although he learns to 'manage' and 'integrate' Johannesburg 'from the standpoint of Orlando', the city was never home. He remained 'intensely rural', and 'it was the first half of his life that really mattered when it came to roots'. Notwithstanding his wider political and social loyalties, 'there were deep-rooted historical identities that could not be denied ... The first experience of human solidarity ... in the family, in the clan, in the tribe ... constituted the real identities, the nurseries for larger solidarities'. His leadership is patrician and inborn. He is gifted with powers of 'breathtaking oratory', compassion 'for the poor' and, above all, the social empathy that enables him to assume a 'rough and ready disguise' and move unrecognised in the crowd ('it felt good to be one of the people').

His social universe is one that is organic, in which, to cite his early mentor, Anton Lembede, 'individual parts exist merely as interdependent aspects of one whole'. Political conflicts in this world can be intensely personal, involving as they do betrayals between kinsfolk, which recur dynastically. 'Sabata's great-grandfather ... had been betrayed by his brother Sabata; now the grandson, K. D. Matanzima, was betraying Sabata and would eventually depose him. They were all Madibas, and should have stayed together at all times; but Madiba was split from Madiba.' Authority is also personal: in 1960 at his Orlando home, Nelson received deputations of Thembu and Mpondo tribesmen, who reported on the Mandelas' errant kinsfolk terrorising an 'illiterate region ... not deemed worthy of literate recording'. For Mandela can listen to them with the sympathy and insight of a personality 'whose instincts were still rooted in rural politics'.

In this depiction of a rural notable and communal patriarch presiding over an organic, interdependent society there seems little scope for either the liberal or the 'national democratic' conceptions of democracy that helped to shape the earlier discourses about Mandela. Neither is there much room for the popular sovereignty favoured by modern trade unions and civic organisations in the obeisance to the messianic leader which was prescribed by spokespeople for the Release Mandela Campaign (RMC) during the 1980s. For Aubrey Mokoena, the RMC's Transvaal chairman, Mandela was 'the pivotal factor in the struggle for liberation. He has the stature and the charisma which derives from his contribution to the struggle.'[37] Mokoena's language was not atypical. Mewa Ramgobin told his audience at a Soweto RMC meeting in July 1984, 'I want to make bold and say in clear language that the human race must remain grateful, that the human race must go down on its knees and say thank you for the gifts it has been endowed with in the lives of the Nelson Mandelas of this country.'[38]

Peter Mokaba, at the time president of the South African Youth Congress, chaired the rally held in a Soweto stadium on 24 February 1990 to celebrate Mandela's release. He had this to say: 'Comrade President, here are your people, gathered to pay tribute to their messiah, their saviour whom the apartheid regime failed dismally to silence. These are the comrades and the combatants that fought tooth and nail in the wilderness ... they toiled in the valley of darkness, and now that their messiah and saviour is released, they want to be shown the way to freedom.'[39]

The attribution of redemptive qualities of leadership to Mandela reached its apogee during his visit to the United States in June 1990, four months after his release. While the ANC had intended it as a fundraising trip – in this respect it was quite successful, with donations totalling $7 million – the occasion served quite different needs for his African American hosts as well as for many people in his various audiences. As a New York newspaper report put it, 'the Mandela visit has become perhaps the largest and most vivid symbol that after many years on the edges of New York City power and politics, the black community has arrived'.[40] For *The Village Voice*'s Harlem correspondent, 'the visit of the freedom fighter positioned us, for a minute, in the center of world politics. It made us the first family. And gave us, again, an accessible past, so that the African part of the equation suddenly had a lot more sense.'[41] The notion of familyhood featured frequently in the comments recorded from spectators: 'We are all from Africa. This is like family. He's a symbol of who we are.'[42] There to welcome Mandela was the city's first black mayor, David Dinkins; there to organise his security was the city's second black police commissioner; and there to determine the events in his schedule were the legions of black community leaders in Brooklyn and Harlem 'who together with more than 500 black churches had turned New York's African Americans into the largest ethnic voting bloc in the city'.[43] So in an important respect, Mandela's American journey helped to consolidate the leadership credentials of an African American elite of municipal bosses, civil rights luminaries and show-business personalities.

Juxtaposed with the triumphalist language that accompanied Mandela's progress was the perception that the South African visitor supplied a missing moral dimension of authority, that his presence in America could rekindle hope in ghetto communities affected by social pathologies and political decay. Benjamin Chavis, the influential former director of the United Church of Christ Mission, captured this feeling eloquently: 'We have a new Jerusalem. When he gets back on the 'plane, we have to keep that fire alive and thank God that Mandela has lit a fire that was extinguished in the 1960s. I think you're going to see a lot of African Americans break out of the cycle of hopelessness we've had.'[44]

Veterans of the Civil Rights movement repeatedly confided to journalists their conviction that Mandela's coming 'had filled a void which had been left by the deaths of Dr Martin Luther King and Malcolm X'.[45] This was a widespread perception. While waiting for Mandela's arrival, schoolteacher Mark Reeves and his class spent 'all week studying Mr Mandela and relating him to Martin Luther King and the Civil Rights movement'.[46] New Yorkers 'turned him into an instant American celebrity, a civil rights leader they could call their own'.[47] Winnie Mandela's presence evoked similar emotions. Brushing aside the troubling controversies then surrounding her in South Africa, Julie Belafonte, one of the main organisers of the Mandela tour, told reporters: 'We don't know what happened over there … and in any case it's irrelevant in relation to the positive power she has displayed and the pressure she has been under. She's a wonderful role model for women.'[48]

Some 750 000 people lined the streets of New York to cheer Mandela's progress whilst in many other cities outside the eleven stops of his tour, programmes of festive events were arranged.[49] Taraja Samuel, an administrator in the New York education department, 'felt a blessing from God that I could be a part of this'.[50] Malcolm X's widow, Betty Shabazz, introduced Winnie Mandela to the congregation of Harlem's House of the Lord Church by saying: 'This sister's presence in our midst is enough. She shouldn't have to speak. To have gone through what she has gone through, and to see her so present, so composed! There must be a God. There's got to be a God.'[51] At a meeting in Bedford Stuyvesant, Brooklyn, *The Village Voice* correspondent watched the sun shine through 'his silver Afro hair like a halo … this is a truly religious experience, a man back from the dead to lead the living, and an authentic African queen'.[52] Even the more measured official rhetoric that accompanied the tour resonated with chiliastic expectation. In his welcoming address, David Dinkins likened Mandela to a modern-day Moses 'leading the people of South Africa out of enslavement at the hands of the pharaoh'.[53]

Mandela deftly tapped into the historical well-springs of the emotions that greeted him, with gracious acknowledgement of a pantheon of appropriate local heroes. Each of his speeches included a recitation of their names: Sojourner Truth, Paul Robeson, Rosa Parks, Marcus Garvey, Fannie Lou Hamer, Malcolm X and Harriet Tubman. But his self-deprecatory meditations on the evanescent quality of human genius – 'each shall, like a meteor, a mere brief passing moment in time and space, flit across the human stage'[54] – remained unheard. Despite his protestations that he was merely a representative of a greater collective entity, the ANC, any such professions of mortality were drowned in the clamour arising from the procession of an American hero embodying American dreams.

In the perceptions of white South Africans, no strangers to millennial political traditions,[55] the incarnation of Nelson Mandela as national hero has signified the possibility of personal and communal salvation or baptism in a new 'rainbow' patriotism. Warder James Gregory's memoir, *Goodbye Bafana*, celebrates in an ingenuous fashion 'a cleansing process, one of ridding the anger,'[56] which he experienced in his dealings with his famous prisoner. The book's title draws parallels between his relationship with Mandela and the lost innocence of a 'pre-apartheid' childhood friendship with a Zulu boy on his father's farm. As Mandela leaves prison, Gregory's mind 'returns to [his] boyhood and to the farm where [he] played with Bafana all those years ago'.[57]

In a less intrusive fashion than Gregory's exploitative text, many others personally seek to appropriate a portion of Mandela's aura and, in so doing, lay to rest old demons. 'The icon of the '90s is a picture of yourself with President Mandela … In homes where, during the apartheid era, the word "struggle" was used so loosely that it could mean your wife had broken a nail or the maid hadn't pitched, Mandela's benevolent face now gazes out of large silver frames placed on study desks. He watches you from wood-panelled libraries or from the walls of board-rooms. In these places the "Me and Mandela" factor works as a talisman against the past, pushing it out of sight and into the dark recesses of time.'[58] Not content with donations to the ANC and undertaking the reconstruction of Mandela's old primary school, Bill Venter, chairman of Altron (an electronics firm which became a major industrial company in the 1980s as a consequence of winning defence contracts), made the birthday poem he wrote for Nelson Mandela required reading for his employees, including it in a little red book, *Memos from the Chairman*, which was circulated to all staff. The poem reads:

> Your wisdom has woven a tapestry
> Much more lovely than any artist's hand
> With a vibrancy that only we can understand
> We, who are Africa's people
> And feel the heartbeat of this land.[59]

As the new 'father of the nation', Mandela can summon expressions of loyalty from the most unexpected sources. The conservative *Citizen* newspaper, rejoicing in South Africa's new-found international acceptability, noted 'the respect, almost awe' with which South Africa was now held, informing its readers that 'we take even greater pride in the recognition of President Mandela's stature in the world. He is a great man who towers above other leaders, both at home, in Africa, and abroad.'[60] The more traditionally liberal *Star* newspaper profitably tapped into a similar vein of sentiment when it filled a 'commercial feature' on 18 July 1994, Mandela's birthday, with congratulatory advertisements from businesses and other organisations.

Since his release, Nelson Mandela has undertaken a series of imaginative gestures of reconciliation and empathy with white South Africa. These have included his professed recognition of Afrikaans as a 'truly African language', a 'language of liberation and hope';[61] his appearance at the Rugby World Cup final dressed in a Springbok jersey and cap; presiding over corporate fundraising dinners on Robben Island; and, of course, a sequence of well-publicised social encounters with old adversaries, including Mrs Betsie Verwoerd (the wife of whose grandson represents the ANC in parliament) and his prosecutor at the Rivonia Trial, Dr Percy Yutar. This last event moved one Johannesburg journalist to refer to Mandela's 'superhuman forgiveness' more or less seriously as 'holy magnanimity', a phrase adapted from the concept of 'holy disbelief' that Eliezer Berkovits uses to describe the loss of faith in concentration camps.[62]

What have been the political effects of this canonisation of democratic South

Africa's first president? In the 1960s, charismatic heroes represented a central focus in the interpretation of African politics. David Apter described how the legitimacy of new institutions was both strengthened and weakened by Kwame Nkrumah's charismatic authority, a sacred authority which remained 'an important device by which political institutional transfer' was effected.[63] Certainly, Mandela's moral and political authority performs some of the positive functions assigned to charismatic authority by the analysts of political modernisation thirty years ago.

In a country in which liberal democratic institutions and procedures are not especially popular,[64] his identification with them may have enshrined them with a degree of legitimacy which otherwise they might have lacked. Mandela's moral endorsement of political compromise is generally perceived to have been indispensable in the success of South Africa's 'pacted' political transition. Transition theory, with its focus on the choices and decisions made by political elites, is especially receptive to 'Great Men' readings of history.[65] Within the domain of foreign policy, Mandela's personal appeal has enabled South Africa to elicit special treatment. As Paul Neifert, a USAID representative, lamented at a House of Representatives hearing: 'Our relationship with the new South Africa has become overly personal, substituting a reckless form of hero worship for a sober analysis of long-term national interest.'[66]

Mandela himself has made attempts to democratise his myth, to assert his secular authority over the more sacred dimensions of his appeal. In his speech on leaving prison he told his audience that he stood before them 'not as a prophet … but as a humble servant of you, the people'. In his autobiography he insists on his status as 'an ordinary man who became a leader because of extraordinary circumstances'. In this spirit during the ANC's election campaign, the organisation borrowed from American politics the device of a people's forum, in which members of the audience would direct questions at Mandela while standing on a podium so that they could confer with him as individuals, as equals, not as anonymous voices from the floor. In explaining the break-up of his marriage he observes that his wife 'married a man who soon left her; that man became a myth, and then that myth returned home and proved to be just a man after all'.

Although it is wise to be wary of courtiers' tributes to their master's humility[67] – these have been a frequent feature of modern autocracies – in Mandela's case his unwillingness to take his authority for granted is often very evident. He was 'never sure whether young people liked him or not', he confessed when announcing the donation of his Nobel Prize money to children's charities.[68] And he often tells interviewers an anecdote from a private visit he made to the Bahamas in October 1993. 'A couple approached him in the street and the man asked: – Aren't you Nelson Mandela? – I am often confused with that chap – was Mandela's mischievous response. Unconvinced, the man then whispered to his wife to inform her of their unexpected find. – What is he famous for? – his wife inquired in a hushed tone. Unsatisfied with her husband's inaudible response the woman asked Mandela outright – What are you famous for?' Mandela concludes the anecdote: 'I hope that when I step down no one is going to ask me: what are you famous for?'[69]

Perhaps it is Mandela's vulnerability as an 'ordinary man' that has done most to reduce the sacred dimension of his appeal. The Mandela divorce hearings prompted the publication of his wife's letters to her lover, Dali Mpofu, in which she reportedly referred to her husband with the dismissive diminutive 'Tata [father]'. When Mandela gave evidence in the trial, he told the court that this letter left him feeling 'the loneliest man'.[70]

At the beginning of 1996, in trying to prepare the ground for his successor, Mandela took the unusual step of publicly criticising 'the exaltation of the president, and denigration of other ANC leaders, [which] constitutes praise which I do not accept'.[71] Mandela frequently acknowledges his own mortality: 'I don't want a country like ours to be led by an octogenarian … I must step down while there are one or two people who admire me.'[72]

In all this modesty there is an ambiguity, though. His preference in many of his public statements for the impersonal 'we' rather than 'I' could be read as the testimony of democratic humility – in Jacques Derrida's phrase, the presentation of 'himself in his people'.[73] But another reading might suggest a different sense in which a leader perceives himself to be the totality of popular aspirations. The people's forums cited above did not just draw upon American electioneering. They also had a local historical resonance in the public assemblies in which chiefs customarily secured consensual popular sanction for decisions. Mandela's preoccupation with reconciliation may be just one facet of a deeper preoccupation with unity, and the politics of maintaining unity can be deeply authoritarian.

The admirable formal adherence of Mandela and his government to the tenets of liberal democracy – the ANC's respect for the independence of the Constitutional Court is an especially notable example of this – has quite a different discourse running alongside it. Black journalists who criticise the ANC, according to Mandela, 'have been co-opted by conservative elements to attack the democratic movement';[74] prominent individuals like Archbishop Desmond Tutu should not criticise the ANC publicly, as this 'created the impression of division within the movement';[75] and South African politicians should emulate the example of Zimbabwe in fostering the politics of unity. The mood such rhetoric evokes is at its ugliest when Mandela uses his personal authority to defend the misdemeanours of his subordinates. For example, there was thunderous applause from ANC benches in parliament following his defence of his instructions to the security guards who fired into an Inkatha demonstration outside the ANC's headquarters in Johannesburg.[76] The existence of such a discourse should surprise no one. In modern South Africa, messianic politics has been employed to demobilise a popular insurrection in one of the world's most unequal societies and, in such a context, the institutions of liberal democracy depend upon the protection afforded by highly authoritarian forms of charismatic authority.

Until his departure from public office in June 1999, Mandela's stature amongst South Africans remained undiminished, notwithstanding the wavering levels of public approval for his government and his political organisation which opinion polls discerned. Just before the 1999 general elections, public satisfaction with his 'performance' as president stood at 80 per cent. This feeling was shared across racial boundaries. In a poll conducted in November 1998, 59 per cent of white South Africans believed Mandela 'was doing his job well', despite the general antipathy to the ANC most whites shared.[77] Even after his retirement, South Africans continued to invest their hopes for national reconstruction in Mandela's iconic status. A proposal to mint 'Mandelarands' in place of Krugerrands was motivated by the belief that such a venture would harness the savings of African Americans in the cause of restoring the fortunes of the gold-mining industry.[78]

The legends and narratives associated with Mandela's life undergo constant mutation. One important contributor to this process is his former wife, Winnie Madikizela-Mandela, as she now prefers to be called. In March 1999, she ceremonially presented her wedding ring to 13-year-old Candice Erasmus, the daughter of a retired security policeman who once spied on her and who had recently joined the Madikizela-Mandela household. This gesture, she said, was a 'symbol of reconciliation' with her former tormentors, but the occasion also marked the opening of a rhetorical offensive against her ex-husband. He was guilty, she informed journalists, 'of using Apartheid legislation which denied property rights to African women to eject Winnie and her daughters' from the home they once shared. Mrs Mandela had been administering the house as a museum, financing the enterprise through the sale of jars of soil from the garden. Mandela's lawyers responded to Mrs Mandela's protestations by noting that the 'property was sacred to the Mandela family', for in its vicinity were buried the umbilical cords of his first children, 'in accordance with African custom'.[79] One month later, during the election campaign, Madikizela-Mandela travelled to America, where she presented to television viewers a very different picture of her marriage from her previous testimony on the subject – one in which her one-time husband was portrayed as having been cold and neglectful throughout their union, interested only in his political ambitions. On her return to South Africa she urged voters to support Mandela's successor, Thabo Mbeki, at the polls, saying that South Africa needed a 'young man' at its helm.[80]

Mandela's age and concomitant infirmities are a theme developed in the first full biography of Thabo Mbeki, in which an exhausted and querulous octogenarian president is depicted as visibly irked by the procedures of 'weaning

[him] from authority … taking place at a quicker pace than he would have liked'. Indeed, the book's authors maintain, many of the accomplishments of Mandela's administration were, in reality, 'a reflection of Thabo's work'.[81] Such disparaging efforts by Mbeki's admirers are unlikely to find much official favour. Instead, the new ANC leadership seemed much more predisposed to emphasise Mandela's record as an 'Africanist' traditionalist and, as such, a guiding genius, together with the new president, of a South African-led 'African Renaissance'.

The ANC's preferred model of consensual democracy, 'co-operative governance', is very much in the 'organic' vein favoured by Mandela in his patriarchal, meditative mode.[82] During the 1999 general elections, opposition hecklers at public meetings were exhorted to return 'home' to the 'family',[83] and Mandela's brief public appearances were directed mainly at securing the loyalty of chiefs in the former apartheid 'homelands', to whom he delivered a series of homilies on the merits of respecting age and custom, and amongst whom he celebrated his wedding to his third wife, Graça Machel, widow of the first Mozambican president. At these festivities his old adversary and cousin, the ex-Transkeian politician and paramount chief Kaiser Matanzima, was in prominent attendance. Graça Machel's anointment as a 'full member of the Mandela clan' became the occasion of a final act of reconciliation, one in which the rift between apartheid's African collaborators and 'progressive' nationalists was symbolically closed through the incantations of a praise singer: 'Hail Dalibunga! [Mandela's praise name] … Hail Daliwonga! [Matanzima's praise name] … the bones of Dalindyebo, Sabatha, Ngangelizwe [Xhosa kings] are shaking now that the Thembu nation is united in this ritual.'[84]

Nelson Mandela's cult is likely to long outlive its subject. As black South African notables – modernist and traditional – close ranks in South Africa's second bourgeois republic, Mandela's many personages as well as the myths surrounding them will remain the most powerful source of ideological legitimisation at their disposal.

1 | THE ALLIANCE IN POWER: WHO RULES SOUTH AFRICA?

In the months following the April 1994 general elections, the leaders of the African National Congress (ANC), in struggling to come to grips with their new portfolios and ministries, often observed that there was a fundamental distinction between controlling the government and coming to power. The ANC, they said, was in government but it was by no means yet in power. 'Are we in power or merely in office?' asked Tokyo Sexwale, then premier of Gauteng, at a provincial ANC conference in November 1994, a refrain which also predominated in key addresses at the ANC's national conference that year. The ANC as the embodiment of 'the democratic majority ... has won only some of the important elements of that political power necessary for the advancement of the struggle', then deputy president Thabo Mbeki told the assembled delegates.[1]

Five years later, in 1997 at the ANC's 50th national conference in Mafikeng, delegates were told that they should not 'be blinded by form', for although blacks occupied the highest political offices in the land, in reality 'colonial relations in some centres of power remain[ed] largely unchanged'.[2] In particular, an ANC discussion paper reminded its readers in October 1999, the power of the 'English liberal section of the former ruling bloc' had yet to be reduced.[3]

All these arguments reflected, of course, an increasing resentment of the compromises a negotiated transition to democracy had required, not the least of which was the acceptance of coalition partners. But at a more profound level, the distinction ANC leaders make between governing and exercising power expresses a conviction that majoritarian democracy requires something more than control of the executive and domination of representative institutions. Moreover, while the state exhibited continuities with the pre-democratic bureaucracy, the ANC's claim to be governing would be tenuous. 'Politicians have become prisoners of civil service rules,' deputy president Jacob Zuma complained one year after the ANC's second electoral victory, referring to the government's frustration 'at the lack of implementation of its policies'.[4]

These considerations were based on the belief, deeply entrenched not just in the political-activist community, but also influencing much of the political analysis generated from academic institutions, that power – real power – was invested somewhere other than in government. An ANC discussion document expressed this concern in November 1996. There remained, it argued, a 'wide variety of important centres of power which, thanks to the Apartheid inheritance, are decisively controlled by the white and privileged section of the population'.[5] By 2001, matters had not changed significantly for the authors of an ANC National Executive statement: 'The ideology and cultural worldview propounded by various representatives of the white upper classes today form the bedrock of dominant national thinking.'[6]

In this book I intend to qualify this picture. Of course, political power is not a state monopoly and it is not confined to parliament, cabinet, officialdom, party leadership, and so forth. But I shall argue that what the ANC likes to call, in referring to the 1994 general elections, 'the democratic breakthrough' did indeed signify a profound change in the distribution and shape of power relations in South Africa. The distinction between government and political power is not a simple one. The two are not synonymous – but neither are they separate. In this discussion, I want to begin looking at the political complexities brought about by the 'democratic breakthrough' by trying to answer the question 'Who rules South Africa?'.

The ANC's victory at the polls was not just the triumph of a political party. Rather, it signified the political supremacy of a broader liberatory movement whose constituents included the ANC itself – an organisation that until its legalisation and homecoming in 1990 had been constituted by a 15 000-strong exile body which was largely, though not exclusively, oriented towards guerrilla warfare, and which by 1991 had built a branch structure inside South Africa embracing a membership of 500 000.[7] Another vital part of the movement was the Congress of South African Trade Unions (COSATU) labour federation, with an affiliate strength of 1.2 million members in 1994. The South African National Civic Organisation (SANCO) helped to embody the legacy of the lively localised tradition of community politics that had been led by the United Democratic Front (UDF) during the 1980s. A rapidly growing South African Communist Party (SACP) included in its leadership a substantial share, though not all, of the ANC's leaders and much of the movement's intelligentsia.

The liberation movement was a social alliance, given formal expression by the relationship between these different formations. An alliance between the ANC and the SACP had existed since the establishment of Umkhonto weSizwe (MK), the ANC's military wing, in 1961 and the subsequent formation of a Revolutionary Council on which members of both organisations served. COSATU, formed in 1985, had by 1987 adopted the ANC's Freedom Charter (though not without misgivings among some of its more left-wing officials). The civic movement and other constituents of the 1989 Mass Democratic Movement (MDM) – a formation which brought together trade unions, the UDF and certain churches in a Defiance Campaign – were also aligned with the ANC when the latter organisation began reconstructing itself inside South Africa. However, as Alliance partners the civics never enjoyed the same status as the labour movement and the SACP in ANC circles. COSATU's status as the ANC's labour ally was confirmed by the decision taken in 1990 to transfer to the federation the assets of the old exile union centre, the South African Congress of Trade Unions (SACTU), then undergoing dissolution. In June 1990, COSATU–ANC workshops were held in Harare to plan policies for a post-apartheid government.

Despite these early affirmations of accord, the next few years would witness evidence of rising tensions between the ANC's leadership and trade unionists. The latter complained of ANC 'unilateralism' in its decision to suspend the guerrilla war in August 1990 and in its advocacy at the beginning of 1991 of an all-party congress which should negotiate the route to a constituent assembly. For a while, trade unionists demanded a separate delegation at any such negotiations, and indeed they drew up a separate set of constitutional provisions. These included proportional representation and a presidency limited to two terms, both features of today's Constitution that did not appear in early ANC constitutional proposals. COSATU was to drop its demand for separate representation but its spokespeople continued to display considerable independence as well as impatience at any conciliatory predisposition they perceived among ANC negotiators towards the government. They also became increasingly resentful of the ANC's tendency to substitute negotiation for mobilisation as well as the exploitation of mobilisation as a merely auxiliary tactic to create public resonance for the arguments that negotiators used. From 1993, however, senior trade unionists began to invest their political efforts in elaborating the ingredients of a 'reconstruction accord', a pact that would supply the basis for an ANC election manifesto and would constitute the condition for COSATU's support during the poll.

The genesis of the Reconstruction and Development Programme (RDP) stemmed from this tacit bargain between the ANC's leadership and COSATU. The RDP's first four drafts were chiefly the product of policy expertise associated with the trade union movement. Three further drafts were debated at meetings which built up a wider range of consensus between the ANC, the trade unions, the SACP, MDM affiliates and a range of sectoral non-governmental organisations (NGOs). The key COSATU planners involved in drafting the programme in its early stages were Alec Erwin, Jay Naidoo and Bernie Fanaroff. As the RDP evolved, its contents drew upon an increasingly broad diversity of tributaries. Since 1990, the ANC itself had moved a considerable distance away from its traditional *dirigiste* preoccupations. In 1990 the ANC–COSATU workshop in Harare had embraced a set of proposals that would have included an extension of public ownership, state regulation of credit, a prescribed high-wage economy, and a central role for organised labour in policy formulation. Redistribution would serve as the principal agency of economic growth.

Through 1991, though, ANC economists began to shift ground. The 1992

Draft Policy Guidelines included the suggestion that the public sector might need to be reduced; they noted the necessity for legal protection of property rights; and they reflected an increased sensitivity to the requirements of international competition for South African manufacturing.[8] Later critics of ANC policy-making suggested that 'top ANC economic staffers', including the then policy principals Tito Mboweni and Trevor Manuel, had been intellectually corrupted by their participation in private-sector think-tanks, training courses, scenario-building exercises and social encounters with officials from the World Bank.[9]

The RDP reflected both the earlier and the later economic predispositions within the ANC as well as other discourses. Some 41 pages out of a total of 147 addressed economic concerns.[10] Its argument opened with an acknowledgement that the South African economy was characterised by 'deep structural crisis', including unproductive manufacturing, inefficient labour, over-subsidised agriculture, a growing government deficit, and an exodus of private capital. Remedies should include unbundling and deracialising corporate ownership, a strategic role for the public sector – which might have to be either enlarged or reduced (the ambiguity reflected conflicting imperatives for the drafters) – a 'living wage' and training for workers, the removal of subsidies from unproductive enterprises, land reform and fiscal restraint. Development projects should involve and 'empower' ordinary people, and they should be the outcome of popular initiatives and wide-ranging 'people-driven' consultations. Economic growth would be substantially boosted by the expansion of consumer demand. This would follow the construction of huge numbers of cheap houses and the extension of electrical and piped water supplies to poor people and communities. In its final form, the RDP represented a careful balance between the 'growth through redistribution' policies advocated by the left and the emphasis on growth as the harbinger of redistribution in more orthodox economic analysis. As such, it certainly reflected the ANC's engagement with an increasingly diverse range of social actors in the four years that had elapsed since its homecoming.

So, who has ruled South Africa since the ANC's accession to power? The most literal answer to this question would be those people who constitute the 'governing class': presidents, premiers, members of cabinets and executive councils and – in the most extended sense – parliamentarians as well as the heads of civil service departments. If we were to consider elected members of the executive only, including the president, the deputy president, cabinet ministers and their deputies, the following picture emerges: today, in early 2002, 42 people are governing South Africa. Most of them belong to the ANC, but Thabo Mbeki's administration continues to embody a coalition. Three cabinet positions are held by Inkatha members. Inkatha members also hold two deputy ministries, and the president of the Azanian People's Organisation accepted Thabo Mbeki's invitation to join his government as a deputy minister in early 2001.

Like Nelson Mandela, Thabo Mbeki seems to have based the selection of his administration on 'descriptive representation' as a key consideration.[11] Altogether 29 ministers and deputy ministers are African, four are Indian, four are white and three are coloured. In total, 14 are women – a reflection of the ANC's professed commitment to gender equity. Out of 27 cabinet ministers, 14 spent substantial periods working in the ANC's exile bureaucracy. In addition, both the president and his deputy president ascended to ANC leadership in exile. Of the ten ANC cabinet ministers who were politically active inside South Africa during the 1980s, three were trade unionists, four were prominent in the UDF, and two held positions in church-based organisations. All but three cabinet ministers hold higher education qualifications, three of them academic doctorates. Aside from the 14 who throughout their careers were engaged in full-time political activity, the most common professional backgrounds they share are teaching, medicine and law. Including Jacob Zuma, only four members of Mbeki's government had been active in Umkhonto weSizwe. At least six cabinet members publicly maintain their membership of the SACP. In 1999 in the National Assembly, 119 of 400 parliamentarians were women (96 in the ANC caucus) and, as in 1994, whites were over-represented: parliament included 232 blacks, 104 whites, 42 coloureds and 22 Indians at the time.

Table 1.1 Racial diversity in the National Assembly, 1994 and 1999

	African		White		Coloured		Indian	
	1994	1999	1994	1999	1994	1999	1994	1999
ANC	170	193	40	31	19	27	23	15
DP	0	3	7	31	0	1	0	3
NNP	9	0	61	22	8	6	4	0
IFP	25	19	13	10	0	3	5	2
Others	4	17	9	10	2	5	1	2
Total	**208**	**232**	**130**	**104**	**29**	**42**	**33**	**22**

Source: For 1994 statistics: Andrew Reynolds, *Electoral Systems and Democratization in Southern Africa*, Oxford University Press, Oxford, 1999, p. 245. Information about parliamentarians elected in 1999 supplied by political party offices, National Assembly, April 2002.

The sociological generalisations that can be drawn from office-holders of national government are true for the 97 members of provincial executive councils: racially they represent a fair demographic cross-section (nine whites and nine coloureds, though only two Indians), and they include 18 women. The vast majority hold degrees or diplomas, many come from the liberal professions, especially medicine and teaching, and a significant number of industrial workers and factory technicians testify to the continuing importance of trade union bureaucracies as training grounds for political leadership. In the provinces in which the

ANC governs, executive councils do not recruit from business or from agriculture. Civil-service head appointments have become political appointments, changing with cabinet reshuffles. In these positions appropriately qualified ANC technocrats predominate.

The social identity of its office-holders is at best an uncertain predictor of the behavioural predispositions of government. One might expect that a common biographical experience of insurgent politics, trade union organisation and neighbourhood civic activism, as well as a shared upbringing in working-class households, would instil in government office-holders a particular empathy for poor people and a predisposition towards radical social reform.[12] Conversely, their 'direct class location' and their professional qualifications and status outside politics mostly define them as members of a managerial group which, in a developed industrial country, would normally align itself with socially conservative interests. However, their family relationships and membership of historically oppressed communities complicate – or 'mediate' – their social identity and perceptions of interest and solidarity, or 'consciousness'.[13] Indeed, ANC leaders repeatedly maintain that their bedrock social constituency is the poorest of the poor, that the organisation 'shares [their] experience of poverty'.[14] How valid are such claims?

Representatives of big business complain about a government which they perceive, or claim to perceive, to be acting in tandem with the interests of organised labour (who, they argue, constitute a relatively privileged social stratum). From within government itself, Inkatha ministers agree that labour reforms have 'entrenched the position of the trade unions ... within our system of government' resulting in 'an ever growing culture of indolence'.[15] COSATU – and some communists – agree that democracy has been hijacked by the representatives of international capital, who have succeeded in corralling the ANC within the hegemonic confines of 'neo-liberal' economics. Left-wing intellectuals suggest that this capitulation has been entirely wilful: 'the soul of the ANC' was won through monetarist financial policies 'by a basically conservative black nationalist petit bourgeoisie leadership, led by Mbeki'.[16] More circumspectly, an SACP document in 1998 warned of a 'serious strategic threat to the national democratic revolution ... the attempt by capital to stabilise a new deracialised capitalist ruling bloc under the mantle of the ANC'.[17] *Vox populi* opinion broadcast on radio talk shows or expressed in newspaper correspondence columns suggests widespread popular disenchantment with either a replication of previous hierarchies of privilege or, conversely, a mean-spirited racial antagonism directed at white South Africans.

Another common perception is that the predominance of exiles in the top echelons of the administration has rendered the political leaders particularly insensitive to the feelings and aspirations of ordinary people while at the same time reinforcing authoritarian bureaucratic traits in government. Opinion polls tended to favour the Mandela administration, indicating up to 1998 – among poor people in particular – modest expectations and a degree of satisfaction with the government's performance, as well as trust in its national leaders.[18] However, in late 1999 a household survey conducted by Statistics South Africa (SSA) recorded an increasing number of Africans expressing a belief that their quality of life had declined, as well as a growing sense of political disempowerment.[19] What is to be made of all this?

Those who perceive the state as an instrument of a particular section of society – capitalists, organised labour, white people, poor people, rich people – may be missing the point. Politics follows its own course, and command of the state invests politicians and administrators with considerable social autonomy, but an autonomy that is constrained by social actors, by ideology and moral beliefs, and by perceptions of the possible. I do believe this. Part of my conviction stems, no doubt, from my own sympathies and preferences. The ANC leaders I have met seem likeable and impressive and I find it hard to regard people who in the past made such costly personal sacrifices, as servants of selfish or sectional concerns. But aside from such sentiments, there are more analytical grounds for taking their independence as politicians seriously.

Presidents and cabinet ministers may take office with particular policy predispositions or narrow social biases, but once in power they will be influenced also by the distinct interests of the state they command. This includes the preservation of order and the defence of national interest. Both these objectives can give rise to conflict between statesmen and -women and dominant as well as subordinate class interests.[20] Moreover, in South Africa, the governing class controls a state which in comparative terms – when considered alongside the bureaucracies of other comparable developing countries – is strong, efficient and powerful.[21] For example, foreign public debt is unusually low, which makes South African financial policy-makers much less susceptible to monetarist pressure from international lending agencies.[22] The managers of public finance do not need to serve other masters than those to whom they profess loyalty.

'Who influences the state?' is a better question than 'Who rules it?'. First of all, what is the political significance of the Alliance? Have the years since 1994 witnessed 'the Alliance in power', as the title of this chapter suggests? Not if you take seriously the angry rhetoric that COSATU's leaders have directed at the government and especially at the macroeconomic measures embodied in GEAR – the Growth, Employment and Redistribution strategy – with their emphasis on deficit reduction, government 'rightsizing', tariff reduction, privatisation and productivity-linked wage rates. GEAR was drafted secretly and presented to the ANC's National Executive in mid-1996 as a *fait accompli*. As an exasperated COSATU discussion paper noted at the end of the year, when it came to making policy 'the Alliance engaged only with the product'.[23] Since then, COSATU's hostility to the ANC's macro-financial management has increased, if anything; in

2000 'it [was] now clear', according to Tony Ehrenreich, deputy secretary-general of COSATU, 'that GEAR [was] an economic framework demonstrably structured in favour of foreign and local capital'.[24]

The abruptness of GEAR's appearance helped to engender the conviction amongst trade unionists that the strategy represented a sharp policy turn-around. The White Paper on the RDP which the government published after the 1994 election promised that 'structured consultation processes would be developed at all levels'. These consultative procedures would include a National Economic Development and Labour Council as well as regional and local development forums which would embrace representatives from all the main 'stakeholders'.[25] The White Paper also described the functions of a minister with special responsibility for the RDP whose tasks would include policy formulation, the coordination of different departmental projects, and the development of further institutions. The minister, Jay Naidoo, formerly secretary-general of COSATU, was appointed directly after the election.

Jay Naidoo held office in this capacity for less than two years. On 28 March, the government announced the closure of Naidoo's office: in future its responsibilities would be divided between the Department of Finance and different government departments. The notion that a senior politician should be responsible for monitoring departmental projects ensuring their coordination in a 'holistic' programme was dropped. Regional governments also closed down their RDP offfices and 'redeployed' their RDP 'commissioners'. Naidoo himself was to be consoled with an appointment as minister of posts and telecommunications. After this development, GEAR's announcement on 14 June was widely interpreted to signify an abandonment of the RDP, or at least the desertion of its commitments to social equity and participatory 'integrated' development.

GEAR's origins lay in the work undertaken by a team which was set to work on designing macroeconomic strategy at the end of 1995, working under Alec Erwin, the deputy minister of finance, and comprising professional and academic economists including people involved in the RDP's drafting. The team's original purpose was to attempt to reconcile RDP goals with the macroeconomic requirements of investment and finance markets, but its arguments and recommendations began to be affected by the currency crisis which occurred after Trevor Manuel's appointment as minister of finance. In March, the team presented an early version of its recommendations to deputy president Thabo Mbeki's office. A final draft of the document was shown to the ANC's National Working Committee and its National Executive's 'economic transformation' sub-committee. A carefully selected group of COSATU and SACP officials also looked at the document before its public release but these consultations were more to seek endorsement than to incorporate politicians and trade unionists into the drafting process. GEAR's production was a technocratic exercise and helped to underline the growing influence within Mandela's government of Thabo Mbeki's office and the two ministries with which Mbeki worked most closely: finance, and trade and industry. Despite the leadership former trade unionists have supplied to these departments, in general COSATU has viewed their influence over macroeconomic policy as inimical to workers' interests, exemplified by fiscal conservatism and 'dogmatic adherence to unplanned trade liberalisation.'[26]

The debates over GEAR, though, have tended to divert attention away from those areas in which labour has made solid gains, often despite intense opposition from business circles. Labour legislation is an obvious case in point: the Labour Relations Act of 1995 has widened the scope for extending collective bargaining agreements throughout industrial sectors, and the more recent Basic Conditions of Employment law imposes longer leave obligations on employers and increased overtime premiums. To be sure, labour may have appeared to lose on symbolic issues – the constitutional status of lock-outs and the 40-hour week are examples – but there can be no question that trade unions have been significantly fortified by legal changes since 1994.

Trade unionists might respond that such gains are illusory in a situation of shrinking employment (business claims that unemployment is accelerated by these labour reforms, as investors seek more 'flexible' labour markets elsewhere), but compared with other national economies undergoing economic 'restructuring', the fall in formal employment in South Africa has been comparatively mild (with public-sector jobs not decreasing at all), and wages have actually risen in real terms. Official statistics released in October 1998 suggested that in non-farm employment, the number of new jobs (289 108) roughly balanced the number of jobs lost (278 901) between 1994 and 1998. More recent figures indicated that formal non-agricultural employment fell from 6 645 000 in 1995 to 6 564 000 in 1999. In the same periods agricultural employment grew by about 250 000, but this was after a period of steep losses: agriculture, forestry and fishing had lost 815 000 existing jobs between 1995 and 1996, while only a small number of new jobs were created.[27] Informal-sector employment grew by about a million from 1995 to 1999. Official unemployment figures rose from 1.8 million in 1995 to 3.2 million in 1999 as a consequence of about 500 000 school leavers entering the job market annually.[28] However, in those sectors which have been most strongly organised by trade unions, employment levels have been fairly stable.

Organised labour can also derive satisfaction from the slow pace of privatisation and its own success in helping to define the process of privatisation. Arguably, broader access to health care, increased public expenditure on education and the efforts to reform social welfare all represent a significant expansion of the social wage. The rise of wages in real terms as well as this expansion runs against international trends. What is true, though, is that such policies have seldom reflected a systematic joint process of strategic direction by the ANC and its partners. The various Alliance summits and conferences, when they have been held at all, have usually been occasions on which ministers and other members of the government have been taken to task for the shortcomings of policies already under implementation. As COSATU observed in December 1996, 'the locus of decision-making on key political issues has not been in Alliance structures but in individual ministries'.[29] Nor has the SACP, despite the conspicuous role that some of its members play in government (it is represented by six cabinet ministers, two provincial premiers and 65 MPs),[30] shown any more evidence of exercising a corporate influence. This is partly a result of the divisions within the party elite, which have widened since the paradigmatic rupture accompanying the demise of communism in Eastern Europe.

Outside the formalised structure of the Alliance, with what justification can Nelson Mandela and now Thabo Mbeki and their colleagues claim to be a 'people's government'? Initially, considerable effort was invested in participatory development procedures in which local projects such as water reticulation, housing construction or improving local roads would be inspired and managed by locally representative bodies. The adoption of the RDP was accompanied by the assembly of hundreds of local development forums, which were supposed to function in partnership with state agencies in conceiving and funding such projects.

Some of these forums survive, but project implementation has mostly been a top-down affair, partly because of difficulty in achieving consensus in divided communities, but partly also as a consequence of the requirements of scale and speed. With these considerations in mind, the RDP programme will be discussed in chapter 3. The absence of responsive and legitimate local government until its election in 1995 and 1996 also posed an obstacle for the 'people-driven' progress of the RDP. In addition, the ANC's own lack of preparation for municipal politics meant that even after their entry into town halls many ANC councillors were ineffectual (and often corrupt too).

In its rhetoric, the ANC invests great faith in its own internal democratic procedures. Since its 50th national conference in Mafikeng in December 1998 it has committed itself to revitalising these. But the ANC's claims to embody 'a parliament of the people' needs to be understood in a context in which paid-up membership had been more than halved between the general elections of 1994 and 1999 – from roughly a million to 400 589[31] – and from a situation in which thousands of its most effective organisers have found employment in legislatures and government and thus become considerably distanced from the communities they used to mobilise so successfully. The latest revisions to the ANC's constitution have extended the interval between national conferences from three to five years, effectively limiting the prospects for the organisation's leadership to become more accountable to its membership and its more inchoate popular following.[32]

What about big business? Like trade unionists, local businesspeople – at least in public – exaggerate the gulf that separates them from government. However, it is useful to distinguish the general interest of business from more specific concerns. Revisions of protective import tariffs, for example, are not a measure that finds unanimous favour in South African business circles. Certain business sectors have encountered particularly hostile attitudes from government departments and their political leadership. The relationships between the Department of Health and the pharmaceutical and tobacco industries would be two cases in point. Others have experienced more sympathetic predispositions. Gambling and liquor are two industries which have developed sophisticated and successful lobbying strategies with respect to both parliament and individual ministries.

In general terms, the government has probably been better for business than any of its predecessors for a very long time – labour reforms notwithstanding – not so much through any direct assistance to business (although corporate taxation remains restrained), but rather through its evident acceptance of what business perceives to be economic common sense in respect of public expenditure levels, exchange controls and foreign trade. But it is different from being a government wedded to the interests of the private sector, even supposing that those could ever be encapsulated neatly by policy.

The rhetoric at the 1997 ANC national conference in Mafikeng about the need to make business more 'socially accountable' needs to be taken seriously, particularly regarding job creation. Though the pace of ownership deracialisation was initially quite swift – 'black-chip shares' as a proportion of the total market capitalisation on the Johannesburg Stock Exchange have grown from 0.05 per cent in 1995 to almost 10 per cent in 1998, although they subsequently declined to 4.9 per cent in February 2001[33] – government leaders still perceive business as representing a different constituency from their own.[34] Even amongst companies in which ANC notables predominate it should not be assumed that the interests of politicians and businesspeople will always coincide. In 2001, there was a bitter dispute over the management of South African Airways between the chief executive officer of Transnet, Saki Macozoma, and the minister of public enterprises, Jeff Radebe; subsequently Macozoma left the parastatal to head up New Africa Media. The same year, the government's award of a third cellular telephone licence found two empowerment groups – both involving ANC interests – in fierce and litigious conflict with each other.

A remarkable expansion of the black middle class has accompanied the advent of democratic government. Today, blacks constitute 10 per cent of the top fifth of earners, up from 2 per cent in 1990.[35] In the 1996 census 700 000 Africans were recorded to be employed in managerial, professional and 'associate professional' positions; this accounts for about half of the people within these categories.[36] A quarter of the income earned by the top earnings group goes to Africans, according to a recent UNISA study.[37] But despite such progress, whites predominate in the boardrooms; only 353 out of 3 406 company directors are black, 161 in empowerment groups.[38] As a result, the social distance between government and business is maintained, making it unlikely that government will be particularly sensitive to every anxiety within the business community, particularly those that trouble local capitalists. During Mandela's presidency, only a small number, namely 32 of the ANC's 252 MPs, registered shareholdings worth more than R10 000, and a mere 20 MPs maintained directorships, many of these unremunerated commitments to NGOs.[39]

There are indications, though, that the gulf between ruling-party politicians and business may become narrower in future. In mid-2001, five influential members of the ANC's National Executive (out of 88) were major figures in the world of black business (Saki Macozoma, Joe Modise, Jay Naidoo, Cyril Ramaphosa and Max Sisulu) and several more were married to prominent businesspeople. Since the 1999 general elections there has been a large increase in the number of ANC personalities who have left the public sector to become businesspeople: Moss Ngoasheng, formerly Mbeki's economic adviser, and Sipho Pityana, up to 2002 director-general in foreign affairs, are two examples of this trend.

In late 1997, deputy minister of tourism Peter Mokaba, an ex-ANC Youth Leaguer and hair-salon chain director, circulated a pre-conference discussion paper that suggested that 'the Freedom Charter [had] always aimed to build a capitalist South Africa'. The ANC should make its priority, Mokaba urged, 'a process that builds the black section of the entrepreneurial class'.[40] Mokaba also challenged the privileged position that the SACP enjoyed within the tripartite Alliance, referring to communists 'who sit in ANC meetings' and who then 'convene under another name and criticise decisions they took as the ANC'.[41] Mbeki's and Mandela's rebukes to COSATU and the SACP in June 1998 for their criticisms of the government's macroeconomic policy reflected the same kind of irritation. These were followed by Thabo Mbeki's condemnation of 'traitors' and 'criminals' in the South African Democratic Teachers' Union (SADTU),[42] and the strictures of minister of constitutional development Valli Moosa upon 'ultraleftist' agitation among municipal workers against privatisation.[43] Meanwhile, Cyril Ramaphosa, in his capacity as the acting chairman of South African Breweries (SAB), warned in his annual report that the 'recent procession of labour enactments' could be 'cost burdensome' and so could inhibit job creation.[44] A further signal of the ANC's move away from its traditional ideological moorings was the angry dismissal by minister of agriculture Derek Hanekom of the National Land Committee's proposal for the scrapping of the constitutional property clause as 'stubborn frivolousness'.[45]

What about the government itself? Do its leadership and managers represent a class in the making, a bureaucratic bourgeoisie of the kind familiar to most observers of nationalist movements that came to power elsewhere on the continent? I do not think so. Several barriers are blocking this development. These include continuities with the old regime (South Africa does not yet have a decolonised public service); the egalitarian traditions which still form a very important part of the ANC's intellectual constitution; the general trajectory of state development in the 1990s, in which the state's role in the economy decreases rather than expands; and the existence of a strong workers' movement as a component of the liberatory alliance. Chapter 7 specifically addresses the topic of political corruption. It is worth observing here how limited its incidence is among elected office-holders, compared with its extensiveness within the civil service. A final barrier to the emergence of a bureaucratic bourgeoisie is the strange resilience of liberal institutions in South Africa, some nurtured by liberation politics, others independent and even in opposition to them. Chapter 8 further develops and elaborates this argument.

So the answer to my question 'Who rules South Africa?' is both obvious and deceptive. A political movement governs, and has real power, as we shall see, to reshape political and economic life. The interests it represents are amorphous – the constituents of a social alliance: organised labour, black entrepreneurs, an emergent managerial class, rural poor, a multiracial intelligentsia informed by competing humanitarian and radical traditions. No single group is dominant, nor is the likely ascendancy of any one of these certain. They struggle for influence in a relatively poor, middle-income, developing country on the margins of the international economy or, from a different perspective, on the borders of what separates the rich industrial world from the desolation of what Frantz Fanon called the 'wretched of the earth'. In such uncertain territory no social group holds undisputed power.

2 | REGIONAL GOVERNMENT

Most government in South Africa today is regional. The regional administrations established in 1994 spend about two-thirds of the national budget (after repayment of the national debt) and employ the vast majority – about 750 000 – of the country's 1.1 million public servants.[1] Some 400 000 of these are the former functionaries of the old apartheid homelands (or putatively self-governing territories, which became labour reservoirs for white South Africa). Regional governments are responsible for those aspects of administration which affect the everyday life of citizenry: health, pension payments, education, housing. When people give judgements about the government's success in making a better life for them they are evaluating, mainly, the performance of regional administrations. Regional governments do not have much discretion in determining policy – the laws they pass in most domains have to conform with the principles underlying policies determined by central government – but they have considerable latitude in interpreting policy and implementing it. Their capacities are also limited by their lack of any significant source of independent finance – their budgets are allocated from central government – but disbursement of such funds gives their politicians considerable real power, nevertheless. No adequate analysis of modern South African politics can overlook the way these administrations operate.

The establishment of nine regional polities owed much to the imperatives of a negotiated transition to democracy in which the ANC was persuaded of the wisdom of making concessions to smaller parties. The case for South African democracy's assuming a federal form was based chiefly on the supposed political benefits of a multi-centred political dispensation in ethnically divided societies. When executive authority is divided between central and regional government, minorities – defined in different ways – would acquire a stake in the system. In post-nationalist politics characterised by a dominant majority party, federal or regional devolution of power held out to small parties, with no hope of winning office at the centre, the prospect of achieving executive control at subordinate levels. Federal governments also protect local or regional interests against big central government. Less conspicuous in the South African advocacy of the merits of federalism was the possibility that it could bring government closer to the citizenry, making it more accessible and accountable, and that the devolution of power might enhance democracy, allowing small communities more capacity to influence or determine the behaviour of politicians. Notably absent, though, from any of the South African motivations for regionalised constitutions were any arguments about efficiency or developmental benefits.

In this chapter, I wish to explore the effects of regional government. I shall look at three separate dimensions of their existence. Firstly, I would like to examine the quality of their public administration. Secondly, I shall consider the politics of regionalism, especially its effect on party politics. Because I will be looking at the northern provinces as case studies, I shall be concerned chiefly with the ANC. Finally, I want to discuss the ways in which provincial governments are regarded by ordinary people. Have they, as the exponents of federalism maintain they should, enhanced the legitimacy of government?

Firstly, I shall deal with administration. When things go wrong in South African government, more often than not they go wrong in the regions. This is not altogether surprising. Several of the regions at their inception were confronted with the task of amalgamating several separate civil services from the old white provincial bureaucracies, whatever administrative arrangements may have existed for Indians and coloured people, and the former homelands, each of which had developed their own managerial styles and most of which lacked technical skills and professional integrity. The new boundaries also brought together competing or rival political elites who were often very jealous of each other's influence. The tensions in the Eastern Cape between Transkeian ANC supporters of an additional 'tenth region' and the more senior political leadership based in Mdantsane (outside East London) and Port Elizabeth would be a case in point. The new political leadership had inherited administrations in which bureaucratic systems had broken down or disappeared. They lacked accurate and reliable information about the identities and numbers of employees and the accounting of public expenditure for over a decade. (In the Transkei, for example, government accounts were not audited between 1988 and 1994.) They did not have basic information about the quality and even the location of government facilities – offices, buildings and the equipment these may have contained. Indeed, an official inquiry conducted in 1997 found that 'the majority of provincial departments do not have complete asset registers or inventories'.[2]

Weak administration prompted the political heads of departments – ministers, or MECs – to become involved in day-to-day management of staff, thereby undermining the authority of their departmental heads.[3] Not surprisingly, those provinces which have since 1994 acquired a reputation for relatively efficient performance of services – Gauteng, Western Cape, Northern Cape, and the Free State – were those which had been least encumbered with the legacies of homeland administrations. In the case of Gauteng, the bureaucracy was reconstructed anew because the decision to base its administrative centre in Johannesburg rather than Pretoria meant that it did not have to assemble itself around the old Transvaal Provincial Administration (many of whose members were reluctant to make the move between the two cities and so opted for early retirement). Thus the new regional government of Gauteng could draw its recruits from the public service training institutions concentrated on the Witwatersrand.

Some of the difficulties, then, which regional administrations have experienced are attributable to shortages of technical or professional skills. In Limpopo, formerly the Northern Province, for example, of 290 doctors employed in public hospitals in 1996 – itself a woefully inadequate total for a population of about six million – only 20 were South African citizens; the rest were foreigners. Not that Limpopo's public service is generally understaffed: it employs one-third more people than the considerably more populous Gauteng. Even Gauteng, though, suffers from a shortage of properly qualified accountants: departmental budgets of R1 billion are being supervised by people who have only basic bookkeeping skills. In Mpumalanga, in 1999, the head of finance told the legislature that his department depended on daily help from consultants: 'Many junior staff did not understand even the basic principles of accountancy.'[4] Even if bureaucracies employed accountants, budgeting often was not linked to planning because of 'a lack of basic coordination between managers'.[5]

In the Eastern Cape and KwaZulu-Natal, schools are especially handicapped by under-qualified teachers – and tens of thousands of teachers on their payrolls do not exist at all. The absence of effective control systems encouraged fraud and wastage. These bad habits have been around for a very long time and have only now come to light. In one province in 1997 it was estimated that R50 million a year was paid out for false petrol reimbursements to the drivers of government vehicles. In one northern district of KwaZulu-Natal it was discovered in 1996 that 97 per cent of the local population was supposedly receiving disability allowances. The recurrent crisis in pension pay-outs in the Eastern Cape is mainly caused by the delays arising from repeated efforts at reorganising a pension system in which huge sums of money were paid to fictional claimants. The provincial audit conducted by the Department of Public Service concluded that over the next ten years 22 000 qualified personnel would have to be recruited annually to make up the province's skills deficit. Skills shortages are often experienced in those fields in which social reform policies have placed the heaviest demands on resources, and the poorest provincial administrations may yet have the heaviest responsibilities in addressing basic needs. As the Ncholo Report noted, 'inherited systems from the past, especially from the Bantustans, were never designed to support service delivery at the massive scales required by the democratic dispensation'.[6]

Central government has attempted to address these problems by discriminating against the richer or better resourced provinces in budgetary allocations, Gauteng and the Western Cape in particular. This caused the two provinces to overrun their budgets in health and education in 1997. Increased funding to poorer provinces, though, has only accentuated their administrative difficulties: they lack the capacity to spend money efficiently. Skilled staff are concentrated in the urbanised provinces; they do not follow the redirection of public funds to the more rural provinces. In fact, teachers, health professionals and technical staff are moving into the private sector instead. The facilities that are most affected by this exodus or budgetary cuts are, of course, most likely to be located in the poorest communities – the Chris Hani Baragwanath Hospital in southern Johannesburg is a case in point. With a provincial shortfall of 1 000 nurses, Baragwanath's intensive care unit for babies was 75 per cent understaffed in March 1999.[7]

Since 1997 the provinces have received their main allocations from national government in single-block grants. In the 2001/2 financial year R117 billion of the state's total revenue of R273 billion was assigned to the provinces in the form of grants, which ranged from R23 billion for KwaZulu-Natal to R2.7 billion for the Northern Cape.[8] Revenues generated by the provinces themselves represent only a small proportion of their total budget; for example, in Gauteng, a comparatively rich province, it represented a mere 6 per cent of its total revenue in 1999. Provinces do not have the formal powers to raise loans. The size of the grants they receive are decided on the basis of recommendations by the Financial and Fiscal Commission. These recommendations take into account census statistics and poverty indicators; provinces with higher proportions of rural people and school-age children qualify for proportionately larger budgets. The provincial governments draw up budgets for submission to their legislatures. Most provincial expenditure is on health, education and social security – 80 per cent in Mpumalanga, for example. With the exception of social security, in which the national department sets the sizes of the various grants and benefits and hence determines the overall scale of expenditure, the provinces have considerable discretion as to how they spend this money.

Of course this discretion is limited by the need to pay salaries, which account for a very large proportion of expenditure. This is especially the case in those provinces which incorporated the former homelands, where the pre-1994 civil services were especially likely to be overstaffed. (In the Eastern Cape, for example, salaries consume about 80 per cent of the health budget.)[9] Salaries are fixed by central government, and overstaffing obviously reduces the scope for provincial policy initiatives. As one provincial manager put it: 'By the time you've paid your staff there is little space for policy. For example, 93 per cent of the education budget is spent on salaries. There's no room to try and innovate things, for example, in textbook purchasing policy.'[10] Such constraints are particularly limiting in the poorer regions. Limpopo Province employs 25 civil servants for every 1 000 people compared to Gauteng's 15.[11] In Limpopo, commitments to salaries and grants and various other fixed obligations account for 80 per cent of expenditure.[12] Public-sector wage increases aggravated the matter, consequently leading to a reduction in expenditure on such items as hospital equipment, medicines or road maintenance. In general, capital expenditure in provincial administrations has declined since 1994.

Even so, the management of provincial finance allows plenty of opportunities for controversy and disagreement. In the Free State, for example, a R308 million deficit resulted in the province being unable to pay its suppliers in 1998; this was the consequence of the government underestimating the cost of its programmes and making insufficient allocations.[13] Similar difficulties in 1999 prompted the closure of hospitals. The Department of Health owed R63 million, and in Bethlehem private food suppliers refused to make any more deliveries to the Phekalong hospital.[14] In the relatively well-governed Northern Cape, in 1997 the government overspent R120 million on education because it failed to budget sufficient sums to pay teachers.[15] In Mpumalanga in 1997, an unusually assertive set of portfolio committees forced the administration to withdraw its 1997/8 Appropriation Bill (the law that enacts the budget) because it hugely exceeded the total of the national government's grant, while also provoking a walk-out by the MEC for finance after the finance committee refused to sanction expenditure of R59 million on government buildings. The minister was later compelled to return and apologise.[16] In the Eastern Cape the MEC for health broke ranks with her cabinet colleagues to condemn the health allocation in the 1999/2000 budget, warning that proposed expenditure reductions would prompt 'total collapse of primary health care services'.[17] She later resigned her portfolio, while the Eastern Cape was praised by the minister of finance in 2000 for its success in introducing financial reforms.

Not all economies, though, are the consequence of generalised fiscal austerity. In Mpumalanga, in 1998, the Department of Transport began replacing tarred road surfaces on major trunk routes with cheaper-to-maintain gravel. In the same year, though, the department undertook the tarring of gravel roads in former homeland areas. Here a symbolic political commitment to 'delivery' to the ANC's poorer supporters took precedence over rational policy.[18] This example draws attention to the very real power which provincial politicians can exercise in the decisions they make about resource allocation and, as in this case, power can be used to build personalised political support. This power may also help to explain why so many provincial MECs feel that they require the permanent services of teams of armed bodyguards, for in patronising impoverished communities they risk generating as many enemies as clients.[19]

I do not wish to spend too much time on the administrative problems of regional administrations. Besides, I am not sure that the overall quality of regional government is much worse than the regional government it replaced. In certain respects it may actually be better. Opinion polls suggest that people in poor rural areas believe they now enjoy better access to government services such as health facilities.[20] Some of the reports of administrative strain, especially in the health services, are entirely attributable to the fact that more people are making claims on government. I now want to turn to a consideration of the political dimensions of our new federal order.

Since 1994, the Western Cape has been governed by parties representing the opposition in the National Assembly. In KwaZulu-Natal Inkatha has predominated in a sometimes uneasy coalition with the ANC (though in 1997 in a constitutional dispute with the National Party the ANC also claimed the status and the entitlements of being the official opposition). However, given the provinces' limited constitutional scope for autonomous policy-making, even when they are governed by the ANC's opponents there is only occasional evidence of serious differences over policy issues between central and regional government. For example, ANC–IFP tensions over the status of traditional authorities prevented enabling legislation for the 1995 Development Facilitation Act to be passed. This law was intended to accelerate development project implementation by eliminating or harmonising local regulations. Such disagreements have been unusual, though. Generally, regional legislatures convene for quite brief periods and pass relatively few laws. For example, the busiest regional parliament in 2000 was that of the Western Cape, which passed 11 laws. Two of these concerned the budget, two more referred to financial issues, two amended the gambling laws, one established a convention centre company, two others amended the Road Transportation Act, and two addressed local government reform. In all instances, only the issues concerning local government involved serious policy disagreements between the regional government and the ANC opposition.

While the provinces are able to enact their own constitutions, only the Western Cape and KwaZulu-Natal have used their authority to do so. In the Western Cape, political consensus was achieved over an initial draft that would have established a mixed-member electoral system (based on constituency and list); this draft was rejected by the Constitutional Court, and the final version, enacted in November 1997, was an anodyne document, in practice ensuring a very similar government dispensation to the other provinces. It differed mainly in respect of its clauses promoting work ethics, market-oriented economics and cultural or community councils. Constitutional harmony between the ANC and the National Party ended when the ANC opposed the premier's decision to enlarge his cabinet from 10 to 14 members, but this did not reflect any deep division over principle. KwaZulu-Natal's proposed constitution, which envisaged a kingdom with its own independent judiciary including a constitutional court and a militia, was rejected by the Constitutional Court in 1996 (notwithstanding reluctant provincial ANC acquiescence in its terms), and the legislature's standing committee on constitutional affairs has yet to complete a new draft.

Outside the domain of constitution-making, of the nine regional governments the Western Cape has been the readiest to assert its autonomy. For example, its Department of Health was the first to sanction free anti-retroviral drugs to prevent mother-to-child HIV transmission. So far there has been no evidence that central government discriminates between provinces on political grounds in its budgetary allocations, though in 1997 the Department of Finance warned the Western Cape that it would risk losing its 'top-slice' funding for academic hospitals if it persisted in implementing a deficit budget.

Federal politics has vastly increased the complexity for the ANC of running its own inner organisational life. Since 1994, in the seven ANC-governed provinces there have been six changes of premiership, two of them – in Gauteng and the Free State – sharply contested. In most of the provinces there have been conflicts between ANC people in government and their respective party leaderships, especially in those instances in which the premiership and the party chairmanship have been held by different people. Political corruption in the strict sense of venality amongst elected politicians has been most evident in provincial administrations, notably in Mpumalanga. Rank-and-file rebellions against national leadership efforts to influence the outcome of regional leadership contests have arisen in Gauteng, Limpopo and the Free State. Provincial premiers have been demonstrably keen to extend the boundaries of their autonomy in policy matters. Tokyo Sexwale's efforts to develop an independent (and very expensive) housing programme with a private construction firm, Stocks & Stocks, was an early instance of this. Mathews Phosa's efforts to conduct a provincial foreign policy with neighbouring Mozambique would be another example.

Some of the difficulties can be explained by the ANC's organisational character in the provinces, where it is a disparate and often awkward sum of its parts. The ANC between 1990 and 1994 expanded its organised following very rapidly and in doing so incorporated a multitude of different local political cultures as well as contrasting styles of political leadership. This was an especially obvious feature of rural provinces, in which governments reflected uneasy coalitions of old-style homeland bosses, veterans of the militant and militaristic youth congresses which mushroomed in the 1980s, and technocrats returned from exile. The case of Mpumalanga is illustrative. Mpumalanga's MEC for safety and security (until his resignation in 1997 in the wake of a car licensing scandal) was the former police minister of KwaNdebele homeland, Steve Skosana. When moving into the ANC, such people also often brought with them intact their patronage networks as well as grandiose expectations of privilege and deference. The habit of Inkatha ministers in KwaZulu-Natal of summoning detachments of civil servants to greet them at Ulundi airport is indicative of this. Nor are these reflexes confined to former homeland notables. The remark that the Mpumalanga MEC for transport and ex-ANC Youth Leaguer, Jackson Mthembu, made in 1997 when questioned about his decision to spend R2.3 million on a fleet of BMW 528s for his colleagues, was revealing: 'I am a leader in my community and therefore have a certain status – you can't be saying I should drive a 1600cc vehicle.'[21]

Regional politics has also been dogged by intra-regional rivalries. In Limpopo competition between politicians from the former homelands of Lebowa and Venda has promoted rival ethnic favouritism in different government departments. Premier Ngoako Ramathlodi's administration was heavily weighted in favour of Northern Sotho politicians, partly as a result of recruiting much of its leadership from the University of the North (the institution, incidentally, that has become the main *alma mater* of today's ascendant generation of national politicians). Ramathlodi himself, who was Oliver Tambo's former private secretary, is viewed resentfully as an outsider imposed upon the local political establishment. In 1996 the regional ANC Youth League nominated Peter Mokaba for the position of provincial chairman. Mokaba was persuaded by his cabinet colleagues in Cape Town to withdraw but conference delegates showed their displeasure by electing Senator George Mashamba instead (by 352 votes to 350). Ramathlodi regained the leadership position in 1998 after a narrow victory over two of his MECs. In the meantime, in 1997, he had attempted to create a degree of consensus in an increasingly unruly cabinet by firing five of his MECs to make room for leaders from the ANC's structures in the former Venda and Gazankulu homelands. Ethnic tensions seemed to have multiplied in the lower ranks of Ramathlodi's administration: the suspension of the director-general of education was followed by rumours of an impending purge of Venda- and Shangaan-speaking civil servants. Subsequently, the premier was compelled by the ANC National Executive to re-appoint to his cabinet former MEC for education Aaron Motsoaledi. Motsoaledi had led the provincial ANC before the 1994 general elections. Before the ANC's 50th national conference in 1997, Ramathlodi published a paper which argued in favour of the ANC ending its practice of making political appointments to top civil-service positions. In Limpopo Province some of the most politically insubordinate civil servants were recent political appointees.

Meanwhile, events in the Free State offered further evidence of leaders at odds with each other. On 20 June 1996 the premier, Mosiuoa Lekota, dismissed from his cabinet the MEC for economic affairs and tourism, Ace Magashule, citing as his reason Magashule's 'insubordination'. This action provoked an immediate outcry within ANC provincial leadership circles. Lekota's critics claimed that he did not consult the party leadership adequately before dismissing Magashule. Lekota claims he did indeed consult both the cabinet and the ANC caucus in general terms several days before his reshuffle announcement. The chairman of the ANC party provincial executive, Patrick Matosa, repeatedly called for Lekota's resignation. Other members of the provincial leadership threatened a vote of no confidence in Lekota but were persuaded against this course of action by ANC secretary-general Cyril Ramaphosa. Over the subsequent weekend a delegation from the national government led by the minister of sport, Steve Tshwete, patched up a compromise in which Magashule was reinstated in the cabinet by being given the transport portfolio (recently surrendered by the National Party). As part of the agreement an advisory committee consisting of senior ANC leaders was to be established to facilitate consultations between the premier and the ANC.

Tensions continued to simmer. A meeting between Lekota and his critics on 26 July failed to resolve matters. Its main outcome was Lekota's loss of a seat on the provincial working committee. On 2 August, the National Working Committee of the ANC declined to debate the 'the issue of confidence or no confidence' in Lekota, to quote Cheryl Carolus. After listening to a report on efforts to resolve problems in the province from Joe Nhlanhla (deputy minister for intelligence services), Steve Tshwete and Makhenkesi Stofile (ANC treasurer-general), the committee decided that 'the status quo' should remain, and Lekota should keep the premiership. Meanwhile the Free State executive issued a statement criticising officials who had conspired to remove 'Comrade Lekota' from office, and who were using 'the organisation for personal and selfish reasons'. However, reports of conflict between Lekota and his executive persisted. Lekota's position was strengthened by a public declaration of support from the regional chairman, Stuurman Mokoena, on 6 September. That week, civil servants marched on the ANC's Bloemfontein offices to demand that it end its 'harassment' of the premier.

There was a history of conflict between Lekota and his party executive. Ace Magashule could be considered one of Lekota's primary political opponents and he was also vice-chairman of the provincial ANC. In 1993 the provincial party nominated Magashule for premier. He subsequently had to be asked to step down to make room for Lekota. At the 1994 conference Matosa and Magashule mounted a surprise challenge to Lekota in the leadership elections. Lekota, who had undertaken no lobbying before the meeting, came third in the delegates' poll.

Conflict between Lekota and Free State ANC leaders reflected local dissatisfaction at having a relative outsider imposed upon them by national leadership in 1994. Though Lekota was born in the province, in Kroonstad, he completed his secondary education in the Transkei, matriculated in Natal and spent his career as a political activist in Natal and the Transvaal. He spent six months in 1991 working as an ANC organiser in the northern Free State before being redeployed at head office, only returning to the Free State during the 1994 election campaign. Commentaries after the conference suggested that the main ground for the rift between Lekota and Matosa–Magashule was the belief that Lekota 'had taken reconciliation [with conservative whites] too far'. In April 1995, Lekota angered his critics further by suspending the MEC for housing, Vax Mayekiso, for supposed involvement in an unsavoury property deal. Matosa said that Lekota had 'acted too fast'. Thereafter, Lekota suspended several senior officials suspected of dishonest dealings, and subsequently ANC legislators complained that these violated procedure.

On the surface, then, there appeared to be two issues separating Lekota from his colleagues: firstly, the resentment of local notables at having a relative outsider imposed in a leadership position over them and, secondly, a clash between the culture of accountability and consultation as understood by many activists who matured in the 1980s and Lekota's more imperious leadership style. In Matosa's words, in the ANC there was 'a tried and tested tradition ... to collectively consult, but the premier seems to forget that he is accountable to the ANC as a political party'.[22] There may have been more to these tensions, though. Lekota enjoyed some support in the regional party leadership, and alignments in the cabinet suggest that a north–south rivalry helped to animate the quarrel. In an earlier dispute over the location of the provincial capital a strongly committed pro-Welkom faction emerged, headed by Mayekiso, Magashule and Matosa, each of them politicians whose support base was located in the northern Free State goldfields. This group also tended to favour 'socialist' rhetoric as opposed to the 'pragmatic' vein which Lekota preferred. The 'northerners' perceived their home area to be underdeveloped in comparison to Bloemfontein and its environs, and they argued that Lekota's administration had been too sympathetically predisposed to white and emerging black elites in the capital. Kaizer Sebothelo, the party secretary, was also part of this group.

It was true that since the 1994 election Lekota had developed good relationships with members of the old regime, in particular with former Free State administrator Dr Louis van der Watt, whom he appointed to his cabinet over the heads of the National Party hierarchy. Freedom Front leaders were also well disposed to Lekota. During the crisis Lekota received public expressions of support from the editor of Die Volksblad and the chairman of the Free State Agricultural Union.

Ace Magashule's antipathy to Lekota may have had little to do with ideological or policy considerations. In August it was reported that he might be facing charges of misappropriating R7.88 million and authorising the payment of cheques into tourist promotion companies under his control. The ANC's initial reluctance to support Lekota in his dismissal of Magashule from his first portfolio apparently arose from the fact that Lekota referred the matter to the attorney-general in June without consulting the national leadership. Lekota may have been correct in terms of official procedure and law, but in choosing this route he offended traditional ANC protocol. As one of his political critics observed, 'Terror [Lekota] has confused the Constitution with convention.'[23] In December 1996, the auditor-general confirmed the validity of the allegations against Magashule. Five officials in the Department of Economic Affairs and Tourism were suspended, three of whom belonged to the same branch as Magashule.

Lekota's supporters in the ANC leadership included Papi Kganare (MEC for safety and security), born in Thaba Nchu and with a background in trade unionism and the South African Youth Congress, mainly in Mangaung (Bloemfontein) and Vereeniging; Sakhiwo Belot (MEC for education), in 1990 a teacher and ANC branch secretary in Bloemfontein; Senorita Ntlabathi (MEC for health), formerly a senior community nurse employed by the Bloemfontein city council; and Cas de Villiers (MEC for agriculture). An unnamed MEC was quoted in the press on 8 September as having said that he or she did not believe that the legislature should become a conveyor belt for ANC provincial executive decisions. In the past, the ANC had been dominated by northerners because the north was where the organisation was most strongly developed, securing its foundations in the trade unions and community organisations established in the industrial towns near the Transvaal border in the 1980s.

The Congress of South African Trade Unions (COSATU) and the South African National Civic Organisation (SANCO) both announced their support for Lekota, reflecting possibly the growth of unionism in the public sector and the spread of civics to Bloemfontein. However, Free State political organisation in 1996 was still volatile and fluid. Since 1994, the ANC had been developing its organisation where before it had none: in the huge squatter communities that were once part of Bophuthatswana and QwaQwa, where the ANC had found it either impossible or very difficult to function openly in the past. QwaQwa activists tended to ally themselves with the Magashule group, for in the former homeland there was strong resentment among civil servants of Bloemfontein's centralisation of administration. In November, there were reports that Magashule partisans had undertaken the bulk distribution of free ANC membership cards in QwaQwa. In his previous capacity as chairman of the ANC's northern Free State region, Magashule had enjoyed a reputation as an excellent organiser, even winning a prize from the ANC's headquarters for his efforts.

Meanwhile, the premier began attacking his rivals on a radio talk show, focusing on Magashule's financial dealings and Matosa's implication in a court case in which the ANC's provincial chairman was charged with attempted murder for drawing a gun on a traffic policeman. Until then, Lekota had never criticised his opponents in public, although his supporters had felt no such inhibitions; during August crowds attending political rallies would be worked into a frenzy with shouts of 'One Free State, One Lekota! Phantsi [Away with you], iOpportunisti, Phantsi!'.

Lekota's radio commentaries prompted the ANC's National Executive to intervene once again. On 4 November Lekota and his cabinet were asked to resign and a caretaker committee for the province was appointed under the leadership of Tito Mboweni, then minister of labour. Despite protests by the Bloemfontein Taxi Forum which blockaded the legislature, a court case against the ANC for ignoring its own constitution, and continuing signals of dissent from the regional leaders of the ANC's trade union and communist allies, Mboweni's team proceeded with the selection and appointment of a new premier, another relative outsider, Ivy Matsepe-Casaburri, former head of the board of the South African Broadcasting Corporation (SABC). She, like Lekota, was a child of Kroonstad, but with a track record of mainly exile politics. In February 1997 the provincial ANC held a sullen conference. Matsepe-Casaburri's candidacy for the chairmanship was defeated by Zingile Dingani, chairman of the legislature's portfolio finance committee and a strong Lekota supporter. At this point Dingani was 'redeployed' to parliament in Cape Town along with Magashule and Lekota.

Matsepe-Casaburri's appointment did not end the ANC's troubles in the Free State. Tension between Magashule and Lekota loyalists continued throughout 1997 and 1998. In August 1998, provincial conference elections reversed the previous year's outcome. As a result of burgeoning branch organisation in Sasol-burg, the goldfields and QwaQwa, as well as the reconstruction of the almost defunct Women's League by his supporters, Magashule was able to ensure victory in the chairmanship contest and secure the election of an executive composed of Lekota's former opponents, including Vax Mayekiso. Ivy Matsepe-Casaburri failed even to secure a nomination. Her efforts during the previous eighteen months to distance herself from the rival factions won her few friends. In the words of one of the delegates, 'she is seen as a person who is neutral. In politics there is no neutrality, a leader has to be firm and decisive. She did not want to be associated with any group.' Zingile Dingani's efforts to reconcile both groups engendered similar reactions. He was not nominated 'because he failed to pursue a certain agenda'.[74]

In Gauteng, political tensions of a different order surfaced in September 1997 with the election of a new premier, Mathole Motshekga, by representatives of 400 or so branches to replace Tokyo Sexwale, in defiance of the preferences of the incumbent party leadership and the provincial cabinet. Motshekga, chairman of the legislature's standing committee on development planning and local govern-ment, had chosen to decline a cabinet position in 1994 despite his senior party rank in the ANC. Although he was deputy chairman of the provincial organisa-tion, he opted instead to devote his energies to consolidating a personal political following within the organisation. This he was able to achieve by building up a network of friendships with local councillors. His victory at the ANC's provincial council elections owed much to support from local councillors, especially those from outside Johannesburg, who felt, rightly or wrongly, that Soweto had received the lion's share of development resources in the province. His popularity was buttressed by his reputation as an 'Africanist', which in turn bolstered his status as a traditional healer and his exhortations for the revival of people's courts. He was also supported by Mondli Gungubele, a former nurse and chair of the port-folio committee for health, and as such a sharp critic of the executive's favoured candidate, the taciturn MEC for health, Amos Masondo. In July 1998, Gungubele replaced Masondo as MEC for health. Masondo, meanwhile, was rather surprisingly 'redeployed' to the ANC's headquarters to manage its 1999 election campaign. In a provincial executive drawn from a mixture of Johannesburg civic activists, communists, ex-trade unionists and technocrats, Motshekga's populism and his intellectual independence were deeply distrusted. This distrust manifested itself in a series of allegations of corruption against him, which were leaked to the press.

In April 1998, an internal ANC commission of inquiry reported on these allegations against Motshekga. It cleared him of corruption charges but found that the premier had been a 'shambolic' manager at the National Institute for Public Interest Law, which he headed in the 1980s. The ANC should second appropriate people to help Motshekga run his government office more effectively, the commission advised. Since then, a succession of rhetorical indiscretions by the premier have continued to embarrass his colleagues while at the same time reports have persisted of continued factionalism directed at the premier.[25]

In addition to its recommendations regarding Motshekga, the commission also advocated a series of measures to halt 'creeping provincialism' within the ANC's ranks. In particular, it suggested that provincial premiers should be appointed by the ANC president. This recommendation was endorsed by the ANC's National Executive in August 1998. In future, the ANC provincial chairperson would no longer automatically fill the post of provincial premier; that is, the two positions would be 'delinked'. Premiers would be appointed by the ANC's National Executive, which was to be advised by a 'deployment committee' chaired by Jacob Zuma as the ANC deputy president. Such a measure supplied for the ANC leadership a constitutional method of preventing the ascendancy to executive positions of awkward personalities such as Mathole Motshekga, but it is unlikely to resolve the deeper causes of conflict in both Gauteng and the Free State – the fear within desperately poor communities that proximity to or distance from political leadership is the crucial determinant in influencing the allocation of public resources.

In a political culture historically shaped by patron–client relations, politicians who fail to develop local bases and personal networks may simply end up pleasing nobody. The Free State history is a reminder of the complexity of internal ANC political relationships. Often tensions are explained through references to the competitive solidarities produced by prison, exile or involvement in mass organisation during the 1980s. As the conflict between Magashule and Lekota, both former leaders in the United Democratic Front (UDF), demonstrated, the networks animated in ANC factionalism cannot be categorised so neatly.

Nor did the assertion of national authority over premiership selection succeed in discouraging factionalism in the provinces. In the Free State, Matsepe-Casaburri remained an unpopular figure within her own organisation, failing to secure a place on the provincial candidate list in the 1999 general elections. She had to be nominated on the national list instead. The national deployment committee replaced her with Winkie Direko as the ANC candidate for premier. Direko was a veteran ANC member who had first joined the organisation in Bloemfontein in 1940 and whose main sphere of activism had been in various welfare organisations. Subsequent disagreements within the provincial leadership under Magashule's chairmanship led to its dissolution by the National Executive and its replacement by an interim committee. Its members swiftly invited contention when they began sharing out amongst themselves the candidatures for the mayorships in advance of the December 2000 local government elections.

Meanwhile, in Limpopo Province, Ngoako Ramathlodi's difficulties with the ANC's provincial executive continued with a group, led by former MEC for health Joe Phaahla, accusing the premier of favouring Vendas and Shangaans. Ramathlodi had, in fact, scrupulously followed a policy of ethnic balance, appointing four Shangaans and four Sothos to his cabinet (as well as two Vendas). Non-Sothos complained of the predominance of Sothos in top civil-service positions as well as more generous public investment in the former Lebowa homeland, partly the result of the post-1999 election decision to move the provincial legislature into the old parliament buildings at Lebowakgomo. Ramathlodi's reluctance to dismiss from his cabinet his MEC for education, Edgar Mushwana, after public disclosures about Mushwana's efforts to secure employment for his wife and breach tender procedures,[26] can be attributed to the premier's perception of his political vulnerability. Mushwana, a former insurance salesman from Gazankulu, was one of Ramathlodi's key supporters against the Phaahla faction. In 2001, the ANC National Executive intervened, in February instructing Ramathlodi to drop Mushwana from his cabinet, and in May, one month before the organisation's provincial leadership elections, disbanding the provincial executive and appointing in its place an interim committee. This decision followed complaints about the inflation of branch support through the bulk purchase of membership cards 'to pump up delegations for the conference'.[27]

In Gauteng, despite rising public approval ratings,[28] in the months preceding the 1999 general election Mathole Motshekga's administration appeared beset by crisis. In February 1999, the premier's former press officer was suing him for wrongful dismissal, his administration was under investigation for alleged corruption in the housing department by the Special Investigative Unit headed by Judge Willem Heath, and a key supporter, East Rand ANC chairman and head of the provincial safety and security committee Pule Malefane, was under arrest for pointing a firearm during a traffic dispute. Two months later, the ANC's deployment committee announced its choices for the premierships after the elections. Despite his leading position on the provincial candidate list Motshekga was to be supplanted by the COSATU secretary-general, self-proclaimed Marxist-Leninist

Mbhazima Shilowa. The 'Africanist' ascendancy in Gauteng was over. In Shilowa's new cabinet, Motshekga himself would be denied a post. Originally he was considered for the lowly sports portfolio, but this went instead to Mondli Gungubele, whose brief term at the Department of Health had engendered much criticism. Seven out of ten members of the Gauteng government executive were now members of the SACP. Only four members of the new government also belonged to the provincial executive elected with Motshekga in 1997. Among those who lost positions was Joyce Kgoali (number three on the candidate list), a key figure in the ANC Women's League. In general, Shilowa's new administration was perceived to be tilted towards the anti-Motshekga Johannesburg-based faction, an impression which was strengthened by Shilowa's selection of veteran Soweto activist Amos Masondo as his political adviser.

Meanwhile, staff who had worked in Motshekga's office complained of being trapped in 'a virtual tomb of despair' as a consequence of their ostracism in favour of 'handpicked party loyalists'. Mathole Motshekga himself managed to retain his chairmanship of the provincial ANC until May 2000, despite several efforts to unseat him. At that point, a year-long history of confrontation between Shilowa's government and the ANC Gauteng leadership prompted the ANC's National Working Committee to dissolve the provincial executive and replace it with an 'Interim Leadership Core' until the next conference, scheduled for July 2001. A process of reorganisation in which local branches would be re-established to correspond with 400 local government wards, represented another means through which Shilowa could consolidate political authority, as this would break up residual local networks of support for his predecessor. A provincial conference, finally held in November, elected Shilowa unopposed. In a peace-making gesture, Angie Motshekga, Mathole's wife and MEC for social services, was chosen as the party's provincial deputy leader.

In these three provinces, the Free State, Limpopo and Gauteng, ANC National Executive intercession may, arguably, have made government more workable, though it probably damaged rank-and-file morale within the party itself. By contrast, the organisation's leadership, whether embodied by Thabo Mbeki, the National Executive or its deployment committee, cannot claim any credit for its decisions in Mpumalanga. Indeed, in this province, external intervention to check local leadership rivalries has had a contagious effect, with local politicians attempting with some success to elicit support by exploiting rivalries between different national ANC notables.

Mpumalanga's political troubles began when its premier, Mathews Phosa, had the temerity in August 1997 to allow his name to be put forward to contest the ANC deputy presidency in defiance of the National Executive, which had already earmarked Joel Netshitenzhe, a key ANC strategist and aide in the President's Office, for the position. Phosa had previously annoyed the ANC leadership with his statements about the need for more devolution of power to the provinces; for allegedly encouraging would-be secessionists in the Bushbuckridge district who wanted to join the 'Republic of Mathews Phosa' rather than remain in the then Northern Province; and for calling for the scaling down of the ANC National Executive. Of all the provincial premiers, Phosa enjoyed the strongest personal support. He was the longest-serving provincial chairperson in the ANC, a consequence of a loyal local following fostered first by his running Nelspruit's only black law firm and then, after exile, by the clandestine networks he built up in the Lowveld as an Umkhonto intelligence chief in Maputo. Phosa's administration drew upon the old KaNgwane political establishment, the youth congresses and the civics associations developed during the era of the UDF (which he had helped to found) and incorporated a number of politicians from the KwaNdebele homeland. Most of the top civil-service positions went to former KaNgwane bureaucrats. Investment attracted by the proposed upgrading of the N4 highway to Maputo helped to boost provincial growth rates as well as Phosa's local popularity.[29] Phosa's political stature was also enhanced by a popular belief that 'the province's record in the delivery of basic services and infrastructure was better than elsewhere'.[30] As Table 2.1 indicates, survey evidence confirmed that he enjoyed higher public approval ratings than any other premier. Popular perceptions appeared to coincide with official evaluations. In August 1997, Pascal Ncholo's official inquiry into the workings of provincial government suggested, apparently, that Mpumalanga was under 'excellent political leadership'.[31]

Table 2.1 Performance evaluation of provincial premiers, November 1998

Positive responses (as percentages) to question: How well do you think [the premier] is doing his/her job?

	Eastern Cape	Free State	Gauteng	KwaZulu-Natal	Mpumalanga	Northern Cape	Limpopo	North West	Western Cape
African	46.8	40.5	49.7	43.4	73.1	53.7	50.4	46.9	27.7
White	9.8	14.7	15.2	25.6	18.7	51.5	20.4	19.0	47.8
Coloured			15.8	25.4		51.3			35.3
Indian			18.9	21.3					

Source: EISA/IDASA/SABC/Markinor – *Opinion '99*

A series of corruption revelations led to fragmentation of the provincial party leadership and tarnished its reputation. In 1997 former KwaNdebele police minister Steve Mabona lost his position as MEC for transport after arranging for a driver's licence to be issued to the deputy speaker of the House of Assembly, Baleka Kgositsile, without a proper driving test. This incident drew attention to widespread dishonesty amongst Highveld traffic officials, sanctioned by the MEC. The following year, controversy broke out over the illegal leasing of the provincial parks to a foreign investment group in return for a huge loan to the Parks Board and kickbacks to various officials, as well as payments to the ANC Youth League. The casualties in this case included Jacques Modipane, the MEC for finance, and David Mkhwanazi, holder of the environment portfolio in Phosa's cabinet and a former KaNgwane cabinet minister. James Nkambule, the provincial secretary of the ANC Youth League and one of Phosa's strongest supporters hitherto, was compelled to resign from his post after the discovery that he, too, had been a beneficiary of the provincial parks deal.

Nkambule subsequently was to lead a delegation of disaffected provincial leaders to the ANC headquarters in Johannesburg where they informed Thabo Mbeki that Phosa was busy spreading 'disinformation' about Mbeki among journalists and produced their own counter-allegations of corruption against the premier. These allegations focused on the construction at public expense of a R700 000 security wall around his private residence. Nkambule also claimed that Mathews Phosa had used taxpayers' money in his campaign for the ANC deputy presidency. Nkambule's accusations prompted the ANC's National Executive to intervene. In February 1999, Phosa was discharged as premier and replaced by Ndaweni Mahlangu, a National Assembly parliamentarian who, in his previous career as KwaNdebele politician, had served briefly as minister of education and had also led the ANC-aligned political party Intando yeSizwe.

After the general elections of June 1999, Mahlangu achieved national notoriety by announcing that in his view it was defensible for politicians to lie, 'because the practice is a widespread and accepted political technique'. The context for this extraordinary statement was his defence of the inclusion into his cabinet of Steve Mabona and Jackson Modipane as well as David Mabuza, Phosa's MEC for education, who had lost his position before the elections after taking the blame for the fraudulent inflation of the province's matriculation marks. James Nkambule was given a senior post in the provincial department of local government as a reward for his repudiation of earlier loyalties, a position he retained until March 2000, when he was dismissed after instigating three anti-corruption inquiries into district councils led by provincial ANC notables. Mahlangu's appointment was intended by Thabo Mbeki to 'end instability', although it is said that he was advised against making the appointment through the deployment committee.[32] However, the Mahlangu administration's reputation suffered because of continuing publicity about the venal behaviour of Mathews Phosa's government. An unusually vigilant local press ensured that Mpumalanga's rent-seekers received more than their fair share of newspaper attention,[33] although many of the administration's problems were of its own making. For example, quite illegally, Mahlangu's colleagues diverted money from flood relief, health and pensions to pay for the escalating costs of a lavish parliament building outside Nelspruit. As a result, pharmaceutical suppliers halted deliveries to provincial hospitals in April

2001 because the provincial government had repeatedly failed to pay its bills.

Meanwhile, financial irregularities prompted Mahlangu to dismiss the MEC for land affairs, David Mabuza, and his MEC for local government, Tsietsi Tolo. Although both were unpopular, their departures intensified infighting within the provincial ANC. Mahlangu used their departures to bring into his government two additional KwaNdebele homeland politicians, Jabu Mahlangu and Mighty Mgidi, while also increasing the Intando yeSizwe veteran component in the legislature. Growing tensions between the executive and the primarily Lowveld-based ANC parliamentary caucus led to a public rift at the Constitutional Court between the premier and Mpumalanga MPs over the content of the Mpumalanga Petition Bill.

In March 2001 the ANC national leadership asserted its authority once again. An ANC 'tribunal' led by the minister for safety and security, Steve Tshwete, was dispatched to the province. In its subsequent report, made public in June, it recommended the dismissal of three particularly corrupt MECs, including Steve Mabona, reputed to be the premier's right-hand man. To balance matters, it suggested the 'redeployment' of several former Phosa allies to the National Assembly. In addition, the provincial executive was to be augmented with senior appointments, including Tshwete himself and his cabinet colleague, minister of land affairs Thoko Didiza. The ANC head office was to send a team to help the province strengthen its administration and reorganise its branches.

Steve Tshwete's visit to Nelspruit supplied an opportunity for James Nkambule to renew his feud with Mathews Phosa. The former ANC Youth Leaguer allegedly amplified his earlier assertions about Phosa's anti-Mbeki rumour-mongering, now linking Phosa with Tokyo Sexwale and Cyril Ramaphosa in an elaborate plot in which the three were supposedly conspiring to provoke attacks on Mbeki by suggesting his complicity in the Chris Hani assassination. A naively credulous Tshwete made these allegations public on 25 April 2001, announcing that there would be a police investigation into the matter. The incident strikingly illustrated how a fractious provincial political culture shaped by competition between rival patrimonial fiefdoms could influence the course of national politics. Ever since 1997 when Mathews Phosa found himself at odds with ANC party bosses over contesting the deputy presidency elections, Mpumalanga politicians were particularly well placed to seek favours from potential patrons in national government. Steve Mabona's willingness to issue an invalid driving licence to the deputy speaker and various efforts by Mpumalanga politicians involved in front companies to engender a relationship with deputy president Jacob Zuma[34] are further examples of such endeavours.

What about popular perceptions of regional government? Survey evidence does not suggest in itself that provincial government has made the government generally more legitimate in the eyes of the citizenry (see Table 2.2). A report by the Institute for Democracy in South Africa (IDASA) on a survey conducted in late 1995 found significantly lower levels of public trust in provincial government than in national government. Some 45 per cent of the IDASA sample trusted national government, whereas only 32 per cent trusted provincial government. Mpumalanga, incidentally, received the highest trust rating (57 per cent).[35] The two provinces that specialists have considered relatively well governed, namely Gauteng and the Western Cape, received relatively poor ratings. This may be a consequence of the social diversity and political divisions within their populations as well as higher political expectations.

Table 2.2 Trust in the Western Cape provincial government, 1997–2000

Responses to question: How often do you think you can trust government to do what is best for people like you? (1 = never; 2 = seldom; 3 = sometimes; 4 = mostly; 5 = always)

	Black				White				Coloured			
	1997	1998	1999	2000	1997	1998	1999	2000	1997	1998	1999	2000
Trust in national government	3.1	3.4	3.0	3.2	2.0	2.1	1.9	2.3	2.7	2.1	2.4	2.6
Trust in provincial government	3.4	3.1	2.5	2.9	2.9	3.1	2.7	2.5	2.7	2.5	2.7	2.6

Source: HSRC Social Movements Project surveys, 1997–2000

Unfortunately IDASA has undertaken no subsequent investigations on this topic, but some trust questions were included in HSRC-sponsored surveys between 1997 and 2000. In contrast to the IDASA reports, the HSRC surveys found that respondents generally seemed equally predisposed to trust provincial and national government. But if the data are broken down according to race and province, significant differences emerge. As Table 2.3 shows, whites particularly and, to a lesser extent, coloured people were more inclined to trust the New National Party-dominated provincial government. This is not surprising. As noted at the beginning of this chapter, one of the considerations which motivated the establishment of a federal dispensation was the hope that it might encourage political engagement and support among minorities by giving the parties which had represented them historically a real prospect of winning executive authority. As Andrew Reynolds has noted, for many whites or coloureds a perception of inclusion within the political system will for a long time to come depend on the presence within government of leaders associated with particular communities and specific (socially conservative) ideological traditions.[36]

Government performance evaluation by survey respondents in 1998 indicates higher levels of public approval of national government than provincial government except in the Western Cape and Northern Cape. In both these provinces about half the white and coloured respondents thought that the regional administration had governed well. In the same survey the proportion of whites who approved of national government was a meagre 19.8 per cent. These findings tend to reinforce the arguments about the relative effectiveness of provincial governments as institutions in promoting the political integration of minorities. Encouragingly, though, they also suggest that racial differences need not prevent positive evaluations of leadership or government among minorities; white endorsement of the Manne Dipico ANC administration in the Northern Cape is a compelling illustration of this.[37]

Table 2.3 Performance evaluation of provincial governments, November 1998

Positive responses (as percentages) to question: How well do you think the national/provincial government is doing its job?

	Eastern Cape	Free State	Gauteng	KwaZulu-Natal	Mpumalanga	Northern Cape	Limpopo	North West	Western Cape
All	39.0	36.7	41.4	34.2	64.5	58.1	50.7	47.6	50.9
White	7.2	24.7	14.3	32.9	23.5	51.5	16.5	17.3	56.5
Coloured	9.4		20.9	26.5		48.5			53.6
Indian			23.2	24.1					
African	44.7	38.8	56.7	35.9	69.9	77.0	52.3	50.9	33.2
All*	60.5	54.5	49.5	48.6	70.6	55.9	83.1	60.1	48.2

* Approval of national government performance

Source: EISA/IDASA/SABC/Markinor – Opinion '99

Even in those instances in which provincial governments received poorer ratings than national government, these need not imply that they necessarily detract from overall government legitimacy. Indeed, they may supply a focus for public dissatisfaction which might otherwise have been directed at national government.

Some of the shortcomings I have described may help to improve public opinion; for example, the existence of a well-organised patronage system which distributes political goods quite widely may make government seem accessible and responsive at least to those citizens who benefit. The border dispute that erupted in Bushbuckridge in 1997 was significant in this respect. Here, people who had been politically oriented towards the networks based in and around Nelspruit, now in the new province of Mpumalanga, found themselves incorporated into the then Northern Province, governed by a distant bureaucracy in Pietersburg, which had weak social links with the district. Local people felt that they would get better treatment from Nelspruit officials. At least Nelspruit could be reached by a two-hour taxi ride, as opposed to an overnight journey to Pieters-burg. Naturally, patronage systems can also lead to feelings of resentment amongst those excluded from their benefits, but such sentiments are less likely to be politi-cally dangerous if they occur within regions rather than between regions, assuming that – as in South Africa – resource allocation between regions is under-taken fairly. Locating the control of the main sources of patronage at the level of the regional governments helps to confine the damage which can result from its deployment. It also helps to broaden access to power and resources. What the border conflict demonstrated was the way in which popular political affiliations are in the process of being reconstructed on the basis of regionalism. In a research project on social movements in which I have been collaborating since 1994, there has emerged an evident geographical redistribution of activist politics, away from its traditional concentration in the larger towns and towards the new regional centres. This augurs well for democracy, I believe.[38]

The ANC's national leadership is reportedly more and more concerned about the costs, both financial and political, of regionalism. One year after the passage of the Constitution, at the ANC's national conference in 1997, Nelson Mandela's speech referred to the need for new theoretical thinking about the shape of the post-apartheid state. ANC constitutional experts are believed to favour the reduc-tion of the provincial governments to mere administrations, removing from them their representative and elected components and subordinating their civil services to the national departments. They can only do this with a two-thirds parliamen-tary mandate. The ANC could probably secure the support of one or other of the smaller left-wing parties to achieve such a goal; the Azanian People's Organisation (AZAPO), for example, favours the dissolution of the provinces. It seems unlikely, though, that the ANC would be willing to risk the consequences of alienating Inkatha, especially given the degree of its evident commitment to peacemaking in KwaZulu-Natal. More plausible is the possibility of reducing the scope of provin-cial power by enlarging the authority of local governments through the construc-tion of unified 'mega-cities' with much greater administrative capacity than today's municipalities. One provincial premier, Makhenkesi Stofile, has suggested that half the seats in provincial legislatures should be reserved for representatives of local authorities, with provincial civil servants being dispersed to different municipal governments.[39]

Both courses would be mistaken. The administrative failings of regional bureaucracies will not disappear if they lose their constitutional status, and the task of supervising them from Pretoria will become no easier. Mega-cities will only relocate the political problems, as well as the patronage networks, lower down the state hierarchy, as is already happening with housing, a field in which local authorities are beginning to assume responsibility from regional government without discernibly better results. Besides, the proceedings I have been describing may not signify breakdown, they may rather represent the conflicts and struggles that are the inevitable effect of change, a process of which the outcome is still uncertain. To help us in our predictions as to how beneficial change will be, we need to look more closely at the government's efforts to reallocate resources to create a better life and evaluate such efforts carefully. I shall turn to these tasks in the next chapter.

3 | THE RDP: DELIVERY AND PERFORMANCE

The essentials of the Reconstruction and Development Programme (RDP) can be captured in a couple of paragraphs. The Programme emphasised two aims: the alleviation of poverty and the reconstruction of the economy. These two objectives were interrelated, the RDP's authors maintained. Balanced economic growth would be impossible without the simultaneous promotion of economic development. Without growth there could be no development. Economic growth without development would fail to bring about 'structural transformation', that is, a more advanced economy and a more equitable and prosperous society. Policies concentrated purely on promoting growth would accentuate existing inequalities and maintain mass poverty, and these would soon stifle growth. The government, the RDP insisted, should play 'a major enabling role' in integrating growth with economic reconstruction and social development.

The RDP proposed five ways to combine growth with development: (1) meeting basic needs, (2) upgrading human resources, (3) strengthening the economy, (4) democratising the state and society, and (5) reorganising the state and the public sector. These activities should involve and empower ordinary people: 'development is not just about the delivery of goods to a passive citizenry'. The RDP should be 'people-driven', that is, it should deepen democracy by enabling people affected by development projects to participate in their planning. Economic reconstruction and social development should be mutually reinforcing. Expansion of infrastructure would stimulate and strengthen the economy and provide popular access to better services. A more modern infrastructure, the RDP suggested, would help to improve South African export capacity.

Such improvements were badly needed, the RDP insisted, for the South African economy was afflicted with a 'deep structural crisis'. Manufacturing was unproductive and dependent on low wages and imported machinery. It made a meagre contribution to foreign exchange earnings and it failed to create new jobs. Within the wider industrial economy, heavily concentrated ownership 'create[d] social tension' and prevented competition. Labour worked inefficiently and its historic repression retarded the accumulation of skills. Heavily subsidised commercial agriculture was often inefficient. Government expenditure required high personal taxation and resulted in a growing deficit. Meanwhile private capital flowed out of the country.

'Neither commandist central planning nor unfettered free markets' could remedy these problems. The public sector would be needed to 'strengthen the ability of the economy to respond to inequalities' and to promote growth. It might even have to be enlarged, the RDP speculated, 'through, for example, nationalisation'. Alternatively, it might need to be reduced. Privatisation measures might promote efficiency, affirmative action, and in general 'empower the historically oppressed'. Government, trade unions, business and civil society organisations should co-operate in redirecting the economy. Labour policies should stress education, training, 'a living wage' and collective bargaining. Affirmative action should include 'massive' training programmes, anti-discriminatory measures in hiring and promotion, job security for pregnant women, and the development of local expertise in preference to the 'import of outsiders'. The public sector would set an example: within two years, 'recruitment and training should reflect South African society in terms of race and gender'.

Economic restructuring should be geared towards increasing national investment in manufacturing, job creation and basic needs. South Africa should become a significant exporter of manufactures. Internationally competitive industries should be strengthened and integrated better with other sectors of economic activity. Anti-trust legislation would be needed to spread and deracialise business ownership. Foreign investors should receive the same treatment as South African businesspeople. Policies should ensure that foreign investment 'creates as much employment and real knowledge transfer as possible'. The government should help small and especially black-owned enterprises through its allocation of contracts and by requiring financial banks to lend more capital to small firms. In agriculture, subsidies and controls should be removed and support services given to those in greatest need – 'poor farmers, especially women'. The expensive pursuit of self-sufficiency in food should be abandoned, and farming should be encouraged to become more labour-intensive and environmentally sustainable.

The RDP also expected the private sector to contribute to fulfilling basic needs. Some of the basic needs proposals were clearly intended to be implemented mainly through government activities. These included the rationalisation of existing health expenditure and services in favour of primary health care; a Public Works Programme to provide employment and supply clean water and electrical connections to communities without them; land reforms to redistribute 30 per cent of the land under commercial agriculture; and the institution of feeding schemes to ensure basic nutritional requirements. Private companies, though, were expected to collaborate with the government in constructing a million low-cost houses and helping the poorest people buy them.

Reconstruction and development should be an all-embracing effort, the programme's drafters exhorted. 'Development forums' would bring together 'all major stakeholders' in formulating and implementing RDP projects. These bodies should represent political parties, NGOs, business and community associations. Organisations in civil society 'must be encouraged to develop their own RDP programmes of action and campaigns within their own sectors'. The RDP should not increase government expenditure significantly, its planners warned. Many of its objectives could be accomplished through the reallocation of government expenditure. Market forces could also achieve certain RDP goals. For instance, deregulating agriculture would, the RDP's authors hoped, release resources for redistribution. Socially desirable investments by the private sector, for example in low-cost housing, would represent a major contribution to RDP financing. Much of the economic growth and restructuring would be prompted by the expansion of consumer demand, which would follow the building of houses and the extension of electricity and piped water. Better labour productivity would follow the institution of education and training programmes.[1]

The RDP has meant different things to different people. There was a 'left' understanding of the RDP which probably conformed with the way most political activists understood the programme when it was first drafted in 1993. Leaders of the Congress of South African Trade Unions (COSATU) and the South African Communist Party (SACP) tended to read the RDP as a 'decisive break' with past policies; in particular, they emphasised those sections in the document 'which demonstrate the economic value of particular types of state intervention in the economy'.[2] Their understanding of the RDP was encapsulated quite well at the SACP's 9th Congress in 1995. The RDP had four essential dimensions, delegates were reminded. These were: (1) redistribution – this should be a central characteristic of government activity; (2) economic reconstruction, along a new growth path directed at 'inward development'; (3) the state's assumption of the role of coordinator of development; and (4) development as a 'people-centred' or 'people-driven' process.

This was not the only way the RDP was understood, though. The government, in its 1994 RDP White Paper, which committed itself to restricting the growth of the public sector as well as endorsing privatisation,[3] seemed to interpret the RDP in a less populist fashion. The ambiguity in the original 'base document' provided plenty of authority for more socially conservative readings of the RDP. Much of the programme's language accorded well with current orthodoxies among development agencies concerning the role of the state, 'not as a direct provider of growth but as a partner, catalyst, and facilitator',[4] with private enterprise participating in the provision of welfare and utilities. Business supporters of the RDP,[5] taking their cue from this aphorism, drew attention to a different set of the programme's features: (1) development as a process that depends upon a partnership between the state and private enterprise; (2) a thinner, more efficient, less expensive state; (3) an internationally competitive economy; and (4) a better-educated and more productive workforce.

There have been other, more cynical views among businesspeople. Especially notorious was a remark in 1995 by the chairman of the Barlow Rand conglomerate, who gleefully told a shareholders' meeting that his company 'would be feeding off the carcass of the RDP for years to come'.[6]

Finally, there were the popular expectations about the RDP. Political parties which polled public sentiment before the 1994 general elections generally found a consistent ranking of the things which people felt a democratic government should achieve: jobs (above all else), water (in rural areas), houses, peace and land. Understandably, this was the way in which the ANC projected the RDP to its supporters, as a programme geared towards meeting basic needs, during the 1994 general elections.

Ordinary people were most inclined to understand the RDP as the provision of benefits and opportunities: a better living environment, improved services and enhanced life chances. It is quite reasonable to begin an evaluation of the RDP by considering the government's achievements with respect to these popular expectations. To what extent has the government succeeded in creating 'a better life for all'?

The statistics are quite impressive. Here are some of the more significant figures.[7]

- Clean water: By the beginning of 1998, standpipes had been installed within 200 metres of the dwellings of about 1.3 million rural people who previously either used ground water or bought their drinking supplies from lorries. In August 1998, the minister of water affairs, Kader Asmal, stated that since he took office 'more than 2.5 million people had been given access to fresh safe water for the first time'.[8] Nearly two years later this achievement had been doubled: by March 2000 a total of 236 projects completed since 1994 supplied clean piped water to 4 847 451 people, three million of whom were inhabitants of former homeland areas in KwaZulu-Natal, the Eastern Cape and Limpopo.[9]
- Housing: By December 2000, altogether 1 129 612 cheap houses eligible for government subsidy had been built since the 1994 elections, accommodating 5 million of an estimated 12.5 million people who were without proper housing. Approximately 232 000 of these houses were upgraded shacks in informal settlements. The pace of housing construction peaked in 1997. According to the minister, Mthembi-Mahanyele, more exacting quality control had brought this annual total down to 200 000. In six years the government had spent a total of R40 billion on housing.[10] In fiscal terms, government commitment to housing slackened after 1996; in that year, some 3.4 per cent of the national budget was spent on housing, whereas by 1999/2000 this proportion had diminished to 1.4 per cent.[11]

- Electrification: By May 2000, around 1.75 million homes had been connected to the national grid since 1994 and another 600 000 connections were planned for the next three years. Most of the electrification schemes had been directed at rural homeland areas. In the same period the proportion of rural homes with electricity had grown from 12 per cent to 42 per cent.[12]
- Land reform: By the beginning of 1999 some 39 000 families had been settled on 355 000 hectares of land using their Settlement Land Acquisition Grants.[13] This was still a long way from the RDP goal of redistributing 30 per cent (30 million hectares) of commercial land within five years. Some 250 000 people had 'received land' within four years, the authorities claimed.[14] In addition, though, the Land Claims Court had by June 2001 settled 12 500 claims for restitution from about 90 000 people who were dispossessed of their land after 1913.[15] Land reform will be considered in detail as a case study of the government's commitment to land redistribution in the next chapter.
- Primary health care: Between April 1994 and December 1998 around 500 new clinics gave an additional 5 million people in the population access to primary health care facilities (3 000 clinics already existed).[16] The beneficiaries of this activity included 77 000 people whose sight was restored through cataract operations by the end of 1998.[17] A polio-hepatitis vaccination programme that began in 1995 ensured that 8 million children were immunised within two years.[18] In 2000, the Department of Health could claim that both polio and measles had been virtually eliminated through vaccination programmes.
- Public Works: A community-based Public Works Programme established after 1994 provided employment over five years for 240 000 people on road-building schemes and the installation of sewerage, sanitation facilities and water supplies, mainly in KwaZulu-Natal and the former Transkei. The programme was evaluated in 1997 by the International Labour Organisation and found to compare favourably with similar undertakings in thirty other countries.[19]

Numbers can be misleading, but these statistics really do signify considerable change. In the case of water, the five million beneficiaries of the new standpipes need to be considered against the 12 million who were without access to piped water in 1994. Before then, most rural water provision was aimed at fulfilling the needs of commercial agriculture, and by 1994, 75 per cent of the water installations that had been established in the homelands since 1980 had ceased to function.[20] Even in the case of the new projects, most people for whom these were intended still had to carry water to their houses. At present rates of progress it will take another thirty years before everyone has tap water inside their homes.[21]

During the apartheid era housing peaked at 50 000 subsidised units for

Africans in 1990. The current rate of homebuilding exceeds the total number of houses erected between 1955 and 1965 – the previous era of really extensive mass-housing construction.[22] Modern Soweto accommodates about 125 000 houses, a figure which suggests the quite impressive scope of the government's programme. Regular surveys undertaken by Statistics South Africa (SSA), the official census organisation, indicate that between 1995 and 1999 the number of households in formal dwellings increased proportionately from 65.8 per cent to 69.9 per cent. However, the same surveys recorded comparable increases in the proportion of people inhabiting informal dwellings (squatter shacks), while the occupation of 'traditional dwellings' had decreased from 15.3 per cent to 11.8 per cent. This meant that people moving from the countryside to the cities created new demand for housing.[23]

Electrification statistics are impressive, but the scope of change they represent may be more modest than the figures suggest. SSA surveys suggest that while households using electricity for lighting had increased from 63.5 per cent of the total to 69.8 per cent, the proportion using electricity for heating had diminished.[24] Though more houses were connected to the electricity grid, many people could only afford to use the power for very limited purposes.

Land reform in the sense in which it is being undertaken today was virtually non-existent before 1994. As late as 1984, the government had still been taking away land from black farmers in the western Transvaal which had been purchased by their ancestors.[25]

A decline in infant mortality, from 51 per thousand in 1994[26] to 45 per thousand in 1998,[27] as a result of free access to maternity care since 1994, as well as immunisation programmes, has signalled the impact of primary health care. In 1996, an opinion poll showed that 63 per cent of South Africans believed that they had better access to health care than before.[28] In November 1998, 77 per cent of African respondents to a poll felt that the government was performing well in its delivery of basic health services. In this survey approval of the government's efforts in health care correlated positively with respondents' extent of social deprivation.[29] Findings from the SSA surveys suggest that public perceptions of government performance may be overly favourable – between 1995 and 1999 use of public health care facilities increased by a modest 1.6 per cent, from 67.8 per cent to 69.4 per cent of the population.[30] Tragically, even the modest improvements in general health which would have been the consequence of wider access to clinics and immunisation programmes have already been eclipsed by the advance of the AIDS pandemic as well as the spread of more virulent strains of malaria. Official estimates of HIV infection rates in March 2001 stood at around 4.7 million,[31] more than ten times the figure in 1990.[32] Between 1995 and 1998 the life expectancy of South Africans fell from 64.1 years to 53.2 years, a decline which life assurers have attributed to AIDS.[33] Associated with AIDS has been a resurgence of tuberculosis (TB). Infant mortality in 2000 was estimated at 59 per thousand, a sharp rise since 1998.[34] With AIDS patients sometimes occupying up to 40 per cent of the beds in public hospitals, the public health system is in crisis.[35] The achievements of the Mandela government as a result of its commitment to expanding primary health care need to be weighed up against policies on AIDS, which have often been indecisive and ineffectual. These will be discussed in more detail in the review of Thabo Mbeki's leadership in chapter 12.

Where there have been gains and advances in the extent and quality of public services these have resulted from reallocations of government expenditure rather than through increased national taxation or higher public borrowing. In line with the recommendations of the RDP's authors, government expenditure has remained more or less at 1994 levels in real terms, while the Department of Finance succeeded in progressively reducing the deficit from 1996 to 2001. The costs of these programmes are evident, though, in a variety of ways. The removal of farmers' subsidies as well as the introduction of land rights for labour tenants (through the Extension of Security of Tenure Act) partly explains the huge job losses in agriculture. In 1994 commercial farmers employed 1.4 million workers; by 1998 this number had fallen to 637 000. Both the agricultural unions and the South African National Civic Organisation (SANCO) suggested that violent crimes against farmers, roughly a thousand of whom have been killed in attacks since 1990, are often committed by the disaffected sons of former farm workers.[36] The increase in the primary health care budget has required the diversion of funds from hospitals. Despite coping with escalating numbers of patients, urban hospitals – including those serving poor communities – have had to contend with staff cuts of 30 per cent.[37] Their services have deteriorated dramatically. In Soweto 950 000 patients attended primary health care clinics in 1994, where they were seen by 800 nurses; in 2000 about 2 million patients visited clinics staffed by 500 nurses.[38] At the end of 1998, Gauteng provincial hospitals were experiencing a 50 per cent shortage of radiographers.[39] Less consequential costs include higher school fees for more affluent suburban parents; rate hikes accompanied by the withdrawal of certain municipal services in wealthy neighbourhoods; and sharp reductions in defence expenditure.

Most fair-minded people would concede that certain sacrifices are reasonable if these reforms and improvements in government services directed at poor communities are sustained and have long-lasting effects. This is when making judgements about the RDP's effectiveness becomes more problematic: we need to consider the quality of services and resources now under delivery to citizens, not just the quantity.

Let us take water as a case study. Water provision is a high-profile programme, of which the government is very proud. Up to 1999, the Department of Water Affairs was headed by a charismatic and popular politician, Kader Asmal, who succeeded in animating the public imagination with what he called 'new South African ablutions'.[40] His successor, Ronnie Kasrils, also enjoys public favour. To its great credit, the Department of Water Affairs took pains to ensure that its efforts were professionally evaluated. To this end, it commissioned an NGO in 1997, the Mvula Trust, which specifically concerns itself with issues related to water supply in rural communities, to undertake an investigation of some of the projects the department had established.[41]

Mvula's researchers focused on three projects, at Winterveldt (in the North West), at Shemula (in KwaZulu-Natal) and at Kgobokwane (in Mpumalanga). These three projects served a total of nearly 300 000 people, about a quarter of those then affected by the department's water provisions. From the investigations of Mvula's consultants it became clear that the most important determinant of the success of the projects was the degree of community engagement with the conception and management thereof. At the outset, the department in principle acknowledged the need for the projects to be planned in such a way that the bene-ficiaries would feel they owned them and hence recognise that they were respon-sible for their upkeep. Crucially, projects were meant to be managed by locally elected committees. These committees would be responsible for administering the fees, which would be used to maintain and operate the pumping and reticulation systems. In practice, this proved to be quite difficult. In only one of the projects, Kgobokwane, did there exist a lively culture of democratically organised CBOs, or 'community-based organisations'. In this area there were branches of SANCO as well as a local network of the Rural Women's Movement. These bodies had elected a water committee in 1994, in anticipation of government action.

In Shemula there also existed a community-based movement, the Amanzi Development Trust. In Winterveldt no such organisation existed, partly because of social tensions which had their origin in conflicts between tenants and freehold landlords in the area. In the case of Kgobokwane and Winterveldt, the planning and management of the projects were entrusted to the local authority. This deci-sion was difficult to justify in the case of Kgobokwane and it owed much to the personal predispositions of the officials concerned. In Shemula, the Development Trust was accorded the task of managing the project. Rural local councils are not always very effective institutions. They are often responsible for huge and scat-tered areas, and before 2000 only had advisory functions.

When examining the way in which each of these projects operated, the Mvula consultants found the extent of community involvement to be the key factor in various ways: in the initial design of the project; in assessing demand and people's willingness to pay for water; in preventing illegal tapping of the water supply; in maintaining the scheme; and in collecting the income from it. None of the projects was covering its running costs at the time of the fieldwork, partly because of inaccurate projections of demand but also because only in the case of Shemula were people actually paying for the water they consumed. When people did pay for their water they appeared not to be using more than they had bought from the tank carriers before. So even when the schemes were working they may not have made a huge difference to people's lives except in shortening the distance over which water needed to be carried. In certain schemes, payment levels have been affected by the operation of other, externally financed schemes, installed by the old homeland governments. As one Mvula manager observed, 'communities with new systems, perhaps rightly, began questioning why they were paying for services when neighbouring villages received free water.'[42]

It was a mixed picture, then. The department's commitment to monitoring its own achievements was impressive. The shortcomings could be attributed mainly to haste, authoritarian inclinations among officials in the field and inadequate research and planning. At the workshop at which Mvula's report was presented it was also pointed out that about a quarter of the new schemes had ceased to function because of neglect and damage to the installations.

What progress has there been since Mvula's evaluation? In 1999, estimates for the failures of water projects ranged between 50 per cent and 90 per cent. For example, a coordinator for the Alternative Information Development Centre claimed that 90 per cent of projects were affected by interruptions or had failed completely.[43] In conjunction with the Department of Water Affairs and Australian Development Aid, Mvula conducted a second investigation in 1999, in which 21 official projects as well as 56 Mvula undertakings were visited. A general finding was that 'training and capacity-building for community management' was 'token and ineffective'. Community involvement in designing systems had been 'non-existent in the vast majority of cases'. Local complaints about project design would be brushed aside: 'in an isolated impoverished area of the countryside, letters from community members and NGOs operating in the area stated that the scheme could never be sustained. The written response from the department was clear – spend the money on the project now or the project will lose its funding.' As a consequence of authoritarian planning too many departmental schemes used technology which poor communities would find far too costly to maintain.[44]

Among the projects visited was the Shemula scheme where payment (through prepaid meters) had declined sharply; only 323 of 7 500 households were drawing water from the prepaid system. The majority of residents had returned to collecting their water from the river bed.[45] Two schemes in Limpopo Province, one in Badimong near Pietersburg and the other in Sinthumule outside Louis Trichardt, together costing R67 million, were reported to be unused. The prepaid metering systems had been damaged because of local hostility to paying for unreliable supplies. In the case of Badimong, local antagonism to the scheme was partly a result of a contest for its control between chiefs and the local council.[46] Such reports of unused facilities help to explain the results of SSA research, which showed that between 1995 and 1999 the proportion of households obtaining their water from rivers, streams and dams had remained unaltered. Table 3.1 shows the results of the SSA surveys: 11.4 per cent of respondents in 1995 collected their water from rivers, streams and dams and 11.8 per cent were doing so in 1999. If they had been beneficiaries of water projects they were clearly not using them. The proportion taking water from boreholes and rain-water tanks had been halved, though – a reflection of the department's practice of closing down these facilities (which had supplied free water) and replacing them with expensive pumping schemes. It seems unlikely that such initiatives could have reflected popular inclinations.

Table 3.1 Changes in main source of water for domestic use of households, 1995–1999

	1995	1996	1997	1998	1999
Piped water	78.5	82.0	82.4	81.0	83.4
Boreholes and rainwater tanks	10.0	5.9	5.4	5.5	4.7
Rivers, streams, dams	11.4	12.1	12.2	13.5	11.8

Source: Statistics South Africa, South Africa in Transition, p. 75

In October 2000, the government announced that after the local government elections people would receive a free basic allowance of 6 000 litres of water a month. This represented a sharp policy reversal, for the allowance represented a quantity equivalent to the total consumption of most rural households that needed to fetch their water. In effect, rural water would become free and water committees would no longer have to recover operational costs for the schemes from consumers. Instead, in the poorer rural local authorities, water committees would receive funding through the 'equitable share transfer payments' which local governments receive from central government. These transfers were originally intended to enable poorer authorities to upgrade a range of services to their citizens; now it is likely that they will be used entirely to support the water schemes. With the abandonment of the effort to instil local financial responsibility and accountability for the schemes, their sustainability must become even more questionable.

At the same time Ronnie Kasrils announced that the government was reviewing its 'demand-led' approach, at least with respect to sanitation schemes. In 1997 the department's White Paper had argued that 'motivation for development [should] come from within communities'; in other words, water schemes and related developments should not be imposed on communities but should rather be the result of decisions within them to commit time and resources to planning and maintaining such undertakings. By 2001, Ronnie Kasrils and his advisers had concluded (in the context of a cholera outbreak) that provision of sanitation had been too slow, demand had been insufficient, and that 'we are committed to focusing far more resources to accelerate the delivery of sanitation'.[47] In the case of water provision, the abandonment of cost recovery has removed a crucial incentive to maintain a demand-led or people-driven developmental strategy.

In this context there is too little space to survey all the RDP initiatives, but housing does deserve consideration, as it is so politically conspicuous. Here there are two types of problems. The first concerns costs and pricing. The housing strategy works as follows: the government awards subsidies up to R15 000 to prospective homeowners who earn less than R3 500 a month. The strategy involves a complex process in which private-sector developers propose schemes that qualify for these subsidies. The state does not actually build the houses.

Initially, the well-publicised delays in housing construction were the result of bureaucratic bottlenecks. It took a long time for the authorities to approve schemes. In addition, it was initially agreed that the Provincial Housing Boards would need a 'Social Compact Agreement' reflecting consultation between developers and community representatives before releasing subsidies for any scheme. Such consultation could be very protracted: in the Eastern Cape developers complained that they often needed to hold as many as eighty meetings before they could start building.[48] To speed up the process, it was later decentralised so that powers of approval were invested in municipalities, and the social compact requirement was dropped.[49] This accelerated the pace of housing construction, but at the expense of efficient control.

This raises the second issue, that of quality. A subsidy of R15 000 does not go very far towards covering the cost of even a very basic dwelling, not once the land has been serviced with plumbing, sewerage and access roads. A serviced plot itself costs between R8 000 and R12 000. In theory, official policy favours the participation of small local contractors and self-help schemes – there are several cases of *stokvels* (informal credit societies) undertaking the task of housing construction – though the initial bids are often made by large companies, which then subcontract. Small contractors usually build more expensive houses because they cannot employ economies of scale or sophisticated construction systems.[50] One research investigation found in 2000 that only 30 per cent of the new houses it surveyed complied with building regulations, including the government's specification that subsidised houses should be at least 30 square metres.[51]

A significant proportion of new homeowners needed to take out loans to pay for their houses; the subsidies can be used for houses costing up to R65 000. Banks agreed in 1995 to make 50 000 loans available, though in practice they remained reluctant lenders to the low-cost housing sector. In mid-2001 Servcon, a special agency established by the government to negotiate settlements between defaulting mortgage holders (and thereby encourage banks to enter the small-loan market) had 33 000 defaulters on its books. Of these, 16 000 were facing eviction. Banks listed an additional 23 000 low-income-group defaulters.[52] At least 5 per cent of the beneficiaries of the new housing projects could afford to own them and from 1998 the government once again committed itself to building public housing for rental by low-income tenants.

Some of the cheapest houses have been built by women's self-help groups based on *stokvel* schemes. In Soweto such a group in Protea, assisted by an NGO, the South African Homeless People's Federation, constructed houses of R10 000 each for its members. The women in the group financed and built the houses by rotating allocations of cash and collective labour, making their own bricks and using second-hand materials. The Protea scheme started without housing subsidies. The same dwellings in Soweto would have cost R50 000 through a normal RDP venture employing contractors.[53]

The Victoria Mxenge Scheme in Philippi near Cape Town is another *stokvel*-based settlement funded through members' savings and a loan from the Homeless People's Federation. The women planned their own houses and built them themselves. Besides 800 dwellings the scheme also features shops, schools and a restaurant.[54] The Homeless People's Federation has supported the construction of 4 000 houses altogether and it largely represents and is controlled by women's organisations, though in 1997 it received a R10 million grant from the Department of Housing. This subvention was allocated following 'an often lonely struggle with government bureaucrats to transform the developer-oriented subsidy system into something able to support people's enthusiasm and capacity to meet their developmental needs'.[55] However, despite government's support for the Homeless People's Federation and notwithstanding official policy, self-help groups often complain of disdainful treatment by subsidy administrators.[56]

Bureaucratic regulations may work against self-help groups but they do not always effectively restrain commercial operators. There is no general standardised set of regulations concerning design, planning or pricing (in several notorious cases the profit margins that private contractors awarded to themselves have been very high). Motheo Construction, a firm headed by a friend of the housing minister, which was awarded a contract to build 10 000 houses in Mpumalanga, is one example of this trend. In East Rand's Phola Park, a company directed by Winnie Madikizela-Mandela, HBM, attempted to win a contract from the Presidential Project Management Committee by skirting regulations and assembling a showhouse twice the size and at three time the cost of other developers' models.[57] Another example of a firm that probably benefits from its political connections is LVR Construction, a company building houses in the Free State and owned by a local political notable and former provincial chairman of the legislature's housing committee, Ace Magashule. Neither has there been a systematic strategy of assessing where housing is most needed, and where shortages are most likely to occur in future.

Many of the completed estates are poorly planned, though certainly an improvement on squatter encampments. There are too many straight rows of boxy dwellings with no social amenities, situated far away from the places where their residents work, constructed as they are on the cheapest land available. Are they always better than what they replace? In Soweto, a Johannesburg architect noted in 1996 that the new housing schemes he visited barely differed, in overall planning, layout, type of construction and quality of finish, from 'the massive building programmes that occurred during the 1950s and 1960s'. Both were characterised by crabbed interiors, regimented streets and dormitory tracts; they were estates, not neighbourhoods.[58] It is difficult to regard such bleak developments as 'empowering' or 'people-driven', however much income they may have generated for local builders.

Even if schemes were participatory in their conception, this had implications for the quality of housing, for community schemes tended to involve upgrading of existing residential areas or the building of homes on land near to where people were already living. Such developments left apartheid geography intact, with black people living on the edges of cities – often near industrial land.[59]

Visual perceptions may be deceptive, though. Community empowerment can happen in different ways. A study of two housing schemes in Tygerberg, near Cape Town, highlights the role collective action can play in influencing official decisions about housing. In Tygerberg's Green Point there was a dispute about the choice of contractor between the council (including the local ward representative) on the one hand and the SANCO branch on the other. In the end, political action by Green Point residents thwarted the councillors' efforts to impose themselves as 'gatekeepers' of the development. Meanwhile in nearby Delft South, a local 'doorkickers' movement challenged a corrupt housing allocation process for 4 000 completed houses by moving its adherents into the new dwellings and then successfully defending their possession through mass confrontations and court litigation. Both episodes may have helped to forge and strengthen a sense of community in these new settlements. Both continue to maintain effective street-committee networks to regulate day-to-day issues between neighbours as well as to ensure popular participation in RDP forums and similar bodies.[60]

In the Tygerberg study, illegal squatters – the 'doorkickers' – are represented as the embodiment of 'communal capacity'. Perhaps this is true. But activism may as easily destroy communal cohesion as it may enhance it. In the informal settlement of Etwatwa outside Benoni, land invasions disrupted the process of allocating title-deeds in which the beneficiaries of houses and land were meant to be those whose shacks were identifiable from an aerial photograph taken in 1996. Tensions between ANC and PAC supporters politicised the distribution of subsidy application forms, and rival leaders attempted to consolidate their followings by selling sites. Here a locally based steering committee could not overcome factional divisions and instead the direction of the project is now in the hands of the council's ward representatives.[61]

How successful has the government been in realising its objectives in the Reconstruction and Development Programme? The answer to this question depends upon whose criteria of success serve as the basis for evaluation. If we keep in mind the 'left' version of the RDP, with its emphases on redistribution, inward economic reconstruction, state coordination of development, and popular participation, the record is uneven. With respect to redistribution, within the limits of conservative public finance a fairly substantial reallocation of resources and services has taken place. The relatively low cost of this and its impact in certain quarters do represent a real indictment of the old regime. So much more could have been achieved when goods and services were cheaper than they are today. Ironically, though, the most recent Human Development Index (HDI) ratings, based on the 1996 census, suggest that general living standards were improving more quickly between 1980 and 1991 than between 1991 and 1996. South Africa's HDI rose from 0.56 in 1980 to 0.68 in 1991 to 0.69 in 1996. Encouragingly, both the Eastern Cape and Limpopo, the two poorest provinces, recorded very dramatic increases in their HDI ratings between 1991 and 1986, from 0.51 to 0.64 in the Eastern Cape and from 0.47 to 0.63 in Limpopo Province. These gains were offset by declines in the indices in the same period for Gauteng and Western Cape, the wealthiest provinces. This decrease is probably the consequence of increasing urbanisation, with people from the poorer provinces moving into the cities, as well as government efforts since 1994 to allocate public resources in favour of rural communities.[62]

HDI ratings are calculated on a scale of 0.1 to 1.0 from a combination of life expectancy, educational attainment and per capita GDP statistics. South Africa's HDI statistics are comparable to many middle-income countries, but they conceal much wider degrees of social inequality than most countries with comparable ratings. Measured on the Gini coefficient scale, inequality in South Africa fell from 0.66 in 1971 to 0.58 in 1998; this figure still makes it one of the most unequal countries in the world.[63] While inequality is believed to be decreasing overall, it is increasing amongst blacks because of the enlargement of the middle class. To date, research is unclear about the effects of government redistributive policies on the very poor, but evidence suggests that between 1991 and 1996 the income share of the lowest 40 per cent of earners declined; that is, during that period absolute poverty might have expanded.[64] This is uncertain, though. In the late 1990s real wages rose by 2.5 per cent a year. The unemployed may not have become poorer but their numbers have increased. Pensioners are probably worse off than ever before: the real value of the old-age pension fell by 20 per cent between 1993 and 2000. Grants to low-income single parents fell in value too, but more people received them.[65] Government expenditure has shifted in favour of poor people,[66] and it is possible that poor people may have benefited from better access to public goods, but this conclusion assumes general efficiency in the delivery of public services. As we have seen in the case of water, the quality of new facilities can be very uneven.

The scorecard for economic progress is even less substantial. At the end of 2001 government had yet to publish an industrial policy that would identify the priorities for public investment so as to encourage certain kinds of economic venture, except in the vaguest terms. The left-wing's argument that growth will be significantly boosted by the new domestic markets for manufactures created by better living standards represents a prospect that is still fairly remote, though electrification could play a very important part in expanding local markets. Annual GDP growth figures since 1994 have yet to exceed 3 per cent, a figure that remains well below the 6 per cent which official planners calculate is needed to make significant inroads into unemployment.

The state's capacity as a coordinator has been quite weak. Development projects, with notable exceptions like water, are implemented through provincial governments, and, as we have seen, both their political complexity and their bureaucratic shortcomings make implementation of development policies extraordinarily difficult. Coordination requires imagination and vision, and the state's managers have often chosen to ignore the NGO sector, which frequently possesses the appropriate experience and knowledge of what is needed. It is also worrying that state policies themselves are often poorly integrated to achieve the most important goals. For example, regulations that compel the use of generic medicines may reduce the cost of public health but this is at the cost of foreign investment by drug companies in a potentially competitive export-oriented industry.

Finally, the state's commitment to people-driven development seems to have been fluctuating and ambivalent. In many areas the trend has run against popular participation. In this chapter we have seen this with respect to water projects and the way in which, in the absence of social compact agreements, the housing programme became a vehicle for small-contractor 'empowerment'. The collapse of the development forums in many neighbourhoods and the evident weakness of community-based organisations make it all the more difficult to engage citizens in development projects. NGOs that might have provided the specialised skills to enable communities to plan their own projects were incapacitated as they lost staff to state institutions (as many as 60 per cent had left by 1997).[67] However, an initial tendency for foreign donors to redirect the flow of project funding into government agencies was reversed in 1998 as a consequence of the perceived inability of state-sponsored bodies to spend international aid efficiently. The National Development Agency (NDA), established by the government as a conduit for foreign aid had by 2001 – three years after its foundation – only spent a fraction of the money donors had channelled into it.[68]

Government bureaucrats may have become more hostile to popular participation as a consequence of increasing pressure on departments to meet quantitative delivery goals. As at least one analyst has noted, since 1999 'government departments have been driven by the need to spend money, meet targets and avoid rolling over funds. The Treasury has become increasingly powerful, and the performance of departments is measured against indicators that focus on spending against budgets … The tone of government has changed. Officials operate less as programme partners (with civil society representatives) and more as programme managers.'[69]

In 2001, an influential ANC commentary expressed exasperation at 'lengthy consultative and consultant-driven processes on actions about which there could be no dispute – is it not common sense that the people, who have the right to meet and associate, need community halls to enable them to do so?'[70] In reaction to mounting official cynicism about its merits, community participation all too often becomes a perfunctory ritual. Though the claim that the government's commitment to fiscal conservatism in its GEAR programme represented 'an abandonment of the redistributive RDP' is unfair,[71] it is certainly true that the closure on 28 March 1997 of a dedicated RDP office headed by a minister within the Presidency ended the official understanding of the RDP as a 'people-driven' process. Today, when government spokespeople refer to the RDP it is simply in terms of the fulfilment of various 'delivery' targets directed at basic needs.

What about the business community's expectations of the RDP? Certainly there is plenty of evidence that the state is willing to share the responsibility for meeting 'basic needs' with private enterprise, sometimes, its critics argue, to the detriment of the supposed beneficiaries of such programmes. It may be significant, for example, that some of the most imaginatively designed housing schemes have been inner-city terraced housing, which will remain within the public sector to accommodate rent-paying tenants.[72] Business would like to see a smaller and less expensive state: given the political pressures for job provision the government has demonstrated restraint in not enlarging the public payroll. South African economic competitiveness remains restricted by low levels of worker productivity and, as corporate spokespeople argue, by legislation that promotes labour market inflexibility. Better-educated and hence more productive workers seem a remote prospect given the recent trend of deteriorating matriculation rates and the government's failure to improve the quality of public schooling.[73]

Politicians, though, are not businessmen; they cannot be expected to arrange their priorities using the same values as stockbrokers. Government programmes have attempted to address a range of concerns across a deeply divided society. The shortcomings of public policy in its conception and implementation have reflected these divisions, but the limited achievements are all the more impressive because of them.

4 | LAND REFORM

South Africa has the most unequal land distribution in Africa. In 1996, some 18.8 million South Africans lived in the countryside. Of these, about 14 million lived in the former ethnic homelands; in other words, about one-third of the population was concentrated in 13 per cent of country. Most of this population was very poor indeed, earning less than R237 per household every month. These represented three-quarters of the people living at this level of poverty. The former homelands represented about 25 per cent of the land with agricultural potential. The rest was owned by about 60 000 farmers, mostly white.

In itself, inequality of land distribution may not be economically or socially problematic. Most advanced industrial countries feature heavily concentrated ownership of agricultural land. In South Africa, though, this inequality is associated with a recent history of dispossession and enforced resettlement, racial barriers on ownership until 1991, and acute overcrowding within the boundaries of the former homelands. Accordingly, the Reconstruction and Development Programme (RDP) acknowledged that a national land reform programme should be 'the central and driving force of a programme of rural development'. Yet eight years after its adoption, South Africa's land is almost as unequally divided as ever. Of all the efforts to address basic needs, those directed at alleviating land shortage have been the most desultory. Less than 2 per cent of farmland has changed ownership as a consequence of government initiatives. What has gone wrong? Why has progress in this sphere been so modest?

Three considerations influenced initial approaches to land reform. It was widely believed that white farmers had prospered mainly because they had received state support. Removal of such support would help to enlarge the land market and lower prices.[1] A generation of historical research demonstrated that in the late nineteenth century and even later, black farmers had done well commercially until the state deprived them of land and prevented them from competing with white farmers.[2] Given this history, it was assumed that black agriculture could be revived quite easily after the removal of apartheid barriers. After all, experience elsewhere in Africa appeared to demonstrate that transferring land from white settlers and giving it to African peasants could make for a more efficient agriculture, capable of supporting a substantial rural population in conditions of general prosperity. In successful land reform programmes elsewhere in

Africa, peasant beneficiaries used the land more intensively than the settlers they replaced and in the long term required less state assistance.

The ANC's agricultural policy-makers were heavily critical of the ways in which the state had influenced agricultural marketing and pricing over the years. State protection, its policy drafters agreed, promoted unnecessary mechanisation, it encouraged environmentally damaging land use, and it caused high prices for consumers.[3] If this picture was valid, then removing or redirecting state support would immediately expose the sector to its inherent vulnerabilities and make it more susceptible to reorganisation.

The problem with this argument is that by 1994 it had been overtaken by changes in government policies. During the 1980s, state aid to white farmers became too expensive and as a result official policy became more businesslike. The National Party (NP) had initially, after its election in 1948, adopted a policy of keeping whites on the land with indiscriminate subsidies, regardless of land usage. However, in the 1980s, the state began to revise policy in favour of a tougher and more discriminating direction. There was a very severe drought in 1982 and poor weather thereafter. In particular, grazing conditions deteriorated. The government became increasingly reluctant to undertake such expenses as payments of huge subsidies to export maize at below cost. All the same the government continued to help farmers through this period. Various forms of aid to 25 000 farmers amounted to R2.7 billion in loans, conversion grants and drought relief. However, in 1984 a White Paper on agricultural policy recommended what it termed 'orderly marketing'. It was still seen as desirable to keep farmers on the land but only if they used it well and performed optimally in international markets. In 1986, the President's Economic Advisory Council proposed help to farmers to convert arable land to grazing in marginal areas. In the following year there were no subsidies to bring down the cost of maize exports.

These reforms were successful. Agriculture became increasingly productive, experiencing a 7 per cent growth through the 1980s, despite a doubling of debt in the sector: by 1996, commercial farmers owed banks as well as the national exchequer around R20 billion.[4] The areas under maize cultivation fell by 25 per cent as shifts took place in favour of specialised forms of cultivation such as horticulture as well as cattle production. Farmers became more capable of coping with risk by shifting to less labour-intensive production, like livestock; by concentrating ownership and forming companies; and by undertaking off-farm income generation. In the 1990s the government withdrew further supports. Under these pressures, farmers' co-operatives converted to companies (making them less susceptible to state regulation) and agricultural employment declined to about 1 million in 1994. With the advent of democracy, white farmers were considerably less vulnerable, politically and economically, than they had been historically.[5]

In 1994, farming within the homelands represented about 10 per cent of national agricultural output. Around 3 per cent of the population within home-land borders could make a living from farming, but for most people cultivation or tending livestock merely supplemented income. Since the 1960s inequality in landholdings and cattle ownership had increased rapidly. People with access to external or off-farm income were then most likely to use their land fully. Much of the land in the former homelands was underused. Family plots were usually between five and eight hectares in size. Of the 1.7 million households that had access to farming land – about 70 per cent of the homeland population – 800 000 used less than one hectare of their allocation.[6] In the early 1990s, researchers found that 85 per cent of homeland households earned less than R1 500 a year; average earnings for each household amounted to R819. Many households were headed by women, who often experienced difficulties in obtaining access to good land.

Some help was available to homeland farmers before 1994. The Development Bank of Southern Africa funded a farmer support programme. Between 1987 and 1992 around 25 000 farmers each received support to the value of R50 000 from this source. But evaluation indicated that the costs of supporting these farmers were higher than the incomes they earned. Financial support to farmers required accompanying investment in infrastructure. Even if farmers were successful in a venture such as vegetable production, they needed better access to markets. The most likely beneficiaries of Development Bank assistance were people who were already quite wealthy in relative terms.

The best success stories in homeland agriculture were the KwaZulu sugar producers. Their enterprises were the outcome of co-operation with larger company-owned estates adjacent to the KwaZulu homeland territory. These companies provided inputs and access to markets. Even so, yields on homeland sugar farms remained comparatively low. Small farmers within homeland borders were unable to replicate the economies of scale of commercial farms.[7] Since 1994 the various kinds of help that homeland administrations offered to commercial agriculture within their borders are no longer available. For example, in the areas of former Bophuthatswana farmers no longer have access to state-maintained boreholes and machinery, nor can they rely on fixed prices for their product.[8]

From 1994, the government committed itself to three kinds of land reform activity: redistribution – in other words, transferring white-owned commercial land to African users; restitution – that is, settling claims for lands lost under apartheid; and tenure reform within and outside the former homelands. The chief emphasis of reform has been on redistribution.

By the end of 1999 about 52 000 households had become beneficiaries of the government's redistribution project, receiving a total of 693 000 hectares, distributed across 439 'designated' or ministerially approved projects. Altogether 130 of these were in the Free State; the next largest number of projects, 52, were established in KwaZulu-Natal.[9] Two key pieces of legislation helped institutionalise the programme. The Provision of Certain Land for Settlement Act of 1993 and the Development Facilitation Act of 1995 both provided for the designation and provision of land and the financial support for people acquiring land.

This early programme of land redistribution in South Africa was much less ambitious than land reform undertakings in other African countries such as Zimbabwe or Kenya. It did not involve extensive settlement of large blocks of land organised through purchase and allocation by a state agency. Instead, individual households or groups of households were assisted to buy land through grants. In February 1996, the Green Paper on South African land policy, drawing on the experience of a series of pilot projects that had been announced by Nelson Mandela just after the 1994 general elections,[10] conceptualised redistribution as an undertaking which should be 'demand-led'. In effect, communities or groups of aspirant farmers would have to take the initiative by identifying land and applying for grants. This approach reflected two background influences. The first stemmed from a land-reform NGO activist community that had been active in the 1980s and emphasised community assertion as the key to progress. The second, in a more conservative vein, had its origin in the government's planners also paying attention to the thinking of World Bank experts and Development Bank land specialists.

Both groups had been in dialogue with the ANC since 1990. They favoured 'market-led' agrarian change, focusing on the role of small farmers in creating a more efficient agricultural sector. The World Bank's advisers argued against any 'confiscation with compensation' approaches because this would require costly bureaucratic agencies and equally expensive litigation. The World Bank's views prevailed over those of the activists from the National Land Committee (NLC), who favoured expropriation, an option which was believed to be ruled out by the Constitution.[11] Since 1992, the agrarian specialists from the World Bank had been engaged in a joint investigation with South African land reform advocates, many of them within the ANC's policy community. The report on their findings, *Options for Land Reform and Rural Restructuring in South Africa*, was extremely influential, particularly in its advocacy of further liberalisation of agricultural policy 'as the foundation of growth for the whole economy' and the proposal that the 'starting point' of land redistribution should be a basic grant 'sufficient to pay for a major share of a rural housing site'.

However, the World Bank's report distinguished between two goals in a successful redistribution programme. On the one hand, the programme should address welfare objectives by enabling the very poor to obtain access to land. On the other hand, it should also promote productive land use. This second objective could be achieved by directing additional grants and agricultural support services towards a more select group of beneficiaries than the very poor, at those with some farming experience and the capacity to match state grants with their own savings or borrowings.[12]

Government policy drew upon the World Bank's recommendations selectively. The RDP's goal was to achieve the redistribution and transfer of 30 per cent of cultivable land in five years,[13] a target taken from the World Bank's report. In the World Bank's proposals land transfer on this scale would involve the resettlement of 600 000 smallholders. The RDP made no reference to the numbers of beneficiaries. This was possibly a recognition that the overall cost of R9.6 billion of even basic grants for the number of people envisaged in the World Bank's recommendation would be unaffordable. The RDP's authors believed that a proportion of the proposed area could be made available from state land; in fact, the homelands comprised about half of state land. Much of the rest is urban.

Beneficiaries of redistribution were meant to take the initiative: they were to form communities that could be assigned legal ownership; they were to indicate a piece of land they could purchase; and then they were to apply for a grant. Land sales were to be on a 'willing buyer, willing seller' basis. To increase seller willingness, the government-owned Agricultural Credit Board and the Land Bank doubled their interest rates.[14] The role of the Department of Land Affairs was to register the groups and to help them create 'business plans'. The procedure included five stages: project identification; feasibility investigation; designation and land transfer; detailed design; and development and support. Successful applicants would receive a grant based on the total housing subsidy for which they were eligible: R16 000 per household. Each plan needed to be approved by the minister of land affairs, Derek Hanekom, a former dairy farmer who had served a five-year prison term for running an ANC communications system from Magaliesburg. In its first incarnation, then, the government's redistribution programme was directed more or less exclusively at the 'welfarist' objective as identified by the World Bank.

Confined as its role was, the Settlement Land Acquisition Grant scheme (SLAG) represented a formidable administrative challenge for the Department of Land Affairs. It was very understaffed. For example, only 169 people worked in its nine provincial divisions,[15] and its district offices were very small, like the district office in Ermelo, which employed only two people. The department was therefore compelled to engage consultants to assist in business planning. These consultants were usually very expensive. Planning of projects was often rather superficial and the 'outsourcing' of the planning function meant that the department built up very little inherent knowledge and experience. The ministry was caught up in and distracted by internal 'transformation' issues, particularly measures for implementing affirmative action and the amalgamation of different apartheid-era agencies that had been responsible for homeland agricultural development.[16] The business planning procedure became very protracted; two to three years was common. By 1997 only R20 million of the R314 million budgeted for the pilot project had been spent.[17] In KwaZulu-Natal at the beginning of 1999, only 12 out of 226 designated projects had reached the implementation phase at which municipal administration could provide services, and more than half of the province's projects were still in the process of being transferred.[18] Budgetary underspending did decline after 1997, but remained a problem: unspent funds totalled R390 million in 1995/6, R619 million in 1996/7, R245 million in 1997/8, and R92 million in 1998/9.[19] The department's inability to spend its money prompted a reduction in funds allocated to it in successive years. By 1999, less than 1 per cent of commercial farmland had been redistributed through SLAG, a fraction of the original RDP target of 30 per cent.

Quantitative evaluations at such an early stage may be unfair. Neither in Zimbabwe nor in Kenya was land reform much swifter in its initial phases. If the South African schemes were successful in creating economically viable enterprises that substantially improved the lives of their members, then the department could justifiably claim success for the first stages of land redistribution.

Researchers' conclusions, based on these criteria, are very mixed. Many researchers maintain that most of the land that has been transferred had been used at least partly for productive purposes – mainly cultivation – despite an official view that many of the applications were essentially designated 'settlement' schemes, that is, for residential purposes. Official figures indicate that only about 10 per cent of the SLAG schemes were essentially residential.[20] How much economic activity occurred on others varied widely. Members of groups that applied for grants often had fairly tenuous social connections with each other. This made planning and subdivision of the land for productive purposes after purchase quite difficult. Officials had originally hoped that settlement communities would undertake some kind of collective or co-operative production, but this would have been very difficult if the group had been formed for the sole purpose of land purchase.[21]

Contrary to early predictions, the market value of land remained high,[22] and if groups only had their settlement grants for purchasing farms, they would have had to assemble very large numbers of beneficiaries   often too many to exploit the land productively or profitably. The most readily available land on the Highveld had been under cultivation for maize or used for cattle farming, both of which entailed very high production costs. The most effective schemes usually involved ex-farm workers. Under SLAG, beneficiaries were afforded little help after transfer. Local authorities were meant to supply certain services, but few could afford such investments. Besides, no state support of the kind could have matched the assistance given to white farmers in the past.

If the aim of the programme was the creation of economically sustainable smallholder agriculture, then clearly Lionel Cliffe's case study of Cornfields,

KwaZulu-Natal, represents failure. Here 10 000 members of households who were originally inhabitants of a 'black spot' freehold community that was removed in the apartheid era, managed to return to their original land and acquire three adjacent farms through the SLAG scheme. They were undertaking 'block farming', that is, common ploughing and then subdivision of the ploughed area between households. They had also succeeded in negotiating the installation of piped water and the construction of access roads. However, even with the planned addition of poultry-rearing, land-based activities would only be able to support a small minority of the households. Most of the titleholders were migrant workers; for them the scheme represented a residential stand and the prospect of income supplementation.

Even further away from the programme's goals was the Botshabelo project Colin Murray encountered in 1995. Botshabelo is a removals-era township situated halfway between Bloemfontein and Maseru (Lesotho). By 1990 a number of white farms had been incorporated into the township as a consequence of an earlier intention to try to persuade the QwaQwa homeland authorities to absorb it into its administration. The farms were leased back to their original white owners until 1993 but fell into disuse during this time because of cattle theft and an increasing feeling of insecurity among the white leaseholders. The land was slowly taken over by herd owners from the township and used as common grazing area. In 1991 an ANC land committee, community representatives and the minister, Derek Hanekom, agreed that the farms should be subdivided into 21 units, which groups could then buy with their land acquisition grants at agricultural value rather than market price.

Members of the National African Farmers' Union (NAFU) as well as a breakaway group from NAFU which could not afford its R25 monthly subscriptions resisted this agreement. Together they represented the 100-odd stockholders who were grazing their stock on the land. In fact, even at the reduced asking price the proposed farming units were no viable proposition to the syndicates of about eight grant applicants who would need to buy these together. At most, the whole area had grazing sufficient for about 1 500 cattle and the same number of sheep or goats. Like the Cornfields titleholders, the stockholders who were grazing their stock here were using the land to supplement their income as taxi operators or supermarket owners.

A detailed study of the post-purchase history of one of the farms, Diepwater, owned by a taxi operator and four of his drivers, suggests that its acquisition represented a means of income supplementation for quite a wealthy group – at the expense of four ex-farm workers who, as the former employees of a white leaseholder, could remain at Diepwater, notionally protected by the Extension of Security of Tenure Act. In reality, they were subjected to continual harassment by the new proprietors, who refused them access to water, firewood and grazing, or charged them very high fees for access to these resources.[23]

Another similarly contested scheme was the Gilimburg plan in which thousands of farm workers would be moved off state land originally purchased for consolidation purposes for the Lebowa homeland. The land would be divided into 38 units and applications would be invited from people willing to undertake farming with cattle, citrus and tobacco. The farm workers would be moved into agri-villages, and some would obtain access to the land through the formation of syndicates. However, most would have to find their livelihoods elsewhere. Despite its promotion under the auspices of the SLAG scheme, local perceptions of the Gilimburg project were that it was merely a revival of an apartheid resettlement scheme.[24]

In Solane, near Malelane in Mpumalanga, 200 families pooled their grants to spend R3 million on fallow land, which they planned to turn into a citrus and sugar estate. With a water quota to enable them to irrigate 100 hectares and an agreement for the supply of technical training from the staff at a nearby sugar mill, the Solane Farmers' Association planned to work the land co-operatively. The project would provide full-time employment for about eighty people, and pay out profit dividends to all its members. Members could also graze their cattle and operate partly commercial food gardens next to their houses. According to the regional planner of the Department of Land Affairs, this venture expressed the essential intentions of the government's programme: 'land reform isn't about chopping high-potential agricultural land up into small plots for resettlement any more. It is increasingly about taking fertile but fallow land and putting it under production.'[25]

In a similarly entrepreneurial vein, 600 workers in Mpumalanga's Lomati Valley were confronted with eviction when the owners of the Inanala mango orchards faced bankruptcy. After threatening to burn down the trees in protest against a take-over from a sugar company, which proposed to clear out the workforce, the workers attracted support from the Mpumalanga government and an NGO, the Land and Agriculture Policy Centre (LAPC). The LAPC helped the workers to assemble a business plan, according to which the farm workers would pool their grants and solicit private investment to buy the farm. After purchase, it continued to run along traditional lines with contracted managers. Wages for the farm workers have risen fivefold since their take-over. They could also look forward to making joint decisions about the investment of a R5 million profit at the end of 1997. Immediately after sale, a day-care centre was built for young children, and running water was laid on at the workers' compound.[26]

If Lomati had represented a typical instance of a SLAG scheme, then the programme would have represented a major achievement. Such projects are clearly sustainable; they represent a significant broadening of land ownership; and at least as far as the workers and their families are concerned, they bring a substantial improvement in the quality of life. Many projects, though, resemble

Cornfields or Botshabelo in their outcomes. These land settlements by themselves cannot provide full livelihoods for the communities who live there. The South African Agricultural Union was by 1997 expressing alarm at 'the loss of agricultural land' these projects represented, in which 'settlements often translated into one cow one family'.[27]

The union's criteria for evaluating productivity may, however, be the wrong measure to judge success in land reform. Left-wing critics of government policy suggest that the authorities' preferred ideal of the full-time smallholder-cultivator is culturally biased and fails to recognise popular predispositions for 'multiple livelihoods' in which farming is only one of a range of activities through which members of households support themselves. Agrarian reform should be directed 'at the growth of multiple livelihood opportunities', for example, by concentrating on land redistribution in peri-urban areas, where access to non-land-based incomes is easier, rather than on the reconstruction of a bucolic idyll of yeoman farming.[28] Limited resources could alleviate poverty more effectively, the advocates of such a strategy maintain, if land were redistributed with the aim of enhancing multiple-income opportunities. If this perspective is adopted, the Cornfields or Botshabelo experiences look more positive.

The government's own evaluation of SLAG was generally unfavourable, especially with respect to larger projects involving groups of more than 100 grant holders. In January 1999, the department's director for monitoring and evaluation told reporters that his colleagues had picked up 'major problems with the larger projects established over the last three years and have realised that the bigger the project, the larger the problem'. Most applicant communities lacked internal cohesion and they managed their new enterprises badly, it was said. The department would no longer be supporting projects with thousands of beneficiaries; too often these were 'rent-a-crowd undertakings' with signed-up nominal urban beneficiaries who never tilled the land.[29] Since 1994, in fact, the general trend had been to support smaller projects. In 1994 the number of households per project was 285, whereas in 1998 this number had diminished to 90. The average size of schemes had contracted from 3 784 to 899 hectares; in other words, by 1998 each household in new SLAG schemes would have obtained an average allocation of 10 hectares if the schemes were subdivided between households.[30] Early evaluations of projects suggested that inhabitants often faced bleak living conditions. A 1997 survey of 62 settlements discovered 40 per cent to have no primary schools within walking distance, that most used wood for cooking, not electricity, and less than half took their water from standpipes. In many cases, the people who moved to these schemes lost access to clean water, electricity and services. 'In most cases,' the department's investigators found, 'project implementers were unable to win commitment from local governments to carry out responsibility for infrastructural development.'[31]

These critical conclusions about the redistribution project prompted a change of leadership within the ministry, as well as a significant policy reappraisal. The Department of Land Affairs had been combined with Agriculture in 1996 after the NP's withdrawal from the Government of National Unity. The deputy minister of agriculture, Thoko Didiza, was appointed as Derek Hanekom's deputy. After the 1999 general elections, Hanekom was not re-elected to cabinet; Thoko Didiza took his place. Well before the elections it was evident to insiders that the two politicians were in disagreement over policy. Hanekom had enjoyed a friendly relationship with the NLC, the NGO which represented the cause of landless people and from which many of his senior managers were drawn, whereas Thoko Didiza, the daughter of a farmer, was closer to the black 'emergent farmer' lobby embodied since its formation in 1991 by NAFU.[32] She also had strong backing from the more 'Africanist' sections of the ANC Youth League. In 1997, NAFU had adopted a resolution of no confidence in Hanekom because of the government's reluctance to provide the kinds of support to black farmers which historically it had given to whites. At that point, black farmers were paying the standard 19 per cent interest rate on their Land Bank loans.[33]

Hanekom's dismissal was accompanied by a shake-up in the top ranks of the department. This was interpreted both as an affirmative-action-motivated purge of the 'Kensington cabal'[34] of white officials, particularly those with a background in the pre-1994 NGO activist sector, and as a redirection of departmental policy towards the right. In particular, the removal of deputy directors-general Stanley Nkosi and Sue Lund was perceived as a repudiation of the priority given to poverty alleviation through addressing the needs of the landless.[35] Shortly afterwards, the chief executive of the Land Bank, Joe Slovo's widow, Helena Dolny, was forced to resign from her post amid accusations and counter-accusations of racism.[36] Among the charges levelled against Dolny was that she was reluctant to make loans to emergent farmers, despite 33 000 micro-finance loans to black farmers. The Settlement Land Acquisition Grant programme was suspended in June 1999 pending a policy review. The 148 proposed land acquisitions still in the pipeline would have to be re-approved.

The department's new approach to land redistribution was announced on 11 February 2000. As expected, its main focus – or, to quote Thoko Didiza, its 'core business'[37] – was to be the emergent farmer sector. The new policy would place much less emphasis than the earlier one on the extension of land rights to the poor. To adopt the World Bank's terminology, it was less 'welfarist' and more 'productionist' in orientation. The principal goal was to be the creation of a new group of 70 000 commercial farmers within 15 years. The initial target group of the programme would be the 50 000-odd members of NAFU. In the first five years of this undertaking the government would spend R1 billion a year settling farmers on 2 million hectares of what is at present state-owned agricultural land.

A new grant procedure would create opportunities for aspirant commercial farmers. Successful applicants would be those recognised as having the potential 'to contribute to local economic development'. In contrast to the earlier 'demand-led' approach in which the beneficiaries were expected to take the initiative, this 'supply-driven' programme would require a much more extensive range of government activities, including the initial purchase and servicing of land. Three levels of grants would be available, the amounts depending on the applicant's own ability to mobilise savings and raise loans. To receive a R30 000 grant the farmer would have to contribute R10 000. For medium grants between R35 000 and R100 000, the farmer would have to raise R40 000. For large grants, farmers would need at least R135 000 of their own capital. To qualify for the medium to large grants, recipients would need to have had five years of farming experience.

The programme still allowed for the allocation of small grants to poorer people who would use the land merely to extend a 'food safety net', that is, for subsistence farming or as an income supplement, but this would no longer represent the main emphasis of land redistribution.[38] The needs of the rural poor would in future be addressed through the second sphere of official land reform activity – land restitution – and this would be speeded up, the department promised.

The programme reflected official impatience with the slow pace of land transfer to date. By helping smaller numbers of farmers purchase larger expanses the de-racialisation of commercial land ownership would be accelerated. Using the criteria of commercial viability as a key determinant in grant-making would ensure that agricultural productivity was not disrupted. The state assumed the role of a land distributor, either by selling off its own land (hitherto leased to commercial farmers) or by purchasing land before subdivision and sale. Thus the department could assume a more active planning role or, alternatively, could delegate such functions to the district councils that were established after the 2000 local elections. The department signalled its recognition of the fact that progress in land redistribution might require more vigorous state intervention by directing tougher language at white farmers. In future, officials announced, land owners might have to be induced to sell their farms at 'equitable' rather than market prices.[39] In certain cases, departmental spokespeople warned, the government would use its legal right to expropriate land: 'Farmers are just going to have to come down in their prices.'[40] Meanwhile, the minister informed journalists, she was seeking advice about the management of land reform from the Zimbabwean officials she had met during a visit in August 2000.[41]

The government's first attempt to expropriate land at a fixed level of compensation was unsuccessful. After initially trying to purchase a farm in Lydenburg for nearly half its market value (after taking soft apartheid-era loans into account) the authorities paid the farmer R1.3 million, R450 000 more than they first offered and only R200 000 below the market price. The government's legal advisers decided that the law as it existed would not allow expropriation; in their view the definition of 'public interest' that would provide constitutional grounds for expropriation excluded land reforms.[42] Their caution may have reflected a recognition that market prices for land were generally low – well below its productive value – according to Agri SA, the body representing commercial agriculture.[43]

The department's policy switch provoked considerable criticism from the left. In October 1999 the NLC accused the new minister of slowing down reform. Nearly two years later, committee representatives were still maintaining that the department was holding up redistribution, blaming its neglect of the landless for a recent wave of urban land occupations. On several occasions during 2001 the NLC expressed its support for popular land seizures.[44] The head of the University of the Western Cape's Land Studies programme, Ben Cousins, published a fierce indictment of Thoko Didiza's 'weak' leadership. Since her appointment, previous 'investments in human capital' were being 'carelessly squandered' as a consequence of the abandonment of training projects and resignations of key staff. The new programme had been adopted as policy without any consultation with either parliament or civil society. In all likelihood the programme would 'use scarce state resources to benefit a small group of better-off people'. The minister had sidelined officials with land reform experience and was instead preparing to implement the programme through former staff from the old Department of Agriculture, people with little experience of supporting new farming schemes.[45]

By September 2001 the first beneficiaries of the new grants were taking possession of their farms in the Free State and Mpumalanga. It is too early to make predictions about whether the grants will mainly be directed at the poorer borrowers, as departmental officials claim. Among the intended beneficiaries of the programme are farm workers and labour tenants who will be mentored by their employers. NAFU members, though, tend to be people who have accumulated savings from other kinds of activity and then invested in agriculture. A fairly typical representative figure would be the Mpumalanga lemon farmer Paul Nkosi, who began leasing land in the mid-1970s with the profits generated from running a chain of grocery shops.[46] In Bethlehem in the Free State, the local branch of the Land Bank had 90 'low-risk' black loan holders in 2000, many of whom were substantial proprietors like Petrus Mofokeng, owner of a 640-hectare dairy farm.[47] NAFU members are not peasants. But even if most of the borrowers take out the larger loans, once implemented the programme would certainly represent a significant change in ownership patterns. Even the larger landholdings would require extensive subdivision of existing farms and, as a consequence, more labour-intensive cultivation methods.

In the early 1990s about half the rural poor depended primarily on agricultural wages for their livelihood. A key concern in land reform advocacy has been the preservation of existing rural land markets, another justification for caution in redistribution.[48] Thoko Didiza's defenders insist that the commitment to poverty alleviation remains,[49] both with the 'food safety net' component of the programme and with respect to restitution. It is to this aspect of the department's activity that we shall turn now.

During the Hanekom era progress in land restitution was very slow. Claimants needed to prove that the state had dispossessed them of land as a consequence of racial discrimination after the passage of the 1913 Land Act. The claim then needed to be researched and validated or disqualified before being taken through an official arbitration process. If arbitration failed, the claim would have to be tested in a Land Claims Court. If the court decided that the claim was valid, then the claimants might either receive their original land (which would be bought for them by the state) or, alternatively, be awarded financial compensation. Given the complexity of this procedure it is not surprising that settlement could take a very long time. Documentary proof of original land ownership strong enough to withstand legal contestation was often difficult to find, and the various agencies involved in the various stages of the process were desperately understaffed.[50] Disagreements between the land claims commissioner, Joe Seremane, and the minister also led to a delay in decisions until Seremane's dismissal in 1998.

By March 1999 only 241 out of 63 455 claims had been settled, although these did involve 13 584 households, which represented a total of 83 378 beneficiaries.[51] Around 80 per cent of the claims involved urban land, for example Johannesburg's Sophiatown or Cape Town's District Six. If these claims are settled in the favour of the claimants, 300 000 people in towns and as many as 4 million inhabitants in the countryside stand to benefit from the process.[52] Two years after the cut-off point for submission, 12 500 claims had been settled, a reflection of a determined effort to speed up restitution by settling claims before the arbitration stage and awarding claimants financial compensation rather than land. Only 40 per cent of the money expended on restitution was used by the state to buy land for claimants.[53] The department had purchased 100 farms in respect of the 12 500 settled claims. Most of these would have been subdivided into tiny allocations to individual households.[54] For rural claimants, though, a more typical outcome might be in line with the settlement of the Chatha claim, which affected a community that had been dispossessed of ancestral land in the Ciskei during the 'betterment' resettlements of the 1950s. The R10.5 million settlement awarded to the community implied a compensation of R31 679 per household, of which half would be paid directly and the other half was to be used to fund development projects. In addition, the beneficiaries would receive ownership rights to the land they currently occupied. Half the claimant households were headed by women. If all the claims are recognised, some 3.5 million people stand to benefit.[55]

About 20 per cent of claims involve rural land. If all these were resolved in a way comparable to the Chatha settlement, land restitution would certainly represent a significant contribution to rural poverty alleviation. But the Chatha community may have been unusually well-organised. Rupert Isaacson's narrative of the disappointing outcome of the Xhomani San community's land claim against the National Parks Board underlines the importance of social capital in enabling communities to benefit from restitution. In the Xhomani case, restitution may have represented a moral victory, but it has yet to bring any significant material advances.[56] However, restitution administrators do claim that since 1999 the department has adopted a 'developmental perspective' towards restitution; in other words, beneficiaries who receive land can also expect support in terms of the 'necessary infrastructure, input, skills and know-how'.[57]

The Chatha settlement included change in land tenure. More generally, the rights of people who at present occupy land they do not own has been a key preoccupation amongst South African agrarian reformers. Official policy-makers have concerned themselves with two groups: labour tenants and the inhabitants of areas of communal tenure in the former homelands. The Land Reform (Labour Tenants) Act of 1996 instituted a registration system through which labour tenants on commercial farms could register ownership rights to the land they used for their personal plots. At the time there were about 30 000 labour tenants in Mpumalanga and even more in KwaZulu-Natal.[58] In each province the department sponsored two mobile units to register labour tenants by the legal deadline of 22 March 2000.[59]

The legal status of communal land was to be altered so that its occupants could use their rights as surety to raise loan finance – an indispensable condition for the reconstitution of agriculture in the former homelands – by means of the Land Rights Bill. However, this Bill, the result of four years of research and consultation, had been withdrawn for redrafting. The original Bill stopped short of conceding full ownership, but rather gave people permanent rights to occupy land. Occupiers of communal land (including women) would receive individual title but the way they used the land would be subject to group consensus, which was to be organised through local landholders' rights committees. The Bill was perceived as an attack on the land allocation role of traditional leaders.[60] Thoko Didiza, in announcing the withdrawal of the Bill, indicated that state land in the homelands would have its legal ownership transferred to individuals and to communities defined in various ways, and in certain cases to tribes. The inclusion of the category of tribes was interpreted by her critics as a measure that would perpetuate the power of tribal chiefs and the existing inefficient and inequitable patterns of land allocation.[61]

These fears seemed confirmed when the minister released a new draft of the Communal Land Rights Bill in November 2001, which defined 'traditional' communities as 'juristic persons' to whom land could be transferred. Thereby the Bill effectively ensured that in such communities chiefly control over land would be maintained. The Bill also drew criticism from leaders of the South African National Civic Organisation (SANCO) and, more surprisingly, from an ANC MP, Lydia Ngwenya, the leader of a commission on the role of chiefs in land management. Land affairs director Sipho Sibanda was disparaging about this opposition, noting that it mainly emanated from 'progressive liberals'.[62] At least in certain provinces, however, fieldwork suggests that there is widespread hostility towards the role of chiefs in land allocation, and considerable resentment of the inequities in allocation.[63] Moreover, both tribal and individual ownership of formerly communal land might well 'undermine the natural resource-based livelihoods of the rural poor' as well as 'promote the capture of key resources by local elites'.

South African data suggest that household use of foraged resources such as firewood, wild fruit and fodder can supplement household income to the value of more than R10 000 a year. Researchers in this field believe that land-based livelihood on communal land may represent 2.5 per cent of GDP and is a vital 'safety net of last resort'. Hence any change of land rights in communal areas should promote, not reduce, egalitarian access to resources.[64] Given the difficulties on the one hand of giving legal expression to common property rights and the antipathy on the other hand of well-organised rural elites to any alteration of 'tribal' land dispensations,[65] the department's hesitation in introducing tenure rights may well reflect quite understandable caution.

Successful land reform programmes reduce social inequality, alleviate poverty and promote growth. Even if progress towards these goals is uneven in the aftermath of a racially oppressive political order, a programme which brings about substantial transfer of ownership may well contribute to political stability if the transfer breaks up racial monopolies in agriculture. To date, the 550 000-odd beneficiaries of land redistribution represent merely a tiny fraction of the rural poor.[66] Given the likely trajectory of the policies adopted by Thoko Didiza in 1999, the number of people obtaining access to new land in the next decade is likely to grow even more slowly.

The concentration of public resources on 'emergent farmers' may well yield political dividends through the racial diversification of land ownership. It might even create more agricultural employment, but it will not affect the welfare of most of the rural poor. Tenure reform in the former homelands might promote productive agricultural activity. However, alterations in tenure arrangements in the form proposed by the government may merely accentuate rural social inequality, as Thoko Didiza's detractors maintain.

Any substantial progress in transferring land ownership and alleviating poverty would certainly require much more money than the levels of public expenditure on land reform since 1994 (see Table 4.1). Politically, land reform has been assigned a low-priority status by successive governments. ANC leaders suggest that this neglect accords with public perceptions, that while 'the issue of land was important for local people', the 'central issue' for most people is job creation.[67] Such arguments can be supported with evidence from opinion polls, which indicate that even rural people assign land redistribution a low ranking on the list of problems government should address.

Table 4.1 Public expenditure on housing and agriculture compared

	1994/5 ('000)	1995/6 ('000)	1996/7 ('000)	1997/8 ('000)	1998/9 ('000)	1999/00 ('000)	2000/1 ('000)
Department of Housing budget	1 623 159	2 866 792	3 186 306	2 400 000	2 880 000	–	–
Department of Land Affairs budget	346 807	533 935	729 780	688 068	793 664	752 632	846 504
Department of Land Affairs allocation to land redistribution	4 277	175 620	328 671	321 808	390 604	345 470	498 584

Source: Annual Reports, 1994–2000, Departments of Housing and Land Affairs

In mid-2001, after a succession of land invasions on the fringes of South African cities, one of which took place in Bredell on the East Rand, led by the Pan Africanist Congress (PAC), government spokespeople insisted that these signalled impatience with housing delivery, and not widespread social inclinations towards agrarian reform. They may be right, but in 2001 local popular support for illegal land seizures was also evident in three rural localities in the Northern Cape, Mpumalanga and KwaZulu-Natal.[68] However, public perceptions can change quickly. Very similar polling results were available in Zimbabwe several years ago, and in the continued absence of job creation in the South African countryside the symbolic appeal of land restoration may win many fresh converts to agrarian radicalism.

5 | LOCAL GOVERNMENT REFORM

Possibly the most difficult tasks in the creation of an integrated democracy in South Africa are those that need to be undertaken by local government. The reason for this is that the material conflicts between South Africa's different communities are most evident in the local allocation of resources. White South Africans tend to measure government's performance by the quality of services administered in their neighbourhoods: street cleaning, well-maintained public spaces, efficient electricity supplies, regular public transport, smoothly tarred roads, and so forth – the traditional responsibilities of local authorities. Many of the public goods that black South Africans expect as the consequence of their enfranchisement – clinics, street lighting, water-borne sewerage – are delivered by municipal administrations.

Even in the larger towns with their relatively efficient administrations, the ANC's first five years of local authority were to prove very challenging for its municipal managers and political leaders. The case of Johannesburg is illustrative. Like most of the newly integrated local authorities, in 1995 Johannesburg was in dire financial straits. Residents owed the metropolitan council R900 million in unpaid bills and taxes at the beginning of 1996. At the time Johannesburg was also borrowing money from banks to finance its recurrent expenditure. In 1997, the national Department of Finance prevented the council from applying for a foreign loan. Meanwhile there were huge inequities in service provision between the different racially segregated neighbourhoods. For example, before 1995 the Johannesburg City Council spent R3 000 per year on each resident in the northern suburbs, compared to R500 per head in Soweto.

With the introduction of a common voters' roll for municipalities and with the ANC's ascendancy there was now a powerful political compulsion to reduce these inequities. The infrastructure desperately needed a cash injection. In black settlement areas housing, roads, water supplies, drainage, sewerage, electrical supplies and transport had deteriorated as a consequence of very rapid urbanisation during the 1980s and 1990s. By 1990, about half the population on the Witwatersrand lived in 'informal housing', much of it very recent. The freshly settled areas placed tremendous strain on existing services. In particular, in the absence of modern sanitation the risk of polluted water supplies grew. In their first two years of office, Johannesburg's newly elected leaders 'spent aggressively on capital budgets' to address these shortcomings in the city's infrastructure – well beyond what it could afford.[1] The division of responsibilities between the central metropolitan council and the five sub-structures or boroughs – a consequence of transitional local government legislation – had created overstaffed and often very inexperienced managerial systems with confused lines of accountability and responsibility.

Johannesburg's new managers attempted to raise revenue in several ways, none of them very popular. The first approach was to try to increase the revenues available for investment in services in deprived areas. This could be done by increasing taxation levels and introducing the principle of cross-subsidisation from wealthier areas to poorer neighbourhoods. People living in the poorest neighbourhoods were required to pay a 'flat rate' basic tax in return for very simple services (public taps and common container refuse removal). People elsewhere were expected to pay taxes or rates linked to the reassessed land value of their residential property. Meanwhile, a central government programme called 'Masakhane' was instituted to encourage boycotters to resume payment of rates and service charges, electricity and water. 'Masakhane' was to be a programme of public education. It was meant to be exhortative and persuasive in its approach to defaulting township residents, but by late 1996 Johannesburg – like many other councils – was resorting to more forceful methods of encouraging payments: cutting off household electricity supplies, for instance. Even councillors, complained its director, Chris Ngcobo, in 1995 'did not take the campaign seriously and most are too scared to tell people to pay for services because they want to save face'.[2] More severe measures were hardly likely to engender a more co-operative public response. A survey undertaken by the Human Sciences Research Council (HSRC) in August 1995 found that 57 per cent of its black respondents opposed evictions or any cessation of services to those who failed to pay for these. Meanwhile, whites were strongly opposed to any cross-subsidisation: in the HSRC survey only 37 per cent of respondents thought that 'taxes of the wealthy should be spent to upgrade poor communities'.[3]

Not surprisingly, therefore, any efforts to increase local revenues by municipal administrations evoked sharp reactions. In Sandton, a previously autonomous municipality, social tensions between rich and poor assumed their most dramatic expression. Sandton was established in 1969, initially as a garden city, though its growth in subsequent decades was chiefly attributable to the movement of corporations from Johannesburg's run-down central business district to the new municipality's office parks and shopping malls. Burgeoning commercial rates and a generally affluent citizenry enabled the new town's governors to keep residential property taxes low. Households employed their own gardeners to trim roadside verges, required few social services, did not need public transport, and drew their labour from the nearby township of Alexandra.[4] Since the 1995 local elections the suburb had been integrated into metropolitan Johannesburg's 'Eastern Metropolitan Sub-Structure' (EMSS). This happy state of affairs for Sandton's office managers and boutique proprietors was difficult to reconcile with the normal social obligations of democracy. After 1994 Sandton's incorporation into the Johannesburg municipality brought wider financial responsibilities. As part of a sub-structure or borough which included working-class communities such as Alexandra, Sandton ratepayers would be expected to contribute to a wide range of local government services. In addition, a system of cross-subsidies would mean that richer boroughs would help to finance better services and infrastructure in poorer parts of Johannesburg.

A new property tax was introduced in the Johannesburg metropolitan area in 1996. In future all householders and businesses would have to pay a rate of 6.45 cents on every rand in new valuation registers. For traditionally under-taxed Sandton residents, the new rate scales in many cases represented threefold increases. Altogether 24 suburban associations, united under the leadership of the Sandton Federation of Ratepayers' Associations (SANFED), announced a rates boycott and opened a bank account into which ratepayers could make monthly deposits equal to their old taxes plus 20 per cent. By September the boycott was reported to enjoy 80 per cent support, with Liberty Life Insurance, Sandton's largest corporate, announcing its affiliation. Boycott partisans also included local Democratic Party (DP) leaders, especially those once associated with the free-marketeer devolutionist Federal Party, who had joined the DP after the 1994 general elections. Democratic support for the boycott stemmed from the party's objections to the authority of 'third-tier' local government generally, and its dislike of the structure of Johannesburg's metropolitan administration in particular. Before the 1995 elections the DP, together with civic and residents' associations (as well as some ANC activists), favoured a larger number of smaller, and hence more accountable, sub-structures or boroughs. The DP maintained that 40 per cent of the revenues that the EMSS transferred to the metropolitan 'third tier' would be spent mainly on 'a bloated administration and services to mainly white communities' in the other sub-structures, and not on alleviating township poverty. The boycott was to drag on for two years before fizzling out (eventually a court found in favour of the metropolitan council), but by then the city had lost about R200 million in unpaid and unrecovered revenues.

While it was true that municipal revenues were mainly expended on existing services, which were indeed concentrated in historically white neighbourhoods, and that improving township facilities mainly depended on capital grants from central government (such as the R1.5 billion RDP fund for municipal infrastructure), it seems likely that most Sandton boycotters were animated chiefly by resentment of what seemed to them unfairly sudden and steep taxation increases as well as principled objections to cross-subsidisation. Such sentiments were fuelled by a series of reports that exposed the self-serving behaviour of elected and appointed council officials in the Johannesburg vicinity. Huge increases in executive salaries and allowances – in certain cases well in excess of government recommendations – and instances of official extravagance abounded. Few of the ANC's municipal leaders in Johannesburg had succeeded in endearing themselves to the public. A snap survey conducted by *The Star* in November 1996 discovered that most respondents could identify neither the metropolitan mayor nor the borough leadership.[5] In December 1996, the DP successfully opposed, on grounds of a legal technicality, councillor allowance increases in the EMSS. Interestingly, the ANC-dominated borough executive was supported by the National Party (NP) minority. This was an example of a wider trend in municipal politics since the 1995 elections in which ANC councillors found it quite easy to discover common ground with their traditional NP adversaries, who tended to represent poorer white suburbs which, like black neighbourhoods, were the beneficiaries of fiscal redistribution.

Wealthy suburbanites were not the only people to protest against local tax increases. Moreover, protests were not confined to Johannesburg's gentry. The Johannesburg valuation roll included 240 000 properties that had never before been registered. These included many stands in squatter camps as well as more substantial township housing. In western Johannesburg, inhabitants of coloured townships, led by a new civic organisation, SOWEJOCA, rioted during January 1997 because they were angered that the poorer coloured neighbourhoods were not included in the areas that were allowed to pay the lowest 'flat rates'. Three people were killed in the course of these disturbances. People were also enraged by electricity cut-offs as a result of bad debts and the expulsion of illegal occupants from a new council-built housing project. In black townships, branches of the South African National Civic Organisation (SANCO) were a prime force in organising resistance against rate increases and service cut offs. In Soweto in July 1996, 45 SANCO branches led protests against rate hikes that averaged 50 per cent.

Elsewhere in Gauteng, there was growing evidence of a widening gulf between the new ANC municipal leadership and civic activism. Though SANCO officials dutifully organised door-to-door 'Masakhane' tours of Alexandra in September 1996 to encourage compliance with the new rates, in other places civic movements were less co-operative. In Tsakane, recently integrated into the Brakpan municipality, local tax and service payments stood at 10 per cent. In the early 1990s this was not an area in which independent civics had a strong presence; the local ANC branch had tended to absorb activist energies. In January 1997, though, residents were complaining that the ANC had stopped bothering to hold block meetings and councillors never reported back to their wards. Municipal service-charge increases from R30 to R130 per household had prompted the formation of new residents' associations with names like 'Simunye' ('We are one').

Civic resistance stiffened in 1998 when the council disconnected electricity supplies. This sparked off a consumer boycott and led to arson attacks on offices and councillors' houses. In October, mayor Calcott Dlephu was assassinated. In Tembisa–Kempton Park in May 1996, the ANC had to replace its mayor when it was discovered that former SANCO chairman Ali Tleane was not paying for his services. Tleane maintained that to pay anything higher than a flat rate 'would be failing his people'. Subsequently, Tleane and his SANCO comrades announced their intention to reconnect electricity and water supplies cut off by authorities. Delinquent ANC councillors in Khayalami, who were reported by a DP representative, Mike Waters, provided no such rationalisations; they subsequently paid up their arrears while a joint ANC–NP vote resulted in the suspension of Waters. In Benoni, significantly one of the few towns in which power-sharing provisions between the ANC and NP collapsed, the new Benoni Ratepayers' Protection Association (BRPA) mounted a year-long tax boycott. White Benoni citizens were reacting to a perception that within the new municipal boundaries they would contribute 95 per cent of the city budget despite having no representation within the council executive. Only R400 000 of the R12 million expended on the townships of Daveyton and Wattville could be derived from payments from their inhabitants, the BRPA claimed. Nationally, by the end of 1996, money owed to municipalities totalled R5.6 billion, Johannesburg itself accounting for nearly R1 billion of this debt. A quarter of this amount was the consequence of the Sandton boycott.

In general, though, resistance to rates increases tailed off in the course of 1997, particularly when the exhortatory 'Masakhane' approach was replaced with tougher sanctions against defaulters. Johannesburg's cut-off policy was reported by March 1997 to have achieved an impressive rise in payment levels. However, even if everybody had paid what they owed, no council could have financed the kinds of improvement to infrastructure that were needed in former townships. In many of the poorer areas, services continued to deteriorate as councils saved money. On the other hand, with respect to its financial management, Johannesburg represented a success story. Within three years – from 1997 – its council succeeded in reducing an accumulated deficit of R338 million to zero, achieving high levels of payments for service. However, the savings were a result of a sharp reduction in spending on maintenance of infrastructure. There were power cuts in suburban neighbourhoods, leaking water pipes, crumbling pavements, potholed roads, non-functioning traffic and street lights, library closures and a massive reduction of budgets (the Public Library bought no books in 1999). In 2000, just before the election campaign, there was a virtual collapse of emergency services – ambulance and fire brigade – despite these being largely staffed by volunteers.

Johannesburg's capital expenditure was slashed from R1.7 billion in 1995 to R500 million in 1999. Such economies implied that rate increases often coincided with a deterioration in the quality of services – an inevitable consequence of sharing revenues – but also resulted from the council's efforts to save money. The unpopularity of increases was aggravated by reports of councillors themselves not paying their rates and service charges, and by the announcement of very substantial pay and allowance increases for newly elected representatives. (In many of the former white municipalities councillors before 1994 had been paid only token attendance fees.) However, most councils did succeed in shedding jobs and reducing money spent on salaries as a result of the amalgamations that led to their formation; Johannesburg's council labour force, for example, shrank from 34 000 in 1993 to about 28 000 in 1997. Labour cuts added to the council's unpopularity, though, particularly when they resulted in reduced services. Most councils lost skilled people who were hard to replace. By 1997 Johannesburg's Southern Metropolitan Sub-Structure Planning Division was taking two years to process planning applications, because 'staff were out of their depth'.[6] As a result, builders and construction companies were losing work. An additional cause of deterioration in local services was overcrowding; most large cities more than doubled their populations during the 1990s because of boundary reconfigurations as well as migration – without any increase in resources.

Many smaller councils remained hopelessly bankrupt and almost dysfunctional. Where they did succeed in balancing the books, this did not usually lead to better services and was unlikely to do so in the short term. Instead, city managers invested their hopes in the 'mobilisation of private-sector capital resources'. In the past, municipalities had financed major projects through loans from banks, but in many cases their history of bankruptcy made it difficult for them to secure such loans after 1995. Instead, South African municipalities hoped to attract private capital investment through privatisation strategies. Johannesburg's *Igoli 2002* is one of the most sophisticated of these. The planning for *Igoli 2002* began at the end of 1998, its strategy involving the division of the council's responsibilities into three categories. Firstly, there would be 'core functions', which would include health, environmental care (cleaning, litter, etc.), museums, libraries and community facilities (including old-age care). These would continue to be performed by council staff. Secondly, a range of functions would be 'corporatised': electricity and water provision, road maintenance, parks, cemeteries, the Civic Theatre, the Zoo and the bus service. These corporatised functions would each be run by separate 'utilities' – publicly owned entities that would nevertheless operate according to business principles, selling to the council and to citizens an increasing range of services at market rates. Through carefully regulated financial management systems, these would be able to attract private-sector lending. In addition, they would have separate corporate legal status to facilitate recovery of

bad debts. In some cases, the new corporations might involve private–public partnerships. Some 12 000 of the council's present employees would be transferred to
these new corporate utility companies with three-year employment guarantees.
Finally, a range of council undertakings would be sold off to private enterprise,
including the fresh produce mart, the gas works, two city stadiums, and the Rand
Airport.

Though better managed than in many other centres, the changes in Johannesburg's administration represented a national trend, one which has encountered
strong opposition from trade unions. In Tygerberg, outside Cape Town, an ANC-
dominated council attempted to institute private rubbish removal, enlisting the
support of township entrepreneurs who organised neighbourhood refuse depots.
Shrewdly they recruited ANC Youth Leaguers, supplying them with two new
minibuses so that they could 'monitor' the emptying of dustbins. The scheme was
intended to reduce the council's wage bill. Predictably, local branches of the South
African Municipal Workers' Union (SAMWU) opposed the scheme, branding the
council's business partners as community 'sell-outs'.

The most protracted privatisation dispute took place in Nelspruit, where the
ANC-controlled local government hoped to extend piped water and sanitation to
the 90 per cent of its citizenry who did not have access to such services, through
offering a concession to a consortium of British and French companies. SAMWU
opponents of this venture insisted that the water would be expensive, that wages
paid by the company would undercut municipal pay scales and that, furthermore,
the foreign enterprises concerned were 'seeking to dominate world water
supplies'. However, despite trade union hostility, by March 2000 nearly 10 per
cent of South Africa's local governments had begun to run their services in
conjunction with private companies.[7]

Contracting out municipal services was just one of a number of ways in which
national government was proposing to change the way cities and rural communities should be governed and administered. In March 1998, a White Paper on local
government outlined a comprehensive programme of institutional reform. The
Paper opened by noting the 'spatial separations and disparities between towns
and townships' which apartheid had generated and which made cities so difficult
to administer. South African municipalities had inherited authoritarian forms of
decision-making, they were unable to obtain private-sector resources and many
had inadequate tax bases. In future, the Paper's authors urged, local authorities
should govern 'developmentally', providing vision and leadership to coordinate
the operations of both public agencies and the private sector. Municipalities
should encourage an assertive citizenry who would participate in community
affairs in equitable ways. The 'empowerment' of poor communities should be
fostered through cross-subsidisation and central government-funded capital
investment in infrastructure. Simpler procedures and regulations were needed to

encourage corporate investment. Municipalities should 'prioritise' their needs through 'holistic' integrated development planning, which would guide their budgeting. A national 'performance management system' should monitor their progress, and they should develop their policies and 'mobilise resources' in partnership with citizens, community bodies and business.

To achieve these goals, the White Paper proposed, municipalities should become more socially inclusive by enlarging their boundaries and becoming more effective within them. The executive authority of metropolitan government, for example, should be centralised instead of being divided between representative bodies at the centre and the sub-structures. Smaller towns should be amalgamated with their rural hinterlands to enable a wider distribution of the resources generated by their tax bases. Decision-making within councils should be concentrated through the election of executive committees or the constitution of a cabinet by an executive mayor. Municipalities should decide on 'an appropriate mix of service delivery options', including partnerships with private firms or NGOs, outsourcing of services or full-scale privatisation. While the White Paper prescribed various measures to improve municipal tax and debt collection, it also referred to a new system of central government financing of local government in which 'equitable share' transfers would help poorer municipalities cover their operating costs.[8]

In short, the White Paper maintained that most of the weaknesses in the administration of South African cities were the historical outcome of racial segregation and these weaknesses could best be addressed through larger municipalities with greater and more centralised powers as well as wider responsibilities. Critics of the White Paper maintained that it paid insufficient attention to the lack of 'managerial and financial capacity' in many localities and that merely unifying poor towns with poorer hinterlands and giving them additional developmental and planning functions over and beyond their traditional 'service delivery' obligations would make them even more difficult to govern.[9] Despite such objections, most of the White Paper's recommendations were transferred intact into an ambitious legislative programme, which over the next two years would reconfigure the landscape of South African local politics.

Local elections in 2000 represented the first step in implementing this programme. On polling day on 5 December 2000, South African voters, depending on where they lived, elected either metropolitan or local and district councils. Many voters were choosing representatives for completely new authorities established through the provisions of the 1998 Municipal Structures Act.

The six metropolitan councils – Cape Town, Durban, Nelson Mandela (Port Elizabeth), Johannesburg, Tshwane (Pretoria) and the Greater East Rand – embodied considerably larger municipalities than the existing metropolitan councils. Tshwane, for example, would incorporate several commuter townships across the provincial border of the North West, and the Nelson Mandela metropole would join Uitenhage and Port Elizabeth. Ten towns on the East Rand would become one 'uni-city'. Moreover, the new metropolitan cities would have no 'sub-structures' or boroughs: all the elected councillors would hold their seats in a single metropolitan chamber. Half would represent wards and half would be elected through proportional representation (PR); in other words, the number and significance of the proportionally elected councillors would increase. The PR seats would be allocated to parties on the basis of the votes received both in the ward elections and in the PR-list elections. Voters would complete separate ballot papers for each. In other words, unlike in 1995, the allocation of seats would be in full accordance with the PR principle. The wards were supposed to consist of roughly equal populations. The extension of proportional representation and equal wards would bring to an end the 'transitional' compromise in which people living in the former 'statutory' areas (white, Indian and coloured districts) were over-represented.

Outside metropolitan areas, voters elected local councils as well as district councils into which the local councils would be grouped; they would complete three ballot papers. In certain rural areas with no obvious concentrated settlement voters would elect district management committees, several of which would be contained in a district council. Powers and functions would be divided between local and district councils at the discretion of the provincial MEC for local government after the elections. District councils were intended to become key agencies in cross-subsidisation between different councils and would supposedly provide resources for local government in rural areas without significant tax bases. Within rural areas, the 800-odd chiefs and some of the 10 000 headmen would sit on councils *ex officio*, the law giving them no voting rights. Altogether, instead of the 843 local councils elected in 1995–6, there would be 6 metropolitan councils, 241 local councils, and 52 district councils – 299 in all. In Gauteng, for example, 51 authorities were replaced by 3 metropolitan councils, 9 local councils and 3 district councils.

Within these three broad categories of municipality, the Municipal Structures Act allows for considerable diversity in the councils' decision-making arrangements. These can vary from province to province as the MEC for local government decides with respect to each municipality how it will be governed: either by executives elected by the councillors (such executives may be multi-party), or by elected mayors (who would normally be from the majority party and may select an advisory mayoral committee), or through plenaries in which executive authority would reside in the whole council. The MEC also decides whether the councils will establish appointed ward committees, which may exercise powers delegated to them by the council.

Advocates of the new system maintained that it would be more democratic and more rational. It would be more democratic, they contended, because it would end the over-representation of racial minorities and it would be more efficient because there would be less functional replication between different sites of representation in the metropolitan council and between different councils. Savings could be achieved by having 4 000 fewer councillors and fewer officials in a smaller number of councils. It would be easier to organise cross-subsidies between richer areas and poorer neighbourhoods. There would be more effective planning, as the new system would allow for local development schemes on a larger geographical base with better coordination over locally available resources. More generally, economies of scale could be expected to result from combining the existing councils. In response to such arguments, the government's opponents in the Democratic Alliance insisted before the elections that the new 'mega-cities' would result in weaker public accountability and costly centralised bureaucracies administering services less efficiently because of the huge distances over which they would have to be delivered.[10]

Opposition from another quarter had more impact and at least achieved vague promises before the elections that the law might change. It also resulted in three postponements of the poll itself. 'The powers [chiefs] had before the whites came must be restored,' Nelson Mandela told those in attendance at the opening of a high school in Mount Frere.[11] Both Thabo Mbeki and the minister for local government suggested that the new municipal legislation might be reviewed and the Constitution amended to allow chiefs more influence in the new councils. Despite such reassurances, 'traditional' leaders and their political representatives in Inkatha and CONTRALESA (the organisation of traditional leaders) remained hostile to the new dispensation. In KwaZulu-Natal, chiefly opposition was reinforced by political suspicions that a politically biased Demarcation Board had amalgamated districts in such a way as to integrate districts in which IFP-aligned chiefs influenced voting behaviour, with towns in which the ANC would predominate.

But evidence of chiefly opposition extended well beyond the borders of KwaZulu-Natal. Chiefs believed that the new local and district councils would usurp their powers and functions (especially concerning land allocation). They were particularly incensed by the fact that the boundaries of the new councils cut across the old tribal authorities. Though the chiefs were to remain land custodians under the new dispensation, they feared that their authority would be challenged by 'preying vultures' if tribal lands were divided between several councils or if land were affected by municipal development planning.[12] In 1993, the law allowed all chiefs *ex officio* representation on councils, whereas in terms of the 1998 law, *amakhosi* (traditional leader) representation was limited to 10 per cent of any council membership. Chiefs also lost financial power: under the former dispensation money paid to local government structures in tribal districts was administered by their offices. In certain instances, traditional authorities were also opposed to cross-subsidisation; for example, the Bafokeng Tribal Authority in Phokeng deeply resented its incorporation into the Rustenburg municipality. The Bafokeng chieftaincy owned 22 per cent of the Impala Platinum mining company, and in terms of the new civic order it may well have to share its revenues more widely. In other areas, demarcation decisions led to the revival of ethnic sentiments associated with former homeland polities. In one instance, a Malamulele Border Committee organised a Shangaan community to oppose its incorporation into the Thohoyandou municipality. Malamulele's 280 000 inhabitants were originally removed from the Venda capital under the Group Areas Act.

The wealthier inhabitants of small rural towns were unlikely to view the new municipal institutions with enthusiasm. Notwithstanding exceptional instances such as Rustenburg in which the district council would embrace a relatively wealthy rural area, most small towns would be expected to spread their revenues over much more extensive and even needier areas than previously. How powers were to be divided between the new local and district councils was not spelt out in the legislation; this was an issue that would be decided by provincial governments. Many town leaderships were worried that their ratepayers would have to pay for the full cost of operating the district councils.[13]

On the eve of the 2000 local elections, many towns were already bankrupt – a consequence of the incorporation of badly indebted townships into former 'white' councils and the decline in central government funding available to support services in the townships. Brakpan is a good example. By 1999 the city was classified by provincial government as a Category 4 municipality, that is, on the brink of financial collapse. For five years the city had spent a R250 million annual budget, based on the assumption that one-fifth of the revenues would derive from service payments in the adjacent township of Tsakane. However, payment levels in Tsakane remained at around 10 per cent.[14] In smaller rural centres the financial crisis was even more serious because of much smaller commercial and industrial economies. The bankruptcy of Ogies in Mpumalanga, for example, had led to the entire town being denied electricity by Eskom in November 1998 and on several occasions subsequently, as the council had failed to pay for the supply it had resold to residents.[15]

In the Eastern Cape, by mid-1999 some 26 municipalities were perceived to require provincial government 'intervention'.[16] In the Sterkstroom municipality, the local ANC branch was in rebellion against its own council representatives for 'non-delivery', while in nearby Dordrecht two people were shot dead in anti-council riots.[17] Incorporation of such centres into larger districts may not offer them any financial relief. The new laws are vague about the extent to which cross-subsidisation will occur between municipalities. However, unless resources are transferred between cities or government is prepared to increase its grants to local authorities, small-town economies will collapse completely. Meanwhile, demarcation within the more prosperous cities could also be contentious, with opposition parties complaining that the new enlarged municipalities and the wards within them were created with the intention of reducing the significance of their areas of concentrated voter support.[18]

Boundary changes would not make cities easier to govern. An HSRC-sponsored evaluation of local authorities in Mpumalanga conducted in early 1997 suggested a quite different set of shortcomings in their effective management from those which the proposed reforms attempted to address. The researcher's survey of 12 municipalities emphasised the significance of the quality of political leadership and the depth of political organisation as determinants of effective administration. This was especially evident in the report on Middelburg, a medium-sized former market town with a population of 120 000 whose economy since 1972 had been enlivened by the establishment of stainless steel industries. While Middelburg is unusual for its degree of prosperity, industry was not the only explanation for the success of its municipal government. Middelburg's local authority boasted one of the highest rates of service payment in the country and was the only solvent municipality in Mpumalanga. This success was partly the result of a sophisticated system for ensuring service payments through prepaid metering and smart cards: consumers had to pay for other services before they could load their cards with electricity credits.

Since 1994, much of Middelburg's R40 million capital expenditure has been directed at the Mhluzi township community. Projects included a well planned RDP housing scheme, the concentration of squatters in a site and service area, and the expenditure of R24 million on improving township roads and providing new parks. Good relations between the ANC majority and the NP minority within the council also proved helpful: NP councillors were not driven by party or ideological concerns and most were former ratepayer representatives. Conciliatory politics was fostered between 1994 and 1996 through the Middelburg Informal Development Forum. ANC political leadership and local officials also benefited from mutual confidence. ANC predisposition to trust departmental executives was explained by the implementation of well conceived affirmative action programmes as well as the ability of ANC leaders to understand policy technicalities. Generally, ANC councillors in Middelburg were better educated than their peers in other Mpumalanga local authorities – a reflection of Middelburg's unusual concentration of post-secondary training facilities. But what was most distinctive about the ANC in Middelburg's municipal politics was the depth and experience of its organisation. As the researchers noted in their report: 'The ANC and the anti-apartheid movement more generally has always been extremely strong and well organised in Middelburg. Indeed it is ironic that this Conservative Party-dominated town was always known by the resistance movement as the

"Little Kremlin." It was Middelburg activists that originally brought the Black Consciousness Movement to the Eastern Transvaal, and when the Soweto riots broke out in 1976, it was in Middelburg that the equivalent occurred. Most indicative, perhaps, is the fact that Middelburg boasts more former exiles and political prisoners than the whole of the rest of Mpumalanga province put together.'[19]

This encouraging scenario in Middelburg was in sharp contrast with the picture drawn in the other 11 case studies. A few examples must suffice. In the trout-fishing tourist centre of Dullstroom, an ANC majority depended on a sympathetic town clerk and an independent councillor for financial expertise. The council functioned efficiently enough but was unable to make any decisive contribution to the development of the local economy which, with its dependence on tourism, was entirely white-controlled. Local ANC principals wanted to see factories attracted to Dullstroom, an unlikely prospect and one which would be anathema to the weekender fishing fraternity, who owned most of the town's property. ANC councillors' legitimacy has been uncertain since their refusal to grant municipal wage increases in August 1996 and the consequent emergence of a trade-union-based Dullstroom Forum. Councillors relied on an alliance with the local SANCO branch and so were very hesitant to penalise rates defaulters with service cut-offs. In nearby Machadodorp, SANCO also enjoyed considerable success in persuading a divided and insecure group of ANC councillors from taking action against tax boycotters (including conservative whites opposed to cross-subsidisation).

Researchers commented on the absence of any civic culture in the township and a mood of 'passive expectation'. ANC leadership weakness was compounded by the personal conflicts that had followed the deposition of the first ANC mayor, a 'struggle' veteran who could neither read nor write. Other councillors found it difficult to understand the legal language in municipal ordinances. The city's population had doubled in two years – a consequence of an influx of evicted farm workers – but its capacity to pay officials had declined: in September 1996 municipal salaries had to be funded from an emergency grant from the province. In Carolina, generally low levels of mobilisation left room for a series of populist leaders to emerge to challenge the authority of the ANC council. Their operations were facilitated by the ANC's dependence on tumultuous mass meetings as its main channel of communications rather than more structured forms of organisation.

In each of these localities, and hundreds more like them, the ANC's political supremacy was not seriously challenged by historically white parties, nor were its efforts at governing hampered by recalcitrant officials. Rather, weak municipal governance was a reflection of a political leadership unable, for a variety of reasons, to project authority.

For South Africa's new rulers, the creation of accountable municipal administration has constituted one of the most difficult challenges they have encountered. Even in larger towns, in which the ANC could draw upon deeper layers of competent leadership and richer material resources, the first five years of democratic local authority have been a chastening experience. Where the new councillors governed best, in Johannesburg for example, the achievement of financial rectitude was at the cost of deteriorating services and public disillusionment. A new architecture of civic reform was unveiled at the turn of the millennium. In the next chapter we shall consider the opening stages of its construction.

6 | MUNICIPAL ELECTIONS 2000

The 2000 municipal elections were held against the background of the situation described in the previous chapter. Voters would be electing representatives for new institutions with boundaries that were widely contested. In many centres they would be influenced by a recent history of local authorities having performed badly or having attempted to save money by cutting services in poor neighbourhoods. 'Corporatisation' and related policies, though favoured by most political opponents of the African National Congress (ANC), divided the party's own constituency and were explicitly opposed by its trade union allies and by the South African National Civic Organisation (SANCO).[1] At the same time, well-publicised evidence of the venality of individual councillors had prompted widespread distrust in local government, signalled repeatedly in opinion polls. For the ANC, the dominant political force in local authorities, it was an unenviable record to defend electorally.

Not surprisingly, the ANC 2000 manifesto, released in early October and entitled 'Speeding up change', contained only obliquely apologetic references to schemes such as *Igoli 2002* ('the public sector is the preferred option to provide services'), and most of the 'delivery' achievements it cited were those undertaken by the national or provincial governments, not local authorities. The main features of the manifesto were its emphasis on the ways in which local government would become more accountable and less corrupt, a commitment to providing 'free basic amounts of water, electricity and other municipal services', as well as an undertaking to 'working with communities to fight crime and strengthen solidarity' and to forge 'social partnerships' to curtail HIV/AIDS.

Accountable representation, free basic services, working together and fighting poverty: these were the messages intended to animate the ANC campaign. The ANC's target audiences were the urban working class and the rural poor: 'Your vote is your weapon against poverty', exhorted a full-page notice in ANC colours in daily newspapers on 22 November – one of the few instances of press advertising in the campaign. Later the Congress of South African Trade Unions (COSATU) claimed that it had played a major role in shaping the manifesto.[2] The promise of free water was the source of some embarrassment in at least one centre in which water reticulation had been privatised. For the ruling party, this was to be a defensive campaign rather than an effort to win fresh territory. And despite the rhetorical commitment to working in partnership with local communities, national leadership was conspicuously in command. In the first month of poster campaigning, October, only Thabo Mbeki's portrait appeared on ANC placards.

Top-down coordination and control were also intended to characterise the ANC's procedure for candidate selection. In the year preceding the onset of formal campaigning, ambitious plans were announced which were to govern the choice of who would represent the party in the new authorities. Given the reduction in the number of municipalities, 4 000 fewer councillors would be needed and their selection was to be governed by a 'national audit' of incumbent representatives to screen out the venal and the incompetent. Local branches would submit nominations for consideration at a 'national list conference', originally scheduled for September 2000. Branches were also expected to reinvigorate themselves by embarking on a recruitment drive. In the Eastern Cape, for example, in the aftermath of the general elections, the provincial general council announced a target of 200 000 additional members.[3] In the event, it was the party's provincial leaderships that provided the effective sanction for the candidatures, and internal politicking was probably as important as meritocratic considerations in their adoption. A national list committee did apparently review nominations in the course of October but it seems to have merely endorsed provincial submissions.

The plans for mass growth through recruitment failed to materialise. According to the ANC's deputy secretary-general, Thenjiwe Mtintso, this was partly because those in control of many branches were reluctant to surrender their function as 'gatekeepers'. In some cases, she said, families and friends had put together candidate lists in the name of branches that had become moribund.[4] The councillor audit was also interpreted in certain quarters as an authoritarian effort by national leadership to impose control, especially when it was accompanied by proposals from the ANC headquarters at Shell House to bring to an end the autonomous role of SANCO in local politics. Such fears were lent substance by a spate of expulsions of dissenting municipal politicians from the ANC. In one especially well-publicised incident the ANC mayor of Saron in the Western Cape lost his job after failing to nominate as a PR-list councillor an individual favoured by the provincial ANC's deployment committee.[5]

Of course, other considerations were also important in choosing representatives. The ANC's commitment to gender equity meant that one-third of the positions on its lists needed to be accorded to women, even if this required replacing local 'populist' notables with comparatively unknown figures. Conversely, in certain former homelands the organisation obviously felt it could not ignore the realities of local patrimonial politics, which had consolidated during the apartheid era and continued to be exploited by its opponents. Hence the party extended its embrace to include such veterans as the former Gazankulu minister Brighton Tlakula, the candidate for the mayoralty in Louis Trichardt; ANC MP Sam Moeti, one-time secretary to Chief Patrick Mphephu's cabinet in Thohoyandou; Messina candidate Gabriel Ramushwana, the last Venda head of state; and Godfrey Mothibi in Mafikeng, once the minister of justice of Bophuthatswana. In protest against deployment decisions, 172 former ANC councillors were to stand as independents. In the Eastern Cape, SANCO resentment at its minor role in the ANC's candidate nomination process resulted in a full-scale revolt. It decided to support a list of independent candidates drawn from ANC dissenters.[6] These were concentrated mostly in Uitenhage and it is likely that the SANCO rebellion was fuelled partly by union conflicts in the local motor industry.

Despite allegations that Mbeki would 'hand-pick' those who would stand as candidates for the mayoralties in the six metropolitan centres, the inclinations of provincial leadership seem to have been more decisive. In Johannesburg, former Gauteng MEC for health Amos Masondo was nominated, apparently after approaches to more glamorous personalities, including Murphy Morobe (chairman of the National Parks Board), had failed. Masondo was a close ally of the Gauteng premier, Mbhazima Shilowa, and his appointment was also supported by the provincial ANC executive, whose members perceived him as a 'unifier'. Masondo, though derided by press commentators for his lack of charisma, enjoyed a reputation amongst insiders as a dogged organiser from his work as head of the ANC's national elections team in 1999. Though Democratic Alliance (DA) detractors suggested that as mayor Masondo would adopt a conciliatory stance towards trade unions, officials of the South African Municipal Workers' Union (SAMWU) were less confident, remembering his tough record as MEC for health.

In Cape Town, ex-schoolteacher Lynne Brown's nomination also reflected provincial leadership predispositions after the national deployment committee had failed to persuade ambassador Cheryl Carolus to return from London. Despite being comparatively little known, Lynne Brown was believed to have considerable standing amongst coloured women voters, who were viewed as a particularly crucial constituency. According to poll evidence they were more likely to vote and more likely to support the ANC than coloured men.

On the East Rand, the inclusion of Bavumile Vilakazi, an MP and the proprietor of a bankrupt construction company that failed to complete a government contract, attracted considerable local criticism, despite his record as a trade unionist and civic activist during the 1980s. In Tshwane (Pretoria), the will of national leadership held sway with the deployment of the deputy minister for education, Smangaliso Mkhatshwa. Only in Durban and Nelson Mandela (Port Elizabeth) the incumbent mayors, MBA graduate Obed Mlaba and ex-Robben Islander Nceba Faku, were re-selected. Both were perceived to have headed relatively efficient 'business-friendly' administrations. In Nelson Mandela, the ANC was divided from the South African Communist Party (SACP) and unions over the choice of mayor, because of Faku's robust advocacy of privatising and outsourcing. In general, the ANC's decisions in this sphere reflected the party's preference for technocrats and skilful political managers; these were not candidates who could draw upon deep personal reservoirs of public popularity. Lynne Brown's contention that the 'elections should be fought on issues and not around personalities' probably reflected a general perception among ANC electoral strategists and their advisers.[7]

Given its recent construction, the initial reluctance with which the National Party (NP) received initial proposals for unification from the Democratic Party (DP), and the lingering dissatisfaction among many NP activists at their junior-partner status,[8] the Democratic Alliance in its campaigning strategy was remarkably coherent and aggressive. The DA allocated one-third of its budget to the 'black voting market', and actively recruited 'quality' black candidates, many of whom had impressive records of civic activism. They included a former deputy mayor of Soweto, several ex-ANC councillors and former ANC branch officials in Evaton. While the DP's 'fight back' slogan of the 1999 general elections was directed at Afrikaner voters, the DA's theme for 2000 – 'for all the people' – was calculated to attract the main share of the coloured and Indian votes and lay the groundwork for building a black voter base among the 22 per cent of the black electorate its pollsters had identified as susceptible to such advances.[9] As a corollary to this effort, maintained the DA's candidate for the Johannesburg mayor's office, Mike Moriarty, a key component of the strategy was that 'any association or reference to the NNP [the New National Party] had to disappear completely'.[10] Other kinds of historical baggage would also be left behind. In southern KwaZulu-Natal, where new DA branches signified to party officials an 800 per cent increase in active support and where black members outnumbered whites, according to provincial organiser Tex Collins 'anyone who cries that we are a white pinko liberal party, has got their sums wrong'.[11] In the Eastern Cape disgruntled former NNP leaders defected leftwards to the ANC, a move which was interpreted by provincial premier Makhenkesi Stofile as a proper reaction to 'the conquest of the nationalist spirit of their forefathers through the liberal philosophy of those who colonised both Africans and Afrikaners'.[12]

In contrast to the vague generalities contained in the ANC's programme, the DA's manifesto bristled with detailed specific commitments to how it would 'fight against crime', 'localise economic opportunity', 'manage poverty', combat HIV/AIDS, institute ombudsmen to 'stamp out corruption' and 'keep rates reasonable'. In addition to matching the ANC's commitment to a free 'lifeline supply' of water and electricity, the DA also pledged the free supply of anti-retroviral drugs at municipal clinics for HIV-positive pregnant women, as well as undertaking to expand the quantity of low-cost municipal rental housing and providing 'opportunity vouchers' for matriculants and basic-income grants for poor households.

The emphasis in the manifesto on the DA's sensitivity to the needs of the poor reflected its redirection away from the essentially suburban preoccupations of the DP's 1999 campaign to a more inclusive approach. But the most important emphasis in the DA manifesto, which set the tone for the campaign, was its attacks on an ANC which it claimed had 'delivered a better life only to a special few' and had led local governments into administrative collapse and financial crisis – the consequences of 'corruption, highly paid nepotistic appointments and sheer incompetence'. Given the absence of any truly significant policy differences with the ANC (unlike the ANC's allies, the DA approved of such plans as *Igoli 2002*), the main thrust of the DA electioneering would be in attacking the ANC's record and, in many areas, the integrity of its representatives.[13] In Cape Town the campaign keynote was expressed in the DA street poster that appeared in mid-November: 'Keep the ANC out: Vote DA'. In 1996, the ANC had won control of Cape Town as a result of the over-representation of its African population in the transitional arrangements. This time, the loyalties of the coloured electorate would decide the outcome.

In Cape Town, the only metropolitan council in which it had any real prospects of victory, the DA's selection of a brash populist, Peter Marais – 'the coloured Elvis' – as its mayoral candidate signalled its determination to maintain the old NP bases in coloured working-class neighbourhoods and to project itself as the champion of at least one section of the poor. Marais's record of ethnic particularism effectively put paid to the DA's prospects of making significant inroads into the ANC's African constituency in the city.[14] No Africans appeared as candidates in the top 30 positions on the DA's PR-list for Cape Town. Marais's chequered political career had included spells in five different parties, membership of P. W. Botha's presidential council, and a near-recruitment by the ANC just before the 1999 general elections, which lost him his post in the provincial cabinet. Elsewhere the DA's choices for metropolitan mayoral candidates were much less important in determining its electoral prospects, and white businesspeople and professionals predominated.

Much more important would be the DA's investment in locally focused ward campaigning. Here the difference between the ANC's and the DA's approaches was very evident. Many candidates all over the country distributed well-printed leaflets issued by the DA's central office, containing their biographies ('Marcelle has great energy and enthusiasm')[15] and detailing their concerns about local issues ('Pedestrian footbridge across canal at Concert Boulevard').[16] Generally, the ANC's national or provincial organisations did not help to produce or finance ward-specific publicity, except in Cape Town, where the contest for the working-class coloured vote became the key electoral battle and where its candidates included very experienced municipal politicians who could claim personal credit in securing 'delivery'.[17] Though ANC candidates' names and faces did appear on placards two weeks before polling, on the whole the party's approach to local electioneering eschewed any reference to their personalities.

Of the smaller parties contesting the elections – there were more than a hundred altogether, including 54 local groups – few had the resources or the skills to develop electoral strategies comparable in sophistication to the ANC's or the DA's. Thus most of them concentrated on sectoral preoccupations in their messages. Outside KwaZulu-Natal, the IFP barely registered a campaign presence, and its electioneering pledges focused on crime, water and basic health facilities. The last two were of particular significance in a party with a mainly rural support base. In contrast to the *dirigiste* emphases of the ANC and DA manifestos, Inkatha stressed self-help and 'community-driven' development. This reflected its dislike of the challenge modern bureaucratic local government posed to *amakhosi* prerogatives. In its activist dimension, the IFP's KwaZulu-Natal electioneering would be 'spearheaded' by its Women's Brigade, leaders noted.[18]

The United Democratic Movement (UDM) could budget only R500 000 for the elections; its candidates each had to contribute R500 to their registration fees.[19] Directed at a similar social constituency to Inkatha's, its four-page manifesto was distinctive for its focus on corruption, its commitment to regulate illegal immigration, its advocacy of a 'proper balance' between the roles of 'elected functionaries' and traditional leaders, and its concern about the state of rural roads.[20] A glossy leaflet elaborated a further list of 'rural issues', including 'respect for traditional leaders', and also called for 'negotiated, not imposed, municipal boundaries'.[21] That the UDM found time to produce a manifesto at all was an achievement, given the outbreak in September in its Eastern Cape heartland of a bitter dispute between 'Africanist' and 'non-racist' factions.

The manifesto launches of the Pan Africanist Congress (PAC) and the Azanian People's Organisation (AZAPO) highlighted the difficulties impoverished township communities were experiencing: electricity cuts, bond-defaulter evictions and service suspensions. Evidently these parties were hoping to mobilise support around the same sources of discontent that fuelled the emergence of such local independent civic movements as Brakpan's 'Simunye in Christ' organisation or Thokoza's Displacees' Ratepayers' Association. Disappointments resulting from the exclusion of community leaders from party lists helped to spawn another set of local associations; one of the most formidable was the Independent Alliance of Ward Candidates in Cape Town, composed of former coloured NNP councillors and branch organisers overlooked by the DA. Meanwhile, the African Christian Democratic Party (ACDP) projected a complicated libertarian programme blending advocacy of 'Biblical Christian values' and civic voluntarism with antipathy to progressive taxation, including local rates, 'municipal bigness' and 'secular humanism'. Such messages could find their resonance in a strong vein of 'anti-political' social conservatism among lower-middle-class white and coloured voters, especially in the Western Cape. In this election the ACDP had several Christian fundamentalist imitators seeking the same support.[22] In Mpumalanga, the ACDP collaborated with the Freedom Front in setting up the 'non-political' Highveld Ridge Residents' Association to contest the elections.

Victories in South African elections still depend very substantially on the degree to which political parties can achieve a local presence in communities. In this election, compared to the 1999 general elections, there was very little press advertising, and as there was no provision of free broadcast time for the contenders, radio publicity was used sparingly by the smaller parties. For the ANC and the DA, radio advertisements on national and local 'community' radio were a central element in their media strategies. Even so, the main parties emphasised face-to-face contact with voters by means of rallies, roadshows, meetings and house-to-house visits. During the final week of the campaign, the DA undertook a telephone canvass in Johannesburg.

Inevitably such procedures allow for plenty of local improvisation and a selective interpretation by activists of the messages devised in party headquarters. Consequently, local monitoring of campaigning is indispensable in any assessment of its progress and outcomes. In the next few pages we shall draw upon the questionnaire forms compiled by observers deployed by the South African Civil Society Observer Coalition (SACSOC) during the month before polling day.[23] SACSOC observers attended nearly 700 meetings in seven provinces. Here we shall first review in detail the reports from the sharply contested Western Cape, before looking more generally at campaigning in the other provinces.

SACSOC observers attended over fifty events in the Western Cape. Most of the reports concern campaigning, mainly by the ANC, in Cape Town. Attendance at meetings averaged 204, with women predominating. Most meetings reported on were small, with an attendance figure at around a hundred. There were one or two mass rallies, such as the ANC's closing event, the *Siyanqoba* ('We are winning') rally, with a relatively modest attendance of 1 800 boosting the figures. At 15 of these events, observers noted an absence of youthful participants. They also recorded disparaging comments from youth present at other meetings, who said that they were 'sick and tired because people always lie'; they were 'promised free education but they received nothing'; and they 'do not see a reason to vote'. In general, observers concurred that the youth were not politically attentive. Observers also agreed that the ANC was conscientious in promoting gender equality and female candidatures. The other parties obtained mainly negative marks on these issues.

To the discomfort of any 'pinko-liberals' remaining in the DA, Peter Marais's gender chauvinism became a campaign issue when he quarrelled with a female MEC after a disagreement over the content of the DA candidate list. Marais warned his colleagues that the DA 'should be careful not to put a lot of white women on the list'. In an altercation with the provincial MEC for gender equity, Freda Adams of the NNP, Marais told her that 'if I looked like you, I'd run and hide away'.[24] Adams subsequently resigned and announced her backing of the Independent Alliance of Ward Candidates.

In general, the SACSOC observers did not identify any serious obstacles to free and fair campaigning at the events they attended, though several violent incidents – including the killing of a UDM candidate, Gideon Sam, in Nyanga – certainly contributed to tensions between ANC and UDM supporters. Sam's murder may not have been motivated by electoral considerations, though, as he had been a central figure in a bloody conflict between taxi operators and a local bus company. The visit of the DA 'battle bus' to Gugulethu on 25 November 2000 was, in the view of one of the observers who witnessed its progress, accompanied by a 'few intimidations', although it is not clear who the perpetrators were. Indeed, the comment could imply that there were few, if any, intimidatory actions. However, in another incident, a DA bus's journey through Hout Bay ended in a brawl. A DA spokesperson claimed that ANC drivers had tried to force the bus off the road whilst the ANC's Cameron Dugmore accused DA passengers of having been drunk and attempting to provoke ANC members in one of their known strongholds. Two people were hurt.

In Atlantis, the ANC's posters had been torn down by DA supporters. A local DA official provided a justification for this on 30 November: the DA, he said, would like all ANC posters to be removed because they contained no publisher's attribution. The DA did make an official complaint to the Independent Electoral Commission (IEC), although the poster itself was quite inoffensive, its provenance unmistakable and the missing information a legal requirement clearly an over sight. Another poster was at the centre of a more serious dispute in Cape Town. This poster, bearing the legend 'A vote for the DA is a vote for Israel', was purportedly published by an anonymous group called the Friends of Palestine. The DA believed that the ANC's ward candidate and chairperson of Cape Town's council executive, Saleem Mowzer, was involved in producing it. Local DA spokespeople also accused ANC leaders of making anti-Semitic remarks about Tony Leon and his Israeli wife at mosques. Any DA feelings of vulnerability to radical Islamic hostility would have been accentuated by two bomb attacks, one outside a DA meeting in September and another in October near one of its branch offices in a shopping centre.

Even so, DA electioneering remained ebullient. DA supporters at an IDASA-sponsored candidate debate on 22 November annoyed several observers by behaving rowdily and shouting down the ANC's mayoral candidate, Lynne Brown. An encounter between DA and ACDP adherents in Steenberg on 18 November was characterised by some tension, with ACDP partisans waving their placards aggressively at DA leaflet distributors and thumping the bonnet of a car containing DA notables on their way to a meeting. In this instance, residents apparently received the DA canvassers with some hostility. However, door-to-door ANC canvassers in the same vicinity, three days later, undertook their visit in a peaceful atmosphere.

Only in two other cases did observers note tensions. At a UDM meeting on 25 November in Khayamandi, Stellenbosch, the crowd's mood became aggressive – or perhaps defensive – as ANC supporters marched close by on their way to another meeting, singing struggle songs. The second occasion concerned SACSOC observers who travelled to a venue in Khayelitsha, expecting to find a UDM meeting. On arrival they were told that they were at an ANC workshop. The organisers greeted them with great suspicion, presumably because they had asked where the UDM event was being held. The observers were refused entry despite having explained their status. The workshop was a private session, they were told, and informers or *impimpi* were not welcome. Otherwise, observers characterised all the proceedings they witnessed as calm and equitable. They may have been a bit uncritical, though. For example, the ANC's exploitation of opportunities arising from its role in government for electioneering purposes was reported without comment: when senior ANC officials and Lynne Brown presided over the formal openings of a crèche and a library in Khayelitsha on 25 November, they delivered heavily partisan election addresses; and Ebrahim Rasool and MPs delivered presents and electoral information at a children's day-care centre on 29 November. To round things off, just before the election Thabo Mbeki presided over a ceremonial hand-over of residential stands in District Six to their original owners who had been dispossessed under apartheid some thirty years before.

One observer raised the interesting question of whether it was in order for the main speaker at a DA meeting in Fish Hoek, on 16 November, to receive a gift at the end of the meeting. While such behaviour breached no regulation, this seemed a curiously deferential way to treat a candidate soliciting votes at a public meeting. The DA's electioneering style appears to have been more 'top-down' than the ANC's, but this perception may be a reflection of an unrepresentative sampling of events by observers. However, the authoritarian impression which DA campaigning made was reinforced by the comments of one 'ardent' coloured DA supporter, as reproduced in *Business Day* of 25 November:[25] a strong 'boer' government was needed, for only strong whites could stop violence and enforce law and order, Trevor Kleinsmith of Bonteheuwel insisted. 'Our hope as coloured people rests with the DA,' he said. Reports of DA meetings refer to events in chiefly coloured neighbourhoods. However, at the party's launch, Africans were 'bussed in' from the townships and speeches were preceded by a performance of Brenda Fassie's 'Vulindlela' (the ANC's campaign song in 1999). Obviously, as noted in one astute commentary, the DA seemed to feel that it could be perfectly assured of its white support base.[26]

To a much greater extent than in other provinces, the content of speeches focused on micro-issues or locality-specific concerns. This was especially characteristic of events organised in coloured neighbourhoods and may reflect the relative experience of candidates in municipal politics as well as the existence of strong civic organisations. Several of these appeared to have been active in the campaign, usually in alliance with the ANC. Civic organisations sponsored at least four of the events that hosted ANC speakers. A meeting in Grassy Park that was held jointly by the ANC and the residents' association discussed, amongst other matters, defective traffic lights at a local junction. A UDM gathering in Khayelitsha focused on the provision of street lights and bucket toilets in C Ward and measures to promote relief from traffic-related air pollution. This meeting provided an interesting indication of the social base of UDM support, when Bantu Holomisa enjoined 'people in the hostels' not to vote for the ANC, because to the ANC 'they were location people'. Toilets were also a central concern at several ANC meetings in Khayelitsha, partly because of the sponsorship of a scheme called 'Project Toilet' by an ANC MP with assigned constituency responsibilities for Khayelitsha.

In all neighbourhoods, African and coloured alike, crime – especially rape and child abuse – seems to have been a key preoccupation. In Gugulethu, for example, participants at an ANC meeting on 22 November discussed the formation of a neighbourhood watch, and in Steenberg on 23 November residents at an ANC house-meeting told candidates about the insecurity arising from local crime and very poor policing. Candidates from all the parties – DA, UDM, ANC and ACDP – spelt out similar promises about free water and electricity. In the ANC's addresses these undertakings appear to have been explained in detail: an audience in Gugulethu was told that the allowances would provide a family with 6 000 litres a month and enough electricity to burn a single light globe for 30 evenings. In several locations, the ANC was campaigning against DA incumbents. In such circumstances its speakers made the most of their opposition status, criticising the DA-dominated authorities for evicting indebted tenants at Happy Valley on 23 November or noting the poor quality of construction in a local housing project in Strand on 24 November. Because both parties enjoyed majorities in different municipalities in the Western Cape, both could attack each other's record in office. Peter Marais, for example, gleefully compared the ANC's house-building record – Cape Town's city council constructed 500 units – with the achievements of the DA-controlled Southern Peninsula, where 3 500 houses had been built – more cheaply, he claimed, than by the council.[27]

In general, negative campaigning – that is, invective directed at other parties – seems to have been much more conspicuous in Western Cape electioneering than elsewhere. This was predictable enough, given that the battle for power between the DA and the ANC would be a close one. DA rhetoric directed against the ANC appears to have been especially fierce. The ANC encouraged prostitution and rape, mayoral candidate Peter Marais alleged at a major DA function held at the Civic Centre on 28 November. On the same occasion, Marthinus van Schalkwyk of the NNP noted that 'Mbeki was honeymooning' despite the ANC's failures to deliver. All the government could do was give people land without houses or, at best, two-by-two-metre 'hokkie' shacks; and the only jobs the ANC could provide were jobs for friends and family. Not to be outdone by his new associates from the NNP, Tony Leon spoke in a similar vein at a meeting in Newclare on 27 November. Unlike the ANC, Peter Marais 'understood the plight of the poor', he said. The ANC promoted crime in the Western Cape, whereas the DA would show no mercy to criminals. Criminals' rights were protected by a Constitution which, Peter Marais noted, had been 'drafted by communists'; the ANC could not administer budgets and only provided for its friends and comrades; and finally, unlike the ANC, the DA would ensure fair rates and no increases in the suburbs.

But ANC propaganda against the DA was equally unpleasant. A leaflet distributed in Mitchell's Plain showed the premier, Gerald Morkel, saying 'thanks Tony' for keeping blacks out of the provincial cabinet. It also accused the DA of wanting poor coloured neighbourhoods to subsidise property rates in affluent white areas.[28] By the end of the campaign, the vituperative tone of the proceedings in the Western Cape was being echoed by the ANC's national leadership, which had through most of the electioneering avoided attacks on their main opponent. At the beginning of December Mandela instructed a Johannesburg audience that they 'should not be misled by a party that cares only for blacks on the eve of elections'. 'No white party', he continued 'can run this country … no matter how they cover up by getting a few black stooges.' Meanwhile, Thabo Mbeki told a wind-up rally in Khayelitsha that 'there are other people who tell they love you. But where were they when we were fighting apartheid? They were on the other side, the side that locked us away in Robben Island.'[29] ANC campaigning in Cape Town was based upon a tacit recognition that it would be most unlikely to retain its hold on city government. Defence of its 'pro-poor' record in the city and emphasis on the DA's 'policies of white domination' appeared to its local strategists to offer the best long-term prospects of 'building solidarity between African and coloured oppressed'. This required the concentration of its efforts on 'core' support and maintaining a low profile in areas where the DA was popular so as to avoid provoking a high turnout amongst DA voters.[30]

Other notable features of local government electioneering in the Western Cape included the prominence of AIDS as a campaign issue. Both the ANC and the DA paid considerable attention to AIDS, with Lynne Brown making undertakings for the provision of cheap drugs and soliciting compassion for AIDS patients on several occasions. More contentiously, the ANC on 23 October issued a statement contending that the DA's proposal to provide anti-retroviral drugs in Khayelitsha could be equated with 'the biological warfare of the apartheid era'.[31] Audiences at meetings appear to have been less participatory than in other provinces; observers noted that fewer issues were raised from the floor except at house-meetings (which seem to have been confined to the Western Cape). When people attending meetings spoke from the floor it was usually to complain about the performance of ineffectual councillors (Gugulethu, 22 November), especially when these had been re-selected as candidates (Khayelitsha, 2 December). To the ANC's credit, the need to make councillors popularly accountable was a frequent theme addressed by its speakers. Ward 99 in Khayelitsha was contested for the ANC by one Hitler Mdoda; this activist's name achieved for him a certain notoriety in the press, but to judge from reports he seems to have been a busy and conscientious candidate. One final and curious feature of the campaign seems to have been the relatively late stage at which candidates were introduced to their wards at public meetings, and candidate introductions seem to have continued until 1 December in Khayelitsha.

What were the most distinctive features of the electioneering in other provinces in which SACSOC observers reported? In the Eastern Cape, within the old borders of the Transkei, the main debate between the ANC and its principal opponent, the UDM, concerned the effects the new municipal institutions would have on local life. At a UDM function, Holomisa told party officials that party agents should not be youngsters and that voters should elect councillors with a clear understanding of Xhosa custom. The UDM would show respect for traditional leaders and ensure that the new demarcations and the municipal administrations which would arrive in their wake would not harm them or their people (9 November). ANC speakers evidently felt on the defensive about the demarcation issue: people should not listen to other parties that were misleading them about demarcation; people should not be afraid of it; and indeed, demarcation would help to improve the lives of their communities as the new authorities would be empowered to deliver clean water, electricity and access roads to rural neighbourhoods, an assembly in Mtombe was reassured on 15 November.

A small group at Mnyolo, Engcobo, on 9 November included several very rowdy UDM supporters who created considerable tension. Even without their presence, the ANC speaker would have had an initially unsympathetic audience. Argument from the floor indicated a widespread sentiment that people were unwilling to vote because they did not want services – if they had to pay for them. It was generally believed that the residential site allocations each household received from the tribal authority would become liable to rental charges from the new council (an issue on which the draft legislation was ambiguous). The concern about paying rent for stands in communal areas was widely shared at three meetings in Mqanduli. In general, the SACSOC observers suggest that despite firece competition, there were no obstacles to free electioneering. However, the rivalry between the two parties occasionally erupted into covert violence: the houses of the UDM's mayoral candidates for Umtata and Mbashe were burnt down.

Some eighty meetings in the Free State, better attended by women than men, testified to a generally orderly electoral environment; most complaints about breaches of the regulations concerned poster vandalism and harsh language. The worst instance of rhetorical aggression involved the incumbent ANC mayor of Moqhaka (Kroonstad) describing two black DA ward candidates as representatives of a 'boere party'. The mayor may, however, have been confusing the Democratic Alliance with a local civic, essentially a representative of the Freedom Front, calling itself Alliance 2000+. This body was heavily critical of the DA for holding rallies on Sundays in breach of Christian principles. Otherwise the most salient features of Free State local electioneering were the prevalence of door-to-door canvassing by both parties in the same vicinities – sometimes on consecutive days – without any activist misbehaviour; the possibly related political disaffection of young voters; and absence of any references by candidates to locality-specific concerns. ANC representatives in particular, wherever they were, appeared to be using a common script. To compensate, those in attendance seemed to have plenty to say about the track record of their municipal administrations. The most common issues raised from the floor were local concerns about the allocation of building sites and the lack of progress in RDP housing projects; shortages of medicine in local clinics; the absence of old-age care; councillor corruption, especially in the area of housing allocation; objections to the ANC's procedures for appointing candidates; water cut-offs; and evictions.

Despite a large number of complaints about the previous record of councillors, observers here noticed, in contrast to certain other regions, no references to the necessity for accountability, or for measures that could make future councillors more accountable. Indeed, outgoing ANC councillors could be quite unabashed by shortcomings in their performance. The Phutaditjhaba council before its dissolution decided to award R1 million to its members as honorariums, notwithstanding the municipality's inability to pay its Eskom electricity account.[32]

SACSOC reports for Gauteng indicate that merely sustaining its existing support base would constitute the principal challenge for the ANC in this area. At one Soweto meeting in Doornkop on 3 November, the issue of councillor corruption in housing allocation was discussed, extensively it seems; at another meeting in the same location two days later, environmental pollution from a nearby mine dump was addressed. In Molapo, people attending an ANC meeting on 12 November expressed their unhappiness at having an unknown candidate imposed upon them. This was one of the few meetings the observer characterised as tense: it featured 'finger pointing'. Apparently there were internal conflicts within the Molapo executive. Unhappiness with the ward candidate was also evident at another meeting held on the same day in Molapo, attended mainly by 'elders'. At Doornkop, again, people at a meeting on 13 November expressed anger at 'ANC people' misusing their powers to evict residents. In Diepkloof on 9 November, ANC candidates were asked why the party only came to the community when it wanted their support in elections. This particular occasion was jointly hosted by SANCO and may have featured an unusually assertive audience for that reason.

In the Vaal area, local residents who were calling for a boycott in protest against confiscation of rate defaulters' properties forced Mbhazima Shilowa to abandon a walk-about in Ncala section, Evaton. In Alexandra, a scandal over the allocation of low-income houses at the Tsutsumani All Africa Games Village pointed to other sources of communal dissatisfaction with the ANC's municipal leadership. Amongst the new homeowners were three ANC councillors, including the chairman of the party's Alexandra branch, Philip Ziqubu. ANC spokespeople defended the new householders: though their councillor allowances were indeed higher than the R3 500 needed to qualify for allocation of one of the houses, banks did not regard these as salaries and so they could not obtain bonds. Meanwhile, 400 people occupied vacant housing in Tsutsumani on 26 November, and the Alexandra Civic Association led a protest march to the Union Buildings in Pretoria.

In certain Soweto neighbourhoods, the DA was able to exploit localised perceptions of injustice. For example, it recruited a militant faction within the Lawley squatter movement, whose members were embittered by municipal efforts to evict them and by what they perceived to be political favouritism in site allocation. Shortly before the elections, the DA's Lawley candidate councillors were arrested for their involvement in a violent conflict with a security company sent in by the council to evict them in September 1999. They were also charged with destroying shacks belonging to local ANC leaders in October.

In the Northern Cape, SACSOC observers noted two quite serious violations of electoral procedure. In Kamiesberg on 18 November an ANC speaker suggested that if the town did not elect an ANC council, the government would not give it money, and at Postmasburg, the electoral code-signing ceremony on 20 November featured complaints about an ANC candidate who had allegedly threatened pensioners with the withdrawal of their pensions if they did not support her. Pensioners' complaints also dominated an ANC meeting at Victoria West on 9 November. Another alleged ANC indiscretion concerned its regional executive in De Aar, which reportedly circulated a memorandum to branches recommending that they should by the election ensure that town clerks were replaced with ANC cadres. Such zealousness may have had other more legitimate and constructive manifestations, though, for SACSOC reports indicate that door-to-door campaigning by both the main parties was particularly frequent and especially well organised in this province.

Pensioners were also threatened by ANC activists in Limpopo Province, it was claimed at a meeting on 22 October in Greater Letaba. Pensioners here had apparently also been told that if they failed to vote for the ANC, they would have their pensions withdrawn. A SACSOC observer heard the same complaint at a DA meeting at Makhado, Louis Trichardt, on 2 December. Pensioners also had other causes for anxiety. Some 100 senior citizens walked out of an ANC meeting in Seshego near Pietersburg after being informed that they would have to pay for their services under the new dispensation. Their obligations would include R58 for water meters and about R2 500 in back payments for water, councillors said.[33]

At many meetings in Limpopo Province, both speakers and audience were animated by fears of traditional leaders as well as by resentment over demarcation borders. The ANC went to considerable pains in Mulima on 16 November when opening its constituency office to ensure that traditional leaders were conspicuous in the assembly of notables who presided over the ceremony. Officials from CONTRALESA (the organisation of traditional leaders) and SANCO were present at an ANC meeting in Thohoyandou on 24 November. They attempted to iron out their differences, but were obviously unsuccessful with respect to the leadership of the Malamulele community. Its paramount chief, Cedric Minga II, continued to advise residents not to vote. To the chagrin of IEC officials, he was allowed to broadcast a boycott call on a local radio station on the day before the poll.

What is impressive from these observations is the extent to which centrally defined strategic intentions were indeed understood and implemented by local activists. In the case of the ANC this may have been its undoing. Too frequently at neighbourhood meetings, ward candidates would recite the list of pledges contained in the national manifesto and pay little attention to local preoccupations. For example, the ANC seemed to be genuinely caught off guard by the worries of people living in former homelands about the possibility that they might have to pay rates on their tribal land allocations. This issue arose time and again at meetings SACSOC observers attended in the North West, in the Eastern Cape and in Limpopo Province. It was also a widespread concern in KwaZulu-Natal. Eventually Thabo Mbeki confirmed during a tour of the rural Natal Midlands that people living on tribal authority land would not have to pay rates individually.[34]

Table 6.1 summarises SACSOC observations at what were mainly ANC meetings. It indicates a striking disparity between the key themes for speakers and the issues that were important to those attending: new entitlements such as free water against new obligations, accountability versus corruption, and advocacy of equitable gender representation contrasting with resentment of unknown or imposed candidates. Only in the Western Cape did ANC candidates develop locally focused election appeals, drawing on decades of experience in municipal politics within the coloured community. Attendance figures suggest rather higher levels of interest in the campaign in the more rural provinces. In six of the provinces monitored by SACSOC, women outnumbered men at the meetings observers attended. Younger voters seemed under-represented in audiences.

Table 6.1 SACSOC pre-poll observations

Region	Average Attendance	Tension	Not free and fair	Gender ratio W/M	Speaker themes	Issues from floor
East Cape	450	5/124	2/124	4:3	Delivery, corruption, demarc., tradition	New taxes, broken promises
Free State	217	14/184	12/124	111:116	Free water and elect., delivery, AIDS, corruption	Corruption, housing allocation, candidate selection, cut-offs and evictions
Gauteng	13–650	2/15	0/15	3:2	ANC achievement, tolerance	Cllr corruption, candidate imposition, scrapping of debts
N Cape	150	7/73	2/73	3:2	Cllr accountability, racism, AIDS	Nepotism, pension delays, unknown candidates
Limpopo	670	0/23	3/23		Chiefs' fears and demarcation	Chiefs' fears and demarcation
North West	14–700	8/43	1/43	2:1	Cllr accountability, tolerance, gender equity	New taxes, demarcation, pay-out delays, chiefs' fears
W Cape	204	4/232	1/232	86:118	Local issues, rape, free water and elect., crime, AIDS, cllr accountability	Cllr performance
Totals		**40/694 (6%)**	**21/694 (3%)**			

One positive dimension of campaign centralisation was the extent of adherence to the Electoral Code of Conduct. In the North West particularly, provincial ANC leaders stressed the theme of tolerance in their addresses at local meetings, though there was at least one allegation by a United Christian Democratic Party (UCDP) candidate that he had been told he could not canvass in Khuma, Stilfontein, as 'that is purely ANC territory'.[35] In the Eastern Cape, SACSOC reports make it quite clear that whatever the tensions between UDM and ANC adherents, in none of the localities observers visited was 'territory' closed off by any one party to its rivals. In KwaZulu-Natal this was not the case: the province was not monitored by SACSOC, and in the months preceding the election campaign there were several murders of ANC and IFP notables, including two nominated candidates, though it is not certain that all these killings were politically motivated.

Despite the IEC's optimistic predictions of a 60 per cent poll, the voter turnout on 5 December 2000 was very comparable to turnout statistics for the 1995–6 local government elections. In the previous elections, 8 550 497 voters participated, representing 49 per cent of voters registered on the voters' roll. In 2000, the 8 882 734 voters who cast their ballots represented 48 per cent of the voters' roll. IEC officials were predisposed to blame 'apathy', especially amongst first-time voters, for low turnout figures. They were also highly critical of their own delay in mounting voter education.[36] But for many voters non-participation should be read not as political indifference, but rather as a form of political response to their experience of local government.

For the main contenders the overall results were very comparable to 1995–6 (see Table 6.2). The ANC increased its percentage slightly and the DA achieved a few percentage points less than the combined DP–NNP total in 1995–6. White right-wing support diminished to insignificance. In KwaZulu-Natal the IFP registered gains at the ANC's expense in several of the smaller towns: Dundee, Ladysmith, Greytown, Richards Bay and Newcastle. Demarcation Board decisions also enhanced IFP influence in several centres. In the Eastern Cape, the UDM took significant numbers of votes from the ANC, as it did in 1999 shortly after its formation, winning a majority of votes – 51 per cent – in Umtata. In Gauteng, the ANC increased its share of the vote by nearly 7 per cent and in the Northern Cape its support expanded to two-thirds, in comparison to just half in 1995. The ANC lost support in Limpopo Province but did well in the Western Cape, winning 40.15 per cent of the vote, 3 per cent more than in 1995–6.

The contraction of the 'other' category in the table reflects the decreased importance of smaller local groups and a general trend away from fragmentation in favour of the major national or regional parties. Of the smaller parties, though, AZAPO's performance was especially heartening for its leadership: its 44 000 votes and 26 municipal seats (17 000 more votes than in the 1999 general elections) resulted from its contesting only 10 per cent of the councils. The PAC won a few ward elections in Barberton and on the East Rand. Civics or residents' associations also did well on the East Rand (with 7 PR seats, including two for 'Simunye in Christ') and amongst white residents in certain Free State towns, but the SANCO challenge in Uitenhage failed to win representation. In the North West, the UCDP did well in Mafikeng, winning 24 seats as opposed to the ANC's 30 seats, and also obtaining 7 out of 18 seats in the rural district of Ganyesa. In its supposed Hurutshe ethnic stronghold, it was disappointed, taking only 11 out of 34 seats – possibly a consequence of party leader Lucas Mangope's controversial local status after being convicted for fraud.

Table 6.2 Local election results, 2000

(1995–96 results given beneath the bold 2000 figures)

	EC (%)	FS (%)	G (%)	KZN (%)	MP (%)	NC (%)	Lim (%)	NW (%)	WC (%)	Total (%)
ACDP	**0.7**	**0.5**	**1.1**	**1.0**	**0.8**	**0.6**	**1.8**	**0.6**	**2.9**	**1.2**
	0.8	0.3	1.0	0.6	0.4	–	0.3	0.3	1.7	0.77
ANC	**74.0**	**72.4**	**59.5**	**35.2**	**80.5**	**64.15**	**80.4**	**72.1**	**40.1**	**59.4**
	80.9	67.3	52.8	32.6	76.0	49	86.2	74.3	37.1	58.02
AZAPO	–	**0.5**	**0.4**	**0.1**	**0.3**	**0.5**	**1.4**	–	**0.1**	**0.3**
DA	**11.8**	**18.0**	**31.8**	**15.3**	**12.9**	**29.1**	**7.9**	**10.3**	**51.6**	**22.1**
	10.75	13.5	30.5	15.85	11.0	32.9	4.2	7.8	53.2	24.2
FF	**1.1**	**0.9**	**1.0**	**0.2**	**0.2**	**0.5**	**0.6**	**0.9**	**0.2**	**0.6**
	0.8	2.5	6.3	0.3	3.2	4.9	1.5	4.5	1.6	2.66
IFP	**0.5**	**0.3**	**2.3**	**45.6**	**1.6**	**0.3**	**0.2**	–	**0.2**	**9.1**
	0.0	0.5	2.1	43.8	0.4	0.2	0.1	0.0	–	8.73
PAC	**1.7**	**3.0**	**1.6**	**0.2**	**2.0**	–	**2.5**	**0.9**	**0.2**	**1.3**
	1.8	1.8	1.1	0.2	1.5	0.6	2.2	1.7	1.0	1.2
UCDP	–	**0.7**	**0.2**	–	–	**2.9**	–	**12.7**	–	**1.0**
UDM	**11.1**	**1.0**	**0.9**	**0.2**	**1.0**	**0.3**	**2.0**	**1.2**	**1.4**	**2.6**
Other	**0.0**	**2.4**	**0.1**	**2.2**	**0.7**	**2.7**	**3.2**	**1.3**	**3.3**	**2.4**
	3.9	12.2	4.8	5.6	6.0	10.5	3.0	9.8	6.1	5.3

As expected, the ANC won comfortable victories in four of the six metropolitan municipalities, losing Cape Town to the DA and failing to achieve an absolute majority in Durban (see Table 6.3). An exceptionally high turnout of 70 per cent amongst white Capetonians and very limited participation in black townships partly explain the scale of the DA's victory in the city and in the Western Cape more generally. The ANC claimed increased support among working-class coloured voters in smaller municipalities in the Karoo and the Overberg, but it only won a single ward election in the coloured districts of the Cape Town metropolitan area. The ACDP obtained eight seats and independent ratepayers captured three, collecting their votes in old NNP wards. The UDM's three seats represented its best total outside the Transkei. The ANC's gains in Tshwane were mainly a consequence of the municipality's expansion across the border of the North West to embrace the commuter townships of Winterveld, GaRankuwa, Mabopane and Soshanguve.

By contrast, in Durban the main parties' shares of the votes appear to have remained stable since the last local elections. The DA's following seems to have diversified, as its victories show in a predominantly black ward in Clermont–New Germany and its gains at the expense of the ANC and the Minority Front in Indian townships. In Chatsworth, DA gains against the Minority Front may have been increased by the commissioning at the eleventh hour of a local radio commercial that insisted that 'a vote for the MF is a vote for the ANC'. Even so, in Durban the Minority Front won 10 Indian wards. The ANC's response to the Durban outcome was unusually ungracious: provincial chairperson S'bu Ndebele took it upon himself to announce 'to all Africans, coloureds and Indians who voted DA, be warned there's going to be consequences for not voting ANC. When it comes to service delivery, we will start with the people who voted for us and you will be last.'[37]

Table 6.3 Metropolitan local government election results, 2000

(Percentages of total votes cast are given on the first line, followed by the actual number of seats won, and, on the third line, the number of seats won in equivalent areas in 1995–96 results)

	ANC	DA	IFP	PAC	UDM	ACDP	Other*
Cape Town	38.54	53.49	0.28	0.46	1.45	3.83	1.91
	(77)	(107)	(1)	(1)	(3)	(8)	(3)
	(127)	(203)	(0)	(0)	(0)	(5)	(6)
Durban	46.94	26.14	17.4	0.6	0.16	1.19	8.47
	(95)	(53)	(35)	(1)	(0)	(2)	(14)
	(170)	(103)	(27)	(0)	(0)	(0)	(25)
East Rand	56.73	31.35	3.18	2.45	0.62	1.1	4.57
	(99)	(55)	(6)	(4)	(1)	(2)	(9)
	(113)	(72)	(3)	(0)	(0)	(0)	(11)
Johannesburg	59.23	33.71	3.57	1.24	0.61	0.41	1.23
	(129)	(73)	(8)	(3)	(1)	(1)	(2)
	(174)	(95)	(6)	(1)	(0)	(0)	(4)
Nelson Mandela	66.16	26.69	0.28	1.1	2.18	1.12	2.7
	(72)	(31)	(0)	(1)	(2)	(1)	(1)
	(56)	(32)	(0)	(0)	(0)	(0)	(5)
Tshwane	56.31	35.06	0.36	1.06	0.51	2.23	4.37
	(86)	(54)	(1)	(2)	(1)	(3)	(5)
	(122)	(72)	(0)	(0)	(0)	(0)	(26)
Total share	53.98	34.73	4.18	1.16	0.92	1.64	3.39
	(558)	(373)	(51)	(12)	(8)	(19)	(34)
	(762)	(577)	(36)	(2)	(0)	(5)	(77)

* This column includes the smaller national parties as well as civic groups and independent candidates. The 2000 Durban total includes 10 members of the Minority Front, down from 25 Minority Front councillors elected in 1996. East Rand's relatively high 2000 'Other' group reflects the scope of the 2000 civic rejection of the ANC – eight of the nine were representatives of township-based civic organisations. In Tshwane the 'Other' group elected in 1995 included 17 councillors from the Freedom Front; by 2000 many of their former supporters in Pretoria were voting for the Democratic Alliance.

Sources for the statistics: Elections Task Group, *Local Government Elections in South Africa, 1995/1996*, Pretoria, 1996; Electoral Institute for Southern Africa, *Local Government Elections Update*, Nos. 9–10, 2001; Clive Keegan, *2000 Local Government Elections, Complete Results*, SA Local Government Research Centre, Cape Town, 2001.

Variations in party performances between the two elections were chiefly a reflection of interprovincial migration, other demographic shifts and differing rates of turnouts between supporters of different parties. DA spokespeople believe that about 57 per cent of their supporters turned out, as opposed to 42 per cent of the ANC's.[38] ANC spokespeople agree that there was a 'massive' turnout of 70 per cent within the white community, whereas amongst Africans turnout averaged at 50 per cent. Among coloureds it was lower still at 45 per cent.[39] At least as far as the main parties were concerned, there was only sporadic evidence of success in recruiting former supporters of their opponents. In general, the DA won comfortable victories in the suburbs and the ANC attracted massive majorities in townships and rural districts. Displeasure with the ANC's performance was mostly expressed through former supporters staying away from the polls, though in certain areas the civic rebellion had a discernible impact.

Johannesburg's results are illuminating. In Johannesburg, the DA seemed to have established a significant presence in a few black neighbourhoods. Remarkably, in the Jeppestown hostel the DA's 584 votes represented 27.16 per cent of the total and put the ANC candidate in third place. In Soweto, the DA's best performance was in Ward 32, Orlando East, where it obtained 866 votes, or 16.56 per cent of the total. In the two other Orlando wards (30 and 31) the DA obtained 264 and 204 votes, 4.8 and 4.1 per cent respectively. In total, in Orlando East, of the 15 687 votes cast, the DA's share was 1 344, that is, 8.5 per cent of the votes cast. In 1995, of 15 086 votes cast in the three Orlando East wards, the combined DP–NP vote was 504 – only 3.3 per cent of the total. The ANC's share of the vote in these three Orlando wards shrank from 92.5 to 83 per cent between the elections in 1995 and 2000.

However, these comparative statistics do not rule out the possibility that the people who switched their votes from the ANC to the DA in 2000 may have been from the minority of Soweto residents who voted for the old Black Local Authorities (BLA) under apartheid. If this was the case, then they would not represent a growing constituency and the DA's future prospects for growth in townships would appear to be limited. In 1988, participation in BLA elections in Soweto amounted to a mere 10 per cent of the registered electorate of nearly 30 000 voters. The DA vote in all of Soweto in 2000 was around 11 000. However, DA research suggests that the social characteristics of its Soweto supporters were very different from the elderly pensioners who were the most common participants in the BLA elections in Soweto in 1988. The DA spent about 7 per cent of its total campaign budget on polling and focus groups. One poll, conducted by Markinor between 11 and 18 August 2000, suggested that a township DA supporter would earn between R2 000 and R6 000 monthly, would frequently be a newspaper reader, would be employed by government or as a shopkeeper, and would mostly be under the age of 35. Around 61 per cent of those urban black voters whom the poll found susceptible to conversion to the DA's cause were female, 43 per cent were employed (a higher-than-average figure), 37 per cent possessed matriculation certificates, and 18 per cent a post-secondary education. According to Mike Moriarty, door-to-door campaigners in Orlando tended to find that pensioners and old people were unwelcoming. Many were under the impression that support for the DA could jeopardise their pensions. A significant proportion of those attending DA meetings were young, he noted. The relatively successful candidate in Orlando was not unrepresentative of the party's local social base: he was a Vodacom salesperson in his late twenties and his popularity was partly attributable to his prominence as a lay preacher in an evangelical church congregation.

Victories for the DA in Lenasia Ward 9, in two Eldorado Park constituencies and in Newclare pointed to its popularity amongst Indians and coloureds. In Johannesburg, turnout tended to be slightly higher in affluent neighbourhoods, lower in townships and very low indeed in inner-city wards. This followed the national pattern. The IFP was the only other party in Johannesburg with enough concentrated support to win ward elections. Its predicable victories in Jeppestown and Denver–Melrose indicated its continuing influence in Zulu-speaking hostel communities. The PAC achieved over 5 per cent of the vote in three wards, each of which incorporated squatter areas, but in most township wards it was eclipsed even by the DA. The other parties to win representation in Johannesburg – the ACDP, the Christian Democratic Party, AZAPO and the UDM – collected their main support from the PR ballot. The DA's performance in Johannesburg townships was nationally its best in respect of black districts: in Tshwane, for example, the DA's best township ward tally was 184 (Ward 23); in the whole of Mamelodi it obtained only 822 votes compared with the ANC's 35 433.

In summary, the key features of the outcome of the elections were the failure of the ANC to mobilise black voters and the inroads of its rivals on both the left and the right into localities where the ANC had previously enjoyed virtually hegemonic status. The DA's campaign certainly succeeded in broadening its constituency socially. Its share of the vote in several areas was well in excess of the percentage share of the combined DP–NP vote in previous elections. While succeeding in retaining white support, it consolidated its gains of 1999 in coloured and Indian neighbourhoods and – in Johannesburg at least – registered a more-than-token presence in African townships. Ironically, the decisions of the Demarcation Board seem to have facilitated an IFP revival in KwaZulu-Natal, notwithstanding DA and IFP contentions about the Board's partisanship. Beyond indications of a more open political terrain than in earlier elections, prospects for future democratic politics look brighter in the light of the general conduct of electioneering and polling. Only 22 out of 694 SACSOC pre-election reports suggest that the local electoral environment was anything but free and fair. A Human Sciences Research Council (HSRC) exit poll, in which 11 135 voters were interviewed outside 209 stations, found that only 4 per cent of its respondents felt that the elections had not been free or fair and 5 per cent had experienced, they said, a degree of intimidation.

However, good government in South Africa requires more than equitably conducted elections. Much will depend on the capacity of those who manage South Africa's cities in the five years after 2000 to address the crisis in municipal management described in chapter 5. The institutional changes that have been enacted since 1998 regarding the ways in which local authorities are governed are no guarantee that they will be governed better.

The new municipalities elected in December 2000 are officially projected as key 'developmental' agencies. To this end, the Municipal Systems Act requires them to submit 'integrated development plans' (IDPs) to the provinces for approval. These should set out their goals and the strategies to reach them during their term of office. An especially important feature of such planning has to be the coordination of public and private investment proposals. The IDP is meant to supply the guidelines for the way the municipalities spend their money and to provide performance indicators by which progress can be measured. The plan has to be tied to a scheme for land development objectives, which also has to be submitted to the province. The adoption of the plan should involve community participation; one of the developmental aims for local government as spelt out in the 1998 White Paper was to build 'social capital' through empowering citizens. Residents are expected to help prepare IDPs, to contribute to the workings of municipal performance-management systems, and to help councillors make deci sions about the budget. Municipalities are expected to encourage such partici pation through public report-back meetings – each councillor must arrange at least four of these – and councillors can also establish ward committees composed of ten people to represent the 'diversity of interests within the ward'.

In fact, integrated development planning began well before the election. In February 1999, 396 out of 846 local authorities had submitted work plans for approval.[40] In Gauteng all municipalities were in the process of revising their plans after a first round of submissions. Though plans would have had to be reconsidered after the elections because of council amalgamations, the planning process at least was well under way, and in the larger municipalities IDPs were already under public review in 2001. Some 8 000 councillors were to undergo a special training programme in IDP planning funded by a Norwegian government donation in January 2001. Encouragingly, initial sessions reported a 70 per cent attendance rate.[41] In Johannesburg, ward committees were established at gener- ally poorly attended meetings in August in most of the 109 wards. The commit- tees comprised representatives of a prescribed range of organisations: business, civic, women and so forth. Very few committees, if any, were elected. Though meetings were publicised, only those who had been nominated turned up in most cases. Since their establishment, ward committees have met about once a month and have discussed the local implications of Johannesburg's IDP, which is essentially a revamped version of the 'Egoli 2010' document, prepared before the election. Much better attended stakeholder meetings have addressed the plan in all eleven regions. Business representatives are especially alarmed by the ANC's commitment to limiting investment outside the (decaying) central business district.[42] The council has also included in its plans an ambitious target of at least 35 000 houses a year to meet a backlog of 250 000 units.[43]

Meanwhile, in neighbouring Ekurhuleni – the new name for the East Rand metropolitan council – ward committees were assembled from March. Very few were elected, although the council insisted that nominations could not be accepted at meetings attended by less than 50 people. No committees were elected in Boksburg because of a lack of public interest. As in Johannesburg, most ward committees hold regular monthly meetings and councillors are encouraged to arrange public report-backs to residents in their wards. On the whole, most ward committee business concerns re-zoning applications. A draft of the East Rand IDP was prepared in January 2001, but many ward committees were still waiting in November for presentations from council officials. Several public meetings to review the IDP were organised in townships, but none in suburbs.[44]

The implementation of prescriptions arising from the Municipal Systems Act presents smaller municipalities with formidable challenges. In Masilonyane in the Free State, which incorporated Brandfort with several lesser towns, ward committees were elected in April, but few met more than once in 2001. Attendance at such meetings was poor. A draft IDP was in circulation within the municipality and its local aspects were presented to ward committees. However, it is very difficult to elicit public participation in a local authority whose scattered population lives within boundaries that are more than a hundred kilometres apart. Visionary planning is a quixotic exercise when the council's debts to Eskom and the Water Board exceed its annual income. However, co-operation between political parties is fostered through the Free State's adoption of the multi-party executive option for its cities. Common concerns between the ANC and the DA may also result from both sharing an increasing number of black constituencies. Masilonyane is one of the municipalities in which the DA made inroads into voter support in black townships during the election.[45]

In contrast to the relatively early start in the Free State, ward committees had only just been elected in Emalahleni (Witbank, Ogies and Kriel) by November 2001, although the council's IDP had been quite thoroughly reviewed in portfolio committees. Here the council is managed by an ANC executive mayoralty.[46] In Buffalo City (East London, King William's Town, Bisho and surrounds) no ward committees had been established one year after the elections. The original meetings at which they were to be chosen had to be postponed because of difficulty in obtaining nominations from an appropriate range of organisations.[47]

A detailed profile of representation in all 43 of the wards in Emfuleni (the new municipality embracing the Vaal Triangle) supplies very useful insights into the challenges confronting even the most conscientious and effective of councillors. In total, 34 of the wards documented in this survey were represented by ANC councillors and the remaining 9 by the DA. Three-quarters of the councillors after the 2000 elections were serving for the first time, a telling indication of public discontent with the quality of representation between 1995 and 1999, although the proportion of experienced councillors is rather greater among the PR-list elected group. The survey, made in June 2001 and based on focus groups and representative sampling, was undertaken by a consultant at the request of the new council as a systematic inquiry into local perceptions of needs analysis. It was itself a good indicator of the seriousness with which Emfuleni's new civic leaders understood the participatory requirement of planning.

Given the needs that respondents cited, the depth of public disillusion with municipal politics was hardly surprising. Complaints about deteriorating services in white middle-class areas are not necessarily testimony to less effective local government; they may merely be evidence of the rational reallocation of resources to neighbourhoods less well provided for . However, the Emfuleni survey suggests that very little such reallocation happened between 1995 and 2000, despite cutbacks in the range of public facilities available to suburban areas. Emergency facilities (fire brigade and ambulance services) had virtually disappeared, for example. Residents in ten of the poorest black wards complained about the disrepair of local roads and the related absence of storm-water drainage systems – indications of continuing council neglect of the most basic infrastructure. Eight wards appeared to have no system of refuse collection, though focus groups in two others, including a middle-class white suburb, claimed that garbage services had improved since the election. Inhabitants of both Evaton and Sharpeville were especially likely to be affected by water-supply disruptions as a consequence of 40-year-old piping systems that had never been repaired or renewed. In several neighbourhoods, both rich and poor, the system of zoning and building regulation had collapsed. Factories and workshops had since sprung up in these residential areas. In a few wards, prepaid card-operated electrical and water metering systems had been installed. Where these worked, they were popular and the extension of such arrangements was a priority with most ANC councillors. However, in at least one area the equipment had malfunctioned since its installation several years previously and repeated complaints had elicited no response from the council. The most substantial civic improvement since 1995 had been the construction of several low-cost housing estates, but even this achievement has been qualified by delays in issuing title-deeds and the failure to organise land tenure systematically.

Given this legacy, the new councillors generally encountered surprisingly ready responses to their initial efforts to publicise the ward committee system, at least in black neighbourhoods. Here the system was explained at well-attended public meetings. White residents tended to resist civic involvement, partly as a result of feelings that the ward committees were an unnecessary duplication of local residents' associations and also because of a tendency since 1994 in local Afrikaner communities to withdraw from politics generally. Incentives for municipal activism amongst whites had also been reduced by the substitution of private for public services in suburban neighbourhoods, although community police forum meetings remained well attended.

In historically black areas it proved to be more difficult to obtain ward committee nominations. Several councillors complained about the absence of a voluntary ethic, for work on the committees would be unpaid. Finally, most committees were recruited by the councillor personally. Survey evidence suggested that many Emfuleni citizens understand the committees to be agencies in service delivery and project implementation rather than consultative planning bodies, and this perception may result in disappointed expectations once the ward committees have been functioning for a while.

The most impressive findings of the Emfuleni profile concerned the quality of the councillors themselves. Focus group testimony confirmed a generally strong predisposition to communal accountability. Regular public meetings and report-backs appeared to be a feature of civic politics in most wards. Many councillors agreed that their main responsibility was to their communities and only secondarily to the political party they represented. Many played leading roles in various voluntary associations as well as church congregations. Even part-time ward councillors often worked a 50-hour week, spending much of their time addressing the kinds of personal difficulties among their constituents which in a more developed welfare state would be handled by social services. Several indicated that the time they spent on such community work made it very difficult for them to contribute effectively to committee work in the council. This problem was exacerbated by the habit of council officials to schedule portfolio committee meetings at short notice and at inconvenient times. Interviews with councillors also indicated considerable resentment amongst them and amongst voters of PR-list representatives who had much less contact with citizens and very little understanding of conditions in specific localities, and who yet played a leading role in council planning procedures.[48]

The example of Emfuleni may be atypical in terms of the extent of its efforts to develop the ward committees as mechanisms of accountable government, but even here it is clear that citizen involvement in planning is limited to the collection of local assessments about the most basic needs. Local case studies suggest that the planning process is only consultative in the most perfunctory way. In many centres, ward committees have reviewed highly developed documents prepared by consultants and already revised after a preliminary process of submission to the provincial departments of local government. This is the case despite official injunctions 'never [to] underestimate the power of community participation in developing a vision'.[49] Executive mayorships may confine the decision-making process to a smaller group of people than before. This is the view of the Johannesburg DA, which unsuccessfully fought a court action to contest its exclusion from the mayor's executive. The DA itself, though, excluded opposition councillors from the Cape Town mayor's executive and also removed from their posts six key officials known to have ANC sympathies, including the generally respected city manager, Andrew Boraine.

Even so, the assembly of ward committees itself suggests that the returning councillors have taken to heart complaints about poor accountability raised during the election. In respect of other electoral preoccupations, both DA and ANC councils moved swiftly to implement a billing procedure that would allocate free water allowances at least to consumers who had access to piped water in their homes. In Emfuleni, for example, a special committee was constituted for this purpose, though the absence of infrastructure and finance delayed the introduction of free water allowances. An attempt to alter electricity tariffs to cross-subsidise poorer households proved to be even more difficult. In Cape Town, the DA was prevented from imposing rate hikes on high-income suburbs to finance the free provision of water and electricity initiated in May and June. In Johannesburg, Eskom insisted that the national exchequer should provide the parastatal with R500 million to finance free electricity in Soweto and has accordingly delayed its provision until this demand is addressed.[50]

Meanwhile, the Soweto Electricity Crisis Committee (SECC) employs Eskom technicians who had been laid off, to reconnect the household electricity supplies of some of the 20 000 defaulters who continue to be cut off every month. The prospect of a visit by an SECC delegation in October so alarmed councillor Ramodire, the ANC's representative in Ward 20, that he recruited an armed bodyguard and absented himself from his office for two months, much to the satisfaction of local DA activists.[51] In October 2001, Soweto residents owed R700 million in unpaid electricity accounts. When the free electricity initiative comes into effect, it is unlikely to make much difference to them – the allowance represents only about one-tenth of the average consumption in poor households.

Indigent debtors may not be the most troublesome group for Johannesburg's credit control managers, though. In August, more than 650 council staff were under investigation after a discovery that massive reductions on service accounts were obtained through widespread bribery and that council arrears totalled R4.3 billion.[52] By mid-2001, the council needed a R76 million overdraft to settle its accounts with Eskom, a debt it was planning to settle through the sale of a power station.[53] In Ekurhuleni, a municipal manager provoked a political row between the ANC and the DA when he gave out instructions that cut-offs should not be implemented in black townships. In November 2001, national and provincial cabinet ministers attended neighbourhood *imbizos* to listen to residents' complaints and to underline their professed commitment to implementing campaign promises. In rural areas, providing the pledged water allowances has been especially difficult, particularly as the transfer of the responsibility for administering water accounts from the local councils to the new district councils remained a contested issue between different government departments throughout 2001.

ANC commitment to better municipal administration was also evident in its removal of Bavumile Vilakazi from his position as mayor of Ekurhuleni. He was compelled to resign from his post in November 2001 after an ill-judged spending spree, which included the purchase of an armour-plated Mercedes for R500 000, spending a similar sum on his inauguration party, and allocating a further R400 000 to refurbishing his offices in Germiston. Unfortunately, Vilakazi's cupidity was not an isolated example of such behaviour. In Mogale (Krugersdorp), the mayor announced plans for a R400 000 official mansion. In Nelson Mandela metropole, Nceba Faku was discovered in October 2001 to have used his discretionary fund (traditionally spent on charities) to pay traffic fines and tuition fees for relatives. Subsequently he, too, had to defend an ostentatious refit of his office: spending R216 000 on new furniture (including a R12 000 leather chair) and decorations was necessary to 'generate a sense of professionalism', he said in his defence.[54]

The DA encountered its most serious challenge in efforts to discipline errant municipal leadership when party bosses called for the unseating of Peter Marais. This followed reports of fake results in an opinion poll undertaken to ascertain public attitudes towards Marais's proposals for street-name changes. The move against Marais accentuated tensions in the DA resulting from well-founded perceptions by NNP principals that Tony Leon and his lieutenants planned to 'sideline' them in the newly merged organisation. Marais's leadership style had irritated DA leaders from as early as February 2001: telephone respondents in its donor appeals were offering adverse comments on Marais, and a survey suggested that his approval ratings amongst black and coloured Capetonians had fallen sharply after the election.

This survey exercise itself supplies insight into tensions within the Democratic Alliance. Whereas the DP relies heavily on marketing techniques to identify issues of public concern, the NNP in Cape Town depended on 'historical relationships with coloured leadership to bring out the vote'.[55] Marais himself enjoyed almost messianic status, at least among the adherents of the New Covenant Christian Church in Mitchell's Plain, whose congregation assembled to supply a defiant musical chorus whenever Marais appeared during the public inquiry into the street-name changes. DP leaders, most of their support still concentrated in middle-class areas, were new to executive power and retained a high-minded aversion to 'big-man' patron-style politicking. In the wake of the street-naming scandal, a succession of additional allegations suggested that coloured DA councillors (several of them close to Peter Marais) and at least one African Party organiser were using their influence in RDP housing allocations in Cape Town to buy votes and favour family members.[56] It may well be true that the NNP will find it easier to govern those cities in which they still enjoy substantial voter support in poor communities in conjunction with the ANC. During the reign of the transitional local authorities, NNP councillors often sided with the ANC when the Democrats raised 'good governance' issues.

If the experience of the Uthukela District municipality in KwaZulu-Natal is typical, then the progress in implementing any integrated development planning outside the metropolitan councils may be very slow indeed. In the area around Ladysmith and Estcourt the council represents some 500 000 people. Formerly the district council functioned as a regional service council and received a portion of the national revenue. Taxes and levies raised within its own jurisdiction covered only about half of its budget and in August 2001 it needed another R8 million. The 2001 National Revenue Act allocated no money to the operating costs of district municipalities.[57] The 1998 White Paper proposals on 'equitable share' transfers for poorer municipalities' running expenses were evidently overlooked by the national Treasury. Uncertainties about revenues did not prevent the IFP-led municipality of Mandeni in KwaZulu-Natal from hiring Professor Musa Xulu as its municipal manager at R400 000 a year plus a car allowance of R320 000. His previous administrative experience had been with the Department of Arts, Culture, Science and Technology, where he had held a position as director-general, from which he had been dismissed because of tendering irregularities. Shortly before Xulu's appointment, Mandeni received a threat from Eskom that its electricity supplies would be cut because of an unpaid bill.[58]

An equally surprising managerial recruit to the new municipal order was the new chief executive of Tshwane, Dr Thoahlane Thoahlane, whose R830 000 package was defended by way of reference to his previous salary at the National Development Agency, which had had to spend R2.5 million to remove him from his directorship before the end of his contract.[59] Meanwhile, in Middelburg, Mpumalanga, tensions generated by the ANC's top-down nominations procedure may well have dissipated the reservoir of 'social capital' which had accumulated under a highly effective ANC administration during the transitional era. Former trade unionist and mayor Ben Mokoena, whose administration between 1995 and 2000 had twice won the 'Masakhane' award for service delivery, was expelled from the ANC together with ten fellow councillors after their refusal to support staff appointments proposed by the new executive mayor, who had been selected by the ANC's provincial executive despite their objections.[60] Middelburg is now part of the new Highveld District Council. In August 2001, 15 of its councillors decided that the risk of thrombosis from tourist-class seats warranted upgrading their air tickets for a visit to a Chinese trade fair at a cost of R500 000. It remains to be seen whether the new system of performance management, 'unveiled' by the minister in October 2001, will provide an effective antidote to the all-too-evident material shortcomings and human failings of local authority in South Africa's cities.

In the 2000 elections, South Africa's municipal leaders at best received a half-hearted mandate from voters. Despite their comfortable victories in most cities and districts, the ANC candidates encountered widespread evidence of anger and anxiety among even their most loyal supporters. Fresh incursions by smaller parties into the ANC's home bases helped to reinforce lessons about the need for better accountability and more managerial competence in local government. To date, the new authorities have invested serious effort into constructing a new network of representative bodies, the ward committees. These may help to engender stronger predispositions in favour of public answerability among elected officials. However, new systems of representation and reconfigured boundaries in themselves will be insufficient to meet the challenges of supplying effective local administration to South African citizens. For this objective, more equitable resource allocation and tougher ethical standards are needed among office-holders than prevail at present.

7 | COUNTERING CORRUPTION

Very few political systems are completely free from corruption, but it is rarely pervasive in advanced industrial democracies. Political corruption is the 'unsanctioned or unscheduled use of public resources for private ends'.[1] It is taken to be endemic or systemic when it becomes open and routine, when its workings constitute a parallel set of procedures to those of the proper operations of the bureaucracy. When this happens, public resources can be wasted or lost on a vast scale. For example, in the Philippines during the 1970s, 20 per cent of internal revenue was lost through corruption;[2] in Nigeria estimates for the total of corruption suggest a figure equalling 10 per cent of the GDP;[3] in Zaïre similar guesses suggest a proportion of 25 per cent.[4] Some people argue that this kind of diversion of public funds may be beneficial in certain cases,[5] for example those in which the proceeds are expended on productive entrepreneurial activity, but mostly this does not happen.

Analysts of corruption view it as an especial characteristic of government in developing countries. The explanation for this is that in former colonial countries, large-scale centralised bureaucratic administrations are fairly recent and often imposed by outsiders. Hence there may exist a 'wide divergence between the aims, attitudes, and methods of the government and those in societies in which they operate'.[6] In such communities, values which arise from the persistence of kinship, clanship and clientship in social relations may infuse a bureaucracy from below. Furthermore, modernisation can enlarge government very quickly, thereby widening its scope for intervention and regulation well beyond the capacity and supply of properly trained people; as such, governments' obligations expand, and so do the opportunities for corruption. Cases of extreme venality (for example, in Nigeria) often coincide with situations in which the state obtains most of its revenues from external sources – customs revenues, payments from off-shore oil extraction companies, and so forth – rather than from enfranchised taxpayers. In third-world countries, the state is often the major actor in the modern economy – the major employer, the main buyer, and the main seller – and this brings more opportunities for misappropriation by its functionaries, especially if the political system is authoritarian.

However, political scientists have recently begun to pay more attention to corruption in rich industrialised and democratic countries, where it seems to be on the rise. Three developments help to explain this: the decentralisation of administration and the delegation of financial authority; the introduction of market values into public administration; and the growing costs of electoral competition, especially because of the predominance of television in party campaigning.[7]

Is South Africa, then, especially susceptible, if we keep these theoretical points in mind? Not especially, I would argue. Firstly, South Africa is not a typical 'developing country'. The state plays a relatively restricted role in the modern economy of South Africa if we compare it to, say, Nigeria's. Since 1994 the government has been trying to stabilise public expenditure and so the state – the bureaucracy – is not becoming any bigger. The state's historical formation was undertaken when the country was dominated politically by a settler minority, and thus it is less likely than other parts of Africa to be influenced by the persistence of old, pre-industrial cultures of tribute. The South African state depends for a major share of its revenues on various types of personal taxation. This tends to make it more publicly accountable for the way it spends its money than many governments in developing countries.

Democratisation and unification since 1994 may have closed down some opportunities for official spoliation but other potential avenues for corrupt accumulation have opened up. Regionalism has involved a downward delegation of budgetary authority, though this may be compensated for by the dissolution of the homelands, in which administrative corruption was sometimes endemic. However, the transfer into regional governments of homeland civil servants may have helped to infect the new system with the patrimonial habits of bantustan officialdom. Although the overall number of civil servants has not changed, senior management has changed with the infusion of new people – often political appointments – and this may have disrupted morale and eroded the social restraints which normally keep corruption in check.

The new government is doing new things – channelling resources in different directions – and old rules are often difficult to apply. The government's policy, which favours black business 'empowerment', surely makes it vulnerable to charges of favouritism. However, there is a professed commitment to an ethic of 'transparency' and, certainly, much more official information about the ways in which the government spends its money is available than before. A democratic Constitution and the demise of racially and ethnically separated administrations have expanded the area of government open to public scrutiny and inspection. This is one reason why there seems to be much more corruption than in the past.

What about historical legacy? What did the new government inherit? Government spokespeople contend that modern corruption is mainly a carry-over from the past. There is some justification in this point of view. From 1948 ethnic favouritism characterised all civil service recruitment and promotion. Government loans and resources were equally invoked by ethnic and political consider-ations. But these kinds of behaviour may not have been motivated by personal desire for self-enrichment among individual officials, at least not in the 1950s and early 1960s. The auditor-general's reports for this period suggest that the number of financial irregularities was very modest, confined mainly to the post office and, to a lesser extent, the police and the departments of Justice and Defence. Signifi-cantly, though, the auditor-general's reports stopped routinely detailing 'mal-feasances' after 1967.

There is plenty of evidence, though, that as the National Party administration matured, it became more degenerate. By the 1980s, political corruption was common both in central government and in homeland administrations. It was especially entrenched in those domains of government activity which one might term 'strategic' and which expended secret funds. The 1978 Information Scandal may have forced a change of political leadership but it did not end the large-scale private appropriation of public funds. During the 1980s the Department of Defence spent around R4 billion per annum on secret projects. Although much of this would have been expended on arms procurement, this itself supplied plenty of opportunity for private profit, with officials setting up ostensibly private companies in foreign countries and awarding themselves comfortable salaries. Besides arms procurement, secret funds were spent on propaganda and subver-sion, carried out by a variety of front organisations. When one looks at the accounts of these activities one cannot help feeling that in many cases the real purpose of these agencies was simply venal. For example, one military front corporation, African Risk Analysis Consultants, issued to its 49 staff Diners Club cards, each with a R25 000 credit limit, presumably for the more incidental expenses of analysing risk.[8] In Namibia, Military Intelligence set up a company, Inter Frama, purportedly to generate income for the leader of the National Union for Total Independence of Angola (UNITA), Jonas Savimbi. The company became a conduit for ivory and mandrax smuggling in which the profits were shared between commanders of UNITA and the South African Defence Force (SADF). From 1984 onwards, opposition politicians in parliament argued that the Strategic Fuel Fund, established 20 years earlier to stockpile oil, was a vehicle for the private enrichment of its officials.[9]

Quite aside from the mysterious world of covert operations, central govern-ment departments had a history of routine corruption. Especially lucrative fields were prison food supplies and textbooks for black schools under the Department of Education and Training (DET). Court cases suggest that contracts for supplying these items were frequently awarded in a nepotistic fashion. The Department of Development Aid (the last in a line of successors to the Native Affairs Depart-ment), which channelled development funding to homelands, was a fertile fiefdom for dishonest bureaucrats. A government commission reckoned that several hundred millions of rands had been lost to fraud and nepotism in the 1980s through awards of contracts to spouses, payments to firms for fictitious projects, and so forth.[10]

Homeland governments themselves exhibited grand corruption on a major scale. In the former Transkei, independence in 1976 was accompanied by a public takeover of South African property and the subsequent sale at bargain prices of farms, firms and houses to cabinet ministers and their friends. In KwaNdebele, the 1994 Parsons Commission discovered a R1 million kickback to officials for building work that was never done.[11] One member of the KwaNdebele Tender Board, a Mr J. Morgan, managed to secure a contract in 1991 for his own company, Professional Project Services, to supervise the erection of 164 class-rooms. Several of these were constructed in the wrong places and many were not built at all; even so, the company received a cheque for R105 000 in excess of the original agreement. Meanwhile, Mr Morgan's brother-in-law was the beneficiary of another agreement in which his company, Hata Butle Homes, undertook to supply 200 prefabricated toilets, despite the decision of the board to award the contract to a firm that had submitted a lower estimate. The toilets never arrived at their planned destinations.

Amongst the litany of complaints about the Lebowa Tender Board was the purchase of cleaning chemicals worth R15 million, in return for kickbacks, in spite of objections by three of its members. (These chemicals would have been sufficient to supply the whole government for seven years.) A similar deal by Dr G. H. Becker, secretary of the QwaQwa Department of Health, cost about 60 per cent of his department's 1993 budget. The list of such anecdotes is never-ending. It represents chronic or endemic corruption in those spheres, undertaken by senior officials, black and white.

More damaging, often, to public perceptions, is routine petty corruption – when members of the public have to undertake dishonest transactions with offi-cials in order to obtain services of one kind or another (or to avoid sanctions). Before 1994, its incidence probably varied in accordance with the degree of ini-quity of those seeking benefits or services from officials. In homelands, bribery was prolific in pension departments and in magistrates' courts. In KwaZulu in the early 1980s, researchers found that *indunas* and chiefs routinely extorted payments for site permits, work-seeker permits and disability grants.[12] In 1997 the Gauteng Home Truths Commission received 800 submissions concerning the management of public housing between 1976 and 1984: thousands of people were evicted to make room for tenants who had paid bribes to councillors and officials.[13]

Police bribery concentrated on the administration of the pass laws and liquor restrictions, but this did not end with the repeal of these laws. In 1995, a survey by the newspaper *Sowetan* found that 67 per cent of its respondents knew that police officers took bribes, a perception that seemed to be based on historical patterns of experience.[14] Amongst white South Africans, though, familiarity with corruption was probably exceptional rather than normal and most often arose from encounters with municipal rather than national state agencies. This does suggest that certain key departments of the administration were fairly clean, for example the Revenue Service. What shape has corruption assumed since 1994? How serious a problem is it today?

A large proportion of the corruption reports which have appeared in newspapers since 1994 are reflections of behavioural patterns inherited from old regimes. Pension fraud is a case in point. One of the most expensive forms of wastage was concentrated in the pension bureaucracies that administered grants to black people. Between 1994 and 1998, up to R5 billion was paid out to 'ghosts' and double claimants. The Eastern Cape was especially bad in this respect, but the problem affected even the better-run provinces, including Gauteng and the Western Cape.[15] The ending of secret budgets to the military and the sharp reduction of defence expenditure for a while closed down one of the most lucrative seams of venality. As will be evident later in this chapter, the resumption of ambitious procurement projects since 1998 has opened up new lucrative prospects for dishonest officials and well-connected politicians. A special defence account which is shielded from parliamentary scrutiny was established in 1974. It remains, and is still used for major arms purchases.

Police corruption may have worsened since 1994 as a consequence, perhaps, of demoralisation and disloyalty to the new government. In 1998, 10 000 policemen (out of a national force of 140 000) were under investigation for charges of bribery, theft, fraud and involvement in crime syndicates. The sale of cars from official depots of recovered stolen vehicles and licensing rackets remained two particularly profitable fields of police activity. In 2000, some 5 000 traffic officers were interviewed in a survey and 75 per cent admitted to accepting bribes, justifying their behaviour with complaints about salaries that were below R29 000 a year.[16] The falling value of salaries in the Department of Justice contributed to an increase in the incidence of docket losses and the consequent dismissal of charges against suspected criminals. Again, this is not a new problem, as a reading of annual reports of the attorney-general shows, but it is evident that the frequency of such events increased throughout the 1990s.

Thus not all misbehaviour is explicable as the persistence of old bad habits. New kinds of government obligations have supplied fresh opportunities for corruption. The subsidisation of low-cost housing and the provision of free school meals are obvious examples. Mpumalanga's MECs used some R1.3 million from the low-cost housing budget to renovate their 'state houses'. In several of the regions, audits have uncovered up to R143 million unaccounted for in the primary school feeding scheme.[17] Only in the Western Cape, where black business empowerment principles were ignored and the scheme's administration was handed over to an experienced NGO, the Peninsula School Feeding Scheme, has it functioned with complete honesty.

There are several other new sources of stimulation for corrupt behaviour. Non-meritocratic processes of recruitment and promotion, inherent in certain kinds of affirmative action unless they are strictly regulated, can facilitate nepotism. Tendering principles that favour small businesses require very efficient administration if they are to be handled honestly. For example, at least R1.7 million in Labour Department funds were lost on various labour-intensive road projects supposedly administered by local committees. The increasing shortage of skilled manpower in the public service has especially weakened its financial control systems. If bureaucracies become inefficient and delays become routine, this supplies incentives for bribery. The lethargy which seems to affect the issue of identification documents and visas in the Department of Home Affairs is a good example of a delay-ridden procedure which represents an incitement for corruption. In mid-2001 some 300 Home Affairs officials were being investigated for suspected involvement in criminal syndicates dealing in passports and identification documents.[18] A range of new sources of public finance, including foreign development aid, can challenge existing regulatory procedures. The scandal surrounding the *Sarafina II* musical (intended to promote public awareness about AIDS) happened mainly because officials believed that normal tendering rules did not apply to donor money, a resource they had never administered before.

Democracy itself has made the financing of political parties much more competitive. Treasurer-general of the African National Congress (ANC) Makhenkesi Stofile told his audience at Mafikeng in December 1997 that R2 million donations to the ANC had now become customary among black businesspeople. In return for this generosity 'we opted for the role of facilitators for black business in the country', he noted. In KwaZulu-Natal, the Inkatha Freedom Party (IFP) accepted donations from illegal casino operators while the provincial government began preparing legislation to regulate the casino industry. In 2000, after the KwaZulu-Natal Gambling Board received and evaluated 13 bids to establish casinos within the new legal framework, the premier intervened to change the tender regulations in such a way as to favour the bidders the IFP preferred.[19]

Though South African levels of public venality are probably lower than in most sub-Saharan African countries,[20] the incidence of corruption is sufficiently serious to constitute a serious barrier to government achieving its goals. In 1998, the firm of accountants Deloitte & Touche suggested that losses caused by public-sector fraud and mismanagement could exceed R10 billion that year.[21] This figure, 7 per cent of public expenditure, does suggest a scenario in which corruption has become systemic. Once the wastage caused by corruption begins to total even a few percentage points of the government's annual budget, then the loss represents a very substantial proportion of the sums available for public-sector capital invest-ment. This has been the case in South Africa for a long time, since well before the advent of democracy in 1994.

Yet with the election of a popular government political conditions favouring anti-corruption action have strengthened. Modern South African elections are organised through a system – closed-list proportional representation – which discourages the kinds of personalised patronage that may result from individual competition between political notables. South African arrangements for parlia-mentary representation – with (until 2002) a ban on floor-crossing – also favour the strengthening of party discipline. This makes individual favour-seeking less productive and renders the political system less susceptible to rent-seeking. Since its election in 1994, the political leadership of the ANC has consistently adopted anti-inflationary policies, including public deficit reduction, whilst at the same time attempting to extend services and broaden access to them. In this context, national politicians (at least in theory) acknowledge the importance of reducing corruption even if they are not always willing to undertake the political risks attendant on punishing prominent offenders. The virtual abolition of press censorship in the early 1990s and, with the achievement of universal citizenship, generally higher popular expectations about government performance have helped to create a more receptive public environment in which to launch anti-corruption campaigns.

A final general condition favouring public-sector reform in South Africa is that, in contrast to most African countries and many developing countries elsewhere, though the public sector is an important employer it accounts for only a minority share of the formal labour force. This characteristic makes public sector reform much less politically challenging than when the state is the main employer, and ensures the existence of powerful reformist pressures outside the state.[22] There are good reasons, then, to believe that there now exists a more favourable climate for attacking corruption in South Africa than ever in the past. How effectively have the authorities exploited these better conditions?

Experience and analysis of a range of international efforts to combat corruption suggest that an effective anti-corruption programme should incorporate most if not all of the following six elements:

1. Measuring corruption. This can be undertaken through surveys of citizen perceptions as well as interviews with possible participants to discover rela-tive costs and returns from bribery.[23] If such exercises are repeated at regular intervals and correlated with other indicators of institutional efficiency, a fairly revealing picture of trends can emerge.
2. Publicity. The state can raise public awareness of the existence and conse-quences of corruption by means of, for example, the ready provision of infor-

mation about corruption to the media. Allied to this measure would be the promotion of values that are hostile to corruption through, for example, the adoption of ethical codes by public servants and politicians. Effective anti-corruption strategies attempt to mobilise public interest by means of the encouragement of non-government monitoring, the provision of telephone 'hotlines' and other inducements for civic participation.

3. Removing incentives. Removal or reduction of incentives for corrupt behaviour might include improving salaries for politicians and public servants, adopting uniform and precise tendering criteria and simplifying other procedures that govern interaction between officials, and cutting back on certain kinds of state regulation.

4. Increasing penalties. Penalties and disincentives for corrupt behaviour may be achieved by criminalising actions that are currently dealt with through internal departmental disciplinary procedures. In addition to criminal sanctions these should include punishing corrupt officials with dismissal and loss of pension rights, creating independent and adequately funded anti-corruption agencies,[24] and protecting and institutionalising 'whistle-blowing' practices. The scope of punishment needs to be given public emphasis through the conviction of politically prominent offenders, preferably from the ruling party.[25]

5. Political support. Such support for action against corruption must include endorsement of agency and judicial action against corruption, refusal to tolerate or sanction corrupt behaviour by political colleagues, limiting political appointments within the civil service and curbing other forms of political patronage, public disclosure of political party finance and politicians' assets, and acceptance of ministerial responsibility for major instances of departmental corruption. Politicians who are proved to have been guilty of corrupt behaviour should be prevented from reassuming any elected or appointed public office.

6. Bureaucratic reform. Measures here might include the adoption of standardised and meritocratic methods of staff recruitment, streamlining official procedures to reduce delays, rotating public servants between different jobs, and strengthening supervision, financial control and reporting.[26]

Beyond these fairly specific measures, political democratisation and state privatisation are widely perceived as processes that are likely to create environments in which administrative corruption becomes less likely.[27] There is disagreement, though, about the implications of both these processes with respect to their effects on corruption. Democratisation might make corruption easier to detect but it can also increase incentives for corruption, especially during elections. Privatisation can restrict opportunities for certain forms of public corruption by reducing the scope of state economic activity and regulation. However, the adoption of market values in place of older professional codes of conduct can also weaken ethical restraints on corruption. Certainly, by themselves, democratisation and privatisation of government cannot be expected to eliminate corruption.

The six kinds of activity listed above supply a useful set of indicators for the extent to which authorities are committed to taking effective action against corruption. They supply a framework of reference by which to assess South African performance in attempting to reduce the scope of venal government. The remainder of this chapter will consider the effectiveness of South African initiatives with respect to these six activities: measurement, publicity, removing incentives, increasing penalties, political support and bureaucratic reform.

MEASURING CORRUPTION

Good strategies depend on knowledge. How much do we know about corruption in South Africa? Academic study of South African corruption is relatively underdeveloped. Until recently, specialists of South African public administration paid little attention to corruption, and implicit in this neglect was the assumption that it was not a normal feature of official life. There is enough evidence from judicial commissions of inquiry into various departmental scandals during the late 1980s and early 1990s to suggest that such assumptions were wrong. But until 1994, it was quite difficult to undertake systematic research on corruption. Large proportions of state expenditure were allocated to secret votes within the military, and certain areas of bureaucratic activity – the prisons services were one example – were protected from public scrutiny by reporting restrictions.

Even so, more scholarly diagnosis could have been undertaken. This academic neglect was primarily attributable to the major locations of corruption. Those who were its main victims were poor and disenfranchised, and often the subjects of homeland administrations. Relatively privileged white citizens were much less likely to have encountered dishonest officials, for their lives were less affected by bureaucratic controls and restrictions. On the whole, before 1994 the study of South African public administration was undertaken from the perspective of white citizens (and white managers), not black subjects. Since 1994 the scope of bureaucratic public accountability has widened. However, many bodies that spend public money still escape public scrutiny. In 1998, of 648 bodies financed through public funds, only 34 reported to parliament and just 200 had to submit their records to the auditor-general.[28]

Since 1994, much more information has become available. This is largely the result of official investigations into historical instances of corruption, but also of the removal of restrictions on public knowledge about government business. Opposition parties demonstrate considerably more commitment to opposing and exposing corruption in official quarters than before 1994,[29] and newspapers accord the topic much more editorial emphasis. Several agencies have organised surveys that report on public perceptions of corruption. For example, the annual Public Opinion Surveys of the Institute for Democracy in South Africa (IDASA) indicate that perceptions that government corruption is widespread have increased among all race groups (most dramatically among Indians). According to the surveys, roughly one-third of Africans and two-thirds of whites believe that there is more corruption since 1994 than under apartheid, although agreement with this view among whites decreased between 1995 and 1998.[30] The Human Sciences Research Council's annual public opinion polls have included corruption perception questions for the past three years, with broadly similar results. More reassuringly, the expert panel consultations of the Institute for Security Studies (154 telephone conversations between August and October 2000) suggested that levels of corruption have remained unchanged since the ANC government came to power.

Other quantitative research has tried to establish the extent to which citizens have encountered corrupt officials. For example, the 1997 official Statistics South Africa (SSA) Victims of Crime Survey reports that 2 per cent of its respondents experienced one form or another of official corruption.[31] Another survey, sponsored by the Greater Johannesburg Metropolitan Council, conducted in 1999 among some five hundred business leaders, indicated a comparatively low incidence of official extortion: only 1 per cent of the firms surveyed had been asked to pay bribes for licences and permits.[32] As such surveys documenting experiences of corruption (as opposed to merely perceptions) become routine and as longitudinal data sets become available, it will become possible to evaluate the efficacy of government efforts to counter corruption.

It is also possible today, given the extent of information available about particular instances of corruption, to make some informed guesses about its severity. We know from official admissions that within the public service there has been an increase in the incidence of misbehaviour by public servants (though this may be the consequence of improvements in record-keeping). It is known that bribery and extortion are especially concentrated in the police force and the Department of Justice. While this may be an historically inherited trend from the apartheid era there have been few signs of effective reform. It is also public knowledge that fraudulent entitlement claims were responsible for the wastage of huge sums of money administered by the Department of Social Welfare. Here it seems that the government has made extremely energetic efforts to eliminate false claimants. In fact, curbing welfare entitlement fraud has inflicted considerable social hardship as the reorganisation and verification of records inevitably caused lengthy delays in payments. During this process nearly 100 000 grants were cancelled or suspended in the Eastern Cape, to the dismay of disability rights advocates.[33] In the same province, the authorities identified 985 civil servants who had awarded themselves grants totalling R462 950 a month. Another R1.27 million a month had been paid out to 'deceased beneficiaries'.[34] In the North West, all disability payments were suspended for several months during a fraud investigation in 2001.[35]

It appears that the administration of housing subsidies has also been badly affected by fraudulent contracting. In KwaZulu-Natal alone, 53 000 queries concerning housing subsidies were under official scrutiny in 1998.[36] Abuse of subsistence and travel allowances by public servants had reached epidemic proportions throughout the public sector: over two years, in KwaZulu-Natal only, abuse of such allowances exceeded R14 million.[37] This seems to be a form of corruption that has increased since 1994. Several further high-level scandals over tendering suggest that this is yet another area in which public resources are being misused. If the National Party's claims that arise from its 'Corruption Barometer' are accurate – that between 1994 and 1998 the government lost up to R20 billion as a result of corrupt employees' behaviour – then these costs more or less match the savings generated by 'rightsizing' the bureaucracy. Such calculations do not appear excessive. The Special Investigative Unit headed by Judge Willem Heath claimed in 1998 that the R10 billion worth of fraud it was then investigating represented about 5 per cent of the total, although this figure included historical instances of corruption before 1994. 'It was as bad or even worse before the elections, but it was not so transparent,' Heath conceded.[38] However, partly owing to the efforts of Judge Heath and his colleagues, while levels of corruption have not receded the authorities have made significant progress in identifying its location and extent since 1994.

PUBLICITY

Though the Mbeki administration with its calls for 'zero tolerance', 'total war' and 'moral summits' has certainly placed more rhetorical emphasis on the problem of public corruption than its predecessor, and though newspapers certainly pay more attention to corruption than was the case before 1994, there is no systematic official campaign to educate the public about the nature and consequences of bureaucratic venality. This is despite an undertaking in 1998 by the Public Service Commission to mount public campaigns 'to reinforce the fear of detection and punishment'.[39] In 1999 the government-sponsored National Anti-Corruption Summit resolved to establish a National Anti-Corruption Forum. Two years later, the preparations for the launch of this body were only just completed. The Forum's proposed activities do include public education initiatives but its resources for such undertakings may be rather modest. Though the Forum's secretariat will be based in the Public Service Commission, as a non-statutory body its programme will depend on support from three 'sectors': business, civil society and the public domain. There are no plans for any state funding.

Codes of conduct for both public servants and parliamentarians have been planned and one for local councillors has actually been legislated. However, these have yet to influence public perceptions and public expectations. The publication of a register of MPs' financial interests attracted a great deal of press coverage, although a special provision allowing parliamentarians to list certain assets in a confidential section limits its utility. To be fair, MPs' financial disclosure rules in South Africa are amongst the most comprehensive in the British Commonwealth, and much more demanding than any other such requirements in Africa. No such registers have been instituted for members of provincial legislatures, though the Executive Ethics Act requires a declaration of assets by provincial premiers and members of their executives. A ministerial handbook approved by the cabinet in 1995 forbids ministers' family members from serving on the boards of public companies and from owning shares in companies connected with the ministers' duties.

How seriously this restriction is taken seemed rather questionable after the revelation that the wife of the premier, Makhenkesi Stofile, had joined the boards of two companies shortly before these obtained contracts with the Eastern Cape government – contracts that were awarded by a tender board appointed by Stofile's executive. Stofile commented that the handbook was 'nothing else but guidelines … it is not binding'.[40] He used the same justification to explain his disregard of the handbook in spending R20 000 on airline tickets for his wife during 1999.[41] The case of the Eastern Cape MEC for health, Bevan Goqwana, presented an even more serious breach of the Executive Ethics Act. Although the Act required cabinet members and MECs to avoid conflicts of interest, Goqwana was running an ambulance company and submitting patients' medical aid claims. Complaints to the premier had elicited no action.[42]

At less exalted levels, external monitoring of compliance with codes is very difficult. Government departments generally prefer to keep their disciplinary procedures secret and anonymous, even in the case of quite serious offences by public servants. Nor do they always welcome civil society initiatives to counter public corruption. For example, in November 2000 minister of safety and secur- ity Steve Tshwete angrily rejected a proposal for a private-sector agency to monitor police corruption. The police had its own unit, he observed, and busi- ness would perform a more useful public service if it tried instead to fight corpo- rate dishonesty. However, toll-free anti-corruption telephone hotlines have since 1998 been maintained by the South African Police Service and the Gauteng government, and more recently by Limpopo Province and the Department of Justice. In 1998 and 1999, the government hosted two major anti-corruption conferences and all parties, including the ruling party, have focused on the issue in their recent electoral campaigning.

REMOVING INCENTIVES

If paying MPs and senior civil servants salaries that emulate the private sector helps to limit the temptations of rent-seeking, then the South African government has performed fairly impressively. Almost immediately after their election in 1994, MPs adopted recommendations for quite a generous overhaul of their salary structure. Subsequent rises have been in excess of inflation and of any pay-hikes in the public sector. Very senior civil servants have continued to be well paid, a trend initiated during the early 1970s. However, if public-sector salary reviews are to constitute a serious contribution to fighting corruption, then concentrating salary incentives at the top may be counter-productive. In 1999, magistrates and prosecutors had to threaten industrial action before the authorities took their pay claims seriously. Yet court officials were known to be one group of public-sector employees who were particularly susceptible to venal misconduct.

Another way of removing incentives for corruption is by simplifying official procedures governing interaction between officials and the public, and ensuring that the formalities that remain are controlled by honest officials. However, with an expansion of entitlements in certain areas – housing, for example – the scope and complexities of interaction may have increased. A proliferation of agencies administering particular aspects of certain government programmes – housing again is a case in point – has also complicated procedures and expanded opportunities for corruption. Nominally independent regulatory authorities seem to be especially susceptible to political pressures and financial misbehaviour, judging from a succession of scandals and disputes which have affected the functioning of the Independent Broadcasting Authority and the South African Telecommunications Regulatory Authority.

More intricate immigration laws (administered by a notoriously weak and relatively unreconstructed apartheid-era bureaucracy, the Department of Home Affairs) represent another instance of how new areas of regulation can open up fresh fields for rent-seeking, particularly when they are known for their historically weak administrative capacity. Though government tendering procedures have been centralised and subjected to a standardised set of criteria, this does not affect procedures adopted by provincial administrations or parastatal agencies. For example, the Strategic Fuel Fund (SFF), a facility originally set up to circumvent sanctions and now a key agency in black business empowerment, sold off South Africa's strategic oil reserves in 2000 without putting out the transaction to tender. Subsequently, an investigation by the Directorate of Public Prosecutions confirmed that the SFF's chief executive officer, Keith Kunene, had accepted bribes to the value of R360 000 in return for arranging the transaction with Trafigura, a London-based company.[43]

In general, as a result of the government's retreat from the *dirigiste* models of public administration favoured under apartheid, and the proliferation of privatisation and outsourcing of previously exclusive government functions (examples include the provision of low-cost housing, public-interest broadcasting, basic services such as water reticulation, and the administration of social welfare entitlements), the government's regulatory functions have expanded very rapidly – well beyond its administrative capacity. It is likely to be burdened further yet with the taxi industry's R20 billion recapitalisation. This process arose from a new set of rules instituted by the Department of Transport, which in 2001 was beginning to attract bribe offers to government advisers from prospective bidders for a smart-card tender.[44]

INCREASING PENALTIES

In this field, much still needs to be accomplished. The incidence of police corruption is especially alarming, given the central role police agencies should play in any anti-corruption offensive. Reports suggest that corruption within the police remains extensive. In the first two months of 2000, 129 officers were arrested for corruption. The number of police officers charged with such offences between January 1996 and December 1998 totalled 1 153.[45] The nature of such charges indicates that policemen are involved in rather more sinister undertakings than simply the acceptance of petty bribes. Drug trafficking, car hijacking and violent competition by taxi proprietors over commuter routes are all fields in which there have been instances of high-level police complicity with major criminal syndicates. However, police officers can be dismissed only after conviction for a crime in which a prison sentence is mandatory.

Both internal departmental and judicial procedures against public corruption can be very protracted exercises. Often they stretch over several years while the officials concerned remain on the payroll, sometimes even continuing to work in the police force. Under such conditions, even after public exposure, corrupt practices can remain routine in certain departments. A case in point was reports in 2001 on the continuing saga of driving licences for cash in Mpumalanga, three years after a major political scandal involving the same testing centres and officials. However, public-sector trade unions, including those allied to the ruling party, frequently seek to protect their members against accusations of dishonesty; municipal workers' unions, post office workers and the Police and Prisons Civil Rights Union (POPCRU) have on several occasions been accomplices in the perpetuation of corrupt bureaucracy.

The prison warders' union is an especially unapologetic champion of venal officials. After an investigation by the parliamentary public accounts committee, which led to the dismissal of correctional services commissioner Khulekani Sithole, POPCRU's national representative reacted by noting that 'the whole public service and administration has lost one of its most committed and dedicated civil servants'. Sithole's forced resignation was accompanied by allegations of co-operation between the commissioner and senior POPCRU officials in running a 'jobs for pals' scheme throughout the prison bureaucracy.[46]

On the credit side, though, is the passage in 2001 of the Protected Disclosures Act to discourage employer victimisation of 'whistle-blowers' – employees who make disclosures about unlawful activity on the part of their colleagues in good faith and who follow certain procedures in doing so. This reform was badly needed. A conspicuous example of whistle-blower victimisation was the suspension of John Muller, the Mpumalanga traffic officer who originally exposed the fraudulent issuing of driving licences mentioned above, while the culprits remained in their posts.[47] Naturally, the law will not protect elected politicians such as Fish Mahlalela, who lost his position as MEC for local government in Mpumalanga in March 2000 after attempting to implicate his provincial ANC executive colleagues in tender fraud.[48]

The operation of the constitutionally protected offices of the auditor-general and the public protector, the establishment of several anti-corruption units in different departments (including the police,[49] customs,[50] the Directorate of Public Prosecutions,[51] and the Public Service Commission), as well as the operations of the Special Investigative Unit under Judge Heath, represent expressions of government support for dedicated action against corruption, notwithstanding the frequently bad-tempered exchanges between Judge Heath and cabinet members. With its 55 investigators and nine lawyers, the Special Investigative Unit is the most formidable of the various agencies. Originally established by the Eastern Cape provincial administration, its mandate was extended nationally by parliament. It became accountable to parliament through special legislation in 1996 and enjoys extensive powers of investigation, seizure, interdict and subpoena as well as the authority to administer civil proceedings for repayment through its own tribunal. Nevertheless, it is obliged to refer recommendations for criminal prosecutions to the police, and each investigation needs presidential sanction. This requirement may cause delays and alert the targets of any proposed inquiry. Judge Heath himself has been an often acerbic critic of government, complaining in early 1999 that of the 80 000 cases the unit was investigating, only 'two or three' had been presented by government – most of the cases were initiated in response to information supplied by private citizens.[52]

Since a Constitutional Court ruling that Judge Heath's role within the unit may be unconstitutional, its future status has become uncertain, though proposals in June 2001 that it should be attached to the auditor-general's office may enhance its position of autonomy. If this proposal is adopted, the unit's resources, powers and functions would still fall well short of the competencies characteristic of the most successful anti-corruption agencies such as those in Hong Kong or New South Wales, Australia. The Hong Kong agency has powers of arrest and the Hong Kong Prevention of Bribery Ordinance reverses traditional presumptions of innocence. Whether such powers are desirable in a new democracy with a history of authoritarian government remains questionable.

Other South African agencies are also comparatively badly resourced. The Office of the Public Protector, whose mandate includes investigating corruption, employs only 40 investigators. The comparable body in Uganda, a country with a population half that of South Africa, employs 110 investigators.[53] Judge Heath complained in early 1999 that his budget had declined in real terms. Heath was also critical of the frequent failure of the authorities to charge people guilty of stealing official property.[54] One particularly conspicuous instance of government reluctance to involve the Heath unit was in KwaZulu-Natal. After initially agreeing to make use of the unit's services, the provincial authorities instead established their own investigation into charges against the MEC for welfare, Prince Gideon Zulu. This commission, the Venter Commission, subsequently found the MEC innocent of receiving money for contracts, although it failed to check the bank accounts into which the money had allegedly been paid.[55]

It may of course be argued that even a weak official response is probably better than none at all. It seems that most reported instances of corruption are at least investigated by one official authority or another. In 1997 one survey found that 84 per cent of corruption cases referred to in the press had received some form of anti-corruption attention from the government.[56] Indeed, most of the corruption cases reported in the media became public knowledge because they were the subject of official investigations. Another survey found that in the 12 months preceding July 2000, 75 per cent of corruption reports referred to incidents that attracted press attention because of official action; only 11 per cent of the revelations were a consequence of investigative reporting. The rest were outcomes of whistle-blowing and complaints from 'civil society'.[57]

POLITICAL SUPPORT

Here the picture is mixed. Senior politicians' attacks on the work of anti-corruption agencies and the courts are currently detracting from the government's proclaimed commitment to fighting corruption 'as public enemy number one'.[58] Penuell Maduna's untrue and unretracted allegations against the auditor-general before the 1999 general elections and the ANC's criticism of Allan Boesak's conviction are two cases in point. Maduna, then minister of energy affairs, accused the auditor-general of concealing what he took to be misrepresentations in the accounts of the Strategic Fuel Fund. In fact, Maduna had accepted at face value a misinterpretation of the books by an accounting firm specially appointed by himself. The Auditor-General's Office was later vindicated by the public accounts committee and the Public Protector's Office. Subsequently Maduna, by virtue of his being a constitutional lawyer, was given the justice portfolio in Thabo Mbeki's post-1999 cabinet. Shortly after his appointment, the minister hinted that he might have to shut down the Heath unit.

When former Western Cape ANC leader Allan Boesak was convicted for misappropriating funds from the charity he had headed, ANC spokesperson Smuts Ngonyama claimed that Boesak's 'only sin has been the lack of his accounting skills', and his conviction raised 'many questions about the integrity of the courts and whether they have been transformed or not'.[59] In his response to the subsequent confirmation of Boesak's conviction by the Appeal Court, he accused the judiciary of being 'totally biased'.[60] Ngonyama's sentiments probably reflected a view widely held within the ANC. At Boesak's first appearance after his release from prison in May 2001, he presided over an evangelical church service flanked by senior members of the ANC's provincial hierarchy.

Furthermore, the reappointment to public office of politicians and officials implicated in earlier corruption scandals is unhelpful. This was especially evident in the case of the Mpumalanga executive council. After the 1999 elections it included the appointment of three formerly disgraced MECs. This announcement was accompanied by an extraordinary statement by the premier, Ndaweni Mahlangu, in which he defended lying politicians. The people he had chosen, he claimed, represented 'the best team'.[61]

Political appointments in the upper echelons of the public service undermine civil service professionalism and may, therefore, facilitate corruption. Such appointments were excusable in 1994 when the ANC was confronted with a civil service which had for decades been the exclusive field of National Party patronage. They were less easy to justify in 1999, when a post-election cabinet reshuffle was accompanied by the movement of key bureaucrats from one department to another in the wake of 'their' ministers. Related to this kind of behaviour is the general refusal to acknowledge an ethic of ministerial responsibility. Since the *Sarafina II* affair it has become conventional for ministers to blame scandals or maladministration on their directors-general.

Secrecy concerning the sources of political party electioneering funding can be a major cause of corruption. There has been a worrying rise in the incidence of party funding scandals. Party funding for the provincial ANC was one factor in the Mpumalanga Parks Board scandal (see chapter 2), and in KwaZulu-Natal it seems that the IFP and its leaders have been beneficiaries of campaign contributions from both illegal operators and licence bidders in the casino industry. Political parties are a long way from achieving a culture of 'zero tolerance' of corruption within their active membership. Significantly, before the 1999 elections, most Free State ANC branches favoured the nomination of Ace Magashule as premier, notwithstanding the former provincial minister's removal from the provincial government for financial irregularities.[62]

More positive indicators have included several high-level dismissals of officials for corrupt practices, notably in the departments of Correctional Services and

Home Affairs. In both cases the directors-general resigned following hearings by assertive parliamentary back-benchers. A number of elected politicians were removed from office for practices involving venality, mainly in regional governments. Most importantly, a general respect for the independence of the judiciary was achieved, despite occasional rhetorical lapses voiced by ruling-party spokespeople. During the Mandela administration, at least nine provincial executive members were removed from office after corruption findings against them, though none of these cases resulted in any criminal prosecution. Thus government was sending out mixed signals. As noted above, three Mpumalanga MECs who were removed from office were brought back either into the executive or into other senior positions after the 1999 general elections. It should also be noted here that the relevant minister was demonstrably reluctant to comply with recommendations for dismissal of the directors-general of home affairs and correctional services. In fact, the minister, Buthelezi, went out of his way to praise home affairs director-general Albert Mokoena, discovered to have used official facilities to promote the fortunes of his private basketball team, for having been 'a very competent, capable and effective director-general'.[63]

Meanwhile, prison commissioner Khulekani Sithole was vigorously defended by his minister, Ben Skosana, who made special representations to Thabo Mbeki to retain the commissioner in his post. Though the Department of Correctional Services was an IFP-led ministry, this did not deter the public accounts committee's chairperson, IFP MP Gavin Woods, from leading an aggressive investigation into the allegations against Sithole.

Up to the end of 2001, the standing committee on public accounts (SCOPA) was notably non-partisan. In investigating allegations of kickbacks accompanying the contracting of R29 billion worth of arms purchases, which in December 1999 followed the Ministry of Defence's strategic review, ANC MPs initially played an assertive role. The SCOPA inquiry followed the auditor-general's recommendation for a parliamentary investigation after he had found deviations from standard practices in the case of one of the main contractors, British Aerospace. The allegations included the acceptance of R11 million by former ANC defence minister Joe Modise and other ANC notables for helping to arrange the purchase of navy corvettes from a German company as well as for exercising political pressure to influence the choice of local sub-contractors.[64] If the charges prove true, they would represent the most serious political corruption scandal since 1994. Discouragingly, in their response to the committee's inquiry into the arms procurement contracts, government and ANC leaders set new precedents for undermining parliamentary authority.

SCOPA would traditionally attempt to function as a cross-party body, reaching its decisions through consensus. This convention came under severe test when its recommendation that the Heath Unit be included in the commissioning of further investigations alongside the auditor-general, the public protector and the Directorate of Public Prosecutions was rejected by President Mbeki and subsequently criticised by the speaker, Frene Ginwala. The leader of the ANC 'Study Group' within the parliamentary committee, Andrew Feinstein, was demoted in January and later excluded from the ANC's representatives on a drafting group within the committee. Feinstein was reputed to be among the 'most tenacious' committee members 'in establishing the facts about the government's spending'.[65] He was one of the authors of the report that had advocated the inclusion of the Heath Unit in the joint investigation. ANC chief whip Tony Yengeni justified Feinstein's treatment by telling reporters that in future ANC members of SCOPA would operate under party discipline: 'Some people have the notion that public accounts committee members should act in a non-partisan way. But in our system no ANC member has a free vote.'[66] Earlier Yengeni had attempted to prevent SCOPA members from travelling to Pretoria at public expense and had accused Feinstein of 'acting without a mandate' in his support for an official inquiry into the defence contract.[67] Feinstein was to be replaced in his capacity as leader of the study group by Yengeni's deputy, Geoff Doidge, and Yengeni himself would attend study group meetings to supply 'political authority and guidance'.[68] Feinstein resigned from parliament in August, complaining that cabinet ministers, including Alec Erwin, had attempted to 'rein me in'.[69]

Just how disinterested Yengeni's guidance to SCOPA might have been became increasingly questionable after press revelations that Yengeni had been the recipient of a Mercedes 4x4, which one of the sub-contractors in the arms deal, European Aeronautic Defence and Space Company (EADS), had ordered from the manufacturers as a 'staff car'.[70] In receiving the vehicle on what seem to have been extremely favourable terms, Yengeni should have included it in the parliamentary register of gifts and assets. In May, Yengeni was protected by the ANC majority on the Parliamentary Ethics Committee, its members voting against the demand that Yengeni explain how he acquired the vehicle and why he had not entered it in the register. Despite spending R250 000 of his supporters' money on newspaper advertisements protesting his innocence in July, Yengeni resigned as chief whip in October after being charged with corruption and perjury over his acceptance of the car from EADS. The other 29 recipients of generously discounted vehicles from the same company included Siphiwe Nyanda, chief of the defence force; Mandla Msomi, an IFP MP and a former chair of the standing committee on public accounts; and Vanan Pillay, a Department of Trade and Industry official who was involved in the tendering negotiations.

In mid-November, the report on the joint investigation by the Directorate of Public Prosecutions, the public protector and the auditor-general was released in parliament, one month after a constitutionally controversial secret submission of its contents to the President's Office, a move which inevitably generated accusations that the public version had been doctored. The report exonerated members of President Mbeki's cabinet of any wrongdoing but expressed serious reservations about the administration of tendering procedures. It mentioned officials who had received gifts from bidders and criticised the Department of Defence's chief of acquisitions, Chippy Shaik, for possibly favouring his brother's company over a more eligible bidder in a sub-contracting tender. Shaik had not abstained from attending meetings at which the fitting out of new corvettes was discussed; in fact, minutes of the meeting showed that Shaik had been an active participant in the meeting and contributed an extended commentary on the financial risks of using the products of his brother's rival bidder. In particular, the investigation drew attention to a curious decision by the Joint Project Team, the body appointed to decide which computer system should be bought to control the corvettes' fire-power, in which Chippy Shaik also played a key role. The winning sub-contractor was given details of a rival and more competitive bid to help it revise its proposal. The Joint Project Team's 'project officer', Rear-Admiral J. E. G. Kamerman, appeared to have misled the investigation on several occasions.

The investigation could find no evidence against Nelson Mandela's defence minister, Joe Modise, who was at the centre of the original bribery allegations, though the report recommended that in future people who leave senior positions in government should be barred from involvement in companies that negotiate public contracts. The report was censorious about various aspects of the commissioning of the main contracts with foreign suppliers, but its authors did not attribute any of the lapses in procedure they identified to corruption. The approval process was deliberately complex and it would have been very difficult for any individual to influence the allocation of the main contracts decisively. Any attempt to influence the cabinet sub-committee that made the final recommendations through the misrepresentation of the merits of one bid over another would have had to involve an improbably extensive conspiracy amongst the people responsible for the tender evaluation. However, the secretary of this sub-committee was Chippy Shaik, and when the investigation's findings were made public the police arrested his brother, Schabir, for possession of a copy of minutes from one of its meetings.

In the most obvious instance of a less cost-effective bid being chosen, that of the aircraft supplier, the choice was a result of the importance the Department of Trade and Industry attached to the industrial investment commitments that were among the tender requirements. The German Submarine Consortium (GSC) was also allowed, against the rules, to resubmit a bid that should have been disqualified. Though the joint investigation drew no conclusions from this impropriety, its finding left open the possibility that the decision may have been influenced by GSC's local investment undertakings, which included projects in which Modise was later to acquire an interest. In general, the evaluation of these commitments was flawed, but the mistakes were probably made in good faith, the investigation concluded. However, the investigation refrained from pursuing the question why the original terms of the tendering process were changed to favour the British bidder for the aircraft contract. This decision was made at the request of Joe Modise, and one year earlier the auditor-general had called it 'a material deviation from the originally adopted value system'.[71]

The joint investigation's report deferred announcing any findings on a number of allegations that were still under investigation by the Directorate of Public Prosecutions. These included the possibility that officials involved in the acquisition process held shares in companies that won contracts; that a 'role player' in the procurement had told bidders that they would offer sub-contracts to particular South African companies; and that one of the sub-contractors had made 'undue payments'.[72] Though by no means the 'whitewash' claimed by opposition parties, the report was probably too charitable in exonerating government. Quite aside from unanswered questions about Joe Modise's behaviour, a stringent doctrine of responsibility would hold ministers responsible for senior officials' misdemeanours in their departments. Besides, the executive pressure exerted on ANC members in SCOPA through the chief whip's office – an issue which lay outside the scope of the joint investigation – reflected badly on ruling-party politicians and accentuated popular conviction that the government was at fault. Mbeki's remarks in the wake of the report's publication, that any criticism of its conclusions about the government's responsibility could only be inspired by racism, represented a particularly clumsy attempt to inhibit any critical consideration of the investigation.[73] Minister Mosiuoa Lekota's claim that the investigation itself represented a litmus test for South Africa's young democracy which had 'been passed with flying colours' was comparably disingenuous.[74] If the agencies charged with the inquiry had generally performed rather well, this was despite the expectations generated by the behaviour of politicians both in government and in opposition.

Modise's extraordinarily rapid emergence as a major player in the local armaments industry is merely the most conspicuous example of a much wider social process. This process involved attempts by the South African 'military industrial complex' to recapture the political influence it enjoyed under P. W. Botha, by actively recruiting former ANC soldiers and intelligence operatives onto its boards and into its management. Any explanation of how the defence establishment succeeded in reversing government policy over arms expenditure to embark on a programme of procurement which even military specialists suggest was irrational,[75] should focus on the movement of Umkhonto veterans into the arms industry.[76] A few examples will underline this point.

In 2000, Joe Modise's business interests embraced a company called Marvol Management, originally established in the late 1980s to equip Armscor with

Mirage upgrades. From mid-2000 Modise also headed BKS Engineering, a key contractor in the construction of the industrial development zone at Coega in the Eastern Cape, a project in which several of the 'anchor tenants' would be enterprises established through the local 'off-set' investments promised by the major arms procurement contractors. Chippy Shaik's brother Schabir, a former ANC intelligence official, was a director of African Defence Systems (ADS), one of the sub-contractors involved in installing equipment in the corvettes. Schabir Shaik had once served as a financial adviser to deputy president Jacob Zuma, securing for him a badly needed bank loan while Zuma was a KwaZulu-Natal MEC, and earlier had played an important role in securing Malaysian financial contributions to the ANC's 1994 election campaign. ADS was established as a local affiliate of the company Thompson-CSF, and from 2000 also included on its board Lambert Moloi, who had held senior positions in both Umkhonto and the South African National Defence Force (SANDF). Moloi also held a directorship on the parastatal arms company Denel, as well as a board position on Futuristic Business Solutions, winner of several procurement contracts. Another significant connection established between arms manufacturers and ANC guerrilla old-timers involved a British Aerospace donation of several million rands in 1999 to the MK Military Veterans Association. British Aerospace later became the successful bidder in the controversial contract for the supply of fighter aircraft mentioned earlier in this chapter.

BUREAUCRATIC REFORM

Given a slight contraction in the size of the civil service, it is possible that recruitment might have in effect become more competitive, though recent reports of the numbers of officials who have made false claims about their qualifications suggest otherwise. The dismissal of a KwaZulu-Natal MEC for education in August 2000 for appointing a poorly qualified relative to the post of deputy director-general represents an encouraging public endorsement of meritocratic appointment principles by political leadership. Affirmative action criteria can undoubtedly be combined with meritocratic considerations in making appointments, but this does not seem to be happening consistently. The exodus of skilled personnel from the public service as well as the appointment of under-qualified people to middle-management positions at a time when civil service tasks have become increasingly complicated, has increased bureaucratic inefficiency and hence increased the incentives to bypass official procedures illegally. This may be a short-term problem, though. The proliferation of public-sector professional training institutions suggests that the supply of adequately trained job-seekers should soon outstrip demand.

Public reporting of public-sector activity has certainly improved, but we know from the auditor-general's investigations that the quality of financial supervision in many government departments is appalling, mainly as a consequence of the shortage of accounting skills. In 2001 the Treasury stopped payment on all government cheques over R2 000; in future such payments would require special clearance. This move was taken after a random audit found that in the Department of Justice 90 per cent of the basic rules of bookkeeping were being disregarded.[77] In the Eastern Cape, where the government was structured around especially degenerate homeland bureaucracies, the political will to implement reform has been impressive in the past two years. Evidence of effective political leadership includes the reappointment of a combative opposition MP, Eddie Trent, after the 1999 elections to the chairmanship of the public accounts committee in Bisho,[78] and the centralisation of departmental financial controls under the MEC for finance, Enoch Godongwana. In the Eastern Cape's Department of Welfare, no less than 985 government employees who were illegally drawing grants were 'rooted out' during a major clean-up during 1998/9. Discouragingly, though, Trent was removed from his chairmanship in early 2001 in a coordinated move across the provinces by means of which the ANC sought to curb DA influence over parliamentary committees.[79]

FUTURE PROSPECTS

In summary, it can be said that by 2000, diagnosis of South African corruption was much better developed than it had been six years previously. This is partly attributable to a stronger official predisposition in favour of disclosure, and to the attention it has received in less censored media and from various monitoring exercises. This represents a major step forward in any process to combat corruption. There is certainly much greater public awareness of corruption, though government has yet to exploit public interest in a systematic campaign to counter official venality. Some of the preparatory arrangements for such a campaign are already in place: codes of conduct, interest registers and telephone hotlines are in operation or have been established. But aside from politicians awarding themselves pay increases, there is no evidence yet of any serious consideration of a programme to reduce the incentives for public-sector rent-seeking. Indeed, these may have increased as the state's regulatory responsibilities expanded. Much remains to be accomplished in making penalties more effective as deterrents, though a new range of institutional measures, including dedicated units, streamlined legal proceedings and whistle-blower protection, have enhanced the likelihood of detection.

The political will to punish corruption in high quarters remains inconsistent – and non-existent in certain provincial governments. Though elected politicians have occasionally lost office as a result of corruption accusations, not a single ANC minister or parliamentarian has been charged with or convicted for a corruption-related political offence.[80] Moreover, since the chief whip's interference in the

SCOPA investigation on arms procurement, there may well be less willingness among ANC back-benchers to challenge the executive over corruption in high places.

Finally, any efforts at bureaucratic reform are undermined by the lack of financial controls and the exemption of broad areas of public life from strict financial accountability. Despite some positive achievements, much needs to be done before the South African government can claim full commitment to the goal of eliminating corruption. Of the elements that are lacking, perhaps the most alarming is the absence in top leadership of what the executive has itself called for, namely 'zero tolerance'.

8 | DEMOCRACY IN A DOMINANT PARTY SYSTEM

Since 1994, South Africa has possessed many of the institutions and mechanisms which normally constitute a fully fledged liberal democracy. These include universal suffrage, based upon proportional representation, for a range of legislatures – national, regional and local; a multiplicity of political parties; a Constitutional Court which has demonstrated its autonomy from the government in, for example, its review of the first draft of the final Constitution; a Constitution which itself guarantees an extensive range of freedoms, many of them entrenched in a Bill of Rights; a number of commissions concerned with protecting specific kinds of rights, including an Independent Electoral Commission, a Gender Commission and a Human Rights Commission; a Judicial Service Commission which helps to restrain politically partisan court appointments; privately owned newspaper and broadcasting industries, and so on.

Democracies, though, are not created overnight. Authorities on the process of democratisation distinguish between degrees of democratic achievement. Competitive and reasonably well-managed elections as well as legally codified civil rights define a formal or electoral democracy, but fairly elected governments and humane constitutions are insufficient to make a system effectively democratic. In an effective democracy the everyday lives of officials and citizens are shaped by liberal values. This requires associational life which is independent from the state and can defend citizens and assert their rights, as well as a state which is strong enough to enforce its own laws.[1]

In first-generation democracies, strong civil society and authoritative states existed before the institution of mass suffrage. Arguably, when this historical sequence is reversed, that is, when popular elections mandate governments that may be weak and society is organised in authoritarian or patrimonial ways, democratic institutions – like elections or constitutions – may have little influence on the lives of most people.[2] This is particularly likely to be the case in new democracies in developing countries, especially if local power is based on control of access to land, and if the working classes are small or fragmented and the middle classes are mainly employed by government.[3] Ostensibly, South Africa with its modern industry, sophisticated trade unions and independent commercial and professional classes may not resemble a typical developing country, but about one-third of its citizens live in the former homelands, where politics is much more likely to be organised around land and the authority of chiefs.

Few new democracies can immediately claim that citizens have been equally empowered by the rights so recently written into their constitutions. Making these rights real often means extending the government's reach while at the same time making government itself more accountable to citizens. A new democracy which is becoming a more effective democracy should maintain a legal system that protects people more adequately than before and increasingly restrains authority. Its bureaucracy should become more capable, and evidently so. Social organis- ation should add to the power of citizens to exercise their rights and such associ- ational life itself should encourage democratic values. The assertion of rights depends on the political engagement of citizens. This, in turn, requires trust and social solidarity. Democracies are unlikely to consolidate when citizen trust in government decreases or if citizens themselves are mutually distrustful of each other or divided by communal antagonisms.[4] In a democratic society in which citizens trust and feel empathy for each other and in which they view government as legitimate, the political system represented by official institutions becomes 'the only game in town';[5] in other words, democracy has then become socially entrenched or consolidated. In this chapter we shall consider South Africa's record in this regard. I shall begin by looking at the prospects for competitive and demo- cratic party politics before discussing the behaviour and performance of public institutions. Finally, I shall address the issue of whether social support for democ- racy has strengthened.

One very demanding definition of democratic consolidation is that democ- racies only become mature when a ruling party in power at the democracy's incep- tion is subsequently defeated in an election and allows the winners to take office.[6] Even if one allows that democracies can mature without such an alternation in office, in the South African case the objection might be that the formal institution of liberal democracy does not mean very much in a situation in which represen- tative politics is overwhelmed by one large party and in which the prospect of any alternation of parties in government is rather remote. If that party is a nationalist movement that broadly represents a racial majority in a society which has a history of racial conflict and racial oppression, and if it represents the formerly oppressed group most closely, it might be argued that its supporters will be fairly uncritical, or undemanding, and that this leaves its leadership scope for plenty of misbehaviour.

This is an uncharitable view of the dynamics of the South African political system, but it has some validity. In the 1999 general elections, as in 1994, racial affiliations on the whole appeared to coincide with the ways in which people voted. Two provinces were an exception. In KwaZulu-Natal locality in either a rural community or a substantial town divided African votes between the Inkatha Freedom Party (IFP) and the African National Congress (ANC). In the Western

Cape, where coloured voters were split along class lines, the ANC took the middle-class votes, while the New National Party (NNP) found support among poorer coloured voters. Whether voter choices were influenced primarily by 'rational', material considerations or by more emotive preoccupations about racial identity is a subject of vigorous debate between specialists. But as long as most poor people remain black and most whites enjoy relative prosperity, the likelihood of parties finding their core constituencies within one racial community or another remains high.

Hence it is not likely that things will change very quickly, at least not to the ANC's disadvantage. Political loyalties among whites may shift. But until opposition parties attract African voters in substantial numbers, the ANC will remain dominant. Black middle-class voters may share certain material interests with the white suburbanites whose neighbours they have become, but as the principal beneficiaries of the government's affirmative action policies they are unlikely to turn against the ANC for some time to come. The Democrats may have established a few bridgeheads in black townships in the 2000 local elections, but they will need to build an extensive local organisation in the townships before African voters will consider them as a serious choice.

The Democratic Alliance (DA) claimed a total of 146 branches in black townships in November 2001, which suggests that establishing an everyday presence in most African neighbourhoods is a project that is unlikely to be completed by the next general elections. Conversely, the ANC claimed that it plans to invest fresh effort into attracting Afrikaans speakers, both coloured and white. In 2001, the ANC's new electoral strategist, Peter Mokaba, contended that the New National Party (NNP) and the ANC 'had much in common' as 'African parties', and that former NNP voters would have a shorter distance to travel in joining the ranks of the ANC than adherents of the 'liberal international' Democrats.[7] Former senior NNP officials who have joined the ANC encourage this kind of thinking, pointing to their own experience as proof that 'Afrikaner, brown and black nationalism can be reconciled'.[8] This kind of thinking may partially explain the ANC's willingness at the end of 2001 to consider embracing the NNP as coalition partner in the Western Cape.

A split in the ANC would, of course, transform the political landscape, but this is not a serious prospect in the foreseeable future, notwithstanding the disagreements between the government and the ANC's left-wing allies, the South African Communist Party (SACP) and the Congress of South African Trade Unions (COSATU), both of which support the ANC electorally. COSATU leaders prefer access and influence to opposition and exclusion. Workers – those who are employed – have not done so badly since 1994; real wages have increased slightly and new laws, where these have been implemented, have significantly enhanced job security and labour conditions. Tensions between the government and the left will be discussed in more detail later in this chapter. As is evident from the developments surveyed in chapter 3, the ANC – notwithstanding all shortcomings and imperfections in the government's performance – has shifted resources in the direction of its main constituency, the rural poor. For a substantial number of them life is moderately better, or at least there still remains hope that it will become so shortly. Opinion polls do not indicate bitter disappointment among poor people – at worst, they show apathy or resignation.[9] As noted in chapter 6, in the 2000 local elections such sentiments amongst people who had previously voted for the ANC tended to prompt stayaways on election day, not votes for the ANC's competitors. Over four elections, two for parliament and two for local government, party support, at least for the ANC, appears fairly stable. In the 1994 general elections nearly 63 per cent of the electorate voted for the ANC and in the 1999 general elections this figure grew to 66 per cent. The ANC's share of the vote in the local elections rose from 58 per cent in 1995–6 to 60 per cent in 2000. Dramatic changes in these percentages seem unlikely in the absence of a complete reconfiguration of the party system.

At present Inkatha, with its increase from 8 to 10 per cent support from the electorate between 1994 and 2000, represents the most serious competition for the ANC with regard to African voters. However, support for Inkatha is unlikely to expand much beyond its bases in rural KwaZulu-Natal. Since 1994, despite policy differences, it has governed South Africa as a coalition partner with the ANC. Certain ANC leaders believe that given that the IFP and the ANC 'share the same constituency' – peasants and workers – conflict between them 'is not inherent' and that for two organisations with such similar goals to compete with each other 'is self-defeating'.[10] It is not a view which has met with universal acceptance either within the ANC or, less surprisingly, the IFP. ANC left-wingers can point to plenty of differences of principle between their movement and Inkatha. In 1996, SACP leader Blade Nzimande, for example, characterised the IFP as 'singularly pro-capitalist, neo-feudal, and undemocratic', objecting to it also because of its federalism.[11] Another influential communist, Jeremy Cronin, responded to merger proposals with the injunction that any future co-operation with Inkatha should be 'built on honesty, not historical function'. Such honesty required recognition of Inkatha's record of 'narrow ethnic nationalism' and the identification of its leadership as a 'self-interested ex-Bantustan elite'.[12]

IFP representatives also believe that their organisation embodies distinctive values, including opposition to centralisation, commitment to market-oriented policies, and support for inherited leadership, traditional law and communal land, all of which would be obstacles to a merger with the ANC.[13] During the Mbeki administration, Chief Mangosuthu Buthelezi's relationship with his cabinet colleagues and ANC parliamentarians as minister of home affairs deteriorated as a result of disagreements about proposed immigration legislation. But generally

Inkatha ministers have co-operated with the ANC as coalition partners and the demeanour of Inkatha MPs seems to conform with the ANC's notion of the appropriate behaviour for loyal and constructive opposition. This degree of cordiality may, of course, be attributable to Inkatha perceptions that as partners in government they enjoy a degree of leverage in protecting their interests and promoting their concerns. Such leverage would disappear if they lost their corporate identity as a separate party. 'Common objectives' and shared 'primary constituencies' notwithstanding,[14] the IFP is likely to remain apart from the ANC, especially on those constitutional issues which some ANC leaders find irksome, such as the status of provincial government. Several KwaZulu-Natal municipalities, for example Ladysmith and Port Shepstone, have been governed by Inkatha–DA partnerships since 2000, an alliance 'with the better devil'. As Inkatha provincial politicians explained, the DA was more sympathetic to their efforts to defend the powers of the *amakhosi* (traditional leaders).[15]

Since 1999, the ANC has remained just short of the two-thirds parliamentary majority its leadership would need in order to change the Constitution unilaterally. In fact, the parliamentary caucus could quite easily muster the support it would need to do so from smaller parties, notably from the Minority Front, whose leadership claims to supports the ANC, as well as from the Azanian People's Organisation (AZAPO), whose president joined Mbeki's government in 2000 as a deputy minister. In effect, South Africa's political institutions are unprotected by the two-thirds majority entrenched in constitutional clauses, and the authority of the Constitution itself depends very substantially on the degree to which the ruling party has internalised its values and principles.

For the time being, the ANC is likely to predominate as the only significant national party. The opposition parties are becoming increasingly provincial in character. The United Democratic Movement (UDM) is at best sustaining its support levels in the former Transkei in the Eastern Cape, and the IFP is continuing to fend off electoral challenges to its control of KwaZulu-Natal, perhaps with the DA acting increasingly as a provincial power-broker, as it has already begun doing in the municipalities in that region.

The fragmented and fluid character of the opposition is helping to sustain the ANC's electoral supremacy as well as its domination of parliamentary proceedings. In the 1999 elections, five of the 13 parties that won seats in the National Assembly had never been in office before, and three had been established after the 1994 general elections. One of the virtues of South Africa's electoral system of proportional representation is that it allows a very low threshold for entry into parliament, but diversity may be achieved at the cost of coherence. Party loyalties within the minority communities – white, Indian and coloured – are especially volatile. Organisations that find their main support within these groups have ceased to rely on a committed core of stalwart supporters. In general, levels of party identification amongst South Africans have fallen, and increasing numbers of voters find themselves undecided before elections. This is a trait that is especially noticeable among voters who finally support opposition parties.[16]

By November 2001 the DA, which since its inception in June 2000 was intended to bring about a merger between the DP and the NNP, had sprung apart, ostensibly because of disagreements between DA leaders over the dismissal of Peter Marais from the Cape Town mayorship. Marais's dismissal was followed by the DA deputy, Marthinus van Schalkwyk, and other disgruntled former NNP office-holders, rebelling against Tony Leon's leadership of the DA, a split in the Western Cape government, and a decision by the NNP's federal council to withdraw from the DA, thereby reversing its earlier decision that its members would belong to both constituent parties.

Shortly thereafter, a joint statement from the ANC and the NNP announced that the parties would co-operate in government at all levels and that a policy forum would be established 'to seek consensus on policy issues'. Tensions had been developing between Van Schalkwyk and Leon since a stolen document written by Ryan Coetzee, a DA strategic adviser, was leaked to the press in February 2001. This document had revealed plans to sideline NNP leaders within the DA.[17] NNP leaders opposed the removal of Peter Marais from his post in Cape Town because they understood that without him they risked losing the highly personalised political loyalties of working-class coloured voters,[18] a view which was at odds with the conclusions Leon and Coetzee had drawn from opinion polls. Without such support the old and financially bankrupt NNP would have very little to bargain with in the reorganisation of party positions,[19] which was meant to create a new unified structure for the DA before the 2004 elections.

Significantly, NNP officials during 2000 and 2001 were very reluctant to merge their branch organisations into the new DA framework.[20] In withdrawing from the DA, NNP leaders emphasised that their differences with the Democrats involved issues of political substance and not just personal conflicts. They were more predisposed than the DP to the ANC's vision of co-operative participatory government and they, too, like the ruling party, had an historical affinity with poor people, they maintained. The DA's assault on Peter Marais was forcing 'our white, black and coloured communities apart'. The NNP favoured a constructive opposition, not one that had been 'reduced to an angry white voice, mudslinging and character assassination'. It is probably true that the tensions within the DA were not only attributable to personality conflicts.

Despite DP–NPP agreement about policy issues, the two parties were still influenced by quite different philosophies, the one rooted in a liberal conception of individual citizenship, the other still based on community-centred notions of rights and obligations.[21] At its inception, the alliance did not find universal approval among NNP office-holders, particularly those who opposed De Klerk's withdrawal from the Government of National Unity.[22] However self-serving their rationalisations may have been, it is probably true that many NNP politicians have fewer principled objections to the ANC's performance in government than the liberal free-marketeers who lead the DP.

Opinion poll evidence does confirm that NNP supporters tended to be more concerned with the kinds of issues that animated the ANC's social base – job creation, for example – and less inclined than Democrats to choose 'fighting crime' as the first government priority. At least certain ANC leaders also appeared to understand their new coalition arrangements as embodying important nation-building objectives as part of 'a huge national process to reconcile and bring together South Africans'.[23] But while NNP leaders profess to see their future in terms of partnership with the ANC, the legislation that was prepared at the close of the 2001 parliamentary session to enable floor-crossing in the national and provincial legislatures – a provision that was prepared in case there were any legal barriers that might prevent the NNP from withdrawing from the DA – also included measures to allow parliamentary parties to merge between elections. Obviously its drafters were anticipating that the ANC would sooner or later simply absorb the NNP.[24] If that was to happen and the process embraced the NNP's voting constituency, the opposition would be quite seriously depleted, at least in the Western Cape – the one province in which the NNP retains popular support.

The extent to which political parties are institutionalised in South Africa is rather impressive when compared with many new democracies. However, the uncertain boundaries of opposition politics, which may be accentuated by government-induced floor-crossing to the ruling party, may generally detract from the scope and depth of organised political life. This would be a serious setback in the consolidation of South African democracy.

It is very unlikely, then, that opposition parties will become much stronger in the foreseeable future. As adversaries of the ruling party, the opposition is weak-ened further by the ANC's subscription to the norms of coalition or consensual government, which are more common in pluralistic than in two-party systems.[25] Since 1999, the ANC has quite voluntarily conceded cabinet representation to Inkatha and allotted lesser executive positions to other parties, though this has not really required any significant compromises in setting policy.

In its current dominant position, the ANC does not require a coalition to form a government. It certainly weakens opposition, but by maintaining coalition executives the ANC may be reflecting principled preferences as much as political expediency; after all, unity is an imperative amongst the exile politicians who predominate in President Mbeki's administration. Besides, ANC leaders profess to believe, and perhaps really do believe, that the ANC's own internal traditions and procedures strengthen democratic practices, and for this reason the future of constitutional democracy is in safe hands. Pallo Jordan, for example, has suggested that 'collective decisions' within the ANC are normally preceded by periods of 'optimal debate', at least within the ranks of the National Executive. Significantly, though, all the examples Jordan used to illustrate his contention that the party leadership could be overruled by national and provincial executive members referred to the time of the Mandela presidency before the ANC's election to government.[26]

Both Mandela and Mbeki at the ANC's 50th national conference in Mafikeng in 1997 referred to the organisation as the 'parliament of the people'. It is true that delegates on that occasion indicated some willingness to challenge leadership, for example in the (independently audited) secret ballot elections for National Executive members and office-holders, as they had done on previous occasions. Conference delegates at all the ANC's conferences during the 1990s resisted leadership attempts to limit the competition for senior office as well as various inducements and pressures to persuade them to vote for preferred candidates. It was noticeable, too, that Nelson Mandela's speech in Mafikeng evoked one of the loudest cheers when he criticised corruption.

In a similarly encouraging vein, Tito Mboweni suggested in a speech that the ANC would invest considerable effort into developing a policy apparatus that would attempt to incorporate a broader range of people in the organisation and its allies into the discussion and planning of policy. Barely six months later, though, Tito Mboweni was transferred to the Reserve Bank and resigned all his policy positions, including his directorship of the policy unit.

One-party democracy, however sincere the intentions of its leaders, has had a history elsewhere of losing its vitality. The ANC's active membership has shrunk,[27] mainly, I suspect, because politics has become less exciting (as it usually does in liberal democracies) – and not as a consequence of rank-and-file disappointment at not being able to attend policy discussions. A political report presented at the annual general meeting of an ANC branch in Protea Glen, Soweto, is eloquently illustrative: 'It is now time to deal with the state of the organisation. We have met here to examine the ANC. How well it is doing or not doing in so much as Protea Glen is a working-class township with most of its citizens in COSATU unions. Membership for the ANC has always stagnated between a hundred to two hundred ever since the branch's launch in 1992. The support for the organisation is [waning] however [because] our people are of the feeling having voted for the ANC there is no reason to then still pay the R12.00 for ANC membership. The consequence of this general support [for the ANC] has rendered to some extent the branch executive ineffective in that people attend AGM where they get elected and soon thereafter disappear, thus creating a leadership vacuum which is increasingly being filled by people who are not astute cadres.'[28]

In early 2000, it was reported that Thabo Mbeki was contemplating the merits of 'winding down' the organisation between elections and 'winding it up again' just before them. This, apparently, would make for a 'much smaller, less bureaucratic party which would make and implement policies faster'.[29] It is certainly true that the ANC's inner politics has become subjected to tighter restraints. At its 1997 national conference, the ANC amended its constitution in ways which strengthened executive authority. In future, general conferences would be held every five years rather than every three. All ANC structures, including caucuses in parliament, legislatures and municipalities, were placed under the supervision of the National Executive Committee. Since 1999, within the parliamentary caucus, office-bearers such as the whips and committee chairpersons have been appointed by the National Working Committee. The 1997 conference re-endorsed the principle of 'democratic centralism' which, together with a constitutionally prescribed prohibition on factionalism, made it very difficult for any organised mobilisation to assert itself against leadership policy.[30] This is the case particularly when authoritarian interpretations of democratic centralism become reinforced by Africanist advocacy of deference and respect for 'elders in society'.[31]

In theory, delegate assemblies, including the national councils which may be held between general conferences, can supply opportunities for policy debates. In practice, ANC meetings tend to adopt pre-drafted resolutions. Although there is provision for the use of the secret ballot in voting for these, in 1997 it was not invoked. Individuals can and do attempt to influence policy through the issue of 'discussion papers' and these represent at least a semblance of internal debate. Publication and circulation of such papers need leadership sanction, though.

Of course, invocations of the vocabulary of Bolshevik bureaucracy by the ANC's senior officials should be understood as an idealised rather than actual description of the ANC's inner life. There is plenty of evidence that the routines and disciplines called for in the party's constitution have only limited application. Factionalism is a case in point. Notwithstanding its being prohibited, ANC leaders constantly complain about factionalism within the organisation. In recent years such complaints have included references to 'warlordism' and 'power-mongering' within the divided leadership of the ANC Youth League, especially in KwaZulu-Natal, where the Youth League opposed the ANC's coalition with Inkatha.[32] At the Youth League's national congress in April 2001, an 'old guard' supported by more senior ANC leaders was said to favour the re-election of incumbent president Malusi Gigaba. It had to fight off a stiff challenge from rival candidates. After the congress, the KwaZulu-Natal Youth League chairperson was dismissed because he had opposed Giqaba's nomination.

As shown in chapter 2, personal rivalries and factionalism based on patron–client relationships seem to be recurrent characteristics of the ANC's internal politics in certain provinces: in the North West the premier, Popo Molefe, went so far as to suggest that the party was falling apart as a consequence of infighting.[33] Another source of factional rivalry has been competition between party notables for government tenders. As Jeremy Cronin noted wryly, the 'advent of a new generation of ANC-aligned black entrepreneurs has decentralised power, creating multiple power bases within the broad ANC fold'.[34] Nor are the divisions simply a reflection of personalised loyalties to particular individuals. ANC spokespeople attribute 'concerted efforts to sow division within the ANC' to agencies 'opposed to transformation'.[35]

This view first surfaced in a document Thabo Mbeki wrote for the ANC's 1994 conference, which referred to an impending offensive against the ANC in which the opposition would attempt to 'create contradictions' within the ANC and between the ANC and its allies. In particular, it would seek to split the movement on 'the issue of leadership'. Left-wing groupings within the ANC would be encouraged by the movement's external opponents 'draped ... in the cloak of radicalism' to challenge government policies, Mbeki maintained.[36]

One need not accept uncritically leadership contentions that all their critics are inspired by the forces of reaction. Yet in 2001 there was plenty of evidence of dissent within the organisation. In Mpumalanga a crudely printed 'briefing document' sought to mobilise followers who were against the United Democratic Front (UDF) and former prisoners, 'to save the movement from the disastrous path Thabo has put it on'.[37] The appointment of an interim provincial leadership committee in Gauteng in 2000 prompted the rebellious East Rand region to submit a number of protest memorandums: one complained about the absence of anything more than 'minimal contact' between branches and MPs and MPLs.[38]

In July 2001, during a parliamentary recess, those MPs who did visit their constituency offices had to endure jokes about chief whip Tony Yengeni's 4x4 Mercedes. They returned to their parliamentary duties complaining that they had encountered 'mass disgruntlement' among members and party officials, who were reacting to reports of ANC leaders enriching themselves.[39] This theme was taken up by Allan Boesak on his release from prison following a conviction for personal appropriation of charity funding. Boesak, flanked by discomfited Western Cape ANC officials, told an adoring congregation at an evangelical church that 'exiles' had 'turned on the people like easy game'. 'Liberation is incremental,' he continued, 'and the poor are last in line.'[40]

The internal fractiousness of the ANC suggests that the organisation is rather more susceptible to various kinds of democratic pressure than the disciplined monolith depicted both in the critical evaluations of the ANC as the harbinger of an authoritarian order[41] and in its own official prescriptions of Leninist democracy. The ANC's alliance with the SACP and COSATU, two organisations whose memberships overlap with its own, also offers opportunities for the expression within the 'ANC camp' of differences about fundamental issues. Of course, the scope of such opportunities is subject to sharp contestation within this alliance, even with respect to what ANC ideologues prefer to call 'secondary contradictions'.

Thabo Mbeki is predisposed to view even criticism from the left as the expression of conspiracies by the 'enemies of transformation'. He has maintained this position doggedly in the face of increasingly fierce rhetoric from the ANC's allies directed at the government's financial policies. In his speech at the SACP's 10th congress in 1998, he told those assembled that 'objective realities' of the struggle for 'genuine emancipation' were so challenging that 'the basis does not exist for partners in the Alliance fundamentally to redefine the relationship among themselves, including the way they handle their differences'. This was after Mbeki had reprimanded communists and trade unionists for 'spreading falsifications and telling lies' in chorus with 'defenders of reaction'.[42] Such admonitions did not end public expressions of SACP–COSATU objections to government policy, but this may not have been the intention. The angry language of trade union officials may not have been aimed at the politicians and bureaucrats, whom they were ostensibly addressing, but rather at an increasingly restive shopfloor rank-and-file.

The debate within the Alliance over the Growth, Employment and Redistribution Strategy (GEAR) has so far had a somewhat ritualistic quality. This has also been the case in other points of disagreement between the Alliance partners. Any criticism, however strongly worded, is always qualified by protestations of loyalty to the Alliance itself and recognition of the ANC's senior status within it. For COSATU's president, Willie Madisha, 'the tripartite Alliance is the only one capable of bringing about the transformation our country needs – it's a principled alliance'.[43] This was despite the prospect of 'real war' against the government over the way it was 'restructuring' public companies.[44] 'We do not agree with GEAR and certain aspects of state restructuring,' the SACP's leader Blade Nzimande explained in July 2001, but breaking the Alliance 'would be handing our hard-won victory to reactionaries'.[45]

Curiously, COSATU officials rationalise their adherence to the Alliance, despite deep disagreements of principle, by likening the relationship between itself as a labour organisation and the ANC to the social dynamics of employment: 'We do not talk of changing an employer if we find ourselves in a situation not favourable to the workers.'[46] The comment itself illustrates COSATU's own perceptions about its decline from equal-partner status in the Alliance, a decline caused by the exodus of skilled trade union leadership into the government and an erosion of the quality of COSATU's own organisation.[47] Somewhat quixotically, notwithstanding the government's perceived abandonment of the RDP, COSATU's executive committee continued to believe in 2001 that both its own influence and that of the SACP could be used to 'win the ANC back to the ideals of the mass democratic movement'.[48] To this end, COSATU would attempt to seek public support for its opposition to the privatisation of state assets by mobilising members of ANC branches.[49]

The reluctance of the SACP to censure those of its own officials who serve in government and in doing so take up positions in conflict with party policy is another way in which left-wing opposition to the government is qualified by fundamental loyalty. 'Communists in public office work for an ANC-led government and will not at any time implement SACP policies,' an SACP representative explained in July 2001.[50] Two months later, the party refused to endorse its own members' demands that it should censure cabinet members who defied the party's position on privatisation. Since 1999, the movement of several prominent GEAR critics into positions within the government or the ANC bureaucracy where they had to implement or defend such decisions as downsizing or 'corporatisation' served to underline the limits to which the ANC's allies would take any opposition. The SACP's awareness of its falling membership (13 803 paid-up members in mid-2000, down from its peak of 80 000 in the early 1990s) also helps to explain its reluctance to engage in any confrontation over policy with the ANC.[51]

Utterances of even qualified opposition may become more difficult for the ANC's Alliance partners in future. In October 2001 an ANC National Executive document was leaked to newspapers after having been circulated to all the ANC's branches. This document drew attention to 'an organised and loose, conscious and subconscious tendency in components of the Alliance to launch a systematic assault on the ANC from the left'. A general strike against privatisation led by COSATU and the SACP, which deliberately coincided with the proceedings of the World Conference against Racism in Durban, 'severely strained Alliance relations'. The National Executive Committee was concerned about the activities of a group of COSATU members 'who have no home other than COSATU' and who 'would want to transform [COSATU] into a political platform to pursue particular political objectives'. This 'ultra-left' tendency needed to be defeated, for it could 'easily create fertile ground for counter-revolution'. Though this group was a minority, its views were 'often expressed [by COSATU] as official policy'.[52]

Meanwhile an increasingly discernible 'nationalist' position within the ANC hierarchy, supported by the ANC Youth League, has begun to urge that the ANC itself (as opposed to the SACP) should play a leadership role in the trade union movement.[53] The appointment of former ANC Youth League president Peter Mokaba to a key position at the ANC headquarters was another signal of the growing influence of ANC conservatives. At the end of August Mokaba suggested that the Durban strike was a demonstration that, effectively, the Alliance was dead. In 1997, before the 50th national conference of the ANC, Peter Mokaba had suggested in a discussion paper that 'non-Africans' and communists enjoyed a disproportionate influence within the ANC. The paper also reminded its readers of what its author believed to be the organisation's historical commitment to capitalism and attacked COSATU for 'left-wing childishness', a reference to discussions within the trade union federation about the possible formation of a workers' political party. Four years later, in a 'whispering' campaign by government officials it was suggested that one of the inspirational figures behind COSATU's ebullience was 'a stranger to the struggle of Africans', (white) American-born economist Neva Makgetla, the wife of a former ANC exile and herself an ANC member of long standing.[54]

With sentiments like these becoming increasingly acceptable in South African public life, it may be a little optimistic to base any expectations about democratic consolidation on the ability of the ANC's partners to exercise leverage within the Alliance and help maintain within it an open political culture. What may be more important, though, in underpinning the new democracy is not the health of the ANC's internal organisation nor its relationships with its historic partners but rather the state of the institutions of government, which should safeguard its principles.

The most obvious of these institutions is parliament. Here the ANC's record is a mixed one. Some of the early shortcomings of its performance in parliament – ANC MPs asked a mere 15 per cent of the total of parliamentary questions between 1994 and 1996 – could be attributed to inexperience. Since the adoption of new rules in 2000, the number of questions to cabinet ministers has been in proportion to the number of MPs. While statistically the ANC's performance during question time has improved, ANC MPs' questions hardly represent serious challenges to the executive. For many of the MPs, nomination was an acknowledgement of their liberation track record or their relative status in the movement. They have found it difficult to adjust to the hard work and tedium which characterise legislative routine. There have also been occasions on which ANC parliamentary behaviour has been rather obviously constrained by deference to senior leadership. This was evident in the *Sarafina II* scandal (also see chapter 7), when ANC members on the National Assembly portfolio committee for health effectively stifled any criticism of the minister, Nkosazana Dlamini-Zuma, and her department's expenditure of European Union funding on the musical.

The list system through which MPs hold seats at the behest of party leadership means that defiance of leadership prescriptions carries heavy penalties. Except for constituency-based local councillors, elected representatives cannot cross the floor. This may not be such a bad state of affairs at this stage; during the 1960s several African democracies effectively became one-party states before their constitutions changed, as a result of floor-crossing.[55] Disappointingly, legislation in preparation at the end of 2001 (a fulfilment of a promise made to MPs in 1999) will allow floor-crossing, but only at the president's discretion. As a result, it is likely to be sanctioned only when it will work to the benefit of the ruling party.

It is fair to say that ANC MPs have sometimes demonstrated a willingness to confront the executive arm. During the Mandela government this was evident in the hearings on child welfare grants and, more generally, it was a feature of the conduct of the portfolio committee for defence. Education and Justice were two examples of portfolio committees which have worked well with their respective ministers. In these areas MPs have often made decisive contributions to the drafting of particular laws. Until it effectively began protecting the minister during the *Sarafina II* hearings in 1996, the ANC majority on the portfolio committee for health, chaired by Manto Tshabalala-Msimang, was considered one of the groups more likely to assert its role independently of the executive.[56]

Since the 1999 elections it has become less easy to identify examples of committee assertiveness. In October 2001 the portfolio committee for safety and security demanded the exclusion of foreigners from the private policing industry until ministerial intervention. However, here the ANC members on the committee may have been misreading initial signals from their minister, Steve Tshwete. At about the same time, the portfolio committee for telecommunications played a key role in redrafting the telecommunications legislation, though this was after the industry's protests to the minister. In 2001 the most obviously independent ANC parliamentary initiatives were to be found in the joint monitoring committee on the status of women, chaired by Pregs Govender, which challenged government on spending priorities and AIDS policy. In 2001, Govender abstained from voting on the defence budget.

Such assertive behaviour may become increasingly exceptional. A political committee comprising 22 senior ANC MPs 'to provide greater political direction to the ANC's parliamentary caucus' was established during the standing committee on public accounts (SCOPA) hearings discussed in chapter 7.[57] On several occasions during 2001, ANC members of the ethics committee evaded their obligations to hold fellow party members accountable for misconduct, notably in the case of Tony Yengeni and Winnie Madikizela-Mandela. Meanwhile, a decision at the beginning of 2001 to remove DA members from the chairmanships of public accounts committees in legislatures and parliament because of their failure to remain within the conventions of 'constructive opposition' represented an important setback: standing committees are intended to work in a nonpartisan fashion. As shown, the principle of majoritarianism adopted by the ruling party undermined the autonomy of parliament's standing committee on public accounts during the arms contract investigation.

Official projections of parliament as a 'success story of democratic change' emphasise the social representivity of its elected members and staff ('a black management component of over 65 per cent, with women in 25 per cent of management positions')[58] and the expansion of opportunities for public involvement in the legislative process. Between 1994 and 1998, MPs met civil society groups on 204 occasions, and they and their staff fielded more than 300 000 public queries about legislative issues. Most MPs are assigned by their parties to geographically defined constituencies, though the extent to which they are accessible to people who live within these constituencies is at best very uneven. Cabinet ministers emphasise their support for public contributions to policy-making and a lobbying industry has begun to consolidate around parliament. However, a specialised study of public participation in the policy process suggests that it is confined to the very early stages in the policy cycle and that too often the opportunities for 'stakeholder inputs' are organised with the chief intention of 'affirming existing policy directions', or to provide legitimisation for already fixed decisions. Consultations over the content of local government reform between 1998 and 2000 took place rather in this vein.[59]

If such consultations take place outside parliamentary procedures – and without the involvement of parliamentarians – they may well enhance executive authority. Arguably this was true of the corporatist National Economic Development and Labour Council (NEDLAC), established in 1995 to institutionalise 'tripartite' bargaining procedures which had developed since the 1980s between business, labour and government. For example, the 1995 Labour Relations Act was negotiated clause by clause in NEDLAC, and when it was presented to parliament, MPs were urged not to change any of its content.[60]

ANC political analysts are sceptical of views of the state which perceive it as a neutral instrument, 'perched above society', or alternatively as a socially autonomous 'thing in itself'. Hence, they have no hesitation in demanding not merely its political allegiance but also a more profoundly ideological orientation. For the ANC, the state is an expression of class interests and 'the most critical area of contestation among classes'. The state that the Government of National Unity (GNU) inherited was hostile to the aims of national liberation and therefore it could be predicted that 'the old order will resist change both from within and outside the state'. In 1998, as the authors of a discussion paper prepared for an Alliance summit maintained, 'the instruments of the state such as the army, police and judiciary remain largely in the hands of forces that were (and some still are) opposed to social transformation'. A transformation process should entail, 'first and foremost, extending the power of the NLM (National Liberation Movement) to all levers of power: the army, the police, the bureaucracy, intelligence, the judiciary, parastatals, and agencies such as the regulatory bodies, the public broadcaster, the central bank, and so on'.[61]

Given a history of a heavily politicised bureaucracy from the inception of National Party rule, such reactions may be understandable, but even so the willingness of certain ANC ideologues to blur the boundaries between party and state apparatus is a little alarming. A pervasive process of political appointments to senior civil service positions continues seven years after the ANC's accession to power. The habit among ministers of moving with their own coteries of senior officials after cabinet reshuffles may also contribute to reducing civil service impartiality. The wholesale dismissal of senior management at the Department of

Land Affairs after the 1999 elections discussed in chapter 4 is a case in point. Clearly, though, such changes by ministers depend on higher sanction. In 2001, home affairs minister Buthelezi felt compelled to make public (and unsuccessful) calls for the resignation of his director-general, Billy Masetlha, an intelligence operative trained in former East Germany, who had embarrassed the department with his tough measures against illegal Zimbabwean immigrants, gays and non-residents married to South African women.[62]

ANC leaders and government spokespeople are quick to view even legal challenges to their authority as evidence of conspiratorial resistance to transformation. For example, a court summons served on Nelson Mandela represented 'sabotage of democracy' and proof of 'the role played by the courts in frustrating transformation'.[63] Business South Africa's (unsuccessful) challenge of the legal validity of the Medical Schemes Bill, according to a spokesperson of the Department of Health, signalled a 'conspiracy' by 'people bent on frustrating the transformation process'.[64] In fairness to the government, new judicial appointments, while making the bench less socially exclusive, have not reduced its propensity to challenge the executive or resist its occasional efforts at interference.[65]

Mathole Motshekga described preparations for the ANC's 1999 elections campaign in a speech as the 'battle plans for the final onslaught against apartheid and the forces of the counter-revolution'. The ANC needed a massive recruitment campaign to restore membership levels before the organisation could hope to 'crush all forces'.[66] If every kind of opposition to government policy is viewed as sinister and subversive – and this did seem to be the perception reflected in Nelson Mandela's speech at the ANC's 50th national conference in its characterisation of parliamentary opponents as 'implacable enemies' and critical lobbying organisations as unpatriotic 'instruments of foreign governments'[67] – then constitutional safeguards will offer limited solace for liberal democrats.

The vigour of institutions like parliament, political parties and local councils as well as the political impartiality of public institutions depends as much on what happens outside and around them as on their inner life. Robert Putnam, an American political scientist, has argued this in a particularly sophisticated book about civil society, *Making Democracy Work*.[68] He suggests that certain kinds of associational life across a range of different kinds of organisations – work-related, leisure-oriented, cultural or neighbourhood-focused – promote values of trust and interdependence within communities. These values, in turn, predispose people to engage more vigorously with government institutions and, in so doing, render them more responsive and effective. What is crucial to his argument is that the associational life which is critical in the process of making democratic institutions effective, however diverse the purposes of such associations might be, must have a 'horizontal' rather than hierarchical character. The associations themselves – whether they be civic bodies, sports clubs, hobby groups, trade unions or charitable agencies – have to be structured in ways which are relatively egalitarian so that the direction is controlled by their memberships. In vertically organised groups – like certain church congregations or, alternatively, criminal gangs, where solidarity is mainly based on patron–client-style relations around an authoritarian or charismatic personality – associational life does not promote predispositions that favour communal civic engagement.

Putnam demonstrates the validity of these contentions by looking at evidence from northern and southern Italy. The relatively more responsive and democratic regional governments of the north are surrounded by lively civil societies, whereas the authoritarian traditions of the south are underpinned and sustained by the hierarchical patronage of Roman Catholic priesthood and the Mafiosi.

South African civil society is relatively well developed, but it has its vulnerabilities. In the 1980s, localised political energies in townships and in even more scattered rural communities were channelled into the formation of neighbourhood associations. These came to be known generically as the civic movement. They were built on long-established traditions of local bodies, which had led people in issues of basic bread-and-butter politics since the beginning of modern urban life at the beginning of the century, mobilising their support to deal with concerns such as high rents, poor services, self-serving behaviour by local officials and similar issues. The civic movement of the 1980s was unprecedented in its size and scope, for it performed a surrogate function as a vehicle for national liberation politics. This was its strength, but also its weakness, for with the triumph of liberation politics the civics movement lost many of its best leaders. Also, with its incorporation into a national movement, the movement lost much of its original concern with local issues. People in the ANC had mixed feelings about civic associations, at least one powerful sentiment being that they should be collapsed into the ANC branches. The subsequent history of the national civic body, SANCO, formed in 1991, has not been happy, not least because of the tensions and ambivalences which arose from its alliance with the ANC. These did not, however, prevent SANCO candidates from standing against ANC candidates in local elections around Johannesburg in 1995. In chapter 10 we shall explore the fortunes of SANCO in more detail.

The civic movement was only one constituent of a lively culture of associational life which had developed up to 1994. South Africa reportedly had a total of 54 000 non-governmental organisations (NGOs) and community-based organisations (CBOs), about one for every 740 people – more than most developing countries – but relatively fewer than the United States, which boasted one organisation for every 250 citizens.[69] There are probably fewer today. Like SANCO, many of these associations depended on foreign funding to maintain their activities. In 1993 funding amounted to US$307 million,[70] although another two-thirds of NGO funding was sourced locally.[71] After 1994, traditional funders, local and foreign, either withdrew their support on the cessation of the anti-apartheid struggle or redirected their money to government programmes or the politically prestigious Nelson Mandela Children's Fund. But as noted in chapter 3, donor attitudes have since shifted again in favour of the NGO sector. Political independence is no longer rewarded as it used to be. Certain donor agencies – the US Agency for International Development (USAID), for example – are now committed to supporting only 'programs in support of Pretoria's policies', a position adopted after political attacks on a donation it made to the South African Institute of Race Relations.[72]

Dwindling resources affected not only organisations with explicitly political concerns. Charitable bodies, alternative newspapers, adult education programmes, self-help disabled people's groups, research bodies, HIV education programmes, care for the aged and human rights organisations such as the Black Sash are all represented in the range of bodies that have either closed down entirely or curtailed most of their previous activities. In addition to their particular functions and concerns, many of these helped to elicit citizenship through volunteer participation.

Of course, powerful, politically assertive and politically independent trade unions are a very substantial guarantee for democracy. Comparative historical analysis has suggested that the key variable in explaining the international presence and persistence of democracy is 'the relative size and density of organisation of the working class'.[73] Certainly this seems a more useful hypothesis to apply to the South African case than the rather more traditional emphasis in democratic theory on the democratic susceptibilities of the urban middle class, for in this country the main middle-class community has been historically anti-democratic and its black successors are often, understandably, contemptuous of local liberal traditions.[74] COSATU's affiliate membership in 2001 totalled 1.8 million, one-third more than in 1994. This amounted to 40 per cent of the workforce. Members' dues made the main contribution to an annual budget of R25 million,[75] a budget which represents an important degree of financial independence from donors. Increasingly, COSATU's members are public-sector workers, 400 000 of whom are restricted from striking as providers of essential services. Another 1 million workers belong to the National Council of Trade Unions and the Federation of Unions of South Africa.

It is important and encouraging that South African trade unions continue to grow, and continue to maintain critical and challenging demeanours with respect to government, their status as allies notwithstanding. For example, at COSATU's 7th congress in September 2000, certain delegations protested at the presence of the minister of labour and only desisted after pleas from their officials. However, while at a national level procedures such as delegate conferences have retained their vitality, COSATU township-based locals have declined in size or disappeared. These had been the key structures in its capacity to mobilise community support during the anti-apartheid era. In general, membership participation in branch-level union activities diminished sharply after 1994.[76] What was encouraging, though, was that several important trade unionists declined to stand for positions on the ANC's National Executive in 1997. This was a convincing signal of their determination to continue defending their unions' political autonomy.

As noted in chapter 1, some of the key features of the Constitution – proportional representation and a limited-term presidency – may owe their presence to COSATU introducing these into the ANC's constitutional thinking. But trade unions have moved a long way from the idealism and egalitarianism that characterised the early stages of their genesis in the 1970s. In 1998 disputes within the Food and Allied Workers Union over the union hierarchy's financial mismanagement were a symptom of a more general tendency for the movement to become increasingly bureaucratised, professionalised and unresponsive to rank-and-file concerns. And trade unionists – quite appropriately – have limited preoccupations focused on the world of work. They cannot always be depended upon to oppose government encroachments on civil liberties in other spheres.

Civil society is, of course, more than merely the proliferation of structured forms of collective organisation. It also embraces other institutions which contribute to promoting a politically engaged citizenry. Of these, the press is especially important. Nelson Mandela's censures of the press at the ANC 50th conference in Mafikeng in 1997 were disconcerting but should not be taken as particularly menacing. Even in mature democracies political notables often noisily evince irritation or hostility towards critical journalism. More worrying is the tendency among ANC spokespeople to dismiss critical black journalists as surrogates for whites. An especially notorious instance of this was the suggestion in the ANC's submission to a Human Rights Commission inquiry into racism on the media that an article appearing under the byline of a black *Mail & Guardian* journalist about Thabo Mbeki had in fact been written by her (white) editor. More positively, the legal restrictions on press freedom continue to weaken: in 1998 a landmark court ruling by Judge Joos Hefer made it much easier for newspapers to defend themselves against defamation. Meanwhile, the Promotion of Access to Information Act at least provides legal openings for investigative journalism on abuses of public authority. The vulnerability of the South African press has more to do with its own shortcomings than with the government's attitude towards it.

One of the difficulties editors face is that there seems to be a limited public appetite for attentive political journalism. Private proprietors are as inclined as ever to limit conflict with government. Ivan Fallon, the chief executive of Independent Newspapers, told the Johannesburg Press Club in 1997 that he did not want 'a crossfire situation which could result in the situation we are trying to avoid'.[77] Ironically, the two most politically assertive (as well as the two most widely read) mainstream newspapers, the *Sunday Times* and *Sowetan*, are both owned by companies led by ANC notables. The only newspapers with significantly expanding readerships are the few remaining Afrikaans publications. Good local journalism has almost disappeared – very few newspapers supply comprehensive coverage of municipal politics, for example. It is noticeable that much of the investigative journalism which during the Mandela administration uncovered major government mistakes or abuses – the Motheo housing contract or the strange goings-on at the Central Energy Fund – emanated from relatively specialised publications like the *Mail & Guardian* with its tiny circulation, its independent ownership and its restricted advertising base.

Newspapers struggle to compete with the growing range of broadcasting and television stations for the advertising revenues that sustain their production. Deregulated airwaves do open up other channels for critical commentary and debate, but many of the new stations are strongly entertainment-oriented. However, a commercial television channel offers an alternative to the SABC's news service, an important development in a context in which citizens increasingly prefer to obtain their knowledge of public events through television sound bites. During the 1999 elections, the SABC's political neutrality appeared to waver; its electoral coverage was noticeably less even-handed than in 1994.

It would be all the more a pity if the organisational framework of civil society fell apart at a time when ordinary people's values are not overwhelmingly supportive of democracy. For example, two surveys by the Institute for Democracy in South Africa (IDASA) asked people whether, in the event of democracy not working, they would prefer 'a strong leader who does not have to bother with elections' or whether 'even when things don't work, democracy is always best'. In 1995 only 47 per cent agreed that 'democracy is always best', with 43 per cent favouring a strong leader. By 1997 these proportions had changed, with the preference for democracy swelling to 56 per cent and advocacy of strong leadership shrinking to 30 per cent.[78] However, in 2000 the proportion favouring strong leadership had grown again slightly to 37.5 per cent, while supporters of the view that democracy is always best had remained steady at 55 per cent.[79] The minority favouring strong leadership under certain conditions had remained disconcertingly high, nearly double the proportion holding similar views when asked the same question in Brazil and Chile, countries in which nostalgia for authoritarian government is considered to be dangerously widespread.[80]

An opinion poll in 1998 found that just over a quarter of African respondents 'might take part in action with other people to prevent a member of a party they disliked most from living in their neighbourhood'. This is still an unacceptably common predisposition, but support for it has declined substantially from the 50 per cent favouring such action when asked the same question in 1993.[81] Both the 1999 general and 2000 local elections featured much less of the activist bullying which had marred earlier contests. On the whole, there seems to be a decline in determined political partisanship.

Surveys conducted by IDASA between 1994 and 1997 indicated that the proportion of the electorate that strongly identified with the ANC fell from 85 per cent to 56 per cent, suggesting the expansion of a 'swing' vote that might be potentially available to a non-racial opposition.[82] Longitudinal survey research on attitudes to democracy suggest that since 1995, while most South Africans support democracy, support levels have stabilised rather than increased. Moreover, compared to the citizens of other countries in the region, South Africans were relatively disinclined to participate actively in politics, through attending election rallies, contributing to any campaign, making representations to officials or representatives, or writing to the press.[83] This may partly be a reflection of an electoral system that features a very impersonal form of representation and, at local government level, vast districts.

In summary, South African citizens favour democracy, but with weak predispositions in favour of participation it remains questionable how vigorously they would defend its abuse. Such qualifications about civic propensities deserve emphasis at a time when antipathy to liberalism in elite political circles has become pervasive.[84]

A frequent refrain among South African politicians is that the country's Constitution is among the most democratic in the world. But many of the rights and entitlements that have been legislated as a result of its provisions remain more notional than real. For example, South African police and prison officials are still the subject of regular reproofs by Amnesty International for their continuing routine use of torture in detention cells and prisons. The inefficiency of the judicial system as well as the expense of using it effectively continues to prompt large numbers of poor people to resort to unofficial and often extremely brutal vigilante justice. In Limpopo Province, members of about a hundred branches of Mapogo-a-Mathamaga ('Colours of the Tiger'), supported by levies from local traders, routinely engage in flogging suspected criminals. The movement has 50 000 signed-up supporters.[85]

In 2001, the Human Rights Commission's third report suggested that the extent of the state's reach was improving, but quite slowly. For example, social services payments were now being made to 3 million people, an increase of 200 000 over the previous year. Even so, of the 2.6 million people known to be eligible for disability grants, only about 600 000 were receiving them. Some 25 per cent of people entitled to pensions were also not receiving them. However, the beneficiaries of child support as a consequence of recent reforms had increased six-fold.

Since 1994, South Africa has enacted a series of enlightened measures to promote gender equality and established a range of impressive official institutions to enhance women's rights. Though under-resourced, the institutional framework of women's rights in South Africa is an expression of deeply held convictions within the ruling party and certain of its opponents. Abortion rights, for example, were liberally extended largely as a consequence of the strength of feminism within the ANC and the vitality of the lobbying movement which was allowed to help shape the legislation. In 1998 ten times more women obtained access to legal abortions than in 1995. Relatively successful implementation of this right may have been a reflection of sympathetic leadership in the Department of Health, too. Such commitment is not uniform across the government and its bureaucracy. The Domestic Violence Act, the Maintenance Act and the Recognition of African Customary Marriages Act each represent important official commitments to women's rights. But if they are to be implemented properly, each requires a very much more extensive administrative system than the one currently existing. The concession of legal status to customary marriages is premised on women within such unions enjoying full rights over property and child custody. These features of the reform are being opposed by 'traditional leaders'. The Department of Home Affairs maintains that it does not have the staff it would need to register customary marriages. Senior police leadership, shortly after the passage of the Domestic Violence Act, admitted that the police were incapable of enforcing its provisions and, more disturbingly, disinclined to try very hard.[86]

At the beginning of this chapter we noted that democratic consolidation was a more complicated process than merely running honest elections and enacting human rights. In consolidating democracies the political system and institutions such as political parties should nurture citizenship through inviting participation and strengthening accountability. Citizens themselves should embrace democratic values more firmly and more widely. Finally the state's administrative competence should be strengthened, so that the laws which are passed in its legislatures can be fully implemented.

The evidence surveyed in this chapter is mixed and not completely encouraging. South Africa's well-institutionalised political parties represent an asset to the consolidation process. However, there have been unwelcome developments in the continuing fragmentation of opposition as well as the fluidity of its boundaries and the increasing impatience of ANC leadership when confronted with challenges to its policies both within the organisation and from its allies. The ANC caucus in parliament appears to have become more reluctant to exercise an oversight role with respect to the executive, and the latter has strengthened party controls over MPs. Politically inspired 'deployments' within the bureaucracy, though understandable just after the ANC's accession to power, show no signs of abating.

However, the judicial system remains robustly independent of the executive (indeed rather more so than it was before 1994). In general, civil society remains vigorous and well organised. Press and broadcasting have retained their editorial assertiveness despite repressive language directed at the media by members of government and notwithstanding political anxieties amongst their owners. There is evidence of a slow increase in the state's capabilities, though government capacity falls well short of what is needed to make legislated rights and entitlements realities in the everyday lives of citizens. Citizens remain favourably inclined towards democracy, even though for a substantial minority it has yet to become 'the only game in town'. Despite progress, South African democracy remains vulnerable.

9 | TRUTH AND RECONCILIATION

An agreement about amnesty was an indispensable condition for a peaceful transition to democracy in South Africa. Between 1990 and 1992, three indemnity laws were enacted to protect returning exiles from prosecution for political offences and to authorise the release of political prisoners. In late 1992, constitutional negotiators agreed that there would be no legal reprisals for any human rights violations undertaken as a consequence of apartheid legislation and that amnesty should be available for politically motivated actions which were illegal at the time they were committed. A postscript to the Interim Constitution was hurriedly drafted by two members of the technical committee of the Multi-Party Negotiating Forum, Mac Maharaj and Fanie van der Merwe, in November 1993. This called for the 'divisions and strife of the past' with their 'legacy of hatred, fear, guilt and revenge' to be addressed in a conciliatory manner. There was a need for understanding, not vengeance; reparation, not retaliation; and *ubuntu*, not victimisation, the postscript maintained. To further these ends amnesty should be available for 'acts, omissions and offences associated with political objectives', the language implying that amnesty would be extended to individuals rather than in a generalised or collective manner (as government negotiators had originally favoured).

By this juncture, key legal thinkers within the African National Congress (ANC) – Kader Asmal, Albie Sachs and Dullah Omar – as well as a group of politically influential liberal intellectuals and churchpeople concentrated in the Western Cape, inspired partly by Latin American experience, were advocating a truth commission as the vehicle through which to administer amnesty. In 1993, the ANC's National Executive Committee (NEC) suggested that such a commission's mandate would extend beyond the issue of indemnity to harness 'the cleansing power of truth'. Truth would ensure that human rights abuse would never happen again and provide an emotionally fulfilling substitute for revenge.[1] The ANC had recently concluded two well-publicised investigations into human rights abuses experienced by detainees in its own prison camps in the wake of a mutiny among guerrilla fighters in Angola.

Accordingly, after 127 hours of consideration by the parliamentary portfolio committee for justice, the Promotion of National Unity and Reconciliation Act was legislated in July 1995, with the Freedom Front in opposition and the Inkatha

Freedom Party (IFP) abstaining. The Act's drafting in 1994 was strongly influenced by the proceedings of a conference convened by IDASA (then the Institute for a Democratic Alternative for South Africa) in February 1994 and attended by a wide range of experts on 'transitional justice' from South America and Eastern Europe, including José Zalaquett, a member of the Chilean truth commission.[2] A Truth and Reconciliation Commission (TRC) was to be established to promote national unity and reconciliation through the achievement of four objectives over the 18-month period of its existence: (1) the discovery of the causes, nature and scope of 'gross violations' of human rights between 1960 and 1994; (2) the extension of amnesty to those who fully disclosed their involvement in politically motivated violations of human rights; (3) the identification and location of victims of violations and the design of reparations for them; and (4) the compilation of a report, which should contain recommendations for measures to prevent any future violations of human rights.

This law accorded to the South African commission a much wider range of powers than comparable bodies had enjoyed elsewhere. No other truth commission had combined investigative powers with the authority to grant amnesties, nor, generally, had previous commissions possessed the capability to summon witnesses or seize evidence. ANC leaders were convinced that amnesty had to be linked 'to restoring the honour and dignity of the victims' through the disclosure of truth and payment of reparation, and that if amnesty was managed in a separate process it would lack public legitimacy.[3] The South African amnesty procedure was also unusual because the law endorsed the principle of publicly accessible hearings. This was a direct result of non-governmental organisations (NGOs) lobbying the portfolio committee. An earlier draft of the Bill agreed in cabinet would have kept the hearings behind closed doors.[4] The South African TRC was to be the first truth commission to feature public participation in its establishment.[5]

The law provided for the presidential appointment of between 11 and 17 commissioners. Though President Mandela was obliged only to consult with his cabinet before choosing the commissioners, he broadened the process by inviting public nominations which would be reviewed by a committee drawn from a cross-section of parties in parliament as well as members of the 'NGO community'. Altogether 45 candidate commissioners had to undergo public interviews; Nelson Mandela reviewed a shortlist of 25. Archbishop Desmond Tutu was appointed in November 1995 as chairperson of the commission, with Alex Boraine as his deputy. Before his nomination in September by the Anglican bishops' synod, Tutu had been looking forward to retirement. Although his personal beliefs accorded very closely with the spirit of the TRC's legislation, he had made no significant contribution to the public discussions which led to the TRC's establishment. By contrast, Alex Boraine had played a central role in the policy process. Boraine, a former president of the Methodist Church and for twelve years a Progressive Party MP before his resignation from parliament to found IDASA, had been one of the most influential lobbyists during the TRC's official conception. It was Boraine who convinced the minister of justice that the commission should include the word 'reconciliation' in its title and its goals.[6]

At the same time, the names of the 15 other commissioners were announced. It was intended that they should be people 'without high political profile', and this was the case despite the inclusion of two former Afrikaner parliamentarians, Wynand Malan and Chris de Jager. Besides these, the two best-known commissioners at the time of their appointment were Mary Burton, a Black Sash leader, and Wendy Orr, who as a district surgeon had obtained a court order in 1985 to stop the Port Elizabeth police from torturing detainees. Seven of the commissioners were women, eight were African, two were coloured and seven were white. The commissioners included five lawyers, five medical workers (doctors, psychiatrists, a clinical psychologist and a nurse), three clerics (four, counting Boraine, an ordained minister) and three former parliamentarians.

From the beginning, two key suppositions would influence the way in which the commissioners set about their work. The first of these concerned the causal connection between truth and reconciliation. In 1994, the Chilean truth commissioner José Zalaquett had told the South Africans in attendance at the IDASA conference about the conciliatory processes through which 'moral order' could be reconstructed. Reconciliation could be achieved either through punishment of wrongdoing or its forgiveness, Zalaquett proposed. Forgiveness, he suggested, was the morally superior option – 'this is stressed by all major traditions and religions'. Indispensable, though, in such traditions, before forgiveness can be extended, is 'that wrongdoing is known, that it is acknowledged, that there is atonement and the perpetrator resolves not to do it again, and that reparations are made'. Reconciliation and forgiveness must be based on truth.[7] Reconciliation depended on 'uncovering the truth', though the commission recognised that such revelation by itself might be painful and might only be one requirement of many needed in a reconciliation process.[8]

Certain authorities were more optimistic: truth might be the most important source of relief for communities damaged by political oppression. According to Peter Kooijmans, a former chairman of the United Nations Human Rights Commission, 'the most important thing is that people want it to be recognised that they were victims … [they] are not interested in seeing the perpetrators behind bars'.[9] 'Our hope', Wendy Orr recalls in her memoir, 'was that, in that telling, a sense of healing and catharsis could begin.'[10] Acknowledgement based on truth could 'trigger catharsis' or spiritual purification, maintained Kader Asmal and his co-authors in a widely influential book published at the beginning of the hearings, entitled *Reconciliation through Truth*.[11] Significantly, Asmal's argument lent support to the notion that individual kinds of psychological healing could be reproduced on a collective scale as Africans exercised their historical 'prerogative to be forgiving' in a 'civic sacrament of forgiveness'.[12] This was certainly the commissioners' understanding of the function of the public rituals over which they were presiding. As Alex Boraine noted, the first Human Rights Violations hearings in East London were preceded by a church service which included 'the traditional enactment of purification, of repentance, of sorrow, of commitment'.[13] The service was opened with the singing of a Xhosa hymn, 'The forgiveness of sins makes the person whole'.[14] The notion of the commission's role as an administrator of sacrament was not an isolated one. Desmond Tutu remembers that most of the commissioners 'felt that what we were being asked to undertake was profoundly religious and spiritual'.[15]

The second important idea was that a compassionate form of 'restorative justice' accorded with popular moral beliefs in general and the African principle of *ubuntu* in particular. The constitutional postscript that gave the commission its original mandate had referred to *ubuntu* as the spirit that should animate a conciliatory settlement with the past. As the commission explained in its report, restorative justice redefined crime as wrongdoing against people rather than a violation of the state, and instead of punishment it emphasised restoration of both victims and offenders, with the authorities 'facilitating' conflict resolution between them. This judicial shift from confrontation to conciliation would represent a revival of 'African traditional values' and especially those associated with the concept of *ubuntu*, 'humaneness', and its maxim that 'people are people through other people'.[16] For Desmond Tutu, though 'honouring *ubuntu* is clearly not a mechanical, automatic and inevitable process', its corollary, restorative justice, was certainly 'a characteristic of traditional African jurisprudence' in which the central concern is not retribution but instead 'the restoration of broken relationships'.[17]

In a similar vein, Alex Boraine was persuaded that a 'holistic philosophy of forgiveness, reconciliation and *ubuntu*' had characterised the ANC's world-view since its embrace of Africanism in the 1940s.[18] From this perspective, deployed by charismatic leadership, the 'politics of grace' – represented in, for example, Nelson Mandela's symbolic gestures towards Afrikaners – had the 'almost salvific power', it was believed, to 'make or break community'.[19] For this to happen, though, for reconciliation – confession, repentance, reparation and forgiveness – to be a collective social process, argued Charles Villa-Vicencio, the TRC's research director, it would have to evoke not just individual testimonies but wider corporate acknowledgements of moral guilt.[20]

The commissioners were assigned to three committees, each charged with one of the three functions to be performed by the TRC: the consideration of 'gross human rights violations' and the identification of victims; the planning of reparations and rehabilitation; and the administration of amnesty to the perpetrators of violations. These committees were to be supported by what would grow into a substantial bureaucracy. As many as 550 people would work in the TRC's four regional offices in Cape Town, East London, Durban and Johannesburg, as well as in its various departments for legal affairs, research, communications, witness protection, security, records, and so forth. Altogether the TRC was to spend by the end of 1998 a total of R70 million. Most of its funds were made available by government, but a proportion also came from foreign donations.

The commission held its first meeting shortly after the commissioners were appointed, on 16 December 1995 – appropriately enough, on the Day of Reconciliation – in Archbishop Tutu's former official residence. The next few months were devoted to setting up the organisation so that the first Human Rights Violations hearings could be held in East London, on 15 April 1996. The public Violations hearings ended in August 1997, but statement-taking from individual victims continued. Meanwhile, the work of the Amnesty and Reparations committees gathered momentum, while the research department began analysing the information gathered from the victims of human rights violations. After the publication of a five-volume interim report in October 1998, the TRC began to disband, though the work of the Amnesty and Reparations committees continued, supported by a skeleton staff and the four regional offices until late 2001. Parliament debated a 'national response' to the TRC's interim report in February 1999.

The work of the Human Rights Violations Committee received most media attention and probably had the widest public impact. The committee's procedures began with statement-taking. Specially trained 'statement-takers' – both TRC employees and volunteers from community organisations – gathered information from 'deponents' (people who had experienced human rights abuses). Statement-makers were encouraged to offer testimony through public meetings during the visits of fieldworkers to particular communities and through the public hearings of select witnesses who had earlier been interviewed by statement-takers.

Most of the 76 public hearings of specially screened victims and witnesses were televised. Edited excerpts from the television recordings were shown on television news bulletins and in a weekly hour-long programme on Sunday prime-time television. Statement-takers initially recorded victims' narratives more or less verbatim, as listening to victims' stories was viewed as a vital therapeutic function which the TRC should undertake, a process of 'validation of individual subjective experience of people who had previously been silenced'.[21]

This concern with collecting what the commission called 'narrative truth' became less pronounced as the numbers of statement-makers multiplied. The 'protocols' or forms that were used by the statement-takers were revised five times, and each revision left less scope for subjective perceptions as victim experience was categorised through a 'controlled vocabulary' to facilitate its 'capture' in a computerised database.[22] Statement-makers would not be cross-examined, even in public hearings, for the commissioners sought to make their 'interaction' with victims 'a positive and affirmative experience'.[23] Instead, the investigative unit attempted to find 'corroboration' for each statement from other witnesses or from documentation or contemporary newspaper reports. Corroborated statements were handed over to the Reparations Committee.

The Violations Committee collected 21 000 statements altogether. These referred to a total of 38 000 incidents, 10 000 of them killings. Some 17 500 of the deponents told the commission about violations experienced by other people. As one sceptical observer has noted, much of the evidence accumulated by the commission would have been based on hearsay.[24] In defence of the commission, hearsay evidence might have been the only evidence available on particular incidents and, as Tutu has pointed out, 'when it came to hearing evidence from the victims, because we were not a criminal court, we established facts on the basis of probability'.[25]

The public hearings were not so much concerned with establishing facts, for those who testified before them had already given their statements. Public victim hearings had an important ritual function: they were essential ingredients in what the commissioners understood to be a process of communal reconciliation. More broadly, of course, they were intended to serve as 'a powerful medium of education for society at large'.[26] Special hearings focused on the experiences arising from particular events, selected from a chronology prepared by the research department, and on the role various professions, institutions and organisations (including political parties) 'had played in committing, resisting or facilitating human rights abusage'.

The members of the Reparations Committee performed an important auxiliary function at the public Violations hearings: they supplied moral support and emotional comfort for victims at these events. Their main labour was directed at identifying who should qualify for any kind of reparation. During 1998 each of about 20 000 corroborated statements would be checked by members of both the Violations and Reparations committees so that for each abuse of human rights a 'victim finding' could be reported. For a positive finding the violation would have to be gross, within the mandated period (1960 to 1994), politically motivated and corroborated. For each finding, the committee produced a brief summary report on the circumstances of the violation, supposedly for inclusion in the final report, though in the end only a list of victims' names was published. Each eligible victim or their surviving relatives would be asked to complete a reparation application, which would be used to assess the material impact of abuse.

While this work was under way, the committee was also meant to prepare its recommendations for various kinds of reparation and restitution, as the TRC itself had no resources of its own for this purpose and its role was limited to advocacy.[27] By October 1998, when most of the committee's members were discharged, some

5 000 applications had been processed and the rest were to be reviewed by a skeleton staff retained until 2001.[28]

Meanwhile, the Amnesty Committee undertook reviewing the 7 127 applications it had received up to a deadline on 30 September 1997, a date that had to be postponed three times. The applications needed to concern offences committed between 1 March 1960 and 10 May 1994. Oddly, given amnesty's central place in the political preoccupations that led to the formation of the TRC, the scale of applications took the commissioners by surprise,[29] and the President added another twelve judges to the original five members of the committee. Amnesty procedures were much more legalistic than the Human Rights Violations hearings. Applicants were normally represented by lawyers who argued on their behalf, and both applicants and those victims or witnesses who opposed applications could be subjected, within limits, to cross-examination, although evidence was not subjected to the standard rules used in a regular court of justice. Witnesses could be subpoenaed by the TRC to appear at hearings, as was the case in the Human Rights Violations hearings. Amnesty judges initially wanted to hold their sessions *in camera* and needed to be persuaded to allow hearings to be televised.

To be granted amnesty, applicants had to prove that their actions were politically motivated and that the violations were gross and within the mandated period. They also had to disclose all relevant information, including the chain of command responsible for the action, and they had to demonstrate that the violation was a 'proportionate' response to the circumstances (although this last condition was seldom given serious consideration). Applicants did not have to offer any expressions of remorse. Unlike the other two committees, the Amnesty Committee did not undertake any public education about its activities, nor did it supply any emotional support for victims who appeared as witnesses. It worked considerably more slowly – as Boraine's account notes tactfully, 'the judges' approach lacked urgency'.[30] Public hearings began six months after the first televised victim testimonies. By June 1998, the committee had completed its procedures with respect to 4 443 applications. Only 122 applicants were granted amnesty. Of the rest, the majority (3 115 applications) were found to concern actions which according to the criteria employed by the commission were not politically motivated. In December 2001, the Amnesty Committee announced the completion of its work: out of a total of 7 127 applications, only 1 146 (16 per cent) had been successful.

The quasi-religious opening ceremony of the public Human Rights Violations hearings in the East London city hall in April 1994 set the tone for much of what followed. After an overture of hymn-singing led by commissioner Bongani Finca, all stood with heads bowed while Archbishop Tutu prayed and the names of those who had died and disappeared, who were to be subject of the day's hearings, were read out. A big white candle inscribed with a cross was lit. The candle symbolised the bringing of truth. Under the glare of television lamps and accompanied by hymn-singing, the commissioners crossed the floor to the rows of victims to welcome them before returning to sit behind a table covered with white linen to watch and listen.[31] The setting created by these preliminaries deliberately invoked Christian liturgy associated with the extension of the sacrament, for the hearings were not simply about remembrance and bearing witness. Instead, they were dedicated to the transcendence of individual experience and the reconstruction of community through the evocation of suffering and sacrifice.

Belinda Bozzoli's analysis of the 1996 Alexandra hearings suggests how the narratives presented to the commissioners and their 'congregation' constituted a carefully structured civic ritual to achieve these goals. This ritual began with a spokesperson for the township, Patience Pasha, welcoming the commissioners on behalf of the community and reminding them of the key episodes of Alexandra residents' collective experience of apartheid's inflictions. As Bozzoli notes, this was clearly a public folk history, one obviously appreciated by her local listeners. Various other local notables also helped to 'contextualise' subsequent narratives with further testimony on behalf of the 'community'. Obed Bapela, an authoritative local ANC leader, unfolded an heroic (and impersonal) narrative of resistance and repression, referring to the need for forgiveness and reconciliation, and placing at the helm of events the older generation of more conservative local ANC leaders and downplaying the leadership role (and the more violent activities) of the local youth congress activists.

The stage was now set for the individual accounts of pain, loss and anguish. After a formal welcome, witnesses were taken through their individual testimonies. Carefully phrased questions would lead them towards relating their moment of greatest suffering, at which point the Reparation Committee's female comforters would move forward to embrace them. Each would then be thanked heartily and the chairperson would sum up their stories. These summaries helped to emphasise the common themes in the individual testimonies. Bozzoli's argument is that these once-private stories now rendered as public performances were through this transformation calculated to achieve important social effects. Prompting witnesses to reveal their most profound agonies was not merely an undertaking aimed at individual catharsis; rather, the pressure the commissioners exerted on witnesses in the form of questioning was to enable the community to feel empathy with the suffering of each witness, to weep as they wept. Humble victims were hence socially ennobled as communal martyrs. By transforming private grief into public sorrow, communal approval could be won for what Bozzoli calls the rites of closure, in which the commissioners sought to elicit expressions of forgiveness or requested reparation. In their structure, then, these public hearings were directed as much at the commission's reconciliation mandate as its quest for truth.

The procedure followed during the Alexandra hearings was not unique. Richard Wilson's research at hearings held on the West Rand and in the Vaal area also shows how commissioners attempted to convert private experience into a common resource. Wilson suggests that four stages were followed in this process. In the initial phase, commissioners' responses and commentaries universalised individual testimony. For example, after listening in Klerksdorp to Peter Moletsane's account of his arrest and torture when he had tried to report the death of his uncle to the police, Archbishop Tutu told him: 'Your pain is our pain. We were tortured, we were harassed, we suffered, we were oppressed.' Tutu was not claiming personal experience of the treatment meted out to Moletsane, argues Wilson. Instead 'he was constructing a new political identity, that of a "national victim," a new South African self which included the dimensions of suffering and oppression'.

Next, commissioners sought to emphasise that all suffering was of equal moral significance. A white woman whose husband had been killed by Umkhonto guerrillas prompted Desmond Tutu to recollect that 'our first witness this morning [a black man, whose son had disappeared in 1985] also spoke of getting the remains of a body back'. It was wonderful, Tutu concluded, 'for the country to experience that – black and white – we all feel the same pain'. However, audiences often resisted this 'sentimental equalisation of all victims of war', a frequent feature of conflict resolution mechanisms. Wilson refers to the consternation of the commissioners at the hilarity which greeted the story of a mother whose son's body was exhumed and set alight by 'comrades'. The body belonged to a leading figure in 'the Toasters', an IFP-affiliated gang whose speciality was burning their opponents alive. After a moral equality of victims was created, each one would be invested with the heroic significance arising from his or her assigned role in a teleology of sacrifice. But in the commissioners' reactions to witnesses' testimony, there was no room for the private or the accidental or the pointless. Accordingly, Peter Moletsane was comforted by Tutu with 'You are one who is still young, who sacrificed himself for the fruits of liberation that we have now'.

Sello Mothusi, shot and disabled by the police in 1986, insisted, to the visible irritation of the commissioners at the Klerksdorp hearings, that on the day of his shooting he was just on his way to the shops, undertaking an errand for his mother, that he was not involved in politics, that he had 'done nothing wrong'. This would not do. All suffering was meaningful and all its victims were public martyrs in a just war for liberation. Even the mother of the leader of the Toaster gang was told by commissioner Hlengiwe Mkhize 'that people like you struggling for freedom should be recognised'. The closing rite in this liturgy was redemptive. Commissioners would ask those who had offered testimony if they could forgive the perpetrators of the violations to which they had borne witness.[32] Forgiveness and the renunciation of vengeance represented for certain commissioners the most important function of these hearings. As Tutu subsequently explained, the loss of the entitlement to retribution was 'a loss which liberates the victim'. Tutu insisted that the majority of witnesses achieved this kind of release.[33]

Amnesty offered fewer opportunities for spiritual emancipation of this order. The law imposed no obligation on those who applied for amnesty to express contrition, let alone to seek reconciliation. Because testimony could be subjected to cross-examination, as Boraine concedes, 'the atmosphere of compassion and sensitivity of the Human Rights Violations Committee hearings was lacking'.[34] Amnesty procedures provoked much more public disagreement than the human rights hearings and the commission had to defend its work against several court challenges, including an effort by representatives of the Biko family to obtain a constitutional judgment against indemnity.

Additional sources of frustration for the commission were the autonomous status of the Amnesty Committee and its chaotic organisation.[35] The committee was supposed to use what is known as the Norgaard principles in its decisions over whether an offence was politically motivated. It ignored these in granting a collective amnesty to 37 ANC leaders who disclosed neither individual motivation nor specific acts. The commission felt compelled to seek a Supreme Court finding to obtain a reversal of the decision. Another example of the committee's inconsistency was its indemnification of the killers of Amy Biehl, an American exchange student murdered by supporters of the Pan Africanist Congress (PAC) in Cape Town. The general criterion used to determine political motivation was that the offence had to have been sanctioned by a political organisation, but Amy Biehl's murder was repudiated by the PAC.[36]

Commissioners expressed disappointment at the reluctance of members of certain institutional groups to apply for amnesty. Not a single officer from National Intelligence came forward despite the implication of the intelligence service in much of the testimony about the 'dirty wars' of the 1980s. Few senior military personnel presented their cases before the committee, encouraged no doubt by the state's failure in 1997 to obtain a conviction in its prosecution of General Magnus Malan for his complicity in the 1987 KwaMakhutha massacre involving Inkatha militia members in KwaZulu-Natal. Attorneys-general were extremely reluctant to delay court cases against people who might be amnesty applicants.

Not all prosecutions were so unhelpful. Applications for amnesty from the police service were much more forthcoming than from the spies or soldiers, especially after top security police officers were named in the testimony that Vlakplaas commander Eugene de Kock presented to the committee in his bid for indemnity following his conviction in 1996. By contrast, ANC applications for amnesty constituted about half of the total, and these again represented only a small proportion of the people in the organisation who would have committed what the TRC defined as human rights abuses.

One member of the South African Communist Party (SACP) in Zwelathemba, Worcester, recalling various brutal killings by activists of suspected informers and drug dealers, toured the town with a loudspeaker announcing that he would wait in the church hall on a particular day to distribute amnesty forms. On the day he had specified, he waited but no one came.[37] It is possible that local residents may not have been aware of the possibility that they could still, in theory, be prosecuted for complicity in necklace murders committed ten years previously, but it is also likely that they may have felt no particular sense of culpability. A local ANC Youth League official in Queenstown, during the Violations hearings there, confided to Antjie Krog that the commission was 'blowing this necklace business out of all proportion ... it was a way of controlling the community'.[38]

Applications for amnesty were all too often accompanied by justifications and excuses, or very qualified statements of regret. Even when they were not, both applications and favourable outcomes were often received with considerable bitterness by the relatives of the victims of political assassinations, as well as scepticism about the extent to which killers genuinely felt remorse.[39] Andrew Ribeiro, the son of two Pretoria doctors killed in 1986, expressed a widely shared sentiment when he told a journalist that 'victims' wounds have been reopened and we have been left with more tears than before. Reconciliation should balance and in our case this hasn't happened.' Understandably, in their memoirs the commissioners attach considerable importance to those applicants whose avowals of moral guilt and personal remorse were successful in engendering expressions of forgiveness. This may not have been true in the case of every commissioner. Mapule Ramashala's dismissive remark during the amnesty hearings for the Amy Biehl murder suggests that at least one member of the commission was unconvinced about the need for all to express remorse: 'it's irresponsible white people like her who went into the townships and got themselves killed, that gave the struggle a bad name.' [40]

However, pressure exerted on victims at the Violations hearings to express forgiveness suggests that such perceptions were atypical. In first-hand narratives of the amnesties, the same conciliatory incidents again and again are accorded emblematic significance. There was a dramatic early instance of public reconciliation when a member of the Northern Transvaal security police, Jacques Hechter, confessed his role in planning various assassination attempts. After his testimony, he and the Revd Smangaliso Mkhatshwa were able to shake hands; subsequently Mkhatshwa was to invite Hechter and some of his accomplices to his church in Soshanguve to say they were sorry. Brian Mitchell, the commander of the unit responsible for the Trust Feed massacre in December 1988 in which 11 people were killed in KwaZulu, asked the commission to arrange a visit to the community his unit had attacked. The encounter was televised, and Desmond Tutu believes 'the majority' of community members 'were glad he had come'.[41] Initially, though, the families of Mitchell's victims expressed anger at his amnesty, and TRC investigator Dumisa Ntsebeza's account of the same incident suggests that they rejected a TRC attempt to arrange a meeting between them and Mitchell so that he could discuss restitution.[42] Amy Biehl's parents attended the amnesty hearings of her four killers and made a public statement of their support for the favourable decision to grant the amnesty. Subsequently they met two of the men involved in their daughter's murder at a youth club the men had established in Gugulethu.

Before the Amnesty Committee began holding its hearings, Beth Savage, a severely wounded victim of an attack on a King William's Town golf club by the Azanian People's Liberation Army (APLA), told the Violations Committee that 'she would like to meet that man that threw the grenade; I would like to meet him in an attitude of forgiveness and hope'.[43] Subsequently she did meet her assailant, Thembalani Xundu, when he sought amnesty in April 1998. She told a newspaper that her nightmares had ceased as a consequence of meeting Xundu. Another target of an APLA attack, the traditionally conservative Church of England in South Africa, in its submission to the Faith Community hearings reflected on the lessons it could extract from an armed assault on one of its congregations, St James Church in Cape Town. Its statement acknowledged that 'even an apolitical religious group could become caught up in the politics of war' and conceded that 'it had been misled into accepting a social, economic and political system that was cruel and oppressive'.[44]

The hearing on Aboobaker Ismail's activities as head of the ANC's Special Operations Unit was attended by survivors of the Church Street bombing in Pretoria. Ismail apologised to the civilians who had been injured and a picture of him shaking hands with Neville Clarence, an air force clerk blinded in the bomb blast, appeared in every South African newspaper the next day. Clarence subsequently visited Ismail's home, and the two men apparently managed to develop a kind of friendship.[45]

How successful was the Truth and Reconciliation Commission in its self-appointed healing function? Did telling their stories and extending forgiveness have the cathartic effect of what Tutu terms 'liberating the victims'? Were locally divided communities assisted by the commission's activities in resolving their conflicts?

For the 21 000 people who made statements to the commission, telling their stories may well have been psychologically empowering. Most statement-givers were Africans – 19 144 in total, the majority of them from KwaZulu-Natal, the province most affected by violent conflict in the 1980s and 1990s.[46] Lukas Baba Sikwepere, blinded by a police sniper in Nyanga, Cape Town, in 1988, told commissioner Gobodo-Madikizela that 'what has been making me sick all the time, is the fact that I couldn't tell my story. But now I – it feels like I got my sight back, by coming here and tell you my story.'[47] Johan Smit, whose son was killed in an Amanzimtoti bomb blast, told the commissioners that meeting the parents of the man executed for placing the limpet mine, Andrew Zondo, 'gave me peace, because [now] I know what was happening'. A representative of the Khulumani Support Group told the commission that its 'intervention ... brought about the dignity of the people that was lost during the political era ... People had no one to listen to their griefs.' Sandra Adonis, an activist in Cape Town and a witness at the special Youth hearings, later told a researcher that offering testimony 'even if there were no reparations ... was worthwhile. There was a weight on me and the TRC has lifted that weight through the mere fact that I could share my story with others.'[48] Tom Ledgerwood, a victim of torture by the security police, said that his testimony freed him 'from a prison in which [he] had been for 18 years ... The silence is ending and we are waking up from a long bad nightmare.'[49] When asked what he needed from the TRC, Mr Mkhabile, an elderly Poqo veteran who had survived brutal treatment during his prison term on Robben Island, took from his pocket a crumpled piece of paper and read to the commissioners the names of his comrades who had been hanged. 'All he wanted was that we should remember them.'[50]

The commission's report suggests that story-telling restored people's dignity in a number of ways: through removing the stigma of criminalisation, which had affected certain forms of resistance (such as refusal to undergo conscription); or through clearing the names of people who had been unfairly attacked as collaborators or informers. The posthumous rehabilitation of Maki Skosana, one of the first necklace victims, was an especially striking instance of this restorative function.

Even genuine collaborators could achieve a measure of rehabilitation at commission hearings. Mrs Beatrice Sethwale, the mother of a black policeman lynched in Upington, was told by commissioner Glenda Wildschut: 'That is why we felt it is important that you too have the opportunity to tell your story today. I think that many people say, looking back they acknowledge the fact that they didn't give that opportunity and didn't recognise your pain and your grief ... it is important for reconciliation and for healing to take place; that we begin to acknowledge that you too went through a lot of suffering.' However, when asked how she felt about people who 'are now beginning to say they would like to work towards reconciliation first by acknowledging that you yourself have suffered', Mrs Sethwale's reply seemed to offer extremely qualified hope that this might happen: 'I feel I am already dead and that this process will be a long and time-consuming one.'[51]

It is rather doubtful whether the same quality of relief achieved by Tom Ledgerwood or by the Skosana family was attainable for the vast majority of victims who did not present their stories at public hearings and who encountered an increasingly abrupt form of statement-taking. Several deponents interviewed during

Richard Wilson's fieldwork told him that after their statements they felt they had left something out, that 'most of the things I wanted to say I couldn't say' because these seemed to be excluded by the bureaucratic requirements of the 'protocol' the interviewers used.[52]

What about the local social impact of the commission's hearings? Did the redemptive, ritualistic dimensions of the hearings heal rifts in communities? Certain commissioners thought they did. Wendy Orr notes that 'throughout the process of the TRC there has not been one act of vengeance against a perpetrator who came forward or a perpetrator freed from prison'.[53] Trust Feed was one community in which the TRC hearings prompted the subsequent formation of a peace committee to bring together ANC and IFP representatives. However, despite assurances about forgiveness at the hearings in August 1996 concerning the Boipatong massacre, fears of communal hostility continued to dissuade Inkatha members from returning to their homes in the KwaMadada hostel in Sebokeng, and at least one person was subsequently killed by an ANC self-defence unit in Sharpeville on Christmas Day, 1996.[54]

In Alexandra, Obed Bapela's suggestion that repentant informers would be welcomed back into the community provoked derision amongst his audience.[55] Belinda Bozzoli suggests that the absence of voices in the Alexandra hearings from representatives of the youth congresses who were at the forefront of 1980s conflict and their evident marginalisation in the public history under construction during the proceedings may have meant that at best the hearings represented an incomplete kind of 'closure'. Even with their presence, closure might not have been achieved, for, as with the psychological process of individual recovery from trauma and loss, restoring social cohesion must be a long term process, requiring much more than the cathartic ritual of the TRC hearings, however emotionally charged and fulfilling these may have been at the time.

The TRC did not have the resources to undertake long-term counselling programmes,[56] social rehabilitation or local conflict resolution in the wake of its hearings. Yet its failure to enlist the support of the wide range of appropriately specialised NGOs to undertake such ventures in a coordinated way was truly a missed opportunity. NGOs undertook support work, including victim–offender mediation, victim counselling and public education, but organisations that approached the TRC for letters of support to attach to funding proposals for such operations were usually denied endorsement. In Gauteng, 35 organisations concerned with mental health offered their services to the TRC free of charge, but most were not drawn into the hearings process.[57]

Richard Wilson argues that an influential view within the commission was that the reconciliation procedure should not attempt to address individual feelings of vengeance or hatred, but rather through truth-seeking lay the intellectual foundations for new kinds of social civility. These would need at least a decade to coalesce. Russell Ally, a member of the Violations Committee, told Wilson that 'we must reconcile with our past as opposed to promoting reconciliation between individuals'. Wilson's argument is that this view discouraged any efforts to engage with the NGO community in conflict resolution.[58] This judgement may be unfair – it is at odds with the evident value commissioners attached to instances of victim–perpetrator reconciliation. Wendy Orr refers to at least one occasion on which she was actively involved in a follow-up activity arising from testimony offered at the special hearings into conscription.[59] It is also possible that the religious background of some of the most influential figures in the commission may have predisposed them to work with local church bodies to the exclusion of other groups.

The TRC's reparations mission might have had powerful restorative effects in addressing the needs of individuals requiring help and solace as well as neighbourhoods disfigured and demoralised by particularly intense violence. That the recommendations of the Reparations Committee have yet to be fully adopted by the government is hardly the fault of the TRC, though. The process of identifying eligible recipients for individual reparations was clearly laborious. Much of the groundwork had been completed by October 1997, by which time the committee had prepared its policy proposals. This was achieved despite a weak chairperson and consequent personal tensions between members of the committee.

The committee recommended that two kinds of financial restitution should be paid to victims of gross human rights violations to compensate for their entitlement to civic litigation. Those who through injuries or loss of income were experiencing serious hardship should receive a one-off 'urgent interim payment' of between R2 000 and R5 000, depending on the size of their household. Ultimately all victims should receive annual payments over a six-year period of between R18 000 and R22 000, figures based on the 1997 median household income. The total cost of such payments would not exceed R3 billion, the committee argued – an annual expenditure comparable to the pensions paid to liberation movement veterans. The committee also included in its recommendations measures of 'symbolic reparation' (exhumations, expunging of criminal records, memorials) and various forms of community rehabilitation including demilitarisation, the settlement of displaced people, and special programmes to reintegrate perpetrators and their families socially and to provide therapy for survivors. The commission itself arranged for the exhumation and identification of some fifty bodies as a result of requests for the return of the bones of the missing, which were a common refrain at hearings.[60]

The modesty of the TRC's proposals echoed the restraint of the requests which people had made during the Violations hearings. At the Alexandra hearings witnesses proposed that the government give people tombstones, that it should 'help us through education', and that medical help should be offered to victims who were still suffering.[61] The TRC's statistics indicate that 22 per cent of deponents wanted a regular monetary grant and another 17 per cent referred to other kinds of financial compensation. Tombstones were mentioned by 8 per cent. Only 5 per cent sought an apology or acknowledgement from perpetrators, though 20 per cent wanted to know what had happened to those they had lost.[62]

In response, in April 1998 the government authorised urgent interim payments of R2 000 and several thousand people began to receive grants. By 2000, though, a substantial proportion of the R320 million the government had committed to this process still remained in the President's Fund, mainly owing to uncertainties about which government department was responsible for its distribution as well as to difficulties in locating applicants and opening bank accounts for them.[63] In May, the Department of Justice announced that there was still no decision about the larger payments, nor had any money been budgeted for these. Besides, as the ministry's spokesperson maintained, 'It is also necessary to place on record the fact that the majority of people never fought apartheid to be paid. It is therefore an insult to them to suggest they be paid or that they deserve to be paid.'[64] One month later, official attitudes appeared to soften with the agreement to form a trust which would solicit contributions from business. No further commitments were forthcoming from government, except some financial support for the construction of monuments. From early on, it was evident to commissioners that officials viewed reparations as a low-priority concern. As Maria Ramos, director-general of finance, told Wendy Orr in 1997, 'she had much more important issues on her desk'.[65]

The evident lack of official enthusiasm for the TRC's recommendations for individual reparations is unlikely to have been merely an effect of fiscal austerity. The ultimate cost of the policy would represent a fraction of what the government spends on welfare payments of other kinds. Political hostility to the commission seems a much more plausible explanation for the obvious official reluctance to pay reparations. Quite early during the course of the hearings, the commission had one important conflict with the ANC over the necessity of its members to make individual submissions for amnesty. In its submission to the TRC, the ANC took the view that reparations should be financed by white South Africans. Though ANC legal thinkers had a key influence on the commission's original conception, their views were not collectively shared by all members of Mandela's government. Boraine's old associate, Frederik van Zyl Slabbert, contends that 'from the outset, the government was never very keen on the TRC', basing his claim on conversations with members of the President's office. The ANC, Slabbert believes, was always in favour of a general amnesty and a fresh start.[66] This is certainly the view of Barney Pityana, former chairman of the Human Rights Commission.[67]

Thabo Mbeki, though, when the commission began its work, appeared to have different views. At a book launch for Kader Asmal in 1996, Mbeki made a speech about reconciliation. 'The only thing that will heal this country is large doses of truth,' he noted, proceeding to argue that apartheid was a form of genocide as well as a crime against humanity and that reconciliation would only be possible if whites would admit that apartheid was evil and that they were responsible for it.[68] Asmal himself maintained that apologies should be a legal requirement for amnesty.[69] If Asmal's views were typical, then the ANC leaders could be expected to react very unfavourably to any hint of moral equation between its own 'scattered human rights infringements amounting to departures from its primary humanist goals' and 'apartheid's administrators' ... patterns of internal and external homicide and violent abuse' in defence of a 'crime against humanity'.[70] In October 1998, the publication of the commission's report brought to the surface the tensions that had been developing between the TRC and the ANC.

The ANC displayed hostility to the commission's findings despite the commissioners' recognition that the liberation movements had fought a just war against criminal policies and notwithstanding their recognition that the ANC conducted its own military operations with comparative restraint. However, within these qualifications, the commission's references to the extent of human rights abuse attributable to the ANC implied a scale of violation well beyond the few 'scattered infringements' conceded by Kader Asmal. Out of 14 000 killings reported to the TRC, the ANC was responsible for 1 300, third in order after the IFP (4 500 killings) and the South African Police (2 600 killings). Particular 'gross human rights violations' included the ANC's landmine campaign in the Northern Transvaal in 1986, the assassination of 76 Inkatha office-holders, and the routine use of torture by the ANC's security department between 1979 and 1989. The commission also contended that through creating and arming 'self-defence units', the ANC had contributed 'to a spiral of violence' after 1990.[71]

Though Nelson Mandela's speech on officially receiving the report was characteristically gracious, Thabo Mbeki was less so in the parliamentary debate that followed its publication, complaining of 'the erroneous determination of various actions of our liberation movements as gross violations of human rights'.[72] The commission had sent to each political party an advance notification of its findings as it was required to do. The ANC, rather than submit a written response, requested a meeting to challenge the TRC's conclusions. On this being refused (in a decision which found the commission sharply divided), the ANC attempted to halt the publication of the report through a court action, provoking an angry denunciation by Tutu of a 'new tyranny'. The court application failed and the ANC instead had to content itself with angry invective by its official spokesperson Ronnie Mamoepa, who condemned the TRC's 'scurrilous attempts to criminalise the liberation struggle by characterising the heroic struggles of the people of South Africa ... as gross human rights violations'.[73] In a more subtle vein, the SACP's Jeremy Cronin acknowledged that the report had 'reached important and correct conclusions' in its reference to a just war, but also noted that the 'moral asymmetry' between the liberation movements and their adversaries was 'overwhelmed' by a 'gross human rights abuse' storyline in which any moral or contextual distinctions between 'perpetrators' were ignored.[74]

F. W. de Klerk was more successful than the ANC in obtaining a court order to halt publication of the TRC's findings. The offending section on his role was printed over in the report with a black square. Alex Boraine reproduced the section in his subsequent book. In it, the commission had criticised De Klerk for his lack of candour about the extent to which he was aware of ministerial involvement in the bombing of the South African Council of Churches headquarters when he testified to the commission.[75] Even with this excision, the TRC's findings on the former president, his predecessor and their colleagues were considerably harsher than its conclusions about the ANC. The state's security and law enforcement agencies were found responsible for the predominant portion of gross violations of human rights, including torture, abductions, the sponsorship of insurgent forces in the region and hit squads at home. Senior politicians who belonged to the State Security Council deliberately planned the killing of political opponents. However, the commission could find no evidence of involvement by senior politicians or top bureaucrats in a 'centrally directed, coherent and formally constituted third force' engaged in *agent provocateur* activities between 1990 and 1994. A third set of findings supplied extensive detail on abuses committed by Inkatha, and held Chief Mangosuthu Buthelezi 'accountable' for these 'in his representative capacity as the leader'.

None of these findings constituted major revelations, and even in detail much of the content in the five published volumes merely rephrased and supplemented the findings of earlier inquiries, in particular those of the Goldstone Commission. The TRC Report provided a more comprehensive picture of the way in which the state security apparatus was organised in the 1980s than any other single source. It also supplied fresh insights into the history of some of the more shadowy state agencies such as BOSS and its intelligence successors. Both the Violations hearings and the small number of amnesty applications heard before the report was written enabled a more accurate picture of the scope of ANC guerrilla operations to emerge than had been available previously.

Limitations in the degree to which the commission generated new knowledge might not have mattered if it had succeeded in making what was already known to some more widely understood – if it had, in commissioner Mary Burton's words, made truth legitimate.[76] It is rather doubtful that the report achieved even this modest goal, at least in the short term. While ANC supporters suggested that the TRC had 'bent over backwards' to produce findings acceptable to white South Africans[77] and 'criminalised the liberation movements',[78] others complained about a 'pattern of playing down ANC culpability and of maximising blame attributed to the police, army and IFP'.[79] Conversely, Richard Wilson has argued that the TRC's commitment to a 'nation-building' predisposition restrained the report's authors from making more severe findings on the role of state agencies and Inkatha. Its 'weak' conclusions about the third force, Wilson suggests, as well as its unwillingness to pursue questions about chains of command which would have linked rank-and-file violators with those who were responsible for giving orders was a consequence of deference to the requirements of ANC *realpolitik* and the need to secure co-operation with Inkatha in the administration of KwaZulu-Natal.

Much of the criticism directed at the report focused on its methodological shortcomings. Most of the testimony that constituted the primary source of evidence for the report's authors derived from victim statements; only a small quantity of the more stringently tested material from the amnesty hearings was available to them. Those amnesty applications that were available were mainly from policemen. With its primary dependence on victim testimony, the commission was unlikely to generate significant insights into the causes of violence. The motivations of perpetrators and their explanations of why violations occurred were hardly incisive.[80] Corroboration of victim statements often seemed to be very cursory. TRC researchers encountered formidable obstacles in their pursuit of corroborative archival evidence, much of which, in any case, appeared to have been destroyed or hidden from the commission. The researchers' initial use of a magistrate's search warrant to raid a military base in Cape Town elicited strong protests from officials of the South African National Defence Force (SANDF), and hence it was agreed that the TRC would have access only to documentation that the military authorities were willing to release.[81]

The majority of victims who spoke to the commission referred to events after 1984 but before 1990. Some of them may have adapted their stories to the requirements of official conceptions of what constituted a gross violation and hence eligibility for reparations.[82] More importantly, the assumption by witnesses of the predispositions of victimhood also contributed to clouding motives and excluding the possibility that groups may have been both victims and perpetrators. As Cronin observed, 'millions of ordinary South Africans refused to be merely victims; they organised themselves for survival and struggle'.[83]

The commission succeeded in collecting evidence on 14 000 killings, leaving at least another 12 000 deaths known to other investigations unexplored. One reason for this was that the IFP leadership had told its followers to boycott the proceedings, and so IFP members were substantially under-represented in victim hearings. In apportioning blame, the commission was working with an incomplete statistical base. Uncritical acceptance of victim testimony resulted in the reproduction in the report of occasional conflicts between different accounts of the same events. Subsequent amnesty hearings sometimes exposed mistaken hearsay testimony, with ANC perpetrators confessing to killings that victims had blamed on the police. Report findings were sometimes at odds with earlier court conclusions, without any explanation. An example of this was the Amnesty Committee's acceptance of Brian Mitchell's claim that he had not been physically present at the Trust Feed killings, a claim that had been explicitly rejected in the court judgment.

The degree to which the commission sought out victims of human rights abuse may have resulted in political biases in the evidence it collected. The commission's research department produced a chronology, which supplied the basis for the special themes around which evidence was collected. Anthea Jeffery, researcher at the South African Institute of Race Relations, maintains that this chronology diverted attention from other issues which were subsequently neglected, including occasions on which IFP members were massacred.[84] Jeffery's argument is that the omissions in the evidence the commission accumulated worked to Inkatha's disadvantage. Other readers have pointed out that relative availability of evidence could just as easily implicate Inkatha's opponents. For example, because of the degree of candour of the ANC's submission to the TRC, it was much easier for the TRC Report's authors to identify a chain of command within the ANC's hierarchy responsible for violence after 1990 than within Inkatha and the government. Hence, in its treatment of this period, the report makes highly critical findings about the ANC leadership's role.

If the commission's efforts to produce an authoritative truth about the past were so vulnerable to criticism, was it more successful in its other aim of promoting reconciliation? As we have seen, the establishment of the TRC and the character of its operations were influenced by the belief that the exercise of a public ritual of forgiveness in return for disclosure could reconcile South Africans and promote civic empathy between them. A compassionate notion of restorative justice was supposed to resonate with the popular African cosmology of *ubuntu* humanism. Such assumptions are widely questioned. It may well be that individuals can forgive crimes committed against them in return for frank disclosures and that the same individuals can be comforted by the recognition resulting from telling their stories. However, as was evident at the hearings themselves, not everyone present shared such predispositions. Audiences at hearings often expressed impatience with the commission's advocacy of forgiveness. Misgivings about the commission's activities may well have been more pronounced and more widely shared amongst those who did not attend such hearings and who were thus less likely to be influenced by their emotive qualities. Richard Wilson suggests that people's religious backgrounds were an important determinant of their willingness to support the TRC's vision of restorative justice. He maintains that those members of the now dominant political elite whose beliefs had been shaped by their membership of 'progressive' church congregations – especially those associated with the South African Council of Churches and the Roman Catholic Church – were particularly likely to accept the TRC's prescriptions as the expression of 'divine principle'.[85]

Not all churches favoured conciliatory 'transitional justice',[86] and its premises, Wilson suggests, were at odds with popular conceptions of retributive justice, which his fieldwork indicated appeared to have stronger support in the townships he visited after the commission had completed its work. Wilson maintains that the punitive judgments imposed by informal local courts in Boipatong township had been rather successful in addressing previous political conflicts and that public respect for the notions of order which the court represented had enabled former 'sell-out' councillors to achieve a degree of social rehabilitation through the court's protection. Communities 'dominated by an ethic of vengeance', he believes, would view the TRC's 'restorative justice' with disdain. Moreover, the TRC's operations may have helped to lower the public prestige of official agencies of justice yet further and hence contributed to sustained high levels of crime.

Understandably, the commissioners disagree with this view. Boraine believes that the liturgical quality of TRC proceedings was by no means imposed on all of those present. At the inception of the hearing into the Boipatong massacre, as the commissioners walked into a hall which a few minutes previously seemed to have been 'full of ghosts', they were greeted 'quite spontaneously' by the singing of a popular hymn. A religion of 'light and hope', Boraine argues, has afforded 'an enormous amount of comfort and security' to black South Africans.[87] Boraine also makes the point that the departures from formal legal traditions in TRC hearings – the space allowed for weeping and lament, for example – accorded with local public cultures of mourning and remembrance. Even if the TRC's procedures only fulfilled the expectations of attentive members of 'progressive' church congregations, such people would have represented a significant proportion of the township population. Time and again, the public resonance of the language of the Bible – Old Testament and New – was evident in the testimony offered by witnesses at the hearings.[88]

Various efforts have been made to measure public responses to the commission. One particularly elaborate exercise involved the exploration of the propensity to apportion blame or to forgive among a representative sample of 3 031 South Africans interviewed in late 1996 and early 1997 by researchers from the University of Stellenbosch. Subjects were asked to respond to a biographical narrative about Philip, a veteran of the political conflict. They were told either that Philip had been a member of Umkhonto or that he had been a security policeman. In each case he was said to have been responsible for killing people, but with differences in the degree of his moral culpability. Each respondent was offered only one version of Philip's biography. Predictably enough, the researchers found that black respondents judged Philip more leniently when he was an Umkhonto cadre and whites ascribed less blame to Philip as a policeman. In general, all respondents tended to blame Philip if he was in the position of giving orders rather than merely obeying them. Whites, though, were less inclined than blacks to believe that Philip the policeman could harm innocent civilians (as opposed to killing liberation activists). On the issue of forgiveness and amnesty, the researchers established that those who ascribed greatest blame were least likely to support forgiveness and amnesty. A minority of African respondents found Philip the Umkhonto cadre blameworthy (whatever his culpability in terms of his actions) and a majority favoured his amnesty. Inversely, whereas 75 per cent of African respondents attributed blame to Philip the security policeman and only 34 per cent could forgive him, 40 per cent supported his amnesty. White responses were more likely to favour amnesty in the case of the security policeman. Philip's political affiliations made no difference to Indian and coloured respondents, and generally a small majority favoured amnesty.[89]

Such experiments may not tell us very much about the long-term impact of the commission. It is probably true that the majority of South Africans disapproved of amnesty, although the minority who were inclined to accept the validity of indemnity in the Stellenbosch survey was impressively large. If the commission's members were more likely than the opponents of amnesty to be drawn from positions of influence (as Wilson suggests with respect to black South Africans), then the TRC's 'healing truth', its claims about reconciliation, may well become one important source of political legitimisation for dominant groups in the new South Africa.

More survey evidence is available from a poll conducted by a leading market research company, ACNielsen, in May 1996. In this investigation, as Table 9.1 indicates, support for amnesty was highest among black respondents and tended to diminish amongst richer and more socially privileged groups. Support for amnesty seems to have been strongest amongst those groups who Richard Wilson's ethnographic research suggested would be least predisposed to amnesty.

Table 9.1 Amnesty (1996)

Question: Once a person has told the commission about the crime they have committed, they should be given amnesty and not be prosecuted. Do you agree or disagree?

%	Black	Coloured	Indian	White	English	Afrikaans	Nguni	Sotho	Highest income	Lowest income
Agree	41.3	27.6	28.8	29.1	24.8	32.2	37.9	46.5	26.3	44.1
Disagree	35.6	51.3	60.1	45.7	51.3	45.7	35.0	36.4	50.1	30.5

A survey containing more or less the same questions and based on the same sampling procedure was repeated in March 1998. Respondents were asked whether the commission's work would enable South Africans to live together more easily in future. As Table 9.2 shows, black South Africans in both surveys were more optimistic than other groups. Their predominance in the sample ensured that agreement was more common than disagreement (in 1996 out of the total response, 46.6 per cent agreed and 30.5 per cent disagreed; two years later the corresponding figures were 39.4 per cent and 38.2 per cent). Predictions about the TRC's effects were more optimistic at the time it began its work than when it neared completion. Afrikaans speakers (who in this table include coloured Afrikaans speakers) were less likely to take a benign view of the commission than English speakers. Expectations of the commission's work were highest amongst lowest-income groups and might have been higher still in 1996 – this survey excluded farm workers, a group that had 'messianic' expectations of the TRC in 1996 and who were virtually bypassed by the hearings and statement-taking.[90]

Table 9.2 Public perceptions about the future consequences of the TRC

Question: Having the Commission means that all people in South Africa will be able to live together more easily in future. Do you agree or disagree?

%	Black	Coloured	Indian	White	English	Afrikaans	Nguni	Sotho	Highest income	Lowest income
Agree 1996	58.5	40.7	54.0	20.0	32.1	24.5	54.8	64.2	27.0	58.3
Agree 1998	54.2	26.4	24.4	11.9	19.6	13.3	51.8	57.5	11.9	50.2
Disagree 1996	20.6	31.9	34.8	51.8	42.4	48.8	20.2	21.4	50.0	22.1
Disagree 1998	22.1	48.3	55.9	69.3	59.2	67.2	22.7	21.3	69.3	22.5

Much the same distribution of positive and negative responses was evident when fieldworkers asked people about the commission's fairness 'to all sides and all races'. Opinion amongst all groups was less favourably predisposed to the TRC in 1998 than in 1996, though a majority of black and low-income respondents still felt in 1998 that the commission had been fair (see Table 9.3). Since 1996, sharp falls were especially evident in the proportions of white, Afrikaans-speaking and high-income respondents who felt the commission had performed its duties impartially.[91] These findings generally correspond with the insights supplied by other surveys. For example, the South African Quality of Life polls conducted in 1996 and in 1999 asked respondents to rank a list of achievements according to their importance as sources of national pride. Amongst black South Africans in 1996, the TRC was accorded second status – after the 'Rainbow Nation' – with 16 per cent of respondents giving it first place. In 1996 black South Africans assigned it second place again – this time the RDP was the first choice – but now it shared this ranking with sport. Amongst whites, who in both surveys viewed sporting achievements as their most important source of national pride, the TRC appeared to hold little significance.[92]

Table 9.3 The TRC's fairness

Question in 1996: The Commission will be fair to all sides and all races. Do you agree or disagree?

Question in 1998: The Commission was fair to all sides and to all races. Do you agree or disagree?

%	Black	Coloured	Indian	White	English	Afrikaans	Nguni	Sotho	Highest income	Lowest income
Agree 1996	68.2	50.0	65.6	35.2	50.4	33.5	65.0	73.1	42.3	66.3
Agree 1998	60.0	29.7	36.3	18.7	28.8	17.4	58.4	62.2	23.8	57.3
Disagree 1996	12.5	19.2	20.8	37.6	22.8	40.0	12.8	12.1	34.7	15.1
Disagree 1998	16.2	40.1	34.4	61.0	46.8	60.4	15.5	17.2	61.0	17.0

In general, black South Africans seem to have been more favourably disposed to the TRC than whites. Few whites were present as listeners at the Human Rights Violations hearings. Antjie Krog reports on a series of hearings at Louis Trichardt in which stories of 'witchburnings, zombies and bantustan brutalities' were recounted against the sedate backdrop of a cricket match on the field next to the hall; the audience inside the hall was entirely black, whilst outside the match spectators were whites only.[93] Disproportionately few whites were among the million or so viewers of national television's weekly special report on the TRC, and white radio stations in Limpopo Province dropped TRC stories from prime time after receiving objections from listeners.[94] Such objections seem to have come from farming families, a group who had been in the front line of the ANC rural guerrilla offensive in 1986 and 1987. But journalist Kaizer Nyatsumba also remembers an 'avalanche' of letters that the daily newspaper The Star received from white readers professing relief that an 'ugly past was being dissected openly'.[95]

Such reactions suggest something else about white responses which has engendered critical evaluation of the commission. As it focused narrowly on its mandate of 'gross human rights violations', concentrating on occasions when the state broke its own laws through the covert prosecution of a 'dirty war', the commission uncovered truths from which many white South Africans could quite easily dissociate themselves. A wider mandate directed at exploring the more general ways in which apartheid infringed human rights through legalised dispossession and institutionalised discrimination might have created an environment in which it would have been less easy for whites to deny their moral complicity as beneficiaries.[96] Opinion poll evidence appears to confirm white disavowals of responsibility for regime abuses. A survey conducted in July 2000 found that only half of its white respondents agreed that it was their 'responsibility as a citizen to contribute to the process of national reconciliation' (actually, only 16 per cent disagreed, the others were uncertain), while 75 per cent of black respondents recognised such an obligation. Only 18 per cent of whites felt that material compensation should be part of a process of reconciliation.[97]

Another variety of moral resistance to the commission's reconciliation function was expressed in the perception of the commission as politically biased. This view seems to have been widely endorsed by Afrikaners, at least partly because so many of the human rights perpetrators who appeared before the commission – policemen, soldiers and politicians – were Afrikaans speakers. In general, Afrikaans newspapers treated the commission with hostility,[98] making recurrent references to its 'witch-hunting' mission against whites in general and Afrikaners in particular and to Tutu's copious weeping of 'crocodile' tears.[99] The 1996 ACNielsen survey found Afrikaners particularly predisposed to agree with the view that 'The Commission is the ANC's way of punishing its opponents'; some 42.2 per cent of Afrikaans speakers concurred with this sentiment, about twice the overall percentage.

Immediate popular responses may not, however, represent the sentiments that are likely to make the most profound historical impact. Partly to meet the criticism that the focus of gross abuse may have distracted attention from the more commonplace effects of apartheid, the commission arranged a series of institutional hearings to explore the ways in which human rights abuse was condoned or tolerated by 'large numbers of enfranchised, relatively privileged South Africans'.[100] These hearings represented opportunities for expressions of atonement which might have assumed considerable symbolic significance had they been forthcoming from organisations with public influence. On the whole, though, the hearings into business were generally characterised by disclaimers that emphasised the ways in which companies were harmed by apartheid restrictions. Participants also drew attention to their occasional opposition to particular government policies. Interestingly, it was only the Afrikaanse Handelsinstituut (AHI) that was prepared to acknowledge self-critically its historical support of apartheid ideology – support, it noted, 'that was part and parcel of the majority of the white community's thinking at the time'.[101]

Similar hearings on the roles performed by different 'faith communities' elicited a grudging and selective 'confession' from the Dutch Reformed Church (DRC),[102] but this was not the whole story. The decision to make a submission to the TRC was taken by the DRC's provincial synods; in other words, the expression of its limited acknowledgement of its moral culpability for apartheid was the result of discussions that would have affected and involved many congregations. An attempt by Beyers Naudé and Nico Smit to obtain individual endorsement of a confessional letter sent to 12 000 churchmen elicited only 610 signatures but, as the organisers wryly noted, whatever their private feelings, most of the DRC recipients would have been unwilling to sign without official guidance by their superiors.[103] The comment itself suggests just how important elite responses to the commission might have been within the Afrikaner community. In this context, the AHI's self-critical reflections may have had a more broadly representative significance and the exceptional National Party politicians who expressed unqualified contrition may have been more influential amongst Afrikaners than their less remorseful colleagues.

The ambiguity of public responses to the commission complicates any attempt to evaluate the success or failure of its efforts to promote social and political reconciliation. As many of the commission's notables have observed, reconciliation is too complex a set of processes to be accomplished by a single institution and it is probably too early yet to tell whether it has begun to happen. Comparative experiences of 'transitional justice' in other countries may be more helpful in arriving at an assessment of the South African TRC's performance. Any such assessment requires a reasonable set of criteria for success. Truth commissions are probably not the best vehicles for arriving at the most rigorous historical conclusions, but if the record of the past which they produce is one that evokes agreement between groups previously in conflict with each other, then they have fulfilled a useful function.

Reconciliation, though, is a broader project than merely the achievement of a degree of social agreement about the historical record, difficult as this task may be. Comparative analysis of truth commissions suggests that at the very least such bodies should offer comfort to the survivors of political oppression and re-establish their faith in the state's propriety. These goals may be promoted through encouraging or prescribing material and symbolic reparations to victims as well as administering sanctions of one kind or another against their former tormentors. In a broader sense, commissions may aim to reconcile divided communities through evoking compassion and forgiveness between adversaries. Finally, and most ambitiously, commissions have sometimes viewed themselves as key agencies in a process of social and political 'moral reconstruction'. As nation-building instruments, through the advocacy of reforms and by their own exemplary behaviour, commissions may help to engender co-operation and citizenship around a new sense of shared political goals.

Since 1974, more than twenty truth commissions or comparable bodies have been established in the aftermath of oppressive government and civil conflict.[104]

Not all of them were conceived of as alternatives to existing judicial procedures; several were merely investigatory whilst others served the purpose of identifying different categories of offenders for prosecution. All, though, had as their primary function the task of officially acknowledging wrongdoing. The South African TRC remains unique in the inclusion of the administration of amnesty in its mandate. The South African amnesty arrangements are themselves unusual when compared to those made in other political transitions. In Chile, the outgoing military dictatorship was substantially protected by its own amnesty law, passed 12 years before its abdication from office, which provided a general indemnity for crimes committed up to 1978. In Argentina the new, democratic Alfonsín government in 1983 repealed a blanket amnesty issued by military rulers shortly before democratisation, but the successor administration under President Carlos Menem in 1990 pardoned those officers who had been convicted as well as those remaining on trial. In El Salvador in 1991, five days after a commission reported by naming various individuals for prosecution, the government swiftly enacted a general amnesty, though the authorities did implement the recommendations of a parallel investigation and removed a number of officials from their positions. In Uruguay, a blanket amnesty evoked such widespread social dissent that the authorities were forced to withdraw it. In Rwanda, amnesties are available for perpetrators of lesser war crimes, but to obtain these, offenders have to apologise to their victims.

The commission's mandate to administer the South African amnesty and its insistence on the condition of individual application and disclosure represented a creative way of addressing the amnesty requirement that arose from a 'pacted' transition. The South African transition terms also ruled out the possibility of the kind of 'lustration' measures favoured by 'decommunising' societies in Eastern Europe,[105] which involved generalised dismissal of senior functionaries. As a consequence, South African survivors can still encounter former torturers in positions of authority,[106] but short of insisting on apologies as in Rwanda, the TRC's amnesty procedures were probably the best way of trying to reconcile political expediency with at least a form of justice. Applicants were subjected to often hostile cross-examination, their applications were mostly rejected, and even those who were granted amnesty were subjected to a form of 'public shaming'. Compared to what happened in other post-transition societies, in South Africa the administration of amnesty has evoked only limited political opposition. In contrast to the Chilean commission, often cited as one of the more successful, the South African commission reported and named those perpetrators who had not applied for amnesty (mainly senior government officials and Inkatha officeholders) and recommended their prosecution.

Of all the commissions to date, the South African TRC was the best resourced. It employed more than ten times the staff of the Chilean body and had a wider investigatory mandate than many others (for example, torture was excluded from the Uruguayan and Argentinian investigators' concerns). The TRC also worked for a longer period than most, though not so long that the public lost interest (as was the case with the second Ugandan truth commission, which did not submit its report until nine years after being established). It was not restrained by the presence of a politically influential military establishment unreconstructed from the period of repression, as was the case in Chile. Though former generals treated the TRC with contempt and in general the military bureaucracy was uncooperative, the SANDF command structure after democratisation had been substantially altered through the infusion of guerrilla commanders. Thus, throughout the duration of the TRC's operations, there were no doubts about the military's loyalty to the new government. By contrast, military pressure subverted the authority of the commissions in Argentina, the Philippines and El Salvador.

Given its better resources and a relatively more favourable political environment to work in (excepting KwaZulu-Natal, where the commission encountered serious political opposition), it would be reasonable to expect the commission to have succeeded rather better in its reconciliation functions than comparable bodies elsewhere. While polling evidence does indeed indicate that the majority of black South Africans believed that the commission had been fair and had contributed to better social relations, this view was not shared by whites. A wide cross-section of political leadership had acceded to its establishment and a great deal of lobbying accompanied the definition of its mandate. A participatory process of establishing commissions is considered to be an important requirement for their effectiveness.[107] Perhaps, if the commission had been composed in a more deliberately politically representative fashion it might have generated findings that evoked wider acceptance across the political spectrum. Bolivian and German truth commissions were set up on an all-party basis, the Bolivian commission disbanding after three years without submitting a report. The German commission had the far more restricted function of overseeing the administration of lustration.

In South Africa, even with its predominantly pro-ANC composition, the TRC was often seriously divided by political disagreement and racial resentment. Scholarly and legal objections to its report notwithstanding, the publicity that accompanied the TRC hearings certainly increased awareness amongst white South Africans about the brutality of the previous dispensation. As Judge Richard Goldstone, one of the early advocates of a South African truth commission, noted, 'but for the TRC, there would have been widespread denials of the worst manifestations of apartheid, and these denials would have been believed and accepted by the majority of white South Africans'.[108] Court proceedings, Goldstone thinks, would not have had the same effect, and they certainly would have failed to elicit a comparable degree of media attention. Quite aside from television coverage and extensive newspaper reporting during the hearings, a substantial proportion of the TRC Report was published in supplements in most of the major daily newspapers.

The social impact of the commission and, in particular, the way its operations have been perceived by survivors of violations could certainly have been more favourable if the government had paid more attention to its prescriptions with respect to reparations and, possibly, prosecutions. The TRC sent a list of recommendations for prosecution which, to date, seems to have been ignored. In other countries, however, truth commissions have engendered readier official responses only in exceptional cases. In Chile, the surviving dependants of 2 800 abducted and murdered victims of the 'disappearances' between 1973 and 1975 have been granted pensions – an impressive achievement in a country with a resource endowment comparable to South Africa's. A copy of the report was sent to every family and the President made a formal statement of atonement on behalf of the state. The Alfonsín administration in Argentina was unusual in its willingness to prosecute, but elsewhere prosecutions following truth commissions have also been limited. In El Salvador, compensation remains unpaid in spite of its commission investigating no less than 22 000 denunciations. Despite reforms to the security apparatus and dismissals of officials, analysts believe that public expectations have been disappointed and reconciliation has consequently been impeded.[109] The public impact of three African commissions – in Chad, Zimbabwe and Uganda – has been reduced by official inaction and continued abuse of human rights.

Comparative international experience suggests that the South African TRC embodied a more ambitious form of official acknowledgement of wrongdoing than has been attempted elsewhere. The ritualistic dimensions of its activities probably did have a comforting effect on individuals and neighbourhoods affected by violence. More often than not, its activities seem to have evoked wider social approval, at least among black South Africans. The commission certainly endowed the administration of amnesty with a degree of legitimacy which it may not otherwise have acquired. Its final likely effect is incalculable but no less important for that. By compelling powerful officials and political leaders, both past and present, to explain the ways in which their organisations and subordinates behaved, the South African commission did establish a new benchmark for the public accountability of those in authority.

10 | CIVIC MOVEMENTS AND ASSOCIATIONAL LIFE

Despite an authoritarian state tradition there has been plenty of evidence of a lively associational life within black communities over generations. The apartheid state was not totalitarian; its retention of a racially circumscribed democracy as well as its own bureaucratic limitations meant that many areas of social life maintained their autonomy. Black South Africans tended to organise their lives outside the state rather than around it, and much associational life tended to compensate for the state's inattentiveness to their needs rather than seek control of public resources. Because of its lack of engagement with the state there was no particular reason why organisational life should always reproduce the state's authoritarian character. Colin Bundy has traced the formation in the late nineteenth century of early associations of urban Africans, led by modernising elites, representing freehold landholders, ratepayers, tenants and traders. Though they were dominated by local notables, Bundy shows how these 'Vigilance Associations' were increasingly articulated with a popular constituency through the agency of mass meetings, and they helped to nurture the popular political base upon which the African National Congress (ANC) constructed its political following in the 1950s.[1]

Of course there were rival, less democratic but more charismatic claimants to civic leadership. In Soweto in the 1960s, the Sofasonke movement of James Mpanza exploited the prestige of his credentials as a 1940s squatter leader to build a political machine that dominated Soweto's official municipal politics for the next two decades. This reproduced much the same hierarchy of 'big-man' politics which had existed in his shanty community.[2] Today, Winnie Madikizela-Mandela's following in the impoverished settlement of Phola Park supplies eloquent testimony to the appeal of highly personalised forms of charismatic authority. 'The Winnie described by the residents of Phola Park is strong and has foiled all attempts to break her spirit. She is the only politician who is accessible to that community at all times. She is their friend in need and in deed. A couple of people used the expression that they shared the same blanket, and ate from the same plate with her.'[3]

We need to know much more about patterns of community mobilisation and organisation before we can confidently assume that they are based upon horizontal strategies of mutual aid as opposed to the dependence of the weak on the apparently strong. But it at least seems reasonable to assume that today's forms of civic engagement have a long history. Though it took on fresh forms in the 1980s it may have incorporated older traditions, some of them democratic, others less so.

Optimistic predictions about South Africa's future prospects for democratic consolidation are frequently justified with reference to the strength of associational life, and in particular the vitality of a national network of local community-based organisations which made such a decisive contribution to the insurrectionary politics of the 1980s.[4] However, the extent to which such civic movements represented an expression of organisational culture that could be separated from nationalist politics was far from clear. Through the 1980s many local bodies were united in a federation, the United Democratic Front (UDF), which, despite its ideological complexity, served in certain respects as an organisational surrogate for the African National Congress. Many civic activists participated in the ANC's clandestine networks, and civics themselves were caught up in nationally orchestrated campaigns. This sense of corporate identity shared by local associations, and engendered by their role in liberation politics, found its institutional expression in the formation of the South African National Civic Organisation (SANCO) shortly after the UDF's dissolution. Though SANCO's brief history does not represent the totality of local associational life in modern South Africa, its troubled progress since its formation is illuminating in any assessment of the prospects for a political culture of civic engagement in South Africa.

SANCO was established in March 1992 at a launching conference in Uitenhage in the Eastern Cape. Plans for a national organisation dated from 1988 when the project was first suggested. A national interim civic structure was established after the formation of a 'watchdog' for the interests of community organisations was discussed at the UDF's disbanding conference in 1991. The new body drew into its fold a total of 2 500 local associations distributed between ten regions, which were later consolidated into regions reflecting the new provincial boundaries determined by the 1994 Constitution. The distribution of these local civics was very uneven. SANCO documentation indicates 750 civics in the Transkei, 700 in the Border (Eastern Cape) region, 300 in Gauteng and a modest 88 in Mpumalanga.[5]

During the launching conference delegates argued over the merits of a unitary as opposed to a federal constitution. In the end a centralised form of organisation was chosen despite objections from representatives of the powerful Southern Transvaal federation. This decision reflected a general perception that SANCO's internal arrangements should match the unitary constitutional arrangements which it was hoped a democratic state would assume,[6] as well as a fear that a looser federal body would allow the then National Party government to exploit divisions within the civic movement in its proposals to reform local government.[7] An executive committee was dominated by leaders from the Eastern Cape who were generally perceived to favour close alignment with the ANC.

The constitution adopted at the conference required that local branches should dissolve their own constitutions and refrain from any local negotiations with municipal reform bodies. Similarly, local fundraising should cease. Funds would be collected nationally and subsequently allocated to the branches. In practice, this has meant that in many cases local civics have had to depend solely on subscriptions and local gifts for their financing; very little money is distributed from the centre.

SANCO leaders insisted at the outset that the new movement should refrain from pledging loyalty to any party. As its president, Moses Mayekiso, put it, SANCO 'should be closer to the trade union movement than political organisations … [it] has to be independent of any political organisations … we must remain watchdogs for the community'.[8] However, at its November 1993 conference, SANCO resolved to support the ANC in the 1994 general election campaign, although vice-president Lechesa Tsenoli qualified this support: 'We are conscious of the need to co-operate where possible, but we want to retain a culture of being critical.' SANCO would continue, he said, to 'get [its] cue from local communities and not political organisations'.[9] As a consequence of its participation in the ANC Alliance, SANCO lost an estimated 70 per cent of its leadership to parliament and regional governments.[10] On obtaining public office SANCO leaders had to give up their executive positions. As a result, SANCO has had three presidents since 1992. A newsletter reported in 1995 that three of the most important regions, the Western Cape, Eastern Transvaal (Mpumalanga) and Border (Eastern Cape), were inactive or disrupted because of such resignations.[11] In 1997 it was decided to allow parliamentarians and local councillors to retain their elected SANCO positions: 'SANCO will as a consequence be better informed about major policy trends.'[12]

By the beginning of 1997 SANCO leaders were complaining of the 'extreme marginalisation of the civic by the ANC'. 'We don't want to be treated simply just as another non-governmental organisation that will be called upon to make submissions at the tail end [of policy formulation].'[13] ANC cabinet ministers, according to SANCO officials, had on occasion told the civic body to obtain permission from the ANC before initiating campaigns and establishing new local branches. In the ANC's view, SANCO should confine itself to the role of a developmental agency and cease competing with the ANC in the task of forging a popular political identity.

At a summit held in February 1997 to address the deteriorating relations between the two organisations, SANCO presented a report that referred to 'a looming breakdown of political linkages between SANCO and the ANC at various levels of our organisation'. Examples of this trend included the suspension of SANCO from the ANC Alliance in the Transkei and the closure of SANCO offices by ANC officials, anti-SANCO propaganda distributed in Limpopo Province, and the refusal by the ANC to hold meetings with SANCO leaders in Port Elizabeth. Resolutions calling on SANCO to play a more constructive role and on the ANC to be more communally accountable seemed to persuade SANCO's leaders of the wisdom of reaffirming their support for the ANC at the second national conference some months later.[14]

Despite such warm rhetoric at leadership level it was very evident that SANCO's capacity to influence ANC policy had diminished sharply. This was obvious in the contrast that could be drawn from the leading role it played in the Local Government Negotiating Forum of 1993, which produced the agreements for the constitution of the transitional local authorities for 1995–2000, and its effective sidelining in the 'mega-city' debate. At the 1997 conference, SANCO's president produced a litany of grievances, including the government's failure to involve SANCO in the launch of the 'Masakhane' programme and, less plausibly, the ANC's refusal to recognise SANCO provincial chairpersons 'as equivalent' to provincial premiers.[15] At the same time, SANCO's submission to the Constitutional Assembly for a radical decentralisation of government, with the replacement of provincial administrations by 200 district councils drawn from directly elected local committees, illustrates the gulf which had developed between its leaders' thinking and the ANC's policies on municipal government.[16] SANCO was overlooked again in 1998, when invitations were sent out for the tripartite Alliance summit in October that year – a telling signal of the downgraded status of SANCO as an ANC Alliance partner.[17]

SANCO's original conception of its role as a community 'watchdog' echoed the protest culture that had animated the civil movement in the 1980s. One of its first actions in 1992 was a call for a bond (or mortgage) boycott in support of the ANC's 'mass action' campaign, which accompanied the opening of the constitutional negotiations. This was also motivated by banks' decisions to 'redline' certain poor districts, freezing bond programmes within them. SANCO president Moses Mayekiso promised reprisals against banks and building societies that refused loans; this would include occupation of offices and pickets outside them as well as calls for international credit sanctions.[18] Mandela's subsequent disavowal of ANC approval for steps that might endanger future bank co-operation in housing projects may explain, in part, the dispirited response to Mayekiso's exhortations.[19] In any case, the initiative would only have reflected the direct interests of a tiny proportion of SANCO's constituents – those who had purchased their homes.

In 1993, SANCO signed an agreement with the Association of Mortgage Lenders. The rapprochement was short-lived as the banks were reluctant to pay for the salaries, cars and offices of 2 000 organisers whom SANCO wanted to administer loans and repayments. As a bank spokesperson later put it, 'the banks were not prepared ... to permit community-based organisations to position themselves as filters between the banks and their clients'.[20] SANCO maintained its stance on bond repayments, effectively ensuring its exclusion from the negotiations around the 1994 National Housing Accord and its non-involvement in the initial stages of the government's 'Masakhane' campaign, the initiative intended to persuade township residents to resume rent and service payments. In June 1996, SANCO threatened 'mass action' against banks unless they halted 75 000 proposed evictions of bond defaulters, citing poor construction and high interest on arrears as a justification for 'selective boycotts'. However, a disappointing popular response helped to prompt SANCO leaders to sign an agreement with the parastatal loan company Khayalethu Homes: it would end its support for defaulting householders in return for rescheduled repayments. 'If you want to be an instant revolutionary these days and be involved in boycotts, SANCO is no longer a home for you,' declared Mlungisi Hlongwane, SANCO's president,[21] in a message confirmed by Moses Mayekiso. 'Boycotts are yesterday's issues.'[22]

In place of direct protest action, SANCO increasingly characterised its prime function as serving as a key agency in development projects or, to cite its president's words, as 'a massive instrument of delivery'.[23] A strategic document published in 1995 described a programme of local development initiatives which would be executed through partnerships between local government, community representatives and the private sector.[24] SANCO was already involved in 'joint ventures with many companies and organisations who want to be involved in community development initiatives'.[25] Some of these have been on a very large scale indeed: one project in the Eastern Cape which the regional executive has helped to launch, planned to invest R147 million to improve township roads and water supplies.

Such undertakings are not without dangers, though. In September 1995 the Free State MEC for safety and security was reported to have instructed the police to investigate corruption charges against SANCO, the construction firm Stocks & Stocks and a consultancy, Ninham Shand Consultants. Both companies had tendered for a R60 million shopping mall in Bloemfontein. The tender board included two regional SANCO officials. Minutes of the SANCO Free State working committee meeting for 13 June recorded a discussion in which the concern was expressed that 'Stocks has been treated badly' and that this might jeopardise a R150 000 donation it had promised SANCO. A similar payoff may have been made to a SANCO branch in Vereeniging by another building firm in return for SANCO 'assisting with marketing of this project'.[26]

Even more well-intentioned commercial ventures carried their own risks. At the beginning of 1996, following the example of certain trade unions, SANCO set up an investment organisation, SANCO Investment Holdings (SIH). Moses Mayekiso resigned from parliament to become its chairperson. SIH was established with the help of Liberty Life, which acquired 20 per cent of the equity for

R1.5 million. Its intention was to focus on joint ventures with companies with which it would invest in a series of focused areas – privatised state services in the domains of cleaning, catering and security, for example. These would supply vehicles for black-managed small enterprises. SIH plans also included the construction of four entrepreneurial development centres, one of which was opened in the Eastern Cape at the end of the year. SIH was to operate a funeral scheme; its own capital contribution to this venture was to be financed through the sale of R30 membership cards to each of SANCO's claimed 1.2 million members. In return, members would receive a booklet of discount vouchers, supposedly worth R4 000. By mid-1997 only 5 000 such cards had been sold and the funeral scheme had already paid out 40 per cent of the funds it had raised through insurance premiums.

A second attempt to offer SANCO membership through a commercial entity, the JD Group, a hire-purchase furniture company, was equally disappointing. The company was issued with 90 000 forms, 10 000 for each province.[27] None were subsequently returned. In April 1997, reports of fraud and mismanagement of a joint venture by SANCO to sell policies on behalf of an American insurance group further underlined the difficulties the organisation was encountering in its efforts to develop a commercial base.

SANCO's shift into the business world drew heavy criticism from Moses Mayekiso's younger brother, Mzwanele. Mzwanele Mayekiso's publicly expressed reservations led to his expulsion from SANCO – a development which provoked the Gauteng provincial branch to threaten secession if he was not reinstated. 'Your handling of Mzwanele's Mayekiso's expulsion could have the potential to destroy whatever remnants of the working relationship exist between us and the national leadership.'[28] Four years later, on the eve of SANCO's third national conference, SIH's troubled finances were at the centre of a dispute between Moses Mayekiso and Mlungisi Hlongwane, both candidates for the organisation's presidency in the forthcoming office-holder elections. Hlongwane had complained of the failure to publish audit statements since 1998. Mayekiso suggested that Hlongwane, in collusion with a former financial manager who had removed computers and documents from the SANCO offices, was using SANCO's financial difficulties to mount a political attack on himself. In truth, Mayekiso argued, Hlongwane and other SANCO leaders were 'against him' because he had refused to pay for SANCO's office expenses, and this was the reason why he had removed bank accounts from the control of the SIH board.[29]

Mayekiso's comments may have touched on a raw nerve. Quite apart from considerations arising from its developmental mission, SANCO's business operations were motivated by a financial crisis. At the beginning of 1998, the organisation owed more than R1.3 million. SANCO's treasurer was publicly critical of what he described as 'the mismanagement and irregular financial goings-on in the organisation'. From its inception, SANCO had mainly depended upon external sources for funds: major donors in 1991/2 included the US Agency for International Development (USAID) and the International Centre for the Swedish Labour Movement.[30] In 1996 USAID ceased funding general administration, and eight staff members were retrenched at national headquarters. By 2001, only two paid members of staff still worked full-time at the national headquarters, and at least one province, Limpopo Province, had no paid SANCO offficials.[31] Most of its national officials depended on salaries from other full-time jobs. Mlungisi Hlongwane, for example, shortly after his election as president, assumed the directorship of a new telecommunications company with offices in Johannesburg's comfortable northern suburbs. Until January 1997 Hlongwane had served as mayor of the Vaal metropolitan council. His resignation from this post was apparently motivated by the perception that 'there was bound to be a conflict of interest in holding a key position in government and leading an organisation that is supposed to put pressure on local government to ensure that it is accountable and serves the people well'.[32]

Joint ventures may yet sustain the organisation financially as well as give it a certain authority as a 'gatekeeper', governing the entry of private development agencies into black townships. But this prospect is scarcely likely to enhance SANCO's moral stature as a community representative. Trade unions have expressed misgivings about SANCO's bid to take over the provision of 'outsourced' or privatised public services through its SIH operations. Some of its more localised forms of collaboration with private interests may also detract from its support. In Alexandra, the local affiliate helps to run a housing association that administers accommodation in unoccupied factory buildings, charging R200 a month for small partitioned sections. SANCO representatives had stepped in to collect and regulate rents after the factory owners had started charging the mainly immigrant tenants R400 a month. In taking over these functions, SANCO also inherited the conflict between landlords and tenants, who now accused it of exploitation.

Elsewhere, SANCO branches held back from becoming embroiled in tenants' movements, thereby creating opportunities for rival movements. In the inner-city suburb of Joubert Park, the Johannesburg Tenants' Association (JOTA) emerged after the general elections to organise the occupation of six vacant apartment blocks. Its leader, Moses Moshoeshoe, was a trade unionist and an Actstop veteran, as well as a former member of the ANC's Joubert Park branch executive. JOTA became strongly hostile to SANCO, reflecting antipathy between the national civic and Actstop, an inner-city movement which had opposed the formation of a centralised national body.

In Soweto's Dobsonville area, local traders were highly critical of SANCO's apparent endorsement of a shopping mall development financed by the SANLAM insurance group. Despite its claims to be the embodiment of 'people-driven development', the mall supplied no opportunities for small-scale retailers.

SANCO's efforts to redefine a role for itself have included the announcement of 'Operation Mpimpi' ('informer') as 'a gift to Tata Mandela' – an anti-crime drive in which information leading to the arrest and conviction of criminals would earn rewards donated by the Business Against Crime organisation.[33] It seems to have evinced little local interest and failed to elicit any contributions from Business Against Crime. SANCO officials themselves admitted in 2001 that the programme had never been 'institutionalised or operationalised' despite its rhetorical adoption by SANCO's structures 'across the country'.[34] In Moroka, also in Soweto, a revival of street committees by a group calling itself Youth Action Against Crime seemed to have no connections with SANCO's operation. In reality, SANCO and the civic movement which it heads have yet to identify a coherent sense of purpose. As its leaders admitted in 2001, for a long time the organisation had been 'unable to take up campaigns in a meaningful manner', partly as a result of 'the lack of political work done in the Organising Department'.[35] The community development forums, which were intended to be the socially responsive incubators of RDP projects, seemed to be increasingly bypassed during the late 1990s in the planning of development projects, especially with the government's emphasis after mid-1996 on efficient 'mass delivery' by large contractors. For SANCO the forums were intended to be the main focus of the civics' local economic development initiatives.

Significantly, SANCO failed to secure representation on the government's National Development Agency, a major conduit of donor funding for development and, as was noted at the third national conference in 2001, not a single SANCO project received any support after the Agency's establishment.[36] Between 1995 and 2000, SANCO's voice in local government was surprisingly muted despite the large number of former SANCO office-holders who sat as councillors, some of whom stood separately and in opposition to ANC candidates. Indeed, the insistence of SANCO's leadership during the negotiations over local government reform that 'the future of local government must be decided nationally' may well have discouraged the development of an independent vision among local SANCO activists about the concerns of municipal authorities.[37]

At its second national conference, in 1997, SANCO resolved once again to support the ANC in the forthcoming general elections of 1999. Moreover, it pledged its 'unashamed' backing of Thabo Mbeki as Nelson Mandela's successor. Notwithstanding qualificatory language about the possibility of reviewing the alliance with the ANC at some later stage, SANCO's identity as an independent and vital social movement organisation seemed increasingly questionable. Mzwanele Mayekiso's comments in an analysis of the civics published in December 1996 reflected the feelings of unease which at least some of its leaders had about the future of the movement. Civics, he argued, were in danger of becoming 'rubber stamp vehicles', driven by political parties with a principal function of merely supplying mass endorsement for conservative notions of development.[38]

Mzwanele Mayekiso helped to form a rival civic organisation in 1999, the National Association of Residents and Civic Associations. Two years later, in 2001, after his defeat in the SANCO presidential elections, Mzwanele's brother Moses announced the formation of a third national civic movement, the South African Non-Racial Communities Movement, claiming that the civic movement should not attempt to function like a political party and should eschew any political ideology. This position was probably calculated to win favour from ANC leaders. ANC officials could hardly have been pleased by SANCO's resolution at its third national conference in April 2001 that the organisation should adopt the posture of a 'revolutionary social movement', a course of action which should be 'confrontational and championing the cause of the historically marginalised'. The strategic document informing this decision reminded its readers that the ANC was not 'the sole owner and defining sangoma [diviner] on the national democratic Revolution',[39] though in its organisational report at the same meeting SANCO maintained that 'the ANC remains the only political party that SANCO wishes to associate itself with'.[40]

Though diversely motivated, rebellious sentiments spread through SANCO's structures towards the end of the decade. In August 1997, Gauteng branches were reported to be threatening a secession if Mzwanele Mayekiso's expulsion was not rescinded. An interim Johannesburg civic executive committee assembled itself behind the former Alexandra leader, its members including ex-Soweto civic president, Maynard Menu. Later, SANCO officials justified Mayekiso's expulsion on the somewhat technical grounds that he had tried to register his affiliated research organisation as a non-profit company without their approval. Mayekiso countered with the accusation that SANCO's leaders were seeking to control his funding and that, moreover, they had failed to provide membership cards and discount vouchers for the people who had paid fees during the recent membership drive.

Elsewhere, challenges to SANCO's hierarchy proliferated. In October 1997, the Transkei SANCO regional leadership announced its secession from the national organisation, citing its dissatisfaction with the organisation's ANC ties, promising to support independent candidates in the 1999 elections and complaining about the 'dropping of the RDP in favour of GEAR'.[41] The Transkeian mutiny came in the wake of a history of conflict between SANCO branches and ANC local councillors who were widely, and in certain cases – notably in Butterworth – justifiably perceived to be very venal indeed. Fanisile Ngayeka, the regional SANCO secretary, claimed that 'many SANCO candidates who were assigned to structures such as local government were blocked by the ANC', a perception which was quite widespread during the 1995 local elections.

Another source of ANC–SANCO tensions in the Transkei was the conflict between SANCO branches and chiefs. At the end of 1994 CONTRALESA, the organisation of traditional leaders, charged that SANCO members were responsible for the expulsion of certain chiefs and headmen from their districts, for occupying tribal authority offices in the Herschel area, for 'bypassing' chiefs by assuming the right to allocate land, as well as for 'hijacking' feeding schemes. SANCO's deputy president for the Border (Eastern Cape) region allowed that SANCO branches were often hostile to headmen who, he claimed, had no traditional status, but generally they respected chiefs.[42] The continuing tendency of the ANC to attempt to build its support in this area around chiefly authority would have accentuated SANCO dissidence.

In Uitenhage, the ANC–SANCO tensions that prompted the civic to nominate its own candidates in the 2000 local government elections had been escalating since 1997, when SANCO's regional leader, Dan Sandi, was replaced in his municipal leadership role by an ANC official. In May 2001, the ANC accused SANCO office-bearers in Uitenhage of plotting to assassinate the Eastern Cape MPL Elvis Bana. SANCO denied these accusations. Its representatives told reporters that Bana was 'threatened by the support SANCO was winning from the ANC in its efforts to combat crime'.[43] In January 1998, another potential mutiny against national office-bearers became apparent when the Northern Cape region demanded an inquiry into SANCO finances. Against this background, in 2000 the ANC published in succession two 'position papers' proposing that its own branches should assume the functions of the civic branches. This process would ultimately lead to the dismantling of the civic movement.

If the national civic organisation disintegrates or is absorbed by the ANC, what kind of social movement will remain in the wake of such a development? How lively and resilient is the associational life represented in the local organisations which constitute SANCO's affiliates? Are they repositories of civic engagement; that is, do they embody the networks that can promote the habits and values which make for good citizenship? Robert Putnam, already cited in chapter 8, and Francis Fukuyama both supply a set of criteria which can help us answer these questions.

Putnam contends that voluntary associations facilitate good government and economic progress because they reinforce habits of social compromise, the spread of information, mutual trust and collaboration, and an ethic of civic obligation. The more dense and overlapping the social networks in which citizens are involved, the more likely it is that they will trust each other, co-operate and develop the confidence to engage with government. The values and reflexes produced by associational activity are what Putnam terms 'social capital'. Like other forms of capital, it accumulates with use. Putnam believes that the networks that generate social capital must be fairly egalitarian. Vertical networks such as those represented in patronage systems are never fully reciprocal in their exchange of benefits or resources. Because of this and their authoritarian dimension, they cannot foster trust and other forms of social capital.

In the 'social capital' field Francis Fukuyama enjoys an iconic status similar to Robert Putnam. In his focus on social trust, Fukuyama's objective is not so much to explain the presence or absence of democracy, but rather the capacity of societies to 'create prosperity' as well as to undergo progressive economic change. An indispensable asset in this social predisposition is the belief amongst economic actors that 'they form a community based on mutual trust'.[44] This belief, according to Fukuyama, may spring from rather more complex considerations than merely self-interest. Solidarity within the community may have become an end in itself, a moral virtue prized more than economic benefits. Through a series of national case studies, Fukuyama argues that certain kinds of social structure are more likely to generate trust and solidarity than others. In particular, societies in which extended family cohesion remains strong are less likely to generate large-scale patterns of economic organisation. Such societies are characterised by low levels of social trust and ultimately encounter barriers to their economic development. They also experience difficulty in any efforts to democratise their institutions.

In certain respects, South African civics appear to resemble Putnam's ideal of egalitarian and democratic associational life. South African civic organisations and their supporters certainly perceived themselves as the expression of 'power in the hands of the people' – the agency through which people demonstrated their 'ability to run their day to day lives'. In its formative phases, the ideology of the movement was democratic and egalitarian,[45] and it continued to be so throughout the 1990s. The secretary of a new SANCO branch in Queenstown in the Eastern Cape supplied an eloquent expression of civic virtues when he described the aims of his committee. SANCO 'would be educating citizens on their rights and municipal by-laws affecting them' and it 'would endeavour local government to put a friendly face on Queenstown and make people feel welcome'.[46] In its organisational report in 2001, SANCO's leaders proudly maintained that the movement was alive and kicking at grass-roots level, with 'comrades at branches tackling all sorts of community and service issues'.[47]

There is plenty of local evidence to support such claims. In 1999, in Kwa-Thema on the East Rand, a SANCO branch claiming 'only' 1 000 'card-carrying members' led a series of sometimes violent protests – stonings and arson attacks – culminating in a well-attended march against the council to protest against its treatment of electricity-bill defaulters.[48] In Tembisa, a SANCO branch president, Ali Tleane, was deposed from the mayorship of the Kempton Park–Tembisa metropole for not paying his bills in protest against rate increases. Subsequently

SANCO led a programme that defiantly reconnected the electricity supply to residents who had been cut off.[49] Tleane later joined Mzwanele Mayekiso's dissident civic federation. In Mdantsane, outside East London, a SANCO rally on 22 March 1999 was held to protest against the violent behaviour of taxi syndicates. It was attended by 5 000 people and supported SANCO's call for a taxi boycott despite efforts by local ANC leaders to defer any action in favour of further negotiations.[50] In Witbank, in 1999, the SANCO branch campaigned for the removal of a corrupt councillor, vowing to 'ensure that it will strengthen the alliance with the ANC so that no corrupt individuals are enlisted into leadership positions'.[51]

Interviews with officials in civic organisations conducted as part of the Human Sciences Research Council's Social Movement Project have served to corroborate the impression of civic associations sustained by responsive followings and locally derived resources. Information collected in mid-2000 from officials in six SANCO civics in townships in Gauteng – Kagiso, Tshepisong, Wattville, Meadowlands, Spruitview and Katorus – indicated that local membership can vary between 25 and 'more than a thousand'. Three of the associations claimed to have more than 500 members. With the exception of the Kagiso civic, which received a small grant from the petroleum company SASOL, all depended for their finances on membership fees and donations from within their communities. The two largest branches, Tshepisong and Wattville, employed paid officials, as did Meadowlands with its 200 members. Membership subscriptions ranged between R15 and R35. At best, these officials would therefore have been remunerated very modestly. In its annual report for 2000, Wattville civic suggested that its membership had grown from 400 to 4 100 in a year. The report described a busy programme of activities, including agitation against Eskom electricity cut-offs, rather more successful efforts to secure pensions and disability grants, and effective resistance against evictions.[52] Five of the six branches whose officials were interviewed claimed to hold meetings for their members more than once a month and to be involved quite frequently in the more decorous forms of 'mass action': meetings, rallies, demonstrations, petitions and, more rarely, boycotts.

This emphasis on forms of protest which suggest engagement with political authority is itself suggestive. Officials who were interviewed perceived members to be largely unemployed, with ages ranging mainly from 20 to 55.[53] Testimony from such interviews does not substantiate claims about 'civil society in decline'. Nor does popular support for the civic movement necessarily indicate deep-seated political alienation, notwithstanding the emphasis in press reports on protest and SANCO–ANC dissent. In Duduza, near Nigel, the local SANCO branch was reported to be establishing 'area structures' in shanty settlements in anticipation of helping people to participate in the planning of low-cost housing projects. Through its local committees it was encouraging 'the community to pay for services to assist development'. In addition, SANCO would ensure 'that the local manpower and contractors get to carry out these projects'.[54] Civics could also perform a 'gatekeeper' function in lightly administered communities. For example, in Mpumalanga's Mosogwaba Tribal Trust, the SANCO branch had undertaken the task of dividing the community into sections, numbering houses and naming streets. The branch had been prompted to undertake this responsibility because 'companies like furniture companies and Telkom find lots of difficulties to drive around the area to do services … they approach our office and ask for help. If they cannot reach us, they fail to reach their clients.'[55]

However, the local functioning of these organisations has often reflected existing social divisions and inequalities. As noted at the beginning of this chapter, local social movements are often built around strong dominant personalities and dependent followings. Civics may as often be built around the vertical affiliations of patronage as they are constituted on the basis of horizontal notions of citizenship. Fieldwork conducted among yard committees, which constituted the base organisational structures of the Alexandra Civic Organisation (ACO) during the 1980s and early 1990s, revealed considerable differences in their social dynamics. In one yard the committee in 1990 was dominated by representatives or associates of the descendants of the family which historically owned the stand; these exercised authority through client relations with their former tenants. In another yard the committee was led by former tenants of a landlord who had never lived in the yard himself and with whom these tenants therefore had never developed any close social attachment. Here it was much easier 'for people to organise themselves into a structure based on an ideology of social equality'.[56]

Later there developed considerable tension between the ACO and the local ANC branch. ACO members stood as ANC councillor candidates in 1995 but their civic background does not seem to have made them any more communally responsive. In 1997 a researcher was told of a general perception that ward councillors did not bother to attend report-back meetings. ACO officials were moreover reluctant to use tried and tested protest tactics against the authorities. 'Yes, ACO can march against the ANC but the problem will be that the ANC has been chosen by us. So we will be marching against ourselves. But the point is there is nothing that is happening. And they [the councillors] are not showing us what we were expecting from them.'[57]

Fieldwork in Soweto revealed other organisational characteristics, which at least raise questions about the extent to which local civics represent reservoirs of 'social capital'. In Mzimhlope the local civic was affiliated to the Soweto Civic Association, a township-wide body with 45 branches. Like many other such associations it had no formal membership – everybody in the area was deemed to be a member. It held annual general meetings which were quite well attended but the same executive members tended to be re-elected each year. One of these administered an advice office, though residents complained that he was not even-handed, citing as an example his failure to report to the police a suspected murderer known to be a friend of his. Besides, he tended simply to note down complaints rather than take any action in response to them. In 1995 the civic did not hold a consultative meeting before preparing a list of its nominees for the Johannesburg council elections. Young people often spoke dismissively about the civic; apparently its leaders had brushed aside their suggestions about peace proposals in the conflict with Inkatha-aligned workers in the neighbouring hostel.

The links between Soweto civics and the ANC and its allies tended to prompt people to use other channels when addressing difficulties in which ANC-linked organisations were involved. For example, people in both Jabavu and Meadowlands relied on the Parent Teacher Association rather than the civic in disputes concerning the conduct of primary school teachers who were members of the South African Democratic Teachers' Union (SADTU).[58] In 1996 there were other grounds for discontent with the leadership provided by the Soweto Civic Association: its officers had failed to accede to branch requests for reports on the expenditure of R600 000 collected in various fundraising events.[59]

Different kinds of organisation have resulted from successive waves of mobilisation. In Leandra in Mpumalanga, the civic association built its following in the 1980s among the more urbanised residents of the municipal township, Lebohang.[60] The ANC, by contrast, established its branch among the more recent arrivals inhabiting the surrounding squatter settlements, who were at odds with the older residents over the allocation of limited resources. This conflict has been expressed by competition between SANCO- and ANC-aligned councillors for leadership positions. In this context, and in many others in which local-level SANCO–ANC rifts appeared in the course of the 1995 local elections, a multiplicity of associations tended to reinforce conflict rather than encourage communal collaboration through overlapping patterns of mobilisation.

The absence of such conflict, though, may not necessarily imply communal solidarity. A letter in a Middelburg newspaper referred to complaints of Mhluzi township residents who failed to obtain help from SANCO in difficulties with the local council. These difficulties apparently included evictions of rent and payment defaulters. (As noted in chapter 5, the Middelburg council was one of the most effective local governments nationally). Nor did SANCO concern itself with the plight of the owners of new houses, whose walls had cracked and roofs were leaking. SANCO ward meetings were increasingly preoccupied with ANC election campaigning and few people attended them. A new body, the Middelburg Mhluzi Concerned Committee, was gaining adherents.[61]

In Springs, SANCO opposition to new service charges imposed by the ANC-dominated town council had resulted in the formation of an alliance with the socially conservative Greater Springs Independent Ratepayers' Association in appealing against Valuation Board decisions.[62]

Anecdotal evidence is thus hardly conclusive about the degree to which local associational life promotes the social trust and civic virtue which Robert Putnam has suggested is such an indispensable source of support for democratic institutions. Quantitative evidence is also ambiguous. Ostensibly, South Africans demonstrate high levels of civic engagement. One kind of evidence that supports this assertion is findings from opinion polls which indicate popular participation in civic associations. Periodic polls conducted by the HSRC's Social Movement Project[63] between 1994 and 1998 suggest that public participation in the civic movement has remained fairly substantial since the formal establishment of a liberal democracy in 1994. Of the black South Africans who were interviewed in the samples consulted in the surveys, 8.5 per cent claimed active involvement in civic groups in 1994 and 8.1% in 1998. Across the provinces with statistically significant shares of the sample, heavily urbanised Gauteng appeared to have the highest level of active participation in civics amongst black South Africans – 6.6 per cent in 1994 and a surprisingly high 21.3 per cent in 1998. The mainly rural Limpopo Province had the lowest participation at 2.4 per cent in 1994 and 2.8 per cent in 1998.

These kinds of survey findings need to be interpreted with caution. They are at best impressionistic and, given the absence of formal membership structures in many civics, respondents' conceptions of active involvement might represent very different degrees of participation. However, other surveys attribute a similar communal significance to civics. For example, in the EISA/IDASA/SABC/Markinor Opinion '99 poll conducted in September 1998, respondents were asked from which source they got most of their information about governments. Nationally, 5.6 per cent of the sample identified their civics as the main source, making it the most important non-media authority after political parties (6.4 per cent) and family and friends (26.7 per cent). Amongst black South Africans this proportion was 7.6 per cent.[64]

There are persuasive signals, then, that within black South African communities, a particular kind of associational life is deeply entrenched. Moreover, in support of Robert Putnam's thesis, there are consistent correlations in the HSRC surveys between involvement in civics and perceptions among respondents that they could influence government. Civic activists interviewed in the surveys tended more often than those uninvolved in civics to feel higher levels of satisfaction with neighbourhood conditions, and also tended to reflect more positive beliefs about the efficacy of (peaceful) protest.

A similar finding emerged from the Democracy and Social Capital survey.[65] In this undertaking, data were collected during fieldwork conducted in December 1997. Nearly 900 people were interviewed across twenty townships by students from the University of the Witwatersrand. The choice of field site was opportunistic: to save costs students were encouraged to work in their home neighbourhoods during the vacation. Within each location, up to 50 respondents were selected randomly. Most sites were in townships and most respondents were black South Africans. In the survey, 41 per cent of civic activists felt that 'all had benefited' from recent government development schemes, a considerably larger proportion than the average across the whole sample, which was 29 per cent (though in both cases, half the respondents felt that the benefits went mainly to 'the well-to-do'). Positive correlations between civic activism, confidence in citizen's capacity to influence government, and perceptions about the government's commitment to general welfare seem to lend support to rhetorical claims by leaders of South African civic organisations that their associations and programmes embody the expression of 'power in the hands of the people', and that they are agencies through which people demonstrate their 'ability to run their day-to-day lives' and their empathy with values which are democratic and egalitarian.[66]

Where such organisations thrive, do they draw upon the reservoirs of interpersonal trust which Putnam and Fukuyama believe are so important in predisposing people to extended forms of collaboration? On this score, the evidence arising from opinion surveys is less supportive. The majority of residents interviewed by the Democracy and Social Capital fieldworkers in different communities around Johannesburg, where levels of activism are relatively high, disagreed with the statement 'Most people are basically honest' – a standard test employed internationally in surveys to establish degrees of communal sociability. The locations included Soweto townships, the Indian suburb of Lenasia, as well as two inner-city apartment building areas. In all these areas most respondents did not believe that the majority of people were honest. General scepticism about public honesty seems to have been more widespread among the Johannesburg respondents than in the other sites in which people were interviewed (see Table 10.1).

Table 10.1 Disagreement with the statement 'Most people are basically honest'

	Berea (Johannesburg)	Dobsonville (Soweto)	Hillbrow (Johannesburg)	Lenasia (Johannesburg)	Protea (Soweto)	Moroka (Soweto)
Percentage in disagreement	68	85	77	70	62	80

Yet, with the exception of the two inner-city locations, Hillbrow and Berea, the majority of respondents felt ready to participate in collective protest to bring grievances to the attention of authorities. Moreover, with the exception of residents in these two neighbourhoods, there was fairly extensive evidence of participation in civic association. Strikingly, lack of faith in people's honesty was most pronounced among shack dwellers (94 per cent) and most evident among young people aged between 17 and 24 (79 per cent). Both groups also displayed a higher-than-normal propensity for civic activism.

In comparable investigations undertaken in three townships in Mpumalanga (Balfour's Siyathemba, Middelburg's Mhluzi and Witbank's Lynville), a more benign set of perceptions was evident. In two cases, Balfour and Middelburg, the responses indicated a general belief in people's honesty. In Balfour only 20 per cent of respondents disagreed with the statement and in Middelburg 39 per cent did. In Witbank, a majority – 62 per cent – were in disagreement. In Mpumalanga, trust in people's honesty increased with age: only 15 per cent of the respondents over the age of 55 did not feel that most people were honest.

As the samples were very small, the evidence from this kind of investigation is hardly conclusive, but at least such studies raise questions about the extent to which social trust underpins associational activity in South African local communities. Conversely, these also look at the degree to which associational life itself encourages trust. And while SANCO civics and ANC branches (which functionally are often very similar) do not monopolise local associational life, they often constitute its most conspicuous ingredients. SANCO's inability to fund its operations from membership subscriptions is put into perspective by such financial achievements as raising R80 000 to build a memorial to an Apostolic Church leader in Katlehong. In such initiatives, apparently, 'it is nothing for someone, a wealthy taxi owner, for example, to give a R2 000 or R3 000 donation'.[67] Church congregations, *stokvels*, burial societies and sports clubs are all potential contributors to the construction of civic communities, and in some cases their inner life may resemble more closely the egalitarian ethos which Robert Putnam believes is indispensable in the accumulation of social capital.

The prevalence in South Africa of very small-scale associations such as *stokvels* and burial groups, constituted normally through the networks supplied by friendship, represents a dense matrix of associational life. People within such groups tend to trust each other,[68] but the intimate face-to-face sociability between neighbours which they engender does not seem to generate a broader sense of social trust. Amongst all the respondents to the Democracy and Social Capital survey only a minority of 36.1 per cent could agree that 'Most people are basically honest'. Amongst participants in religious or cultural groups that minority was smaller, at 29 per cent; amongst political party participants only slightly larger, at 36.6 per cent; amongst civic activists, 37 per cent; and amongst *stokvel* subscribers, 39 per cent.

Associational involvement, it seems, only fosters a slightly greater propensity than normal amongst South African township dwellers to believe in other people's honesty. Nor are responses any more trusting when the question is posed in a more parochial context. In addition to the question about honesty, people were asked if they agreed with the statement 'Members in your own community are always more trustworthy than others'. Only 21 per cent of respondents overall within the Soweto neighbourhoods concurred with this view. Discouragingly, membership of burial societies or *stokvels* did not seem to make any difference to the level of confidence in the community.

If adherents of civic organisations seem fairly distrustful in response to questions about honesty, they do nevertheless demonstrate a stronger predisposition to invest their energies in collective action. In the Democracy and Social Capital survey, respondents were asked the question 'If the road in your town needs fixing, do you feel it is best to make a personal approach to influential leaders, or is it best to form a group and state your demands publicly by demonstrating or using some other form of mass action?'. If the answers to this question are cross-tabulated against civic activism, the results do indicate a slightly greater susceptibility for collective action among civic members (see Table 10.2).

Table 10.2 Organisational participation and susceptibility to collective action

	Civic participation	No civic participation	All respondents
Best to approach leaders	58 (42.9%)	240 (47.6%)	298 (46.6%)
Best to form a group	76 (56.1%)	247 (49%)	323 (50.5%)
Don't know	1 (1%)	17 (3.3%)	18 (2.8%)

A propensity for collective action does not seem to depend upon a general predisposition towards social trust, though: 50.5% of all respondents agreed that forming a group was the most effective way of addressing problems, whereas agreement that most people were basically honest was shared by a much smaller proportion of the respondents (36.1%). As we have noted, participation in civic organisation does not coincide significantly with a trusting predisposition, it seems. In total, 36.6% of the respondents who had taken part in civic associations were inclined to believe that people were generally honest. This does not represent a dramatically higher proportion than the 32.4% of those who had not been involved in civics and who agreed in people's general honesty.

This absence of generalised trust may explain why the government has achieved considerable success in encouraging the formation of self-help housing groups among relatively intimate and small church-based *manyano* groups or street-based *stokvels*,[69] but has found formation of much wider community-based developmental initiatives, such as water management committees, far more difficult.[70] While mutual trust may not be an indispensable accompaniment or consequence of the kind of collective protest action around which popular participation in South African civic association has been orchestrated historically, it is probably a prerequisite for sustained community management of such large-scale undertakings as water reticulation. Whether SANCO branches serve as repositories of social trust or not, very frequently they find themselves in an adversarial position in relation to ANC-controlled local councils, so they are often non-participants in locally initiated development projects.[71]

In trust-generation, Putnam's argument stressed the importance of cross-cutting associational ties, ties which are woven by membership of a multiplicity of organisations, including those which unite people across neighbourhoods and have nothing to do with material concerns. These kinds of associations may be much weaker and more ephemeral in South African towns than in the civic communities of northern Italy.[72] However, the data in Table 10.3 from the Democracy and Social Capital survey suggest that individual townships contain quite an impressive range of different kinds of associations. Certain of these appear to evoke the extent of participation which make it likely that their boundaries and active followings overlap. These include *stokvels*, burial societies (both usually very small groups), churches and political organisations. A note of caution is needed here, though: Goodwill Ditlhage in his research on Meadowlands, Soweto, found that *stokvel* and burial society members generally did not support civic movements.[73] The Democracy and Social Capital survey data suggested that members of *stokvels* were slightly less likely to attend civic association meetings than non-members, though burial society subscribers were more likely to do so than non-subscribers. More conclusively, the figures do indicate that many people belong to a multiplicity of organisations.

Table 10.3 Civic life in South African townships

Civic association	Lenasia (Johannesburg) (%)	Moroka (Soweto) (%)	Kgomo (Lebowa) (%)	Mhluzi (Middelburg) (%)	Atteridge (Pretoria) (%)	Mamelodi (Pretoria) (%)	Makweng (Turfloop) (%)	Lynville (Witbank) (%)
Civic	9	18	18	4	27	26	22	14
Youth	18	10	14	9	20	18	18	26
Women	16	9	18	15	20	13	17	9
Trade union	0	12	31	8	33	9	16	21
Trader	7	8	8	0	3	17	7	13
Professional	7	10	0	5	14	7	18	40
Cultural/ religious	59	48	33	13	57	47	31	47
Political	15	29	29	8	56	48	28	25
Street committee	6	20	48	30	42	35	42	21
Stokvel	0	36	18	22	56	27	7	8
Burial	18	42	75	25	68	58	40	33
Sports	23	58	44	14	20	24	29	28
Student	12	47	15	18	21	33	14	29

If so many people are involved in such a range of associational organisations, then why do the inhabitants of these communities display such low levels of social trust? Putnam maintains that the kinds of organisations that make up the fabric of social life are a key determinant of trust. The associations need to be horizontally structured and depend upon truly egalitarian forms of co-operation, rather than on hierarchy and patronage. In his Italian case study, he therefore argues that neither political parties nor church congregations are significant incubators of social capital.

Such generalisations are less easy to defend in South Africa. The respondents in the Democracy and Social Capital survey represented a wide range of religious persuasions. Nearly half of the group belonged to elite churches (Dutch Reformed, Anglican, Methodist, Roman Catholic, evangelical) and the rest mainly to various Zionist congregations. Charismatic or prophetic churches are probably more likely to produce politically passive or authoritarian dispositions than the more institutionalised elite denominations.[74]

In respect of political parties, the South African situation may not be comparable to the Italian scenario in which, Putnam contends, electorally oriented parties have a mainly clientalised structure. In South Africa, during the 1980s, political and civic organisations emphasised the need for popularly accountable and mandate-bound leadership. At least in the case of the civics, this ethic seems to have been sustained quite strongly. For example, in September 1995 respondents in an HSRC survey were asked to agree or disagree with the statement that 'Popular participation is not necessary if decision-making is left in the hands of a few trusted, competent leaders'. Amongst ANC supporters, 40 per cent were in agreement and 40 per cent against, with 20 per cent being uncertain. Significantly 56 per cent of SANCO adherents disagreed with the statement and only 33.4 per cent were in agreement.[75]

Organisations may feature a democratic inner life and democratic attitudes among their followers but, as we have seen, they do not seem to represent reservoirs of social trust. These South African findings, incidentally, appear to coincide with research on social capital in other African contexts. Fieldwork in Uganda and Botswana indicates very low degrees of correlation between trust and experience of participation in voluntary associations and only insignificant variations of trust between members of hierarchical or horizontal organisations.[76]

However, though trust between individuals and within local communities appears to be weak in South Africa, there is a range of evidence suggesting that since 1994 popular trust in political institutions has been robust, especially when citizens evaluate the performance of national authorities as opposed to local administration. For example, a national survey in late 1995 conducted by IDASA found that 53 per cent of respondents were pleased with the conduct of the national parliament, though only 42 per cent had a similar degree of confidence in regional government. This finding has been echoed in the insights arising from the annual HSRC Social Movement Project surveys.[77] A 'Reality Check' commissioned by the Independent Newspaper Group discovered that 85 per cent of Africans polled expected 'central government to do the right thing', while smaller proportions of white, coloured and Indian respondents held this expectation. Across the whole population, confidence in central government was thus shared by 79 per cent of the sample. In this survey there were no significant distinctions between trust in central government and regional government.[78]

In the Democracy and Social Capital interviews respondents seemed less enamoured of this thought, although their responses were quite positive. The greater proportion in the sample (47 per cent) believed that central government was 'interested in the needs of people likely [my]self', in contrast to the 35 per cent who felt that central government did not care about their needs. Regional government fared slightly worse, with 45 per cent perceiving it as interested in their needs. Local government obtained comparable endorsements from only 40 per cent of the sample.

The weakness of social trust and the comparative resilience of popular confidence in public institutions may be difficult to reconcile with Putnam's understanding of social capital (or civic culture) as a causal factor in democratic performance. But in general, these features of South African political culture are in line with comparative work elsewhere on the relationship between civic values and democracy. At least one influential analysis indicates that variations in interpersonal trust appear to be irrelevant in democratisation and that low social trust can co-exist with public faith in gradual reform – that is, public belief in the efficacy of institutions.[79]

These relatively favourable perceptions of government are likely to stem from two sources. Firstly, there needs to be a genuinely reformist administration with a continuing capacity to implement 'basic needs' programmes so as to make visible commitments to improving material living conditions.[80] Secondly, legitimacy is associated with heroic leadership from an era of liberation politics. Confidence in central government is quite likely to be a consequence of an historical process of democratisation that had featured high levels of organised popular mobilisation. The less favourable perceptions of local government may reflect its minor role (by 1998) in the provision of the more successful basic needs programmes as well as the deterioration of municipal services that has accompanied the growing levels of debt in most local authorities.

Relatively strong and effective central government compared to fairly weak local authorities represents, of course, a rather unpromising environment in which to explore the connections between local levels of social capital and institutional capabilities. Putnam's arguments focused on popularly accessible and fairly powerful regional and local authorities.[81]

The legitimacy of national leadership has, for the time being, compensated for any administrative shortcomings in regional and local polities. While liberation politics may have nurtured legitimate authority and encouraged the assertion of popular rights and entitlements, such politics did not always foster liberal values of citizenship. The extent to which organisations such as the ANC or the constituents of the Mass Democratic Movement (MDM) were 'horizontally' democratic as opposed to hierarchical and authoritarian in their internal arrangements varied considerably. In many instances mobilisation certainly included an element of coercion. As we have noted, this does seem to have produced a political culture in which most people trust central government, a critical ingredient of citizenship.

In many localities, South African associational life is diversified and lively, but such local movements are not always incubators of the kinds of beliefs and habits that strengthen democracy. Often they reflect the inequalities within the communities to which they belong and the fierce struggles for scarce resources that take place in them. For a generation, at least, the moral aura surrounding charismatic authority may have helped to compensate for the weakness of trust between citizens, by helping to nurture civic engagement in South Africa. It will not perform this function forever, but its current credentials, which were conferred on it through the achievement of liberation, may represent an opportunity. This unusually legitimate authority can itself attempt to foster the patterns of associational life, which in turn can engender more sustainable qualities of citizenship that arise from communities of trust. It would be profoundly tragic if such an opportunity were squandered.

11 | THE AFRICAN RENAISSANCE

Since its appearance in a speech by Thabo Mbeki in June 1997, the idea of an 'African Renaissance' has increasingly assumed an almost liturgical status in South African public life.[1] Today, references to African regeneration are an almost obligatory feature of any major social gathering. A writers' conference in Cape Town in February 1998 was entitled 'African Literature in South Africa: Towards a Renaissance'. The guest speaker at a banquet held in Johannesburg in August to honour the businesswomen of the year called for women to assume a key role in the African Renaissance. The national director of National Adult Basic Education said at an adult education workshop in Mafikeng that 'the call to Africa's renewal for an African Renaissance was a call for rebellion'. Gauteng's Crown City, 'the heart of South Africa's coming Silicon Valley', on 3 May 1998 provided the setting for 'the African Renaissance show', a three-hour performance by the 'custodians of the legacy of culture' before a 'select' corporate gathering of three thousand 'VIP guests'.

The earliest public reference by a government leader in South Africa to an African Renaissance was made by Thabo Mbeki in his parliamentary address on 10 June 1997. He reminded his audience of 'the obligation to contribute to the common African continental effort, at last, to achieve an African Renaissance, including the establishment of stable democracies, respect for human rights, an end to violent conflicts, and a better life for all peoples of Africa'.[2] Two months before, in the United States, Mbeki had told the Corporate Council Summit of 'a new miracle' which 'slouches to its birth', an African Renaissance which 'may not be obvious' but which 'is upon us'. 'What we have been talking about', he went on to explain, 'is the establishment of genuine and stable democracies in Africa,' democracy supported by a generation 'which has been victim' to the failed systems and violent conflicts of the past. 'It is this generation whose sense of rage guarantees Africa's advance to its renaissance.'[3]

By the end of the year, commitment to an African Renaissance had become a 'strategic objective' incorporated into the programme statements endorsed at the ANC's 50th national conference.[4] An African Renaissance and International Cooperation Fund was established within the Department of Foreign Affairs to promote democracy and development across the continent, and the first of what is intended to be a network of national chapters of the African Renaissance opened its doors in Johannesburg in 1999.

From the time of Mbeki's address in 1997, two visions of an African Renaissance have predominated in the speeches of politicians and other public spokespeople. The first is the idea of modernity. The African Renaissance is something that will be brought about by means of fibre-optic cables, liberal democracy and market economics. A fairly typical expression of this view was the kind of rhetoric that accompanied a continental telecommunications conference in Johannesburg in May 1998. 'Global village', the 'information super-highway', 'cyberspace' – these were the phrases that were summoned to describe a brave new world in which African citizens would click their way into a new millennium of prosperity and progress.

Such visions are not new, of course. In the 1960s, hydroelectricity was the key element that would install a dynamic motor into the African political economy – power stations coupled with the rational bureaucracy brought about by the vanguard party and nation-building ideology. To be fair, today's modernist vision is rather more plausible. It springs from technological developments that are more accessible to ordinary people and probably do have greater meaning for their ordinary lives. It is impossible not to be moved by reports such as the story in a newspaper telling of small co-operatives of South African rural women who through basic computer literacy can now market their pottery, acquire information about farming techniques and teach themselves language and bookkeeping skills. These things are happening, and to those who are affected by them they are powerfully liberating. But we are a long way from such possibilities becoming even remotely within reach of universal experience, in a continent where about 1 per cent of inhabitants have access to a telephone and half of those who do must wait hours for a dialling tone. In the Ivory Coast, one of West Africa's more prosperous countries, of the 4 000 computers sold every year only a few hundred are bought by citizens and private businesses; the rest are used by government.

In its South African form, the African Renaissance as described in modernist rhetoric often allies itself with the confidence of being a regional power. At the telecommunications conference mentioned above, the relevant minister – perhaps unconsciously – echoed Cecil John Rhodes's famous ambition of constructing a communications highway, from Cape Town to Cairo. The Engen oil company, sponsors of a conference on the African Renaissance and owners of one of the largest networks of petrol stations on the continent, advanced the same vision in their projection of 'an enabling system called The African Dream'. Engen's programme deftly combines commercial interests with pan-African ideals in its intention 'to link the splendours of Africa through a continuous network of Afrikatourism routes from the Cape to Cairo – a route colonialists failed to achieve, but which is within our grasp'.[5] It is quite probable that unlike Rhodes, the authors of this African dream expect the traffic on these highways to be two-way. But this is not always the case. In the opinion of one influential newspaper columnist, 'Africa screams for a brave African nation to step on the plate and lead the continent out of the abyss. South Africa with its economic and political clout is the only country with the ability and the moral capital capable of doing this.'

Nor is this kind of thinking limited to local commentators. As eminent a scholar as Ali Mazrui called in 1996, at a conference in Johannesburg, for a 'recolonisation' of Africa, with the establishment of a system of trusteeship that would oversee the affairs of Africa's dysfunctional state system. Such a management function would be undertaken by five of the continent's regional hegemonies, with South Africa presiding over its subcontinental hinterland. Mondli Makhanya, writing three weeks before the Southern African Development Community (SADC) military intervention in Lesotho in mid-1998, cited this small enclave as but one example 'of countries in Africa which are ripe for recolonisation'. 'South Africa,' he continued, 'as the dominant power on the continent, should begin piecing together a coalition of stable nations which could implement this project.'[6]

South African politicians still regard such proposals with disfavour, but local businessmen have been less bashful. After South Africa, the continent's second gold producer is Ghana. Its swelling mining sector today features investment by virtually every significant South African mining corporation. Anglo American is now the largest investor in Mali; Gencor, the biggest West African mining operator, is opening mineral deposits in Burkina Faso. And this is true not just in the mining sector: in 1998 Telkom was about to resuscitate the Senegalese telephone system; Shoprite-Checkers has set up stores throughout the SADC region; Maputo's famous Polana Hotel now belongs to the Protea chain. As one travel writer put it as early as 1993, for South Africans Mozambique was becoming 'a paradise – recolonised'. Such power does not necessarily engender popularity or solidarity. A man selling T-shirts outside a hotel in Burkina Faso expressed his resentment of the visiting South African football team: 'They are not really Africans, they have their own plane, they bring their own food and water, and they think they are above the rest of us.'

The modernist vision of African Renaissance assumed a strategic dimension in the process of pan-African diplomacy during 2001 with the formation of a New Partnership for Africa's Development (NEPAD). NEPAD was originally entitled the New African Initiative (NIA), a declaration adopted as a 'leadership pledge' by the presidents of South Africa, Nigeria, Senegal, Egypt and Algeria. It combined two earlier manifestos, President Thabo Mbeki's Millennium African Programme (MAP) and the Omega Proposals drafted by President Abdoulayé Wade of Senegal. In essence, NIA–NEPAD argues that the behaviour of Africa's governing class will determine whether the continent will benefit from global capital flows. Hopeful signals are the adoption of liberal constitutions and the spread of democratic cultures sustained by 'voices in civil society, including organisations of women, youth and the independent media'. Development will depend on the maintenance of democratic government, regional co-operation and good 'corporate governance'. To compete in the global economy Africa needs to upgrade its infrastructure, especially in information technology, invest in 'human capital', and promote exports and economic diversification.

Sharp increases in inward flows of capital will be indispensable for the realisation of such objectives. In 2000 FDI inflows into Africa were below 1 per cent of the world total.[7] Increases will not be achieved as long as external investors perceive Africa as a high-risk continent, a perception that is the consequence of conflict, deteriorating infrastructures and weak governments. In other words, Africa's shortage of capital is a consequence of its political weaknesses and not intrinsic to its economic situation, the authors of NIA–NEPAD maintain. The solution to the continent's problems is the reconstruction of its own institutions. A Heads of State Forum will ensure that African governments adhere to a leadership code.

In certain respects, the NIA proposals represented a weaker set of commitments than those originally set out in Mbeki's MAP. Mbeki's programme paid more attention to the role that civil society could play in promoting democracy and suggested, in a much more explicit fashion than NIA, that the continent's progress could result from a partnership between Africa and developed countries which would be anchored in formalised mutual obligations. MAP suggested that a condition for membership of the Heads of State Forum should be good conduct. The NIA declaration is much vaguer on this issue and is also ambivalent about the relationship between the Heads of State Forum and the African Union, the successor body to the Organisation of African Unity. These shifts in content were clearly a consequence of the diplomatic bargaining that accompanied the fusion of Wade's Omega Proposals and MAP. The Omega Proposals emphasised the reconstruction of infrastructure, and Wade needed to be persuaded that participation in the initiative should be based on democratic behaviour,[8] a requirement which Mbeki emphasised in his original efforts to solicit Western support for MAP.[9]

Then there is a second Renaissance language which refers to heritage and legacy and suggests that the impersonal forces of modern bureaucracies, international markets and electronic technology can somehow be humanised and adapted to African needs. This is a renaissance in which African communities succeed in reconstructing themselves around tradition, legacy and heritage, around the values and relationships that characterised pre-colonial institutions and values. As noted in chapter 9, much of this kind of thinking in South Africa has focused on the concept of *ubuntu* in the last few years, the idea of humanness, of people realising their humanity through their interaction with others. *Ubuntu* was first given systematic written exposition in the novels of Jordan Ngubane, founder of the ANC Youth League, member of the Liberal Party and professor at Howard University in the United States. *Ubuntu*, Ngubane maintained, was the common foundation of all African cultures; in essence it involved 'a consciousness of belonging together'.[10] *Ubuntu* discourses have helped to generate a mini-industry. There are today *ubuntu* consultants, there is even an Ubuntu Institute in Pretoria which arranges seminars on such topics as '*ubuntu* marketing and public relations' and '*ubuntu* management'. At the Ubuntu School of Philosophy (held at the Rustic Pheasants Nest Restaurant, Tierpoort), the 1997 theme was 'The After Mandela (AM) Factor – Will *Ubuntu* See Us Through?'

A Human Sciences Research Council (HSRC) presentation at another such gathering suggests that *ubuntu* is more than simply a set of values governing personal relations, that it represents a sub-system which can supply the found-ations for democratic institutions. 'The remnants of the African systems have survived years of colonialism and oppression, and have been preserved by many African societies. Some of the practices can today be found in urban areas where Africans live, namely in townships and white suburbs. One need only drive around on a Sunday afternoon in any urban area in South Africa and observe African people assembled, some dressed in uniforms, discussing matters of mutual concern, applying the system of African democracy in their deliberations and association. Many African men and women belong to structures called *stokvels*, something akin to a credit society … Deliberations at their meetings are simple: everyone follows the discussion, resolutions are clear and all participate equally.'[11]

As eminent an authority as Constitutional Court judge Yvonne Mokgoro has argued that *ubuntu* principles could help to shape the future of South African jurisprudence. Key *ubuntu* values such as collectivity, unity and group solidarity could inspire realignment of the adjudication process so as to promote 'peace and harmony between members rather than the adversarial approach in litigation which emphasises retribution'. In a social order constructed around *ubuntu* insti-tutions, law 'is bound to individual duty as opposed to individual rights, demands or entitlement'. In such an order, Mokgoro believes, group interests should prevail over individual rights.[12] In this vein, the prison service in 2001 announced its embrace of a 'concept of restorative justice', a concept which, according to minister of correctional services Ben Skosana, is 'as old as natural law and African values' and based 'on the redefinition of crime as injury to the victim and the community, rather than as an effrontery to the power of the state'.[13]

Over the last four decades of post-colonial African experience there have been many other such efforts to recapture and institutionalise pre-colonial social ethics. In Tanzania the government's *Ujamaa* philosophy tried to base developmental initiatives on co-operative agricultural production in the villages, assuming that such collective endeavours corresponded with pre-colonial values of sharing. Less equitable or benign were the efforts in Zaïre of constructing a state ideology around notions of African authenticity, in which the Mobutu personality cult, a bizarre amalgamation of African patriarchy combined with the vocabulary of French revolutionary republicanism, was instituted as a civil religion in place of Roman Catholicism. Kenneth Kaunda's philosophy of humanism was a more kindly effort to translate the egalitarian ethos of village life into a modern socialist public policy. In Botswana, government spokespeople suggest that the endurance of the pre-colonial *kgotla*, the consensual elders' council, supplied the essential fabric of the country's democratic life and helped to explain the survival of multi-party democracy.

Indeed, there is plenty of evidence to suggest that many social arrangements and the ideas that animate them continue to have more meaning for ordinary people than the bureaucracies introduced by colonial conquerors or the economic ethics promoted by the market economy. In many areas of West Africa, traditional secret societies have reappeared, after a long period of dormancy following their persecution by different colonial administrations. In Sierra Leone, youth joined the Poro societies upon initiation and these provided, through horizontally linked age-sets, a form of communal sanction on chiefs who abused their power. With the collapse of local administration in many parts of the countryside, Poro societies are reassembling. They and traditional occupational brotherhoods have provided the local militias which have helped to oust the Koroma military dictatorship.

There are plenty of other examples of the resuscitation of traditional networks and their enlistment in democratic causes: the role of spirit mediums in Zimbabwe's Chimurenga, or war of liberation; the messianic Naparama movement of Mozambique, which fought alongside FRELIMO regulars in the war against Renamo; and the Mai Mai guerrillas of the eastern Congo, who have fought every Kinshasa government from 1965 until the present. How such forms of associational life can be integrated into structures of government that can perform national developmental functions is a conundrum that continues to haunt African state-makers: Yoweri Museveni's 'no party' democracy is just the latest in a succession of efforts trying to address the particularistic and localised character of conceptions of community in many parts of Africa.[14]

Neither the modernist concept nor the heritage notion of Renaissance is completely plausible as a political programme. The modernist discourse assumes that technology and markets and even prescriptions of government are neutral or ideologically colourless, whereas they are not. They express relationships of power and domination, and engagement with them need not be empowering. They often assume an administrative capacity in government and other institutions which simply is not present in many parts of the continent. Even in South

Africa, which is governed by a more capable administration than many, the limits of what government can manage are rather obvious. This is evident in its achievements as much as its failures. The provision of piped water to two million rural people through public taps represented for the minister of water affairs, Kader Asmal, a 'unique achievement even by world standards'.[15] The hyperbole is understandable in its context, but in fact the achievement is paralleled by the efforts of the Tanzanian administration in the early 1970s and falls well short of what Victorian municipal engineers installed in British cities a hundred years ago. One should keep in mind also the regression which has featured in the history of many post-colonial African countries: in Congo, for example, the road system is now only 20 per cent of its extent at independence in 1960; in Ghana it took ten years from 1984 to restore roads to the state they had been in 1957.

Quite aside from the issues of relative state capacity across the countries of the continent, the degree to which African leaders share Mbeki's vision of a democratising continent developing in partnership with the industrial West is rather questionable. This remains the case despite the separate endorsements Mbeki's MAP received at gatherings of the OAU, the G-8 countries and the European Union. Despite the African Union's constitutional undertakings in favour of 'democratic principles, popular participation and good governance',[16] a reformist grouping within the union, led by the original NIA progenitors, compete for influence with what one analyst has called a 'counter-revisionist bloc wedded to an authoritarian status quo'. This group includes Libya, Zimbabwe, Ivory Coast and Burkina Faso.[17] In January 2001 only seven countries out of 54 potential member states had ratified the union's treaty, although 37 had signed it provisionally.[18]

More worrying is the wavering within the reformist group to which South Africa belongs, to make a strong commitment to democratic principles. South Africa's most powerful ally, Nigeria, is sharply divided over the merits of a secular constitutional democracy, with several northern states having introduced Sharia law despite opposition from the federal government and from non-Muslims within their own borders. Nigerian official support for NIA–NEPAD is low-key in comparison to South Africa's, and the head of the Nigerian planning commission, Isaac Aluko Olokun, disagrees with the South Africans on the question of whether African countries can be excluded from membership, a key consideration for backing by the G-8 countries and the European Union.[19] In Europe and the United States, official perceptions of the sincerity of African commitment to NEPAD's principles are likely to be influenced by the efforts of continental political leadership – especially those 15 heads of state on the NEPAD implementation committee – to sanction non-compliance. In this context Zimbabwe is likely to represent a test case.

External evaluations of African diplomacy, in general, with respect to Zimbabwe's progressive abandonment of constitutional order, and of South

Africa's efforts in particular, are likely to be very critical. South African attempts to induce a return to liberal government in Zimbabwe through 'soft diplomacy', to quote Trevor Manuel, were influenced by earlier experience of the failure of more aggressive promotion of human rights values, which minister of foreign affairs Alfred Nzo insisted in 1994 were the 'cornerstone' of South African foreign policy. At least with respect to Africa, such values remain important to South Africa, not least because the government recognises their significance in conditioning external perceptions of investor risk in the continent.

In 2001, South Africa turned down the prospect of an extremely attractive trade and oil exploration agreement with Sudan, citing reservations about that country's human rights record.[20] However, the failure to elicit African support for sanctions against the Abacha administration in Nigeria (which taunted Mandela's government as 'token black leaders of this white country') convinced ANC foreign policy specialists that in future 'there is no way in which South Africa and the ANC can stand alone and outrightly condemn [without consulting other African countries]'. As Mavivi Myakayaka-Manzini, head of the ANC international affairs desk, explained, 'We did that in Nigeria ... and what happened? Everybody stood aside and we were isolated ... we acted as this bully ... people resent being bullied.'[21] South African concern not to be perceived as a bully is especially pronounced in the SADC region, where historical memories of Pretoria's support for insurgent movements reinforce continuing resentment of asymmetrical trade relations and restrictive immigration policies.

In the second half of 2001, the comradely fraternity ('relations sealed in blood', to quote Myakayaka-Manzini) that characterised early party-to-party attempts to influence the Mugabe administration was no longer so evident. Thabo Mbeki and his ministers occasionally gave cautious expression to their mounting alarm at events across the Limpopo.[22] Even so, South Africa remained determined to induce change in Zimbabwe through collective African persuasion, in particular from President Olusegun Obasanjo and the SADC foreign ministers.[23] At the same time South African diplomacy efforts were directed – with some success – at soliciting foreign financial support for properly administered land reform in Zimbabwe in return for compliance with the terms of the Abuja agreement, in which Zimbabwe undertook in September to end illegal land invasions. By the end of that year, after three months of continuing land seizures and state-instigated political violence, even such senior ANC insiders as the president's brother, Moeletsi Mbeki, were calling for a tougher approach north of the Limpopo. But such calls went unheeded by a ministerial SADC delegation that visited Harare in December. In its final communiqué it found itself able to 'welcome the improved atmosphere of calm and stability'.[24] Shortly afterwards, the ANC dispatched a delegation to Harare for talks with leaders of Mugabe's ruling ZANU-PF party. It is unlikely that the Zimbabwean officials viewed its arrival with much apprehension, for even before its departure the delegation's leader, Mosiuoa Lekota, pronounced himself to be 'deeply satisfied' with the explanations he had been given for the Zimbabwean government's decision to ban the presence of foreign poll monitors during the forthcoming presidential elections.

In the absence of Western support for Mbeki's modernist vision (investment inflows into Africa have continued to decline since the 1990s), national reinvention of tradition may acquire fresh adherents. Looking to the past is all the more tempting in a continental environment in which many of the institutions introduced through colonialism – infrastructure, bureaucracies, notions of borders and nationality – have disintegrated. To prescribe reconstruction by reverting to traditional values rests on questionable premises, though. Firstly, it assumes that these values are uniformly useful across society and, secondly, that they are universally prevalent. Thirdly, it supposes that people are unable to adjust their beliefs and practices in response to changed circumstances and external forces.

There is nothing wrong with codes of behaviour such as *ubuntu*. The concept expresses a compassionate social etiquette which, if everybody adhered to it, would make life most agreeable. It might prove quite difficult, though, to reconstruct a political order on the basis of collective solidarity rather than civil liberties. Besides, not all traditional belief systems are egalitarian or benign. What constitutes tradition is always a contested issue, but tradition is often invoked to justify oppression and cruelty. Whether the tradition that is invoked existed or not is a rather academic question. Tradition is summoned to justify the persecution of homosexuals in Zimbabwe and many other places; tradition is used to defend the absence of democratic representation in Swaziland as well as the extraordinary royal investment corporation, the Tibiyo Taka Nqwana; tradition is used to justify the minor status of South African women in the former homelands; and tradition is employed whenever African rulers arrogate power and resources to themselves and their clients.

The invocation of tradition ignores the extent to which Africa has changed. Today, half of the continent's population lives in towns, not in villages or homesteads, and in circumstances in which traditional ideas of reciprocity and social responsibility are very difficult to sustain. Within the first decade of the twenty-first century it is likely that most Africans will speak English, not just as an occasional medium of communication in the workplace but as the language of everyday life.[25] Television has become accessible to even the poorest urban communities. Transcontinental patterns of trade and migration are also beginning to reshape African notions of distance, locality and community. Consider, for example, the ten thousand Nigerians who live and work in Johannesburg, or the tens of thousands of Congolese who keep South Africa's public health system functioning, or the street market vendors who sell Ethiopian prayer scrolls to wealthy suburbanites. Consider, too, the case of the Samburu warriors of Kenya, a pastoral people whose local economy depended upon cattle herding and whose homesteads subsisted on cash incomes of a few hundred rands a year – until 1992, that is, when many people were recruited for a UN peacekeeping force and dispatched to Bosnia. Here they earned US$4 500 a month, money that was later to be invested in bottlestores and teashops. Here was a new entrepreneurial elite shaking loose the community bonds of a society built around cattle and grass.

Not that the capacity of people to embrace new ideas need be corrupting or destructive. East of Nairobi is the Machakos district, described by a British colonial soil inspector in the 1930s as a dustbowl, 'an appalling example of environmental degradation ... in which the inhabitants are rapidly drifting to a state of hopeless and miserable poverty and their land to a parched desert of rocks and stones and sand'. Since then, the population has risen five times, and today the landscape is a green garden of fertility and industry, from which farmers export mangoes to the Middle East, supply coffee to the breakfast tables of Europe and grow most of the tomatoes consumed in Nairobi. The change came about through the experiences of African soldiers who served in India during World War Two. They returned home inspired by the terraced hillsides they had fought across in the Eastern Theatre and determined to imitate the technique locally.[26] Terracing had been advocated and implemented by British colonial bureaucracies in more than a dozen African colonies. The difference was that in this part of Kenya the technique was adopted by local people and adapted to their environmental and social needs, rather than imposed upon them.

In the Machakos experience, women have played an increasingly important role in agricultural innovation. This is another point that deserves emphasis: over the last century in African communities, time and again the division of labour and the relationship between genders and generations have changed. With these changes there have been shifts in values, ideas, knowledge and power. In such a context, trying to reconstruct tradition is misguided. There is no such thing as one fixed set of traditions. Even if there were, they might not be very useful. Contemporary African philosophers such as Cameroon's Marcien Towa and Benin's Paulin Hountondji concur that 'the traditional values of African societies cannot justly be characterised as philosophy in the sense of a systematic methodology applied to defined areas of analysis such as logic or ethics'. In this vein, Kwasi Wiredu of the University of Ghana writes disparagingly of 'the spectacle of otherwise enlightened Africans pouring libations to the spirits of their ancestors ... That our departed ancestors continue to hover around in some rarefied form ready now and then to take a sip of the ceremonial schnapps is a proposition that I have never heard rationally defended.'[27]

In South Africa, public calls for an African Renaissance are quite rightly understood to imply a process of political, economic and cultural re-engagement of the country with the rest of the continent, as well as a process of recognition of South

Africa's identity as African. What being African means has become a key preoccupation of Renaissance commentators. For Thabo Mbeki, Africans are those people who view the continent as their home in the fullest emotional sense. 'I am an African,' he told the Constitutional Assembly on 8 May 1996. 'I owe my being to the Khoi and San ... I am formed of the migrants who left Europe to find a new home on our native land ... I am the grandchild of the warrior men and women that Hintsa and Sekhukhune led ... I am the grandchild who lays fresh flowers on the Boer graves at St Helena.' 'Afrikaners are Africans,' he reminded a meeting of the Afrikanerbond three years later, adding that 'binary oppositions' of the past, such as black and white, Africa versus Europe, and conquered and conqueror, should be discarded.[28]

For other authorities, however, finding one's home in Africa means more than a sense of shared history. For Sipho Seepe, a principal at Vista University, 'one's geographical location should not be collapsed and confused with one's cultural orientation'.[29] 'Declaring oneself an African', William Malegapuru Makgoba maintains, is not 'simply being located in Africa'. Makgoba believes that whereas there is 'no need to entertain a genetic cause of African thought', amongst all authentically African cultures 'there are profound and prolonged areas of convergence' and that 'there is something specific and particular about African thought processes'. These, he thinks, include *ubuntu*, 'looking at things holistically, looking for meaning and symbolism in phenomena, consensus or group identity' and 'the inclusion of the unseen or spiritual dimension of life'.[30] Presumably, those who do not share such 'thought processes' are not African.

The West African writer Kwesi Kwaa Prah, now based at the University of the Western Cape, is even less shy of essentialist conceptions of African identity: 'the fact that most South Africans or people of African historical or cultural descent are black is only one characteristic, a bonus which generalises and typifies Africans.' But while he argues that 'colour has become an easy and fortunate identifying attribute of most people who regard themselves as African', he insists that 'culture, history and attachment to these and consciousness of identity and not skin colour, primarily define the African'.[31]

In practice, though, cultural conceptions of African identity are often accompanied by a racial emphasis. The Gauteng premier, Mathole Motshekga, in addressing an African Renaissance conference in Midrand, took as his theme the concept of *kara*, an idea, he said, which was to be found in many African languages. *Kara*, Motshekga told his audience, was a root word for the name of God, the same God who made the sun. 'There is therefore a close relationship between the way Africans saw God, the creator of all things, and the life-giving force of light we call sunlight. African people are people baked by the sun, while *kara* is a word for divinity.'[32]

Proclamations of an African Renaissance are neither original nor new.[33] As early as 1937 Nnamdi Azikiwe, the future president of Nigeria, published his intellectual manifesto, *Renascent Africa*.[34] Azikiwe was one of the first African leaders to recognise the political opportunities represented by generational consciousness. His contention 'that youth is the sine qua non in the political evolution of the various nations of the world' inspired a legion of youth movements which assumed the leadership of nationalist organisations across the continent, from Cairo to Johannesburg. Leonard Barnes, a former British civil servant, in his *African Renaissance*,[35] written shortly before the victory of revolutionary peasant insurgencies in Portuguese Africa, perceived the best prospects for an African rebirth to be in a rurally oriented African socialism. His prescriptions included disengagement from world markets, planned village settlement, and limits on urbanisation to counter 'the menace of the towns'. In this vision Sékou Touré's Guinea offered the most instructive lessons of 'peasant truth'. Nearer to home, in Hammanskraal outside Pretoria, a Black Renaissance Convention assembled in 1974 'to re-examine our cultural heritage in the light of modern and contemporary developments'.[36] The intellectual genealogy of Mbeki's deployment of the Renaissance concept may also include a speech by Malaysia's prime minister, Mahathir Mohamad, delivered at the beginning of 1997, shortly before Mbeki's visit to the Federation, in which the Malaysian leader referred to an 'Asian Renaissance' constructed on the foundations of information technology and Islamic social principles.

Calls for an African Renaissance punctuate the history of the continent's intellectual community, although such exhortations may today have a much wider and more socially profound impact. What is historically unprecedented about Mbeki's optimistic vision is that it is reinforced not just by the authority of the South African state but also by the corporate culture of Africa's most powerful economy. A journalist's description of a 'Celebration of the African Renaissance' sponsored by the South African Broadcasting Corporation underscores this point: 'From the moment one walked into the expansive foyer illuminated by a score of flaming torches on tripods, you could feel you were in for a different experience. The atmosphere was exotic, understated and quintessentially African, and the music was quiet, rhythmic and soothing ... each table had as its centrepiece an African footstool, depicting tradition. An arrangement of thornbush and porcupine quills conveyed Africa's rustic nature and the wealth of its animal life. A giant protea in the centre of the quills and thorns symbolised the beauty of Africa, according to a page headed "table detail." The banquet hall was flanked by huge murals of San rock-paintings with cubes of African thornbush signifying "A new Africa dawning."'[37]

After a 'multimedia' stage show, those in attendance watched a live television transmission of Thabo Mbeki's latest oration. On departure each guest received a bound copy of Mbeki's seminal speeches encased in a wooden box in the shape of a book with a hinged cover. Quite aside from the aesthetic vulgarity of these arrangements, this final conferment of canonical authority on Mbeki's texts is a little alarming. Personality cults, no matter how benign, are an African tradition quite difficult to reconcile with the tenets of democracy. Notwithstanding the fact that Mbeki grounds his Renaissance concept in democratic values, culturally specific projections of African regeneration can have an authoritarian dimension. Mokgoro's communal *ubuntu* jurisprudence, however humane its intention, is one example of this tendency.

South Africa's rebirth as 'a member of the African family' has clearly animated the collective imagination of the South African 'Afrostocracy' specifically, and members of the new black middle class more generally. A rise in 'African pride' is signalled by the rhetorical promotion of 'an African intellectual base', the exaltation of ethnic *haute couture*, and a trend towards employing 'vowel English', the pronunciation of English using mother-tongue vowel sounds.[38] The organisation of a Kwanzaa carnival in Johannesburg in December 2001, as a 'celebration of African heritage', is a reminder of just how complicated the reconstitution of tradition can be. Kwanzaa was first celebrated in Los Angeles by African Americans who believed that they were adapting a Yoruba harvest ritual. In a less self-conscious vein, African indigenous churches are recruiting fresh support from 'street-wise and sophisticated township people, [who] kneel in front of old rural Shembe men, who a few years ago would have been objects of scorn and prejudice that is often associated with the urban–rural divide'. Today, Shembe and other Zionist churches represent to their new converts 'an identity that draws on tradition to reinvent Africanness'.[39]

What is one to make of Mbeki's Renaissance? It is striking how within a very short time it has assumed the status of a collective discourse, articulating a sense of social purpose within South Africa's new intellectual and business leadership. Its advent followed four years of very rapid expansion of a new entrepreneurial and managerial class. Evidence of this trend includes the accelerating black share of market capitalisation on the Johannesburg Stock Exchange, from 11 black-owned companies worth R4.6 billion in September 1995 to 28 companies representing a capitalisation of R66.7 billion, 10 per cent of the total shareholdings listed in February 1998.[40] In the civil service Africans filled 30 per cent of managerial posts by 1996, compared with only 2 per cent in 1994.[41] Between 1994 and 1997, the number of black South Africans earning more than R5 000 a month jumped by 52 per cent, from 310 000 to 472 000.[42] Significantly, Thami Mazwai, the proprietor of Mafube (South Africa's first black-owned publishing house), presides over the South African chapter of the African Renaissance. In his words, the company represents 'a monument for the black community'. A leading pan-Africanist and advocate of 'patriotic journalism', Mazwai combines robust defence of capitalism with antipathy to the 'conservative liberal establishment'.[43]

In December 2001, the South African chapter was reported to be in financial difficulties. Few donations had materialised from the local business sector, despite efforts by Essop Pahad, minister in the President's Office, to solicit support.

Significantly, the other major political advocate of continental regeneration, the Ugandan president, Yoweri Museveni, has constructed his programme around market economics, regional integration and the 'restoration of sovereignty' to African 'wealth producers'.[44] But it remains to be seen whether a new class of African proprietors will be more predisposed than previous generations of nationalist leadership to be infused with the 'democratic rage' against corruption and tyranny which Mbeki attributes to it. The Afrocentrist historical nostalgia that characterises many of the efforts to develop the Renaissance project – the key authorities in this context are Ivan van Sertima and Cheikh Anta Diop – may be rather more inviting for members of the new 'patriotic bourgeoisie' than the conceptual difficulties arising from Mbeki's challenge to 'put behind us the notions of democracy and human rights as peculiarly Western'.[45] All too easily the idea could become debased into a series of self-congratulatory maxims in which the recollection of the African identity of ancient civilisations – 'the presence of melanin in the skin fragments of Egyptian mummies'[46] – becomes the founding myth for a new imagined community in which racial sentiment rather than political principle is the animating idea.

12 | THE MBEKI PRESIDENCY

In new democracies the quality of political leadership matters more than in established political systems, however carefully scripted the constitutional safeguards may be against the abuse of power. Institutions are still fluid and susceptible to being shaped by dominant personalities. Rightly or wrongly, both domestic and external confidence in South Africa's government are decisively influenced by perceptions of the personal qualities of its leadership. Certainly the country's present international status still owes much to the moral stature of Nelson Mandela as well as to the evident affection he inspires amongst South African citizens regardless of their political affiliations or social circumstances. Thabo Mbeki may well in future years accumulate a similar degree of charismatic authority but today, even among his admirers, he is respected rather than loved.

At the time of his accession to the President's Office in 1999, in contrast to his predecessor, not much was publicly known about Thabo Mbeki.[1] The basic details of his career were easy enough to recite. Born in the Transkei in 1942, he belonged to an important ANC household, the third generation representative of a lineage drawn from a 'typically "progressive" or modernising peasant family characteristic of the region at the turn of the century'.[2] His grandfather, Fkelewu, was a Presbyterian convert, a salaried headman and a peasant farmer; his father, Govan, a prominent member of the Communist Party (SACP) and an influential journalist.

Thabo was politically active from the age of 14 when he joined the Youth League at Lovedale College (two years before the normal age of entry). He was expelled from Lovedale in 1959 after helping to organise a class boycott and he subsequently matriculated through correspondence. Later, in Johannesburg, he helped establish an African Students' Association while taking a correspondence degree course from London University and left South Africa in 1962 after a brief spell in detention. Three years later he graduated from Sussex with an MA in economics before working in the ANC's London office and undertaking a brief stint of military instruction in the Soviet Union. From 1971 he served as assistant secretary to the ANC's Revolutionary Council and subsequently represented the ANC in Nigeria, Botswana and Swaziland. In 1975, he became Oliver Tambo's political secretary and speech-writer. He was elected to the ANC's National Executive in 1978, became director of information in 1984, and head of the organisation's international affairs department in 1989. Four years later, in August 1993, he was appointed to the national chairmanship, a honorary position created two years earlier for the ailing Oliver Tambo, who died in April 1993. In August 1991 he was replaced in the role of the ANC's chief negotiator with the South African government by Cyril Ramaphosa, considered to be tougher, less predisposed to compromise, and more inclined to brinkmanship.

During the CODESA talks between the De Klerk government and the ANC, Mbeki participated in the ANC team in the working group that considered transitional government arrangements, a relatively low-profile contribution, and a forum in which the National Party experienced no real pressure to offer concessions. He played a more decisive transitional role in his successful efforts to persuade General Constand Viljoen to bring his following into the settlement. In 1994, his appointment to the deputy presidency more or less confirmed his status as Mandela's successor.

In contrast to the public scrutiny directed at Nelson Mandela's domestic circumstances, Thabo Mbeki's family life was kept firmly private. Mrs Zanele Mbeki worked well out of the limelight, running the Women's Rural Development Bank, an extremely effective NGO that supplies loans to help rural women start up businesses. In this position she drew upon her exile experience as an administrator for the UNHCRR in Lusaka. Thabo Mbeki's only child, Monwabisi, a son born from a youthful love affair, was last seen by members of his family in 1981. He disappeared subsequently, although his mother received reports from his friends, who told her of meeting him in a military camp in Tanzania.

Filling in the gaps in this curriculum vitae is not easy. Mbeki himself eschews confessional statements. As one interviewer noted in 1993: 'Thabo Mbeki has great difficulty talking about himself ... and prefers to talk about the ANC instead, and even then downplays the role he has filled.'[3] Some of his self-contained reticence probably stems from an upbringing in which family relations were very disrupted. Mbeki told one journalist in 1994 that because of his parents' political commitments 'we didn't grow up at home. From the ages of six and seven we were dispatched to relatives and friends. I can count on one hand the political discussions I've had with my father.'[4] Though Mbeki occupied a key position at the ANC's nerve centre of strategic decision-making from the late 1970s onwards, as a firm subscriber to the ANC's traditional etiquette of 'collective leadership' he has never claimed personal responsibility for particular developments.

Even so, his individual impact upon the movement's history in exile was considerable. Even as a comparatively junior official, when representing the ANC in Swaziland, his careful courtship of the first wave of Black Consciousness refugees helped to ensure that many of the key figures in this new political generation found their final home in the ANC. He is generally credited with inventing the 'make South Africa ungovernable' slogan popularised by the ANC in the early

1980s, and conversely, and more reassuringly to white South Africans, he is also believed to have been one of the strongest advocates of negotiated settlement at the end of the decade. One encounter with Afrikaner intellectuals in 1988 even earned him a censure from the ANC's National Working Committee for failing to obtain appropriate authority before the meeting.[5] When delegations representing various South African elites started travelling to Lusaka to meet the ANC, it was Mbeki who was their most prominent host. Well before his return to the country Mbeki had probably become the best known and most receptive black South African politician among businessmen and mainstream journalists. Though Peter Mokaba, the former Youth League president (and in that capacity one of Mbeki's key supporters in the succession contest), referred to Mbeki's guerrilla accomplishments, the president is more commonly associated with the exiled ANC's diplomatic efforts as well as its increasing commitment during the 1980s to social, if not liberal, democracy.

Like many ANC leaders of his generation, Mbeki joined the SACP, recruited into its fold in 1962 by Duma Nokwe while living in his household.in Johannesburg. In 1977 Mbeki became the youngest member of the party's five-member politburo. In 1978 Mbeki's ideological affinities were well on the left of the ANC's political spectrum: in one address to a Canadian conference he referred to 'black capitalism' as 'parasitic' and 'senile', historically obsolete, 'without any extenuating circumstances to excuse its existence'.[6] Though he formally renounced his party membership only in 1990 and despite the prominent role he played at the SACP's 1989 ninth congress in Havana, Mbeki had been at odds with SACP leaders for more than a decade. He disagreed with Joe Slovo over the emphasis which the liberation movement should place on armed struggle (Mbeki argued the ANC neglected mobilisation) and his initiation of discreet talks with elite Afrikaner groups engendered mounting hostility from SACP ideologues who remained wedded to an insurrectionist strategy.[7] One incident which may have caused an early source of tension between him and the ANC's left occurred shortly after his arrival in Lusaka in 1978. His decision to allow the Columbia Broadcasting System access to make a documentary prompted accusations of complicity with the CIA.[8] Oliver Tambo had to use all his charm to persuade him not to leave the exile movement.

However, Mbeki remained friendly with individuals in the SACP, with Essop Pahad for example, who became the minister responsible for the administration of Mbeki's office and who during the Mandela era was Mbeki's liaison with the ANC parliamentary caucus. Pahad was a veteran communist, but this did not signify anything about Mbeki's ideological predispositions. In 1994 leading communists, including Joe Slovo, were known to favour Cyril Ramaphosa's appointment to the position of deputy president, as did Nelson Mandela (who was worried about Xhosa predominance in the ANC's leadership). Significantly, in

1996 Mbeki became the first major contemporary ANC leader to publicly specu-late about the possibility that with the achievement of 'a more normal society', out of the 'broad movement' the ANC represented there would emerge different parties, with liberals and socialists going their separate ways.

How can one explain Mbeki's ascendancy in the organisation? In a characteris-tically perceptive aside in an interview he gave in 1995, he observed, 'I don't have constituencies.' Though journalists like to speculate about divisions within the ANC based, for example, either on ideological factions, communists or African-ists, or even on different trajectories of struggle experience – exiles, prisoners, mass democratic movement members – these supply a misleadingly simple view of the organisation's internal politics. Communist notables can be counted among Mbeki's most prominent critics and can be identified as his strongest allies. Sydney Mufamadi and Mbhazima Shilowa are two important personalities in the latter category. Nor is the ANC's aspirant 'patriotic bourgeoisie' camp uniform in its attitudes to Thabo Mbeki. Peter Mokaba was a Mbeki protégé but Cyril Rama-phosa and Tokyo Sexwale are two former rivals who, once outmanoeuvred in the leadership stakes, redirected their energies towards business.[9] Part of his strength is that Mbeki does not represent a particular ideological predisposition in the ANC.

Mbeki's status as a successor leader was evident a long time ago. In the guer-rilla training camps he and his old Lovedale classmate Chris Hani were earmarked as the two outstanding leaders of the younger generation. In the 1990s genera-tional seniority remained an important consideration in the ANC's pecking order and the organisation frowned upon competitive leadership struggles. In July 1991 at the ANC's conference in Durban, the aged Walter Sisulu had to be elected as deputy president to Mandela, to pre-empt a direct contest for delegate votes between Hani and Mbeki. Hani had insisted on standing before both were persuaded to withdraw in favour of Sisulu. Mbeki's position as ANC national chairman was decided in 1993 not by delegates at a conference but rather by a meeting of the National Working Committee. Initially Mandela had proposed Kader Asmal for the post but he was overruled after vigorous lobbying by Mbeki. By the end of the ANC's exile period, aside from Tambo and Mandela, Mbeki was probably the most familiar ANC personality to the broader public inside South Africa as well as to external audiences. Mbeki probably did not need 'constituen-cies' to secure delegate support at the 1994 ANC conference, though the public backing from Peter Mokaba, a key 'internal' leader of the 1980s, did not harm him. Mrs Madikizela-Mandela's antipathy to his rival, Cyril Ramaphosa, ensured him the support of the Women's League for the post of deputy president. In the 1997 leadership elections, Mbeki faced no opponents. His was the only nomina-tion for the post of ANC president, an isolated carry-over from a more deferential past when most ANC leadership positions were uncontested.

The position of deputy president of South Africa in the first ANC government had a special significance in the light of Mandela's professed intention to serve only one term and his decision to delegate considerable executive authority to his deputy. As the chairperson of most cabinet meetings, Thabo Mbeki was effectively responsible for the routine administration of government after 1994. As Mandela explained to an audience in Singapore in early 1997: 'I am doing less and less work. That is being done by the present Deputy President.'[10] Nor were Mbeki's responsibilities confined to day-to-day supervision of the executive. During Mandela's presidency Mbeki increasingly became the main arbiter of policy issues, and after 1994 successive cabinet appointments testified to his decisive role in government. The dissolution of the RDP office in 1996 and the transfer of many of its functions to the deputy president's burgeoning staff were important signals of his consolidating authority.

This should not be exaggerated, though. Mandela's first cabinet included several independent, strong personalities who were not especially intimate with Mbeki – Mac Maharaj and Tito Mboweni were examples. Others who disagreed with him in public have retained authority: Dullah Omar's clash with Mbeki over the issue of secrecy in the Truth and Reconciliation Commission hearings was a case in point. Maharaj resigned from politics after the 1999 elections, and Omar was transferred from the justice ministry to the less important transport portfolio, and replaced by Penuell Maduna, a key Mbeki associate from his time in exile. With respect to those cabinet appointments under Mandela in which Mbeki's influence was particularly obvious, apart from a concern for ethnic balancing, political criteria (at least those which relate to public popularity or ideology) appeared to be unimportant. That was not necessarily a bad thing: neither ideological conviction nor popular following is a guarantee of effective executive performance. For example, as minister of health, Nkosazana Zuma was not universally liked, but her administration of the portfolio was decisive and her determination to reallocate resources to primary health care had a positive impact upon public health. Mbeki is generally credited with the imaginative and far-sighted choice of Trevor Manuel (a UDF leader in the 1980s) as finance minister.

However, loyalty and personal connections to Mbeki seem to have been at least as important as meritocratic considerations in influencing cabinet appointments, even during the Mandela era. The selection of Sankie Mthembi-Mahanyele as housing minister after Joe Slovo's death was such an expression of Mbeki's personal patronage. Early on, her performance was marred by allegations of nepotism. Tito Mboweni's replacement in the labour ministry in 1998, the comparatively unknown Membathisi Mdladlana, a former school principal, SACTU leader and COSATU parliamentary nominee, was perceived at the time of his appointment as a 'caretaker … someone unlikely to rock the Mbeki boat'[11] and unlikely 'to call the shots at labour'.[12]

Which particular feature of the Mandela government should be associated with Mbeki's influence? His principal achievement was in setting a coherent financial policy agenda. Depending on one's perspective, he probably deserved the principal credit or the main blame for the government's fiscally conservative macroeconomic policies.[13] Though the drafting of the GEAR programme was undertaken by a team of economists working with the minister of finance, the deputy president's office was closely involved in the discussion of early drafts, well before the programme was shown to the ANC's executive, the cabinet or even Nelson Mandela. The task of justifying and defending GEAR in public was normally undertaken by Trevor Manuel and Alec Erwin, though it was Mandela himself who appeared at the 1997 COSATU conference to confront labour criticisms of policy. Mbeki's public statements on GEAR were less conspicuous, although he spoke in favour of the programme in press and television interviews (his preferred method of public communication). At the SACP's tenth congress, in July 1998, following an angry repudiation of GEAR critics by Mandela, Mbeki lectured the assembled delegates on the dangers of 'fake revolutionary posturing', accusing party leaders of trying to boost their following 'on the basis of scavenging on the carcass of a savaged ANC'.[14]

At the time, defending unpopular executive decisions in public against a hostile audience was a fairly fresh experience for Mbeki. Indeed, until that point the exercise of such assertive authority had not been Mbeki's main perceived strength. Nelson Mandela in an interview in 1995 conceded that Mbeki was not at his best in dealing with 'day-to-day problems'. Some 'of our own people' thought that Mbeki was too indecisive, he conceded.[15] Mandela was reacting to Mbeki's awkward handling of Winnie Madikizela-Mandela's resignation from her deputy ministership as well as the attempt by Mbeki's legal adviser to exonerate Allan Boesak from corruption charges. On both issues Mbeki's predisposition to compromise rather than confront was well to the fore. Like his mentor, Oliver Tambo, Mbeki's reflexive inclination seemed to be to placate potential troublemakers and keep them within the fold, until at least their supporters could be won over. Mandela conceded on another occasion: 'He can be diplomatic to the point where many people regard him as weak.'[16] The high premium which Mbeki and other former exile leaders in the ANC placed on organisational cohesion and unity was understandable but it had a less beneficial effect when applied to the business of government.

Not that Mbeki was incapable of acting firmly against opponents. The expulsion from the government and from the ANC's ranks of Bantu Holomisa in May 1996 was convincing evidence of the dangers of clashing with the deputy president publicly. The singularity of Holomisa's situation, though, was that as a latecomer to the ANC he had no support network within the organisation, his popularity with 1994 conference delegates notwithstanding. Though up to his accession to the presidency Thabo Mbeki was careful to maintain courteous public relations with Winnie Madikizela-Mandela, in canny fashion he was also generally supportive of some of her leading critics. Amongst these was Mavivi Myakayaka-Manzini, who in 1996 replaced Essop Pahad as the deputy president's parliamentary counsellor after Pahad's promotion to a deputy ministership.

The experience of holding office may have helped Mbeki to develop a more confident way of dealing with open opposition. This was manifest at the February 1997 ANC Free State conference, which was bitterly divided between supporters of the deposed premier, Mosiuoa Lekota, and his opponents. 'The ANC', Mbeki reminded his audience, 'is a voluntary organisation. If you do not agree with majority decisions, then you are free voluntarily to leave as you are to join.'[17] Sometimes, though, his growing confidence in open forums could be intimidating. Parliamentarians complained that they felt increasingly reluctant to challenge the executive. At one caucus meeting in 1997, Barbara Hogan kept prefacing her remarks with the phrase that she 'did not want to cause any trouble'. To his credit Mbeki intervened and said he was worried that she felt it necessary to say this, and was there, he asked, a more general feeling that the ANC leadership did not welcome dissent. 'Yes-s-s', the MPs whispered in chorus.[18]

Thabo Mbeki's preferred leadership style is that of a political manager, not a charismatic populist. As one commentator put it, 'he works behind the scenes, patching together alliances of disparate ANC factions to produce a power base.'[19] There is much to be said for such leadership, especially in a context in which the ANC has to please so many different constituencies, and also when it is aided, as in Mbeki's case, with an affable personal manner and a convincing television presence, increasingly important factors in South African politics. With his skills as a conciliator working behind the scenes, Mbeki deserves much of the credit for the decline in political violence in KwaZulu-Natal after 1994.

The problem with his behind-the-scenes managerial approach, though, is that the ANC as an organisation is not particularly susceptible to such direction. During Mandela's presidency, this was evident in the resistance of provincial organisations to electing leaders supported by higher authority as well as the difficulties the ANC leadership encountered in securing delegate support for Jacob Zuma in the December 1997 conference elections. Zuma was a friend of Mbeki but his candidature for the election probably owed more to his work with the deputy president in the KwaZulu-Natal peacemaking process. The choice of Zuma was also a significant indicator of the Mbeki leadership style. Zuma enjoyed the reputation for being a highly effective negotiator and a skilful strategist. Amongst top-echelon ANC leaders, particularly those from exile, he was especially trusted and liked by security officials during the early 1990s. Outside KwaZulu-Natal, though, he was scarcely known, in spite of his status as a senior ANC office-holder. As Mbeki's deputy in the organisation and in the government he could be counted upon to be loyal and skilful in all those managerial functions which Mbeki had performed for Mandela. That he had no significant public following outside his province did not seem to be viewed as a shortcoming. Indeed, Mbeki may have perceived this as an asset in a prospective subordinate. But in an ANC increasingly crowded with disrespectful young activists who had no direct experience of the discipline or the inspiration of the struggle decades, age, status and track record count for less and less. As memories of liberation fade, to maintain their authority the leadership will need showmanship and showmen (and women).

Charismatic attributes of leadership can be acquired. They are not simply engrained in particular personalities and, of course, they are often the product of carefully fostered myths. Nelson Mandela's charisma is at least partly attributable to the legends created during his enforced absence from the political stage. Mbeki's lack of a comparatively heroic liberation biography and his 'commoner' family status are factors which in a South African setting may inhibit the acquisition of charismatic leadership attributes. But they do not represent unsurmountable obstacles to such a process. Just before the 1999 general election, Mbeki turned his modest village origins to his advantage when he attended an Amazizi clan welcome that was intended to 'double up as a traditional ceremony to introduce Mbeki to his ancestors' as 'an honoured son of the soil'. This would not be his first such homecoming, his spokesman insisted; Mbeki had often visited Idutywa unheralded, making 'sure to mingle around and keep in touch with people at the rock bottom'.[20] A few months earlier, though, his mother, Epainette, told Mbeki's biographer Mark Gevisser that though she had told her son that the villagers in his birthplace had wanted to see him, 'this is the very last village in South Africa he will come to', a comment that to Gevisser underlined Mbeki's 'stern disavowal of both the sentimentality of ethnicity and the favour of patronage'.[21]

To some observers, Mbeki appears a stilted orator, but during his first term in public office he became an increasingly relaxed public performer. His presentation of the ANC's testament to the Truth and Reconciliaion Commission combined candour with warmth and included an improvised break into song which charmed his audience. It was by far the most impressive of the political party presentations to the commission. Mbeki's 'I am an African' speech at the adoption of the Constitution in 1996 was one of the most visionary and poetic public statements to have been delivered by an ANC leader in recent history, especially in its inclusive definition of Africanism. It represented one of the best statements about South African national identity to have been produced by any local politician.

As we have noted in the previous chapter, one important ingredient in Mbeki's vision of an African Renaissance is his hopeful belief in technological determinism. The other premise which animates his projection of continental rebirth is his conviction that ideas can move millions of people to be 'activists for their own emancipation'. At least in his perceptions, Mbeki remains the leader of a national liberation movement, not a liberal political party, and in his vision of political progress the task of moving the millions in such a direction should be entrusted not to the institutions of state, but rather to a vanguard intelligentsia, new cadres nurtured in the ANC's heroic traditions.[22] Voluntarist faith in the dominant capacity of the will to alter social circumstances has a long trajectory in Mbeki's thinking. In 1969, while undergoing political training in Moscow, Mbeki wrote to a friend about his admiration for Shakespeare's Coriolanus, who was too high-minded to live in the society he saved and who, when threatened by the Senate with exile, replied, 'I banish you. There is world elsewhere.'[23] In Mbeki's understanding, the revolutionary hero, the new intelligentsia and the virtuous party cadre – the 'new persons', in the jargon adopted at an ANC National Council meeting in 2000 – must make their own new world.[24]

Mbeki's attitudes about race are easy to misunderstand. References in his oft-cited 'Two nations' address in May 1998 to whites' economic selfishness and reluctance to commit themselves to a new patriotism can be interpreted as a cynical appeal to the social resentments that exist within the ANC's following. More fairly, they probably signified frustration at the absence of evidence of a corresponding sense of Africanism among white political and business leaders When such evidence arises, it is warmly reciprocated, as was evident in his embrace of former Afrikaner nationalists as fellow patriots.[25] Afrikaner intellectuals, such as Stellenbosch philosopher Willie Esterhuyse, remain among his closest white associates, having won his confidence for the role they played as intermediaries in the 'talks about talks' conducted in the 1980s. In a paper written a few months after the ANC's first electoral victory, Mbeki argued that one of the ANC's main objectives should be to 'retain and increase our support among … the white middle strata'. To do this, he contended, 'it would also be important to deploy a fair number of white organisers to join this effort, to give reassurance that the new power is also based among the "super-powerful" white minority. The message that the organisers must communicate to these communities is that the democratic transformation requires their skills and talents and therefore considers them a valuable national asset and a vital national component of the forces that we require to build a better life.'[26] Unlike the 'I am an African' prose, the language in this document was dispassionately analytical. It was directed at an internal audience, not the broader public, and it recognised the continuing salience of racial identity in political behaviour. It also demonstrated a commitment to including white South Africans within a new patriotism.

Mbeki's vision of an 'African Renaissance' in which an economically powerful South Africa can 'strike out on this new path' to nurture 'the rebirth of the continent' is defined in terms that are easy enough for white South African patriots to embrace, though, as we have noted, not all Renaissance discourse is as socially inclusive. However, even during the conciliatory Mandela presidency, when placating white fears was an important official preoccupation, Mbeki's public addresses tended to emphasise 'transformation' issues. Social harmony was impossible, he insisted, in a context in which 'poverty and prosperity continue to be defined in racial terms. If you want reconciliation between black and white, then you need to transform society.' In Mbeki's perception, though, not all opponents of transformation are white. In a speech in parliament in June 1998 he called for 'a halt to the abuse of freedom in the name of entitlement ... especially by elements of the black elite' who 'hijack sacrifices ... to satisfy a seemingly insatiable and morally unbound greed'.[27]

As Mandela's deputy, Mbeki seemed to engender favourable perceptions amongst businessmen. Positive ratings in such exercises as the surveys undertaken by a Johannesburg business journal in 1996 and 1997[28] testify to the care and effort which he invested in addressing the concerns of this constituency, both locally and abroad. He was especially successful abroad, as Kaizer Nyatsumba noted in 1997: 'In Brussels ... in Rome and in Amsterdam, not once in my 20-plus meetings with top political and business leaders did the question of Mbeki's suitability for the presidency come up, not once.'[29]

Not everyone approved of his courtship of the business community. Mbeki aroused sharp criticism from leading communists for his promotion of a 'golden triangle' of business, labour and government, a term used in a 1997 ANC 'discussion paper', *State and Social Transformation*, widely believed to reflect Mbeki's thinking. But if some communists were critical of the ANC leadership's 'slide into a technocratic "class neutral" approach', as deputy-president, Mbeki was not generally unpopular amongst the left. As the surveys cited above indicated, and more conclusively as a CASE survey also discovered in 1995, Mbeki enjoyed the approval of many senior trade unionists, despite his early support for privatisation of state-owned corporations. As Mandela's heir, Mbeki demonstrated a deft rhetorical capacity for steering a middle course between what he has dismissively called 'the paradigms of ideological dogma', an aptitude which his supporters term 'pragmatism' and such detractors as Tony Leon more unkindly described as 'travelling on both sides of the road'. While businessmen could find reassurance in Mbeki's willing acceptance of the economic challenges of 'an historically unavoidable process of globalisation', labour leaders could draw encouragement from his sharp advocacy of redistributive social reform. As long ago as 1978, Mbeki had written about 'the skill of combining the necessary and the possible'. Twenty years later, one left-wing commentator found the recognition of such an imperative to be a consistent theme in Mbeki's thinking and suggested that as the South African contemporary of a new wave of centre-left politicians such as Tony

Blair or Lionel Jospin, Mbeki's political ascendancy represented the advent of a 'radical democratic project within South Africa'.[30]

Mbeki's apparent pragmatism as well as his obvious commitment to social reform or 'transformation' helped prompt the expectation that his presidency would initiate a technocratic 'politics of management and governance'.[31] This would be a business-like era of 'service delivery', a time for the nation to 'get back to work'.[32] The time-consuming procedures of consensual constitutional deliberation and consultative policy formation were complete, it was believed. In apparent conformity with this 'new dynamic' of 'getting down to business',[33] Mbeki's accession to the President's Office coincided with a considerable extension of its powers and functions. Even when he was deputy president, Mbeki's office employed 100 members of staff and contained within it divisions concerned with youth, gender equality, HIV/AIDS, NGOs, government communications and bi-national commissions with the United States and Germany.

Under Mandela, Mbeki chaired a number of inter-ministerial committees, the main arenas within government for high-level policy deliberations. Mbeki's office also established a Coordination and Implementation Unit which, after the demise of the RDP ministry, became the main agency responsible for implementing programmes in which responsibility was shared by several government departments.

At the end of 1998, Mbeki's office was merged with Mandela's in preparation for the launch of a 'super-presidency'. After the 1999 election the new office was to be supported by 334 staff including three directors-general and a budget of R70 million. Equipped with the personnel to enable it to become 'a powerful coordinating structure for government policy and action', it was predicted that it would exercise considerably more control over cabinet and ensure much more effective 'integrated' deployment of resources in the implementation of policy than during the Mandela era. It was anticipated that the Mbeki administration would enhance efficiency and centralised direction by cutting the number of ministries (following the recommendations of the 1998 Presidential Review Commission) but in fact the number of ministries increased with the elevation of Intelligence to a full portfolio. A substantial number of Mbeki's personal staff came from an ANC intelligence background, incidentally. However, in line with Mbeki's technocratic aspirations, his 1999 cabinet and deputy ministerial appointments (representing an extensive reshuffle) were significantly younger than Mandela's ministers – 19 out 43 were younger than 50 and only two were over 65 – and generally better educated. Nineteen of the 43 had belonged to the ANC in exile, fourteen were veterans of the UDF and another nine owed their political rise to the trade union movement.[34]

Since 1999 certain achievements have helped to justify the optimism in the widespread perception of a newly energised administration. The whole-scale reorganisation of local government, whatever the merits of its long-term outcomes, would have been very difficult to achieve without the coordinated efforts of several different ministries and other government agencies. Education is one field in which a lengthy and perhaps over-consultative process of policy contemplation during the Mandela presidency was followed, with the advent of Mbeki's administration, by energetic implementation of central government directives and effective channelling of resources to the areas of greatest need. Recent matriculation results supply hard evidence of very considerable improvements in public schooling. As we have seen, the Mbeki government has consolidated its predecessor's record in meeting 'basic needs' in the 'facilitation' of low-cost housing and the extension of clean water and public health services, though the pace of expansion of the 'delivery' of such services has not really increased since the Mandela era. Land redistribution was actually halted to allow for a protracted policy review, though arguably the new agrarian programmes to foster black commercial farming, which are being implemented by Thoko Didiza's ministry, will represent a much more ambitious attempt to change racial patterns of ownership than the earlier efforts to alleviate landlessness.

Coordination and centralised control have probably been most important not so much in the organisation of social reform but rather in the strict enforcement of fiscal discipline and consequent curbs on public expenditure, particular with respect to provincial governments. At least in its public pronouncements, Mbeki's government has paid much more attention to the problem of bureaucratic corruption. As we have seen, there has been a proliferation of powerful anti-corruption agencies. Meanwhile, aggressive promotion of affirmative action policies – through equity legislation, public-sector regulations, government contracting and informal pressure exercised on institutions as diverse as sporting bodies or universities – lends support to Mbeki's claims of leadership of a government committed to profound social change.

Nowhere else has the dominant influence of the presidency been more obvious than in foreign affairs, with Mbeki himself spending around a fifth of each year since his accession on foreign missions. His foreign minister, Dr Nkosazana Dlamini-Zuma, spent 202 days abroad in 2000, 89 of them in Africa.[35] Though the president's personal preference for coordinated multilateral African diplomacy, rather than the unilateral exercise of South Africa's power as a regional 'hegemon', has to date been ineffectual in promoting foreign policy goals in Zimbabwe, there is no question that under Mbeki, South Africa's influence as an arbiter of African continental affairs has increased significantly. This has been partly because of Pretoria's downgrading of Mandela's spirited emphasis on the foreign promotion of human rights, in favour of African continental institution-building, obtaining better trade terms and attracting foreign investment to South Africa particularly and Africa more generally. Mandarins may grumble at the effective sidelining of the Foreign Affairs Department in foreign policy determination, but analysts of Mbeki's leadership in this sphere discern strategic ambition and intelligent diplomacy, much of the latter conducted at a ministerial level by Mbeki himself and his cabinet colleagues, especially those concerned with trade, industry and finance.[36]

In contrast to this picture of a visionary, unified and disciplined administration geared to the promotion of domestic social reform and continental restoration there is the accusation of authoritarian or even totalitarian predispositions directed at Mbeki's government by its critics in the press and its parliamentary opponents. The broadside directed at Mbeki's leadership style by James Myburgh, a researcher employed by the Democratic Alliance (DA), is representative of such arguments. Comparing Mbeki's presidency to Hannah Arendt's conception of totalitarian leadership, Myburgh attributes Mbeki's ascendancy within the ANC to his mastery of inner-party struggles and the construction of a network of loyalists occupying key positions, a network which since 1999, Myburgh suggests, has been extended to government and key institutions in civil society. Independent and able party members are 'shunted aside' or confined to technocratic roles or simply discredited. Decision-making on even minor aspects of policy implementation is decided within the president's inner circle, to the detriment of administrative efficiency. In any sphere of activity from which the president's attention has been distracted, indecisiveness prevails.[37]

Since 1999, supporters of such views have been offered a considerable quantity of anecdotal evidence in the behaviour of Mbeki's administration. In April 2001, for example, the minister of safety and security, Steve Tshwete, made public a number of bizarre allegations directed against three of Mbeki's former rivals for senior ANC positions, Cyril Ramaphosa, Tokyo Sexwale and Mathews Phosa, suggesting that they might be behind the spread of rumours that Mbeki was implicated in Chris Hani's assassination. Such rumours were intended to 'set Mbeki up' for attack. The source of these accusations was James Nkumbule, the Mpumalanga Youth League leader who had lost his party position for promoting factionalism in the province. Nkumbule had apparently been reporting to security and intelligence officials for some weeks before Tshwete made his public statement. Later in the year Tshwete retracted the allegations but the damage had been done. They were widely interpreted as a clumsy effort, sanctioned by Mbeki, to demonise potential opponents. They also represented a good example of the risk of contagion inherent in the ANC leadership's efforts to intervene in provincial party politics.

A few weeks earlier, in a telling example of the political nervousness generated by any discussion of succession issues within the ANC, Jacob Zuma, considered in certain ANC quarters to be an ally of Mathews Phosa, and believed to be running his own campaign in three provinces for support in the 2002 ANC conference elections, felt compelled to make a public declaration of his loyalty to

Mbeki and deny any personal presidential ambitions, which he said were the subject of 'unverified so-called intelligence reports'.[38] Mbeki's uncertainties about Jacob Zuma's loyalties were reportedly aroused by the deputy president's failure to show him for two months a letter from Winnie Madikizela-Mandela in which she referred to gossip about the president's alleged 'womanising'.[39] Two months later, Thabo Mbeki's irritation with Madikizela-Mandela was very obvious in the brusque treatment he accorded her when she arrived late at the podium during a 16 June rally at Orlando stadium. In justice to Mbeki, in several public statements directed at other SADC leaders he has stressed the virtue of a two-term limit on presidential office. But his defence of this principle makes the reluctance within the ANC to encourage an orderly succession contest all the more puzzling. The apparent complicity of state intelligence agencies in the ANC's palace politics was a particularly troubling dimension of this sequence of events and an apt illustration of the erosion of the boundaries between party and state which normally protect liberal democracy.

An increasingly elaborate security complex to insulate the presidency from any risk of attack, including a R40 million system installed at his Cape Town residence after a petty burglary, the expenditure of R12 million on special entry facilities at main airports, and the purchase for R400 million of a presidential aircraft all suggest an increasingly imperial presidential hauteur. They are at odds with the modest demeanour Mbeki adopted in his initial public appearances. His arrival at a 1998 World Economic Forum meeting in Windhoek in a hired car with secretary, a bodyguard and his wife contrasted favourably with the cavalcades of limousines and officials who accompanied other African leaders to the same event.[40]

In a demonstration of sensitivity to the dangers of a socially insulated presidency, Mbeki led during 2001 a series of public consultations in rural regions, the so-called *imbizo* programme, in which cabinet members presided over neighbourhood meetings to listen to complaints about local officialdom. Though intended to accentuate executive accessibility and accountability, such occasions divert public attention away from the policy flaws or institutional shortcomings which may be responsible for bad government and promote the impression of an omnipotent presidency.[41] Meanwhile, in a spirited defence against Myburgh's accusations, Kader Asmal took it upon himself to confide to newspaper readers that the president had refused a salary increase, a decision which he insisted should not be publicised.[42]

Further attributes of a nascent authoritarian political order are detected in Mbeki's habit of responding to criticism of his government with accusations of racial malice; his edgy relationship with the press; and interference by his office with government licensing and contracting to promote particular black empowerment interests. His infrequent appearances in the National Assembly and the cavalier treatment cabinet ministers accord to question time,[43] as well as the ferocious animosity between the ANC and the DA, are also often read as signals of presidential disdain for the conventions of liberal democracy. Such understandings may well be overdrawn. Mbeki's exercise of executive authority is a local instance of an international trend in government. A similar litany of complaints has accompanied Tony Blair's centralisation of decision-making within the British government and the Labour Party. President Mbeki's more thoughtful defenders maintain that much of the liberal criticism results from a failure to appreciate the merits of 'deliberative democracy' in which politics 'is structured as conversations aimed at achieving consensus'.[44] In such polities government and politics are inclusive rather than adversarial.

Misgivings about the Mbeki administration's commitment to democratic values are not just limited to parliamentarians schooled in the Westminister tradition, however. Within the ANC and in COSATU there is a perception that 'ANC traditions of open and vigorous debate' are under attack. The trade union federation complained in 2000 that the ANC presidency was seeking to manipulate the outcome of office-holder elections.[45]

However, when historians assess the democratic credentials of Thabo Mbeki's government in future, it is likely that their most critical attentions will focus on its responses to the HIV/AIDS pandemic, surely its most formidable developmental challenge. AIDS – Acquired Immunity Deficiency Syndrome – is a state in which particular cells within the immune system, CD4 lymphocytes, drop in number to below 200 per microlitre of blood, a point at which those who are affected by it cannot produce an effective immune response to infectious diseases such as TB or pneumonia. Since the early 1980s, most medical scientists have understood AIDS to be the consequence of infection by the human immunodeficiency virus, HIV, which damages CD4 cells. HIV is transmitted through sexual fluids, blood and breast-feeding. About a third of children born to HIV-positive mothers are infected at birth. The speed with which people who are infected with HIV develop AIDS, and their relative susceptibility thereafter to 'opportunistic infections' such as tuberculosis, can be affected by environmental conditions such as poverty. The appearance of the virus is believed to be relatively recent. Other diseases are able to destroy immune systems but not in the same way and not as commonly nor to the same extent as HIV.

A minority of doctors and scientists have, however, contested the significance of HIV as a necessary cause of AIDS or even denied its existence. An extreme version of this 'dissident' argument suggests that AIDS itself represents merely the effects of diseases such as tuberculosis which are primarily the consequence of poverty. More generally, AIDS dissidents dispute the validity of HIV testing, contest the statistics derived from such testing, and maintain that the 'anti-retroviral' drugs used to defend the immune system amongst HIV-positive patients and to prevent transmission of the virus from them are highly toxic and can indeed promote the symptoms associated with AIDS.

Government estimates for the number of HIV-positive people in South Africa, based on annual surveys of women attending antenatal clinics in 2000, rose to 4.7 million from 4.2 million in 1999. The implication of such figures, according to the Development Bank, is that the country's population will start contracting in 2016, when the number of AIDS-related deaths will exceed births.[46] The Medical Research Council reported in October 2001 that one in four deaths was attributable to AIDS, with nearly 200 000 expected to die as a consequence of AIDS in 2001. Those who were dying were disproportionately young, with 40 per cent in the 15–49-year age group. Life expectancy at birth, the MRC forecasted, would drop from 54 years in 2001 to 41 in 2010. By 2011, the MRC report predicted, 5 million South Africans would have died of AIDS.[47]

Well before his accession to the presidency, Thabo Mbeki played an influential role in helping to shape government policies with respect to HIV/AIDS. As deputy president from late 1997, he chaired an Inter-Ministerial Committee on HIV/AIDS, a body which was replaced in January 2000 by the South African National AIDS Council, composed of both ministers and 'civil society' notables. In October 1998, he presided over the launch of the Partnership Against AIDS. When researchers at the University of Pretoria attempted to short-circuit the normal procedures for undertaking clinical trials of a new anti-AIDS drug, Virodene, by soliciting government moral and financial support, he and the health minister arranged for them to present their findings to the cabinet and later attacked the Medicines Control Council (MCC) for rejecting clinical trial proposals. The MCC, he said, was guilty of denying AIDS victims 'mercy treatment'.[48] The MCC's reluctance to sanction further Virodene research was understandable. The drug, derived from a dry-cleaning solvent, had been administered to eleven patients experimentally (and illegally) with inconclusive results as well as indications of a high risk of liver injury. Subsequently health minister Zuma tried to dismiss two leading MCC officials, who were, however, later reinstated. The ANC, taking its cue from the deputy president, accused the MCC of censorship and of seeking to promote the interests of multinational drug companies against a potential local competitor.

Hostile rhetoric from government and ANC spokesmen directed at international pharmaceutical companies dated from Mrs Zuma's early efforts to promote the use in public health of cheaper generic medical imports from India and Brazil rather than the more expensive brands manufactured in developed countries. In 1996 Nelson Mandela suggested that opposition to the government's expenditure of R14 million on *Sarafina II*, a musical which was intended to promote public awareness about AIDS, was prompted by the drug companies' antipathy to Mrs Zuma as a consequence of her policy emphasis on preventive rather than curative health care.[49] In October 1998, Zuma announced that the government would cease supplying the anti-retroviral drug Azidothymidine (AZT), up to that point prescribed in certain hospitals to pregnant HIV-positive women, because it was too expensive. The R80 million that wholescale prescription would cost was to be used instead for the public education initiatives sponsored by Mbeki's partnership against AIDS. These would include, Zuma explained, training for 10 000 teachers to promote 'life skills' in schools; the distribution of 140 million condoms; publicity; and strategies to limit the spread of all sexually transmitted diseases. One month later, Mbeki defended the minister's decision about AZT. The medication was dangerously toxic, he claimed. Up till then, the government's justification for withdrawing the drug from hospitals was the cost of the medication itself as well as the support structures required for its effective dispensation. In fact, the manufacturers, Glaxo Wellcome, had since 1997 attempted to encourage the prescription of AZT by offering very substantial price reductions.

For much of 1999, the preoccupations of presidential succession and electoral campaigning brought other issues to the fore, despite the development of public opposition to the government's decision on AZT and the formation of an activist group, the Treatment Action Campaign (TAC). However, on 28 October 1999, in his speech at the National Council of Provinces, Mbeki included a reference to AZT's possible toxicity and asked his new minister of health, Manto Tshabalala-Msimang, to undertake further investigations into its use. Meanwhile, the ANC's annual report for 1999 insisted, AZT would not be made available in public facilities because of unanswered questions about its toxicity and efficacy. For the president, though, the unanswered questions embraced wider issues than simply the prescription of a particular anti-retroviral medicine. Early in 2000, the impending formation of a Presidential AIDS Panel was announced. As Mbeki explained in a telephone call in March to a leading 'dissident' scientist, David Rasnick, this panel would review the hypothesis that HIV caused AIDS. From this date onwards, official AIDS discourses on its causation referred to the causal link between AIDS and HIV as a 'thesis'.

Mbeki first voiced his scepticism about conventional explanations of the aetiology of AIDS in February 2000, earning a rebuke from Dr Zolile Mlisana, the chair of the South African Medical Association.[50] By this time, Mbeki's hostility to the South African medical establishment was quite evident. In a press interview that month, Mbeki excoriated the head of the Medical Research Council, Professor William Makgoba, for failing to read a particular article about the toxicity of AZT.[51] In March, Parks Mankahlana, the official spokesman for the presidency, accused Glaxo Wellcome of being 'like the marauders of the military industrial complex who propagated fear to increase their profits'.[52] The previous month, the president told the ANC's parliamentary caucus that drug companies were financing the Treatment Action Campaign, which was now busy 'infiltrating' the trade union movement.[53] In April 2000, Mbeki's predisposition in favour of dissident arguments about AIDS causation seemed to his critics to be evident from an open letter to world leaders in which he compared Rasnick and his colleagues to heretics, who in earlier ages would have been burned at the stake.[54] However, on 23 May 2000, the president told an American journalist that he had never said that HIV was not the cause of AIDS.[55] That month the composition of the Presidential Aids Panel was announced; about half of its members were drawn from the 'dissident' community including David Rasnick and Peter Duesberg.

Between June and October 2000 correspondence between Mbeki and Tony Leon, leader of the parliamentary opposition, shed further light on the president's attitudes. Initially Leon challenged Mbeki to justify the government's refusal to prescribe AZT to rape survivors. In response, the president cited reports from the American Center for Disease Control in support of his argument that no scientific evidence existed to indicate that AZT could prevent transmission of HIV to rape victims and noted that Glaxo Wellcome had not registered the drug for rape survivors. As Leon noted, such considerations would not normally rule out its precription, particularly as clinical trials of AZT's effect on rape survivors would be restricted by ethical considerations. The debate rapidly shifted ground to more controversial issues. In subsequent letters to Leon, Mbeki referred to 'hysterical' estimates of the incidence of AIDS by epidemiologists and the 'insulting' theory that HIV/AIDS originated in Africa.[56] He reiterated his doubts about the gravity of the epidemic when he addressed the opening session of an international conference on AIDS in Durban on 10 July.[57] In September he moved one step nearer the dissident position when he told *Time* magazine that 'there may very well be a virus – but to say this is the sole cause of AIDS, therefore the only response is anti-retroviral drugs, I am saying that we will never be able to solve the AIDS problem'.[58] On 21 September he reassured parliamentarians that the government's programmes were based on 'viral explanations' of the causes of AIDS but added that 'a virus cannot cause a syndrome', a phrase which became repeatedly used by presidential spokesmen, and effectively represented a repudiation of orthodox views about AIDS aetiology.[59]

By this stage the alarm engendered by the presidential opinions concerning AIDS had spread to senior echelons of the ANC. In April, KwaZulu-Natal's MEC for health, Zweli Mkhize, the deputy leader of the provincial ANC, published a statement attacking dissident scientists for their public disclosures of their conversations with Mbeki, a 'most discourteous abuse of a rare privilege' which, Mkhize maintained, was clearly aimed at associating the president with their views. Mkhize's statement went on to discuss the issue of the toxicity of anti-retroviral drugs, 'another matter that has been misinterpreted'. The reality was that 'few drugs have no side effects'; in fact drugs used for cancer had similar problems. It was the cost of using anti-retrovirals, not their toxicity, that was the central issue.[60]

After Mbeki's remarks in parliament, both COSATU and SACP representatives called upon the president to stop raising questions about the causes of AIDS in public. Subsequently, a three-day ANC National Executive Committee meeting reportedly succeeded in obtaining an assurance that the president would 'definitely try to be quiet about the issue'. A unnamed participant at the meeting told a reporter that during the foregoing months Mbeki had 'exposed a side of his personality which some of us were aware of: terrible conceit and paranoia'.[61] A statement from the Government Information Service confirmed that henceforth 'questions that still need to be answered' (about the link between HIV and AIDS) would 'take a back seat'. The National Executive published a statement on 3 October suggesting that the controversy aroused by Mbeki's views were the result of a 'massive onslaught' against the ANC, its president and the government. COSATU and the SACP were wrong to raise their concerns in public. Pharmaceutical companies were chiefly responsible for hostile interpretations of Mbeki's views. Government policy remained based on the 'thesis' that HIV caused AIDS despite the need for more research.[62]

For the next seven months there were no further public presidential statements about AIDS aetiology. Behind closed doors, though, Mbeki was less discreet. On 28 September, Mbeki addressed the ANC's parliamentary caucus. If newspaper sources are to be believed, MPs were warned about a 'huge propaganda offensive' led by drug companies and involving the CIA to 'promote the thesis' that HIV caused AIDS. In fact, the HIV virus had never been isolated. The attack on Mbeki's views was part of a wider effort to discredit him as the leader of efforts by the developing world to obtain a better deal in the international economic system. The Treatment Action Campaign, funded by drug companies, was the leading agency in this offensive.[63] In late October, the AIDS issue was taken up in electioneering in the Western Cape. Responding to the DA's undertaking to supply free anti-retrovirals in the province, Mbeki noted that South Africans were being 'used as guinea pigs' and the provincial government's prescription of such dangerous medication could be compared to the biological warfare of the apartheid era.

In April 2001, the Presidential AIDS Panel reported. Its members could find no consensus either about the causes of AIDS or as to how the epidemic should be contained. This was hardly surprising, given the arguments expressed by dissidents during its sessions. Peter Duesberg had maintained that AIDS itself was caused by anti-retroviral drugs and only 7 500 Africans were affected. David Rasnick suggested that HIV tests were 'lethal' and should be abandoned. In the prevalence of diseases like tuberculosis now associated with immune deficiency, Sam Mhlongo, head of the department of family medicine at MEDUNSA, insisted, South Africans were seeing diseases which were always there and their apparent spread was attributable to their previous concealment by apartheid health statistics. The Panel produced two parallel sets of recommendations. Dissident advice included the proposal that blood donations should not be screened for HIV.[64] Minister Tshabalala-Msimang noted drily that its discussions 'had not provided ground for the government to depart from its current approach to the HIV/AIDS problem, which is rooted in the premise that HIV causes AIDS'.[65]

The appearance of the Panel's report signalled the end of the presidential silence, however. During a television interview, Mbeki responded to a question by saying that he would not take an AIDS test 'because this would mean accepting a particular paradigm'. Subsequently, during a visit to Britain, the president elaborated on his understanding of the causes of AIDS. Once again he denied saying that HIV was not a cause of AIDS, but went on to maintain that it was only one among several sources of immune deficiency. One could not 'say that immune deficiency is caused solely by one virus'. Poverty was a major contributor to the pandemic.[66] In any case, World Health Organisation statistics indicated that in South Africa HIV was ranked eleventh amongst the 17 most important causes of death. On 27 June, Mbeki addressed the American National Press Club. Here he was asked clearly to state whether he believed HIV to be the primary cause of AIDS. He replied he did not know. Scientists believed it to be and his personal view was not relevant to scientists. 'There is such a condition as immune deficiency', he continued, 'and deficiency is acquired from somewhere including the HIV, but the immune system is compromised by a variety of things, not only the virus.'[67] On 7 August, Mbeki told the BBC's Tim Sebastian that in South Africa crime killed more people than AIDS. The day before, it was later disclosed, he had written a letter to his minister of health referring to the 1995 WHO statistics he had cited in the United States in June, to argue that given the minor status of AIDS as a cause of premature death, government policy should be reassessed.[68]

In October, press leakage of a report commissioned by the Department of Health from the Medical Research Council suggested that whatever the validity of the WHO statistics in 1995, any conclusions to be drawn from them had long being overtaken by events. MRC statistical analysis suggested that 5 million South Africans were HIV-positive. Amid rumours that the publication of the report was being delayed by the President's Office, the MRC's statistical findings were called 'not credible' in an official ANC statement.[69] Mbeki himself refrained from any public comment on the MRC's conclusions. However, in a lecture at Fort Hare University he returned to the theme touched upon in his earlier remarks about the supposed African origins of AIDS. In an oblique reference to both the Treatment Action Campaign activists and the medical establishment, he noted that 'thus it does happen that others who consider themselves to be our leaders take to the streets carrying their placards to demand that because we are germ carriers and human beings of a lower order that cannot subject their passion to reason, we must perforce adopt strange opinions to save a depraved and diseased people from perishing from a self-inflicted disease'.[70] In other words, explanations of the epidemic that focused on its virological cause and sexual transmission and that advocated medical remedies were racially condescending.

Notwithstanding official insistence that presidential opinions about AIDS aetiology have not determined government policy, it seems very likely that Mbeki's views have certainly influenced government responses to the pandemic, at least with respect to the prescription of anti-retroviral medicine. The emphasis in public health programmes directed at HIV/AIDS from 1998 was on the provision of information and the promotion of safe sex, as well as the treatment of opportunistic infections. Even so, AZT was available at certain public hospitals until Mrs Zuma's embargo on its prescription in October 1998. One justification used by health officials and Parks Mankahlana for the refusal to use AZT in a general programme to prevent mother-to-child transmission (MTCT) was that the government could not afford the costs of supporting the orphans who would survive the death of their mothers[71] – though it seems likely that the care of such children is undertaken mainly by grandparents and other kinsfolk. Zuma did not rule out the possibility of future sponsorship of an anti-retroviral programme but cited the need for further research. In March 1999 two ANC parliamentarians, Sister Bernard Ncube and Salie Manie, joined a Treatment Action Campaign fast in protest against the withdrawal of AZT. Other ANC politicians who voiced subsequent public support for the provision of anti-retrovirals to prevent MTCT included Pregs Govender, Winnie Madikizela-Mandela and Nelson Mandela.

In October 2000, the new health minister authorised seven KwaZulu-Natal hospitals to administer a new drug, Nevirapine, to HIV-positive expectant mothers. Nevirapine was cheaper than AZT and was believed to have less severe side-effects. Administered through a single dose to the mother and child during and just after birth, this drug, like AZT, required mothers to refrain from breast-feeding. A necessary corollary of its prescription to poor people was the provision of formula milk and the availability of clean water. Trials in Thailand suggested it could cut MTCT by half. In December 2000, the Department of Health announced that it would begin to prescribe the drug on a general basis in two hospitals in each province. Preparations for this programme, including the negotiation of cheaper supplies of milk powder, had been in progress for two years. MTCT prevention programmes started in the Western Cape in late 2000 and in KwaZulu-Natal.

The expansion of the Nevirapine programme was to become the main casualty of the presidential scepticism of HIV/AIDS aetiology. Despite departmental support for the use of Nevirapine for pregnant women, its launch in the provinces continued to be delayed. The planned extension of its prescription to five more provinces in April 2001 was halted when the minister decided that this needed cabinet approval (despite general agreement among provincial MECs in July 2000). Tshabalala-Msimang's reluctance was in contrast with strong sentiment in her department in favour of a full-scale supply of Nevirapine to all HIV-positive patients, not just pregnant women,[72] a position now supported by the United Nations and by research indicating that such provision would be a cheaper alternative to the hospital care needed for AIDS sufferers. By the end of 2001 the programme was operational in eight provinces, but not in Mpumalanga, where the MEC for health continued to refer to the unacceptable toxicity of Nevirapine and in May evicted from Nelspruit hospitals an NGO which had raised funds to supply anti-retrovirals to rape victims. The MEC, Sibongile Manana, charged that black women were being used as guinea-pigs to test anti-retrovirals and, moreover, she added in an aside, HIV had nothing to do with AIDS. Her decision to evict the Greater Nelspruit Rape Intervention Project was supported by Minister Tshabalala-Msimang.[73]

The prescription of Nevirapine was additionally politicised by a lawsuit mounted by the Treatment Action Campaign to obtain its general prescription for all HIV-positive women. Despite the minister's continued insistence that such a policy would be unaffordable and dangerous, in Gauteng during 2001 twelve provincial hospitals began prescribing Nevirapine to HIV-positive mothers after the provincial premier, Mbhazima Shilowa, 'consulted at the highest level'.[74] Incidentally the ANC's leader in the Western Cape, Ebrahim Rasool, played a key role in the launch of his province's pioneering anti-retroviral programme when he was health MEC. Nevirapine's manufacturers had offered a five-year free supply, a gesture of generosity which may have been partly prompted by the withdrawal in April by 39 drug companies of their litigation against the generic medicine policy embodied in the Medicine and Related Substances Control Amendment Act.

The major costs associated with the prescription of Nevirapine would now arise from formula milk, HIV testing and the monitoring of patients, costs which the minister continued to insist the authorities could not afford. In December, the Treatment Action Campaign obtained a favourable judgment in its court case, but the department announced its intention to appeal to the Constitutional Court, making it likely that ministerial opposition to the generalised prescription of anti-retroviral medicine to HIV-positive women would continue.

As the positive results of Shilowa's initiative suggest, the muddle in government anti-retroviral policy is not the simple consequence of Thabo Mbeki forbidding the use of the medication. Rather it is attributable to the effect within the ANC and government of the political nervousness engendered by his public expressions of support for the dissident case. In an organisation in which leaders were treated with less deference, things might be different.

One discouraging feature of these developments is the evident reluctance among the ANC's governing class to express any opinion at odds with the presidency, despite their private reservations. In late 2000, politicians were quizzed by journalists about their views on the causes of AIDS. Significantly, Mbhazima Shilowa stated unambiguously that there was a causal link between HIV and AIDS. Most of the others who were approached by journalists were less forthcoming. The response of the minister of education, Kader Asmal, was typical. He conceded that HIV may cause AIDS but he was not going to be 'pushed into a corner'. The chair of the ANC's health committee, Dr Abe Nkomo, felt he could not answer the question, though his deputy, Confidence Moloko, had no such difficulty: the infection agent was HIV, he confirmed, and moreover this was the view of the ANC. This claim earned him an immediate denial from Smuts Ngonyama, spokesperson for the ANC presidency. Moloko's statement did not reflect either the views or the policies of the movement, he insisted. Manto Tshabalala-Msimang has earned particular notoriety for her unwillingness to express any opinion that could be interpreted as being at odds with Mbeki's views.[75] She has been a loyal supporter of him ever since their departure together from South Africa into exile in 1962. In late September 2000, when Mbeki spoke to the parliamentary caucus about the conspiracies which promoted the view that HIV caused AIDS, he observed that it was unclear whether his own cabinet supported him against the drug companies. Several MPs at this juncture apparently gesticulated accusingly at Membathisi Mdladlana, the minister of labour, one of the few cabinet members to contradict Mbeki's views in public and say forthrightly that HIV caused AIDS. MPs who had expressed private reservations about Mbeki's stance were among those who jeered at the president's questioners when he answered questions in parliament on HIV on 21 September 2000.[76]

Further indications of the ANC's indulgence towards the president's thinking appeared on the ANC's website in November 2001. A new 'briefing document' listed a set of 'key questions that remain in HIV/AIDS'. These included whether 'an infective agent' existed and, if it did, whether it was a virus, and, if it was, whether it caused HIV, and whether the tests used to detect such a virus were reliable.[77] Such questioning must surely detract from the popular authority of the government's own awareness campaigns. Indeed, NGOs and church bodies have on several occasions suggested that Mbeki's embrace of dissident arguments has increased public resistance to AIDS education. Even the director-general of the Department of Health conceded that Mbeki's scepticism had 'created its own dynamic because he is the president and what he says gets taken very seriously'.

AIDS activists have been less guarded in their comments. Nkululeko Nxesi, director of the National Association of People Living with HIV and AIDS, noted that his organisation encountered rejection of the message that HIV caused AIDS 'on a daily basis' and that 'it [was] affecting what we're doing' with respect to the advocacy of safer sexual behaviour.[78] To be fair, such charges are derived only from anecdotal impressions, and survey evidence suggests that official public education has had a powerful impact and, at least with respect to the use of contraception, has helped to change sexual habits.[79] Even so, popular identification of Mbeki with dissident science has certainly undermined public confidence in his leadership, especially among foreign businessmen.[80]

What explains Mbeki's apparent embrace of dissident doctrine on AIDS aetiology? Certainly, the view of disease as essentially sociological pathology has a long history within the ANC and the Communist Party. In a country as unequal as South Africa, the contention that the primary cause of illness is poverty is reasonable enough. In 1988 the ANC's exile journal, *Sechaba*, published two articles on HIV/AIDS, both by Jabulani Nxumalo, writing under the pen-name 'Mzala'. Nxumalo's work drew upon East German scientific research to suggest that the AIDS virus was imported into Africa through an American military conspiracy. Moreover, the notion that the disease originated in the continent was the expression of racist prejudice. The research claimed that its prevalence was exaggerated by drug companies and that the vast majority of HIV testing resulted in false positives. It is possible that Mbeki was aware of Nxumalo's work when he began raising doubts about HIV being a cause of AIDS but his earlier support for Virodene indicates that his interest in dissident explanations was a recent development, not prompted by Nxumalo's work.[81] To be fair to Mbeki, the relative scientific merits of orthodox and dissident medical science are not easily discernible to a lay reader, even a comparatively well-informed one. In South Africa the dissident view is supported by an influential group of journalists as well as free-market libertarians. Contributing to the complexity of any external assessment of the scientific debate is the absence of complete unanimity amongst scientists who do believe that HIV causes AIDS, both on the issue of whether HIV infection inevitably leads to AIDS and on appropriate medical interventions. Mbeki's political socialisation within the confinements of an exile movement probably helped to predispose him towards challenging the authority of institutionalised establishments, scientific or otherwise. After all, in its internal discourses the ANC still views itself as a revolutionary force. On several occasions, Mbeki has signalled his distrust of existing bases of technical knowledge with his calls for the formation of a new intelligentsia.

The public projection of Mbeki as a philosopher-king by his supporters, as a prophetic public intellectual, is evidently a reflection of his own self-perception and may help to explain his reluctance to make any public concessions to the canonical authority of specialist knowledge. In addition, ostensibly scientifically based denial of the AIDS pandemic has very obvious attractions for a visionary leader championing the cause of African rebirth. In the case of his understanding of the AIDS pandemic, intellectual rationalisation may be powerfully reinforced by emotional proclivities as well as an heroic strategic discourse of leadership in which 'new men' can still make new worlds. If this explanation has any validity, then it suggests to an alarming extent that Thabo Mbeki, like his early mentor, Coriolanus, has begun to inhabit a 'world elsewhere' in his imagined community of a renascent Africa.

In making a concluding evaluation of Mbeki's presidency, the new genre of leadership analysis developed in management studies offers a useful range of conceptual tools. A particularly helpful approach of this kind is Keith Grint's *The Arts of Leadership*.[82] Grint's argument is that successful leadership depends upon four accomplishments: the fostering of identity; the projection of a strategic vision; the use of tactics that focus resources on opponents' weaknesses, not their strengths; and finally, communicative authority.

With respect to identity, leaders should aim to construct 'an imaginary community that followers can feel part of'. The underpinning premises of this part of Grint's argument are heavily influenced by Benedict Anderson's *Imagined Communities*, an exploration of the role of reading, intellectuals and popular literature in the arousal of widely shared perceptions of national identity in the nineteenth century. It is true that Mbeki's projection of an African Renaissance has helped to create a sense of a shared-purpose community among the new managerial elite who assemble at self-consciously Afrocentric gatherings. Paradoxically, too, the projection of South Africa as fulfilling an historic destiny in leading the continent 'out of the abyss' may well resonate with wider and more popular perceptions of South Africa's national superiority as well as the increasingly obvious xenophobia directed at immigrants from other parts of the continent.[83] More generally, though, since 1999 Thabo Mbeki's speeches have tended to emphasise national divisions rather than the broader inclusive sense of community emphasised in his 'I am an African' address. However, his critics maintain that eloquence is not enough. As one sympathetic observer, Xolela Mangcu, has commented, too often the president's philosophy is communicated in terms that do 'not resonate with ordinary people'.[84] Opinion polling suggests that he has been rather less successful than his predecessor in inspiring popular confidence and optimism,[85] and at least one survey has suggested that his preoccupation with racial divisions does not accord with public sentiment.[86] Mbeki's frequent castigation of black intellectuals[87] and the adverse commentary offered on his performance by some of the most prominent 'Africanist' personalities also indicate the limitations of his ideological project. In the Quality of Life Survey cited in chapter 9, very few respondents to the 1999 poll, black or white, were prepared to rank the African Renaissance as a source of national pride.[88]

Grint argues that leaders have to present utopias to their followers. These may be drawn from an imagined past or they may project an ideal future. Not all followers will necessarily be animated emotionally by this vision, but they must have grounds for supporting it derived from self-interest if they are not ideological converts. The best visions are those that resonate with the experience of followers. It is certainly true that the Mbeki administration projects in many of its policies a strong sense of strategic purpose and Mbeki himself is probably genuinely respected by his colleagues 'for his intellect, strategic vision and ability to grasp and articulate the most logical course of action', to cite a particularly flattering testimonial by Ronnie Kasrils.[89] To date, though, Mbeki has yet to achieve consensus among the ANC allies about the merits of his government's policies, especially in respect of GEAR. This failure is at least partly attributable to his preference for a tightly circumscribed policy process.

As a tactician, Mbeki performs best in the controlled terrain of bureaucratic inner-organisational politics. But rather than succeeding in what Grint terms 'the politics of inversion' – the conversion of opponents' strengths into sources of weakness – all too often Mbeki demonstrates reluctance to channel and concentrate resources into directing these from a position of strength. This failing is discernible in his efforts to address the Zimbabwe crisis. Here, too, another of his tactical weaknesses has been very obvious: his aversion to risk and his dislike of confrontation. Both characteristics explained the ANC's reluctance to use him as their key constitutional negotiator in the early 1990s. Grint maintains the best tacticians are susceptible to advice and are capable of changing course. Leaders who allow a degree of freedom to subordinates to resolve problems that their leaders have caused are most likely to succeed. As the controversy over the president's interference in AIDS policy demonstrates, his moral authority in government effectively insulates him from advice and, having adopted a view, he can be rigidly doctrinaire in enforcing conformity with it. It is true that certain favoured subordinates, such as Mbhazima Shilowa, are allowed a degree of autonomy, but in general Mbeki's colleagues appear reluctant to challenge his judgement. Certainly, with respect to AIDS, the president's views have prevented the effective marshalling and direction of public resources and social energy.

Finally, Grint proposes, for leaders to motivate followers, more than just ideological, strategic and tactical accomplishments are needed. Followers need to be persuaded through the skills of rhetoric or the skills of negotiation or through some form of performance. It is seldom that relying on the rational logic of followers works. Leadership is 'the world of theatre'. This understanding of communication differs from conventional approaches, which view successful communication as either transmission or filtering of information. More is needed than this to mobilise followers to take irrational risks, inducing followers to believe in an imaginary world. At its best, Mbeki's oratory is capable of inspiring enthusiasm but, as a leader, too often he appears remote or didactic and even, according to at least one commentary,[90] uncaring. Moreover, the elevation onto the national stage of the ANC's internal conflicts, as exemplified by Tshwete's conspiracy accusations against Mbeki's former rivals, detracts from the president's moral authority and projects the sort of drama which can only demobilise followers rather than inspire them. South Africa's democratic prospects may have been enhanced by the early abdication of Mandela's charismatic power, but since his departure presidential authority has struggled to engage and enthral South Africa's citizenry.

NOTES

PROLOGUE

1. Mary Benson, *Nelson Mandela*, Penguin, Harmondsworth, 1986, p. 13.
2. Nelson Mandela, *Long Walk to Freedom*, Abacus, London, 1995.
3. Richard Stengel, 'Mandela: The man and the mask', *Sunday Times*, Johannesburg, 27 November 1994.
4. Courtney Jung and Ian Shapiro, 'South Africa's negotiated transition: Democracy, opposition and the new constitutional order', *Politics and Society*, 23, 3, September 1995, p. 287.
5. Sam Sole, 'Angry Mandela reads the riot act', *Sunday Independent*, Johannesburg, 17 March 1996.
6. Claudia Braude, 'We need to share Mandela's hidden pain to lay past abuses to rest', *Sunday Independent*, 3 March 1986.
7. Fatima Meer, *Higher than Hope: The Authorised Biography of Nelson Mandela*, Harper and Row, New York, 1990, p. 334: 'I have been fairly successful in putting on a mask behind which I have pined for my family, alone, never rushing for the post until somebody calls out my name ...'
8. Kaizer Nyatsumba, 'Mandela raps praise singers', *The Star*, Johannesburg, 28 February 1996.
9. The address was drafted by Mandela in conjunction with two members of the 'National Reception Committee', Cyril Ramaphosa and Trevor Manuel, both representatives of the political movement that had developed during the 1980s out of trade unions and local voluntary associations, which emphasised popular sovereignty and accorded leaders very limited authority.
10. E S Reddy, *Nelson Mandela: Symbol of Resistance and Hope for a Free South Africa*, Sterling Publishers, New Delhi, 1990, pp. 1–6.
11. See Nomzamo Winifred Madikizela-Mandela, 'A country girl reflects on the media that turned her into a commodity', *Sunday Independent*, 8 September 1996. She wrote, 'I have a sense of being commoditised by the press. My relationship with it began the moment I stepped off the train in Johannesburg on a morning in 1953, a late teenager in my school uniform, with an iron trunk on my head, a food basket in my hand and an ambition in my heart to become a social worker. It was such a momentous step for a rural girl to take. Yet I was not newsworthy in that respect. I had to become a smart city girl, acquire glamour, before I could begin to be processed into a personality. And I began to be processed thus because I made my entry into Egoli at a time when there was an emergent black bourgeoisie and magazines like *Zonk* and *Drum* to reflect that bourgeoisie ... they were on the lookout for role models: they were like talent scouts, looking for people who could be converted into personalities, glamorised and projected larger than life ...'
12. Nancy Harrison, *Winnie Mandela: Mother of a Nation*, Victor Gollancz, London, 1985. For photograph, see Albrecht Hagemann, *Nelson Mandela*, Fontein Books, Johannesburg, 1996, p. 61.
13. Meer, *Higher than Hope*, p. 317.
14. *South*, Cape Town, 21 July 1988.
15. This is suggested in the preface of Sheridan Johns and R Hunt Davis, *Mandela, Tambo and the African National Congress*, Oxford University Press, New York, 1991, p. ix.
16. John Carlin, 'Love affair with Britain', *The Star*, 1 May 1993.
17. Richard Stengel, 'The Mandela I came to know', *The Spectator*, 19 November 1994.
18. See especially Nancy Harrison, *Winnie Mandela*, in which she describes Mandela returning home from his mission abroad to obtain foreign support for Umkhonto weSizwe, carrying a suitcase filled with national costumes for his wife. Mandela's 'fairytale' marriage featured prominently in a television soap opera broadcast starring Danny Glover and Alfred Woodward in more than 80 countries in 1988 (*Sunday Times*, 11 February 1990). Ronald Harwood's screenplay was intended to emphasise 'the remarkable qualities of Winnie Mandela ... [and] the extraordinary bond between the man

and the woman' (Ronald Harwood, *Mandela*, Channel Four Books, London, 1987).

19. This is true not only of black writers. In 1948, Alan Paton's *Cry, the Beloved Country* was the first South African work of fiction to introduce the moral drama of apartheid to an international best-seller audience. The book was subsequently filmed, inside South Africa, with a young Sidney Poitier in its leading role. Some 40 years later, Poitier returned to play the part of Mandela in an American television film about South Africa's transition to democracy.

20. Rob Nixon, *Homelands, Harlem and Hollywood: South African Culture and the World Beyond*, Routledge, London, 1994, p. 178. Alf Khumalo and Es'kia Mphahlele in *Mandela: Echoes of an Era* (Penguin, Harmondsworth, 1990) reproduce a good range of the press photographs of Mandela taken by Khumalo for South African newspapers in the 1950s and 1960s.

21. Sipho Sepamla, 'I Need', reprinted on the frontispiece of Meer, *Higher than Hope*.

22. Steve Davis, *Apartheid's Rebels: Inside South Africa's Hidden War*, Yale University Press, New Haven, 1987, p. 50.

23. Chris Erasmus, 'Mandela: The options', *Inside South Africa*, September 1988.

24. Credo Mutwa, *Let Not My Country Die*, United Publishers International, Pretoria, 1986, pp. 162–4.

25. A 1981 poll of black South Africans living on the Witwatersrand found that 42 per cent of the sample chose 'ANC leaders' as the 'real leaders of South Africa' as opposed to 37 per cent who favoured the ANC as an organisation which 'will be important in their lives' (Lawrence Schlemmer, 'The report of the attitude surveys', *Buthelezi Commission*, vol. 1, H. and H. Publications, Durban, 1982, pp. 244–5). Another 1981 poll of black South Africans in Johannesburg, Cape Town and Durban found 78 per cent endorsing Mandela as opposed to 40 per cent of respondents favouring the ANC (Craig Charney, 'Who are the black leaders?', *The Star*, 23 September 1981). A 1985 national survey of black urban residents found 23 per cent acknowledging Mandela's leadership as opposed to 8 per cent favouring the organisation – in both cases the largest proportions of support for an individual or an organisation (Mark Orkin, *The Struggle and the Future: What Black South Africans Really Think*, Ravan Press, Johannesburg, 1986, pp. 35–6).

26. 'Letters from black South Africans to the president of Inkatha', *Inhlabamkhosi*, Bureau of Communication, Department of the Chief Minister, Government of KwaZulu, Ulundi, February 1984, pp. 7–10.

27. Stanley Uys, 'The ANC generation gap that haunts Mandela', *The Guardian Weekly*, 23 April 1993.

28. Mary Benson, *Nelson Mandela*, PanAf Great Lives, London, 1980.

29. Mary Benson, *Nelson Mandela*, Penguin.

30. 'And that's why they won't release him', *New Nation*, 7 July 1988.

31. Though Derrida also suggests that in Mandela's future actions there will be represented 'the effective accomplishment, the filling out of the democratic form' when the 'seeds of African revolutionary democracy' infuse and fulfil the potential of Anglo-American forms. See Jacques Derrida, 'The laws of reflection: Nelson Mandela, in admiration', in Jacques Derrida and Mustapha Tlili (eds.), *For Nelson Mandela*, Seaver Books, New York, 1987.

32. Nelson Mandela, *No Easy Walk to Freedom*, Heinemann, London, 1973, pp. v–vii.

33. For one version of this argument, see Raymond Suttner and Jeremy Cronin, *30 Years of the Freedom Charter*, Ravan, Johannesburg, 1986, pp. 179–80.

34. 'The Charter on the Mines', *SASPU National*, Last Quarter 1987, supplement on the Freedom Charter, p. 5.

35. Fatima Meer, *Higher than Hope: Rolihlahla We Love You*, Skotaville Publishers, Johannesburg, 1988.

36. Meer, *Higher than Hope: The Authorised Biography*, p. xi.

37. 'Heed Free Mandela Movement, government urged', a press cutting used as Exhibit D 30, in *State vs. Mewa Ramgobin*.

38. Speech at Release Mandela Committee meeting, Soweto, 8 July 1984; Schedule A, Indictment, p. 19, *State vs Mewa Ramgobin*.

39. From the transcript of the rally reproduced in Isaac Saki Shabangu, *Madiba, The Folk Hero*, Lingua Franca Publishers, Giyani, 1995, p. 107.

40. Martin Gottlieb, 'Mandela's visit, New York's Pride', *New York Times*, 25 June 1990.

41. Lisa Jones, 'Nelson and Winnie in the black metropolis', *Village Voice*, 3 July 1990.

42. 'Waiting joyously for an African Godot', *New York Newsday*, 21 June 1990.

43. Gottlieb, 'Mandela's visit'.

44. Peter Applebone, 'American blacks talk of change after Mandela', *New York Times*, 1 July 1990.

45. 'Mandela takes his message to rally in the Yankee Stadium', *New York Times*, 22 June 1990.

46. *New York Newsday*, 21 June 1990.

47. Alessandra Stanley, 'Pride and confusion mix in talk on education', *New York Times*, 21 June 1990.

48. John Tierney, 'Meeting New York on her own', *New York Times*, 23 June 1990.

49. In certain centres preparations began months in advance: 'Rainbow coalition celebrates release of Nelson Mandela', *The Montclair Times*, New Jersey, 8 February 1990.

50. Stanley, 'Pride and confusion'.

51. Jones, 'Nelson and Winnie'.

52. Jones, 'Nelson and Winnie'.

53. Nixon, *Homelands*, p. 187.

54. From his address to the joint session of the US House of Congress, 26 June 1990, in Reddy, *Nelson Mandela*, p. 83.

55. See T. Dunbar Moodie, *The Rise of Afrikanerdom: Power, Apartheid, and the Afrikaner Civil Religion*, University of California Press, Berkeley, 1975, pp. 18–21.

56. James Gregory, *Goodbye Bafana: Nelson Mandela, My Prisoner, My Friend*, Headline Book Publishing, London, 1995, p. 434.

57. Gregory, *Goodbye Bafana*, p. 489.

58. Liz Sampson, 'Me and Mandela', *Sunday Life*, Cape Town, 19 January 1997.

59. Mark Gevisser, 'Grown fat on total onslaught contracts, Bill Venter meets Mandela on the road to Damascus', *Sunday Independent*, 15 December 1996.

60. Editorial, *The Citizen*, Johannesburg, 15 January 1994.

61. Shaun Johnson, 'Allaying anxiety about Afrikaans', *The Star*, 19 September 1991.

62. Claudia Braude, 'Yutar and holy disbelief', *Weekly Mail & Guardian*, 27 March 1997.

63. David Apter, *Ghana in Transition*, Princeton University Press, New Jersey, 1972, p. 323.

64. Recent market research suggests that 60 per cent of the population see no role for an opposition party and more than a quarter would prefer a one-party state (Editorial, *Weekly Mail & Guardian*, 20 March 1997). In 1994 pollsters found that 50 per cent of African respondents of a Witwatersrand sample would not allow members of the party they most opposed to live in their neighbourhood, and that 59 per cent of the same sample would try to stop such party members from canvassing for support in their area (R. W. Johnson and Lawrence Schlemmer, 'Political attitudes in South Africa's economic heartland', in R. W. Johnson and Lawrence Schlemmer, *Launching Democracy in South Africa: The First Open Election, April 1994*, Yale University Press, New Haven, 1996, p. 261.)

65. For a very readable popular reflection of transition analysis with Mandela at its centre, see Allister Sparks, *Tomorrow is Another Country*, Heinemann, London, 1995.

66. Alec Russell, 'Mandela magic leaves the world lost for words', *Daily Telegraph*, 5 July 1996.

67. Peta Krost, 'Focused spindoctor at Madiba's side', *The Star*, 11 January 1997.

68. Esther Waugh, 'Mandela gives Nobel money to children', *The Star*, 11 March 1994.

69. John Battersby, 'Mandela meditates on the ironies of fame', *Sunday Independent*, 24 November 1996.

70. 'I won't be your bloody fool, Dali, wrote furious Winnie', *The Star*, 20 March 1996.

71. *Sunday Times*, 25 February 1996.

72. 'Presidential accolades for nation-building citizens', *The Star*, 11 November 1996.

73. Derrida and Tlili, *For Nelson Mandela*, p. 26.

74. 'Mandela fires newsmen', *The Star*, 14 November 1996.

75. 'Mandela hits out at Tutu, chief whip', *The Star*, 27 September 1994.

76. H. W. Vilakazi, 'Leaders' moral quality must rise', *The Star*, 12 June 1995.

77. Findings from *Opinion '99*, a poll conducted by the Electoral Institute of South Africa (EISA) in conjunction with the Institute for Democracy in South Africa (IDASA), the South African Broadcasting Corporation (SABC) and the survey agency Markinor. Similar percentages emerged from a poll conducted in March 1999 by the Human Sciences Research Council through its Democracy South Africa project.

78. Jonathan Rosenthal and Frank Nxumalo, 'Mandelarand may oust Oom Paul', *Business Report*, March 1999.

79. 'Mandela using Nat laws to eject Winnie', *The Star*, 17 April 1999.

80. Meanwhile, Winnie Mandela's status in public history is undergoing critical re-evaluation, her continuing popularity notwithstanding. A memorial stone commemorating the site of the aircraft crash in which Mozambique's Samora

Machel met his death had its inscription reworded so that the original message of condolence received by the Machel family, reproduced on the stone, had Winnie's name excised. See Paul Fauvet, 'History remade as Winnie's name left off Machel plaque', *The Star*, 23 January 1999.

81. Adrian Hadland and Jovial Rantao, *The Life and Times of Thabo Mbeki*, Zebra Press, Rivonia, 1999, p. 98 and p. 149.

82. For a perceptive exposition of the democratic implications of Mandela's ideas about national consensus, see: Andrew Nash, 'Mandela's democracy', *Monthly Review*, April 1999, pp. 18–28.

83. Ranjeni Mumusamy, 'Come home, ANC tells UDM supporters', *Sunday Times*, 31 January 1999.

84. Xolesa Vapi, 'Hail Queen Graça', *The Star*, 10 April 1999.

CHAPTER 1

1. *The Star*, 7 November 1994 and 25 November 1994; *New Nation*, 9 December 1994.

2. *Strategy and Tactics of the African National Congress*, Presidential Address, 50th National Conference of the ANC, Mafikeng, 16–20 December 1997.

3. Cited in *The Star*, 21 October 1999.

4 *The Star*, 10 July 2000.

5. African National Congress, *The State and Social Transformation*, November 1996, p. 15.

6. 'The balance of forces in 2001', *Umrabulo*, 10, May 2001, Department of Political Education and Training, African National Congress, Marshalltown, p. 5.

7. ANC figures as reported in *The Citizen*, 17 June 1991.

8. For the evolution of ANC economic programmes, see Nicoli Nattrass, 'Politics and economics in ANC policy', *African Affairs*, 93, 372, July 1994, pp. 343–60.

9. Jonathan Michie and Vishnu Padayachee, *The Political Economy of South Africa's Transition*, The Dryden Press, London, 1997, p. 46. See also Patrick Bond, 'The making of South Africa's macro-economic compromise', in Ernest Maganya and Rachel Houghton (eds.), *Transformation in South Africa? Policy debates in the 1990s*, IFAA, Johannesburg, 1992.

10. African National Congress, *The Reconstruction and Development Programme: A Policy Framework*, Umanyano Publications, Johannesburg, 1994.

11. Andrew Reynolds argues that descriptive representation – matching the social mix of governing bodies to the composition of the population – plays a key role in consolidating political stability in previously divided societies. He draws a distinction between descriptive and substantive representation. In the case of the latter, for example, members of a racial minority within cabinet would seek to represent minority interests. See Andrew Reynolds, *Electoral Systems and Democratization in Southern Africa*, Oxford University Press, New York, 1999, p. 59.

12. This is often claimed on their behalf. See, for example, a profile of minister Sankie Mthembi-Mahanyele, who recalls her own childhood in 'traumatic' surroundings and believes 'it is her past experience that prepares [her] for the mammoth task of delivering houses to the needy millions', in Pamela Dube, 'Matchbox memories drive minister's vision', *Sunday Independent*, 25 July 1999.

13. In this discussion of class identity I have borrowed the terminology employed by Erik Olin Wright in his *Class Counts*, Cambridge University Press, Cambridge, 1997, pp. 22–4

14. African National Congress, *Together, Speeding Up Change. Fighting Poverty and Creating a Better Life for All*, Local Elections Manifesto, 10 October 2000.

15. Mangosuthu Buthelezi, as quoted in *The Star*, 16 November 1998.

16. Ebrahim Harvey in the 'Left Field' column in *Mail & Guardian*, 4 August 2000. Also see Dale T McKinley, *The ANC and the Liberation Struggle*, Pluto Press, London, 1997, p. 133.

17. *Saturday Star*, 16 May 1998.

18. Pollsters in late 1994 found African ANC voters demonstrating patience with the new government and confidence that it would keep its promises. In a variety of policy-related questions respondents demonstrated a surprising degree of moderation in their expectations. For example, 61 per cent of the sample favoured smaller housing subsidies than those offered by the government so that more people could be helped sooner. See Lawrence Schlemmer, R W Johnson and Craig Charney, 'South Africa: findings of a survey of political and social attitudes in post-election South Africa', Centre for Policy Studies, Johannesburg, December 1994, p. 20. For a generally positive view of government performance (especially in the spheres of health, education and housing) amongst poorer African respondents to a national survey undertaken in

December1998, see the Independent Newspaper Group's 'Reality check' supplements, published in *The Star*, 21 and 28 April 1999.

19. *The Star*, 1 August 2000.

20. For further discussion in this vein, see Theda Skocpol, *States and Social Revolutions*, Cambridge University Press, Cambridge, 1979, pp. 24–33.

21. Of course, in certain respects, the state has become less socially autonomous and less powerful over the last decade, partly because of its rising debts and also because of its democratisation, which has made public access to the state easier. Even so, South African government bureaucratic capacity compares favourably with most other African governments on the subcontinent for the extent of its social penetration, that is the range of citizenry affected by its actions, its extractive capacity – the social character of its taxation base – and its coercive authority. For the historical reasons for South Africa's state strength, see David Yudelman, *The Emergence of Modern South Africa*, Greenwood Press, Westport, Connecticut, 1983, pp. 214–48.

22. In 1992, South Africa's total foreign debt was US$17 billion, 14.5 per cent of the country's GNP. In terms of figures expressed as a proportion of GNP, only Mauritius and Botswana were relatively less indebted. Mozambique's foreign debt in 1992 was five times its GNP. See Pieter Esterhuysen, *Africa at a Glance*, Africa Institute, Pretoria, 1995, p. 51.

23. COSATU, 'A programme for the Alliance', *African Communist*, 146, 1997/1, p. 22.

24. Malcolm Ray, 'COSATU mounts new offensive on GEAR', *Sunday Independent Reconstruct*, 30 April 2000.

25. Republic of South Africa, *White Paper on Reconstruction and Development: The Government's Strategy for Total Transformation*, Cape Town, Office of the President, 1994.

26. Mbazima Shilowa, 'Challenges of the transition: A COSATU perspective', *African Communist*, 139, 1, 1995, p. 36.

27. Lynda Loxton, 'Job figures released', *The Star*, 15 October 1998.

28. Figures are drawn from an analysis by Jeremy Baskin of Statistics South Africa, PO317, in *Mail & Guardian*, 24 November 2000.

29. COSATU, 'A programme for the Alliance', p. 22.

30. According to Mazibuko Jara, SACP media officer, 13 July 2001.

31. *Sunday Independent*, 9 July 2000.

32. *All Power to the People: Proposed Constitutional Amendments*, 50th National Conference of the ANC, Marshalltown, Johannesburg, 1997.

33. *Sunday Times*, 1 April 2001.

34. See, for example, Thabo Mbeki's remarks on the racial representation of the South African Chamber of Business in Thabo Kobokoane, 'SACOB worried about restrictive labour laws', *Sunday Times Business Times*, 18 October 1998.

35. *The Star*, 5 April 2001.

36. It is likely that most are concentrated in junior positions. A survey of 120 companies in 1998 revealed that Africans occupied 12 per cent of senior management positions in 1998 and 21 per cent of middle management positions; the proportions of whites in middle management was expected to drop to 55 per cent by 2001 (see *Business Day*, 23 November 1998).

37. Susanna Loof, 'Economic freedom eludes South Africa', *The Star*, 14 August 2001.

38. Thabo Kobokoane, 'Infighting, fewer deals make it a slow year for empowerment', *Sunday Times*, 11 November 2001.

39. See the parliamentary register reproduced in *The Star*, 19 February 1998. The two richest members of parliament, Ben and Mary Turok, with shareholdings worth R1.5 million between them, are also amongst the most left-wing.

40. Jeremy Cronin and Blade Nzimande, 'ANC Thatcherites want a party of black bosses', *Mail & Guardian*, 10 October 1998.

41. Wally Mbhele, 'Mokaba tackles the SACP', *Mail & Guardian*, 3 October 1997.

42. Cyril Madlala, 'Mbeki's gauntlet', *The Star*, 12 September 1998.

43. Kerry Cullinan, 'Moosa raps COSATU for privatisation strike plan', *The Star*, 11 September 1998.

44. Ann Crotty, 'Ramaphosa calls for balanced labour law', *The Star*, 30 June 1998.

45. Kerry Cullinan, 'Hanekom defends property clause', *The Star*, 19 September 1998.

CHAPTER 2

1. According to figures released in parliament by the Department of Public Service and Administration. See Ian Clayton, 'Still too many bureaucrats', *Mail & Guardian*, 19 March 1999.

2. Department of Public Service and Administration, *Provincial Review Report* (*Ncholo Report*), 1997, p. 46.

3. *Ncholo Report*, p. 25.

4. 'Consultants needed on a daily basis', *The Star*, 23 February 1999.

5. *Ncholo Report*, p. 42.

6. *Ncholo Report*, p. 9.

7. Charlene Smith, 'Budget cuts send hospitals from bad to worse', *Mail & Guardian*, 26 March 1999.

8. 2000/1 budget statistics in *Business Report*, 27 February 2001.

9. Quentin Wray, 'PAC expert slams East Cape health chaos', *Eastern Province Herald*, 26 June 1999.

10. Ann Bernstein, *Policy-making in a New Democracy*, Centre for Development Enterprise, Johannesburg, 1999, p. 36.

11. Clayton, 'Still too many bureaucrats'.

12. Dudu Molate, 'Cash-strapped province takes on system', *Provincial Whip*, 7 August 1998, p. 4.

13. Walter Sehurutshe, 'Cash crisis in the Free State', *Provincial Whip*, 13 August 1999, p. 5.

14. Simon Zwane, 'Free State welfare and health services in crisis', *The Star*, 11 February 1999.

15. Andy Duffy, 'Another education chief on the line', *Mail & Guardian*, 30 April 1998.

16. Gareth Newman, 'Legislature battles the budget', *Provincial Whip*, 11 August 1997, pp. 2–3.

17. Nick Wilson, 'Dire warning on EC health', *Eastern Province Herald*, 16 March 1999.

18. For commentary, see correspondence columns in the *Lowvelder*, 19 March 1998 and 26 March 1998, and Dumisane Lubisi, 'Gravel replacing tar in hard-up Mpumalanga', *The Star*, 23 February 1999.

19. The MEC for public works in KwaZulu-Natal routinely travels in a convoy with two additional cars transporting bodyguards, according to newspaper reports about a shooting incident on 24 July. These bodyguards are paid from provincial safety and security funds. In Mpumalanga R17.8 million was allocated to security in 1999/2000 (*Highveld Herald*, 26 February 1999).

20. Findings from *Opinion '99*, a poll conducted by the Electoral Institute of South Africa (EISA) in conjunction with the Institute for Democracy in South Africa (IDASA), the South African Broadcasting Corporation (SABC) and the survey agency Markinor. In October 1998 the survey registered that 62.4 per cent of its respondents in rural settlements felt that the government was handling the improvement of health services very well or fairly well compared to 50.5 per cent in

metropolitan areas. Also, 71.8 per cent of residents polled in the Eastern Cape responded to this question favourably compared to 35.8 per cent in the Western Cape. See *Project Nyulo*, vol. 3, Table 86, Markinor, Johannesburg, p. 258.

21. Justin Arenstein, 'Big wheels', *Sunday Times*, 14 December 1997.

22. Jacquie Golding-Duffy, 'Plans to unseat the premier', *Mail & Guardian*, 28 June 1996.

23. Mark Gevisser, 'One Free State, one Lekota?', *Mail & Guardian*, 6 August 1996.

24. Wally Mbhele, 'The poison arrows are out for Ivy', *Mail & Guardian*, 7 August 1998.

25. For an example, see Jovial Rantao, 'Motshekga in firing line', *The Star*, 15 July 1998. According to reports, 'Motshekga sympathisers' alleged that senior provincial ANC personalities, including two MECs, were deliberately encouraging the premier to make mistakes by offering him bad advice.

26. Mushwana had tried to lay disciplinary charges against the superintendent-general for education, Black Consciousness Movement founder Harry Nengwekhulu, after Nengwekhulu had refused to appoint Mrs Mushwana to the principal's position at a Tzaneen school, insisting on proper tendering procedures and refusing to countenance business arrangements authorised by Mushwana. Mushwana had originally been the province's MEC for finance and had been moved from that position after the Semenye Commission had found evidence of serious financial maladministration in his department.

27. Mathatha Tsedu, 'North's leaders vie for power', *The Star*, 4 February 2001.

28. Between September 1998 and January 1999 research undertaken by the ANC's internal elections department showed approval ratings for the Gauteng government rising from 44 per cent to 51 per cent. See Shalo Mbatha, 'Elusive Motshekga plays down furore in his backyard', *Saturday Star*, 30 January 1999.

29. When the Maputo Development Corridor was opened in June 1998, Mpumalanga's economy was ranked third out of the nine provinces' economies, up from sixth position in 1994. See Charlene Smith, 'Phosa heals old wounds in drive for economic success', *Sunday Independent*, 7 June 1998. In 1997 Mpumalanga enjoyed an above-average growth rate of 4.4 per cent – see 'The Mpumalanga Report', in *South Africa Report*, Second Quarter 1997, p. 5.

30. 'The Mpumalanga Report', p. 11.

31. Phosa made this claim in an interview published in *South Africa Report*, Second Quarter, 1998, p. 64. However, the *Ncholo Report* does not single Mpumalanga out for such praise. It is possible that Phosa may have been referring to the more detailed reports on Ncholo's investigations in each province, which were not published.

32. Ivor Powell, 'Mbeki expected to axe Mpumalanga premier', *Mail & Guardian*, 8 September 2000.

33. A survey of 374 newspaper reports on provincial government corruption in 1999 included 97 reports from Mpumalanga, an unusually high incidence reflecting the presence in Nelspruit of a local news agency, African Eye News, which was feeding stories to metropolitan newspapers. See *Corruption and Good Governance: A Media Profile,* Transparency South Africa, Community Agency for Social Enquiry, Johannesburg, December 2000, pp. 8–11.

34. See Justin Arenstein, 'Jacob Zuma drawn into Mpumalanga scandal probe', *Mail & Guardian*, 16 March 2001, for allegations concerning Zuma's involvement in a company connected with the illicit Parks Board commercialisation as well as the payment of his bond by Phosa's special adviser, Pieter Rootman. Lakela Kaunda, the Presidency's chief director of communications, subsequently published denials of these claims in a letter to the *Mail & Guardian* on 30 March 2001.

35. Helen Taylor and Bob Mattes, *Political Parties and the Consolidation of Democracy in South Africa*, Institute for Democracy in South Africa (IDASA), Kutlwanong Democracy Centre, Pretoria, 29–30 September 1997; Marlene Roefs, 'Notes on perceptions of legitimacy of national and provincial government in the Western and Eastern Cape, KwaZulu-Natal and Gauteng', paper presented at a workshop on 'Democracy and Social Capital in Segmented Societies', Department of Political Studies, University of the Witwatersrand, Johannesburg, 9–12 October 1997.

36. Reynolds, *Electoral Systems*, p. 8.

37. Dipico's refusal to move out of the modest township home he occupied with his mother after his appointment to the premiership was one instance of the unassuming personal style which has contributed to his public standing across the social spectrum. For commentary on the 'Dipico factor', see Steven Robins's contribution to *Elec-*

tion Update '99, Electoral Institute of South Africa, no. 15, June 1999.

38. Johan Olivier and Rose Ngwane, 'Marching to a different tune', *Indicator SA*, 1996.

39. Kaizer Nyatsumba, 'ANC will not be bound by dogma', *The Star*, 21 March 2001.

CHAPTER 3

1. All quotations in the paragraphs preceding this note are from African National Congress, *The Reconstruction and Development Programme: A Policy Framework*, Umanyano Publications, Johannesburg, 1994.

2. COSATU, NACTU and FEDSAL, *Social Equity and Job Creation, the Key to a Stable Future. Labour's Proposals on Growth, Development and Job Creation*, Johannesburg, 1 April 1996, p. 5.

3. *White Paper on Reconstruction and Development: The Government's Strategy for Total Transformation*, Republic of South Africa, Office of the President, Cape Town, 1994.

4. World Bank, *Development Report*, Oxford University Press, Oxford, 1997.

5. See especially Consolidated Business Movement, *Building a Winning Nation*, Ravan Press, Johannesburg, 1994. Also in this vein, see J. Michael Cleverley, *South Africa's Obstacles: The RDP's Opportunities*, address by the counsellor for economic affairs, United States Embassy, Pretoria, 22 June 1995.

6. 'Business: confused signals?', *RDP Monitor*, Stock Information Services, 1, 6, February 1995, p. 2.

7. Unless other sources are indicated, these statistics are taken from *The Building Has Begun! Government's Report to the Nation*, Republic of South Africa, Government Communication and Information System, Pretoria, February 1998.

8. 'Asmal punts his achievements', *The Star*, 25 August 1998.

9. *Department of Water Affairs, Annual Report, 1999/2000*, Republic of South Africa, Pretoria, RP 101/2000, p. 15.

10. Barry Streek, 'SA housing delivery unsurpassed', *Mail & Guardian*, 23 February 2001; Barry Streek, 'Housing shortage still desperate', *Mail & Guardian*, 29 June 2001.

11. David Pottie, 'Housing the nation, the politics of low-cost housing in South Africa since 1994', paper presented to the South African Political Science Association, Durban, 2001, p. 10.

12. Mbongeni Zondi, 'Eskom lights up life for

1,75 million customers', *Sunday Independent Reconstruct*, 14 May 2000.

13. Justin Arenstein, 'Land reform faces dramatic change', *Sunday Independent Reconstruct*, 10 January 1999.

14. Derek Hanekom, 'Great progress in land redistribution', *Mail & Guardian*, 24 January 1998. Land reform statistics are contradictory. The ANC's 1999 election manifesto, *Together, Fighting for Change*, cited the Hanekom statistic of 220 000 hectares transferred to 68 000 households. In fact, by the election the area of land transferred under the Settlement Land Acquisition Grant Scheme (SLAG) was greater, but the number of beneficiaries smaller (see Jubie Matlou, 'A beginner's guide to land matters', *Mail & Guardian*, 5 May 2000). Official sources in May 2000 suggested that only 40 000 households had been resettled, not significantly more than in January 1999. The 68 000 figure was the target of the first phase of the programme before its suspension in August 1999.

15. Allen Seccombe, 'SA to speed up land claims', *Business Report*, 29 June 2001.

16. *Department of Health, Annual Report, 1999/2000*, Republic of South Africa, Pretoria, RP 75/2000.

17. *The Foundation for a Better Life Has Been Laid: The Government's Mid-term Report to the Nation*, Republic of South Africa, South African Communication Service, Pretoria, February 1997, p. 16; *Department of Health, Annual Report, 1998/9*, Republic of South Africa, Pretoria, RP 59/1999.

18. Jim Day, 'Zuma's remarkable road to recovery', *Mail & Guardian*, 23 May 1997.

19. Ria Greyling, 'Sigcau to take public works along new roads', *Sunday Independent Reconstruct*, 17 October 1999.

20. Melanie-Ann Feris, 'Historic watershed in the lives of many', *The Star*, 8 October 1997.

21. Caroline Hooper-Box, 'Kasrils offers a drink to democracy', *Sunday Independent Reconstruct*, 15 October 2000.

22. The South African Institute of Race Relations' annual surveys for the late 1950s and early 1960s suggest an annual rate of 'sub-economic' housing construction of between 25 000 and 35 000 a year for Africans, much of it financed through private-sector loans to the government. This level was only slowly revived again in the late 1980s after a long period in which the state built or financed very small numbers of houses for Africans. Also see John Kane-Berman, *Soweto:*

Black Revolt, White Reaction, Ravan Press, Johannesburg, 1978, pp. 58–61.

23. Pali Lehohla, *South Africa in Transition*, Statistics South Africa, Pretoria, 2001, p. 84.

24. Pali Lehohla, *South Africa in Transition*, pp. 90–1.

25. Richard Abel, *Politics by Other Means: Law in the Struggle Against Apartheid*, Routledge, London, 1995, p. 401.

26. Pieter Esterhuysen, *Africa A–Z: Continental and Country Profiles*, Africa Institute, Pretoria, 1998, p. 52.

27. *Department of Health, Annual Report, 1998/9*, Republic of South Africa, RP 59/1999. South Africa's infant mortality rate remains higher than Botswana's and that of several other much poorer African countries.

28. David Robbins, 'Making our health service better for all', *The Star*, 20 December 1998.

29. EISA/IDASA/SABC/Markinor, *Opinion '99, Project Nyulo*, Set 1, Table 125, Markinor, Johannesburg, November 1998. Tables are held in the library of the Electoral Institute of South Africa.

30. Pali Lehohla, *South Africa in Transition*, p. 88.

31. This estimate is based on a survey of women attending public ante-natal facilities and is considered by some researchers to be too conservative. See Belinda Beresford, 'Doubt on accuracy of AIDS stats', *Mail & Guardian*, 23 March 2001.

32. Robin Hamilton, *South African Institute of Race Relations Social and Economic Update: Special Issue on AIDS*, Johannesburg, May 1991, p. 1

33. Clive Rubin, 'Insurers blame AIDS for ten-year fall in life expectancy', *Business Report*, 21 July 2000.

34. Central Intelligence Agency, *The World Factbook*, on the CIA website (http//www.cia/gov/publications/factbook).

35. Peter Cooper, cited on Gauteng hospital admissions in Anso Thom, 'Medical care is a juggling game', *The Star*, 19 February 2001.

36. Graham McIntosh, president of the KwaZulu-Natal Agricultural Union, interviewed in the *Helen Suzman Foundation KwaZulu-Natal Briefing*, September 1998, p. 19; Mbongeni Ngubeni, 'Understanding and dealing with the killings on farms', *The Star*, 9 October 1998.

37. This statistic refers to the King Edward Hospital in Durban. See Ann Eveleth, 'Cash is the only cure for ailing hospitals', *Mail & Guardian*, 6 February 1998.

38. Kerry Cullinan, 'Health care has become the Cinderella service while officials focus on

bringing the budget into the black', *Sunday Independent Reconstruct*, 15 October 2000.

39. Charlene Smith, 'Doctors make way for
Zuma's interns', *Saturday Star*, 21 November
1998.

40. Kader Asmal, 'We must treat our water, that
life-giving essence, as if we found ourselves on a
spaceship', *Sunday Independent*, 18 May 1997.

41. Department of Water Affairs and Forestry,
*Evaluation of the Community Water Supply and
Sanitation Programme*, Workshop Document,
Mvula Trust, Pretoria, November 1997.

42. Ned Breslin, 'There's a hole in South Africa's
water bucket', *Sunday Independent Reconstruct*,
4 October 1998.

43. 'Water Affairs disputes claims that rural
programme is in disarray', *The Star*, 10 May
1999; Peter Wellman, 'Asmal's disaster', *Sunday
World*, 9 April 1999.

44. Edward D. Breslin and Bethuel
Netshswinzhe, *Strengthening Sustainability Initia-
tive: Results of the Mvula Trust/Aus Aid Evaluations*,
Mvula Trust, Johannesburg, 15 February 2000.

45. Charlene Smith, 'Too poor to pay for
services', *Mail & Guardian*, 26 March 1999.

46. Khathu Mamaila, 'Water tanks fail to quench
thirst', *The Star*, 25 February 2001.

47. 'No access to sanitation for 21 million', *The
Star*, 15 February 2001. I am grateful to Stephen
Louw for alerting me to these recent policy shifts.

48. 'Keep politics out of housing', *Housing in
Southern Africa*, October 1999, p. 12.

49. 'Reconsidering the place of community
participation in the housing delivery process',
Inform: Newsletter of the National Housing Forum,
1, 1, 1997, p. 4.

50. A good example of the advantages of
working through large-scale organisations would
be the case of ISCOR. An ISCOR subsidiary,
Balaton Housing, has developed a steel building
system which owners can easily erect for themselves. Some 4 000 of these houses were built in
Phomolong for R7 000 a structure, leaving the
rest of the subsidy for infrastructure: roads, water
and sewerage. See advertisement 'Iscor: Building
the Nation', in *Reader's Digest*, June 1996.

51. Edwin Naidu, 'Housing headache continues',
The Star, 14 February 2000.

52. Dianne Smith, 'Crumbling foundations',
Saturday Star, 14 July 2001.

53. Ryan Cresswell, 'Unique housing scheme a
dream come true for women', *The Star*,
25 February 1998; *The Star*, 23 July 1998.

54. Leanne Dickerson, 'The houses that women
built with vision and trust', *Sunday Independent
Reconstruct*, 28 March 1999.

55. Letter, *Mail & Guardian*, 21 May 1999.

56. For details of an Ennerdale women's group,
see Bongiwe Mlangeni, 'Stokvel makes dreams of
own houses a reality', *The Star*, 20 November
1995. For obstructive official attitudes in respect
of a community self-help project, Sivukile in
Mpumalanga, see Susan Miller, 'Individuals pull
together to uplift community', *The Star*,
6 February 1996.

57. Celean Jacobson, 'This is the house Winnie's
building', *Sunday Times*, 15 December 1996.

58. Alan Lipman, 'Apartheid ends, but they're
still put in little boxes, little boxes all the same',
Sunday Independent, 3 March 1996. For unflat-
tering comparisons between 'Verwoerd's
matchboxes' and 'Madiba's rabbit hutches', see
Maja Mokoena, 'We can learn from the occasional
good deeds of bad people', *Business Report*,
24 November 1998, and Vincent Thusi,
'Apartheid matchboxes better than popcorns
being built today', *The Star*, 10 July 2000.

59. David Pottie, 'Housing the nation: the politics of low-cost housing policy in South Africa
since 1994', paper presented to the South African
Political Science Association Meeting, Durban,
2001, p. 8.

60. Sophie Oldfield, 'The centrality of community capacity in state low-income housing
provision in Cape Town, South Africa', *International Journal of Urban and Regional Research*,
24, 4, December 2000, pp. 858–72.

61. Robert Simmonds, 'Troubled housing project
to go ahead', *Sunday Independent Reconstruct*,
19 December 1999.

62. *Human Development Index*, Press Release,
Statistics South Africa, June 1991.

63. *Report for the Office of the Executive Deputy
President's Interministerial Committee on Poverty
and Inequality*, Republic of South Africa, Pretoria,
13 May 1998.

64. Murray Leibbrandt and Ingrid Woolard, 'The
labour market and household income inequality
in South Africa', *Journal of International Development*, 2001; Steven Friedman and Ivor Chipkin,
'The politics of inequality in South Africa', paper
presented at the Centre for Policy Studies, Johannesburg, August 2001.

65. Nicoli Nattrass and Jeremy Seekings,
'Democracy and distribution in highly unequal
economies: The case of South Africa', *Journal of*

Modern African Studies, 39, 3, 2001, pp. 477–83.
66. For statistics, see Trevor Manuel, 'SA dare not ignore sufferings of the past', *The Star*, 22 September 2000.
67. Adam Habib and Rupert Taylor, 'South Africa: Anti-apartheid NGOs in transition', *Voluntas: International Journal of Voluntary and Nonprofit Organisations*, 10, 1, 1999, p. 19.
68. David Macfarlane, 'NDA mired in controversy', *Mail & Guardian*, 24 August 2001.
69. David Everatt and Sifiso Zulu, 'Analysing rural development programmes in South Africa 1994–2000', *Development Update*, 3, 4, 2000, p. 11.
70. Peter Mokaba, 'The state and social transformation: Observations on the South African developmental state since 1998', *Umrabulo*, 10, May 2001, Department of Political Education and Training, African National Congress, Marshalltown, p. 41.
71. Gerald Kraak, 'The South African voluntary sector in 2001', *Development Update*, 3, 4, 2001, p. 143.
72. For details of such schemes in Newtown, Johannesburg, and Payne Park, Germiston, see Hopewell Radebe, 'Rental home projects for low wage earners', *The Star*, 5 October 1998, and Adele Shevel, 'Germiston leads way in housing project', *The Star*, 23 July 1998.
73. Between 1989 and 1998 the matriculation repeater rate (the proportion of students who re-enrolled for a second year in Standard 10) rose from 19 per cent to 40 per cent. See Jacqui Reeves, 'Classroom failures strain education budget', *The Star*, 1 September 1998.

CHAPTER 4

1. According to minister Derek Hanekom, increasing numbers of white farmers would be willing to sell their land as a consequence of government refusal to 'bail out indebted farmers'. See Ray Hartley, 'Hanekom faces rocky terrain', *Sunday Times*, 4 February 1996.
2. Colin Bundy, *The Rise and Fall of the South African Peasantry*, Heinemann, London, 1979, pp. 65–108.
3. African National Congress, *Agricultural Policy*, Westro Reproductions, Johannesburg 1994, pp. 11–18.
4. Norman Chandler, 'Winds of change reach platteland', *The Star*, 19 December 1996.
5. The argument in this paragraph follows Stefan Schirmer, 'Policy visions and historical realities:

Land reform in the context of recent agricultural developments', *African Studies*, 59, 1, 2000, pp. 143–67.
6. Lawrence Schlemmer, 'The situation in South Africa with special reference to rural productivity', in Shaun Vorster, *Land Reform in Southern Africa: Conference Report*, Democrat Union of Africa, Cape Town, 2001, p. 41.
7. On the inefficiency of the small-scale sugar sector, see Ingrid Salgado, 'Coca-Cola slams farmers', *Business Report*, 29 November 2001.
8. Malachia Mathoho and Tobias Schmitz, *Poverty, Civil Society and Patronage: A Study of Two Farmers' Associations in the Northern Province*, Centre for Policy Studies, Research Report, 80, Johannesburg, 2001.
9. Figures vary. These statistics for the redistribution programme were cited by the director-general for the period 1994 to 1999 (see Gilingwe Mayende, 'Didiza's doing what she should', *Mail & Guardian*, 25 August 2000). Slightly different figures are provided by Lionel Cliffe, who obtained the following official figures for November 1999: 447 projects, 55 424 households, 714 407 hectares, and 360 256 people (see Lionel Cliffe, 'Land reform in South Africa', *Review of African Political Economy*, 84, 2000, p. 275).
10. The pilot projects were sponsored as a Presidential Lead Project for the RDP to 'kickstart' land reform. They were very hastily designed and then administered by provincial governments. Subsequent land redistribution schemes were managed by the Department of Land Affairs, which maintains its own offices down to district level.
11. Experts disagree on whether the Constitution bars expropriation of land. The property clause permits expropriation to serve the public interest but there are different views on whether land reform falls within the scope of public interest. See Brendan Pearce, 'National Land Committee presents its vision', *The Star*, 29 August 1995.
12. World Bank, *Options for Land Reform and Rural Restructuring in South Africa*, paper presented to the Land and Agricultural Centre, Land Redistribution Options Conference, Johannesburg, 12–15 October 1993, pp. 1–3 and pp. 41–2. For an analysis of the interaction between the World Bank and the ANC's policy-makers, see Gavin Williams, 'Setting the agenda: A critique of the World Bank's Rural Restructuring

Programme for South Africa', *Journal of Southern African Studies*, 22, 1 March 1996, pp. 131–66.

13. African National Congress, *The Reconstruction and Development Programme: A Policy Framework*, Umanyano Publications, Johannesburg, 1994, p. 22.

14. Norman Chandler, 'Winds of change'.

15. Jovial Rantao, 'About 400 000 people have now acquired land says Hanekom', *The Star*, 18 April 1997.

16. For details, see Colin Murray, 'Land reform in the eastern Free State: Policy dilemmas and political conflicts', *Journal of Peasant Studies*, 23, 2/3, 1996, pp. 209–11.

17. Jim Day, 'Land redistribution flops badly', *Mail & Guardian*, 11 April 1997.

18. Ann Eveleth, 'Slowly the sands are shifting', *Mail & Guardian*, 9 April 1999.

19. Barry Streek, 'Land ministry underspends', *Mail & Guardian*, 26 May 2000.

20. Cliffe, 'Land reform', p. 281.

21. Cliffe, 'Land reform', pp. 282–3.

22. Andile Mngxitama, 'Bold steps may avoid pitfalls of a stalled land reform programme', *Sunday Independent*, 30 April 2000.

23. Colin Murray, 'Changing livelihoods in the Free State: 1990s', *African Studies*, 59, 1, 2000, pp. 130–3.

24. Jim Day, 'Reforming the bantustan way', *Mail & Guardian*, 11 April 1997.

25. Justin Arenstein, 'Land reform grants drive commercial farms', *The Star*, 24 November 1998.

26. Eddie Koch, 'Workers and boers create fruit synergy', *Mail & Guardian*, 26 July 1996.

27. *Land Info*, 4, 6, November 1997, p. 6.

28. For more argument in this vein, see Gillian Hart, 'The agrarian question and industrial dispersal in South Africa: Agro-industrial linkages through Asian lenses', *Journal of Peasant Studies*, 23 2/3, April 1996, pp. 245–77, and Ben Cousins, 'Livestock production and common property struggles in South Africa's agrarian reform', *Journal of Peasant Studies*, 23, 2/3, April 1996, pp. 166–208.

29. Justin Arenstein, 'Land reform faces dramatic change', *Sunday Independent Reconstruct*, 10 January 1999.

30. *Land Info*, 5, 5, November 1998.

31. 'Quality of Life Report', *Land Info*, 6, 1, 1999, pp. 14–15.

32. Mbongeni Zondi, 'Quiet revolution in National Land Committee', *Sunday Independent Reconstruct*, 29 August 1999.

33. Anne Eveleth, 'The gift of land proves useless without support', *Mail & Guardian*, 28 November 1997.

34. Kensington, a gracious but modestly priced Victorian suburb near Johannesburg's city centre, was a favoured residential location in the early 1990s for returning ANC exiles, including several prominent SACP personalities.

35. Farouk Chothia, 'Three senior Land Affairs officials axed', *Business Day*, 22 June 2000; Jaspreet Kindra, 'Hanekom appointees shown the door', *Mail & Guardian*, 4 August 2000.

36. Nicole Turner, 'Land Bank now ploughing new furrow', *The Star*, 22 February 2000; Mungo Soggot, 'Why Jack doesn't like Dolny', *Mail & Guardian*, 23 July 1999.

37. 'The reason we put a moratorium on all new land proposals was for all of us to be clear … what is the product that we want to support? What is our core business?' (Thoko Didiza, as quoted in Dudley Moloi, 'Winds of change at Land Affairs', *Land and Rural Digest*, 8, September 1999).

38. For discussion of the new policy, see Ben Cousins, 'Zim crisis: Our wake-up call', *Mail & Guardian*, 5 May 2000; '2 million hectares of state land to be redistributed', *The Star*, 9 May 2000; Ben Cousins, 'Meaningful land reform must involve people at the grass roots level', *Sunday Independent Reconstruct*, 20 February 2000; Edward Lahiff, 'Delivery must be accelerated', *Sunday Independent Reconstruct*, 28 May 2000.

39. Linda Ensor, 'Government will buy farms for land reform', *Business Day*, 21 June 2000.

40. Louise Cook, 'White farmers under pressure', *Business Day*, 22 June 2000.

41. Barry Streek, 'Didiza seeks Zimbabwe advice on land reform', *Mail & Guardian*, 18 August 2000.

42. AFP, 'Lydenburg case shows legal loopholes in land reform plan', *Business Report*, 17 May 2001. Also see Allan Secombe, 'SA to expropriate its first farm', *Business Report*, 14 February 2001; Rapule Tabane, 'Reprieve for farmer as government gets cold feet', *The Star*, 26 March 2001. For comment, see Geoff Budlender, 'Land reform is not a grab', *The Star*, 3 April 2001, and Lynda Loxton, 'Land redistribution lacks legal grounds', *Business Report*, 6 April 2001.

43. Hannes de Wet, 'Restitution too slow, say commercial farmers', *Business Report*, 4 October 2001.

44. Mbongeni Zondi, 'Minister and NLC to discuss differences', *Sunday Independent Reconstruct*, 17 October 1999; Zakes Hlatshwayo, 'Land grabs are rooted in the slow pace of reform', *The Star*, 10 July 2001.

45. Ben Cousins, 'Didiza's recipe for disaster', *Mail & Guardian*, 18 August 2000.

46. Jubie Matlou, ''n Boer maak 'n plan', *Mail & Guardian*, 12 May 2000.

47. Abbey Makoe, 'Black boers change the colour of Free State farming', *The Star*, 7 May 2000.

48. See the argument in John Sender, 'Rural poverty and land redistribution: Some macro-economic issues', paper presented at the workshop 'Land and Agriculture Policy Centre Redistribution Options', 13 September 1993.

49. Mayende, 'Didiza's doing what she should'.

50. André Horn, 'Land restitution: The South African programme in the African context', paper presented at the biennial conference of the African Studies Association of South Africa, 'Africa in a Changing World', Broederstroom, 8–10 September 1997.

51. Jubie Matlou, 'A beginners' guide to land matters', *Mail & Guardian*, 5 May 2000; Brendan Templeton, 'All land claims will be settled in five years' time', *Sunday Independent*, 7 May 2000.

52. Barry Streek, 'Didiza to revive land bill', *Mail & Guardian*, 19 October 2001.

53. Hlatshwayo, 'Land grabs'.

54. AFP, 'Lydenburg case'.

55. Ashley Westaway, 'Land reform for the poorest', *Mail & Guardian*, 13 October 2001.

56. Rupert Isaacson, *The Healing Land: A Kalahari Journey*, Fourth Estate, London, 2001, pp 264–72.

57. Louise Cook, 'Pace of land restitution speeding up', *Business Day*, 29 November 2000.

58. Andile Mngxitama (in 'Labour tenants. The forgotten people', *Land Update*, January 1998, p. 9) suggested that the KwaZulu-Natal labour tenant population totalled 1.2 million – but this figure is too large (it exceeds the numbers of the entire permanent agricultural labour force). The official estimate of the total of labour tenant population and their families is 250 000 (*Department of Land Affairs, Annual Report, 1997*, Pretoria, RP 96/98, p. 8).

59. Sizwe Samyende, 'Last-minute drive to register labour tenants', *Sunday Independent Reconstruct*, 5 December 1999.

60. Stephen Greenberg, 'Chaos in communal areas', *Land and Rural Digest*, 7, July 1999.

61. Ben Cousins, 'Meaningful land reform must involve people at the grass roots', *Sunday Independent Reconstruct*, 20 February 2000.

62. Drew Forrest, 'Uproar over land bill', *Mail & Guardian*, 23 November 2001; Jaspreet Kindra, 'Land Affairs officials push for the African way of life', *Mail & Guardian*, 30 November 2001.

63. See Richard Levin and Daniel Weiner, 'Peasants speak: The land question in Mpumalanga', *Journal of Peasant Studies*, 23, 2/3, April 1996, pp. 278–301.

64. Sheona Shackleton, Charlie Shackleton and Ben Cousins, 'Re-valuing the communal lands of southern Africa: New understandings of rural livelihoods', in Overseas Development Institute, *Natural Resource Perspectives*, 62, November 2000.

65. For instances of chiefly hostility to tenure reform, see *Mail & Guardian*, 8 November 1996, and *Sunday Independent Reconstruct*, 31 October 1999.

66. This total is derived from the statistics provided by Derek Hanekom in an official departmental publication ('Progress in land and agriculture reform', *Land Info*, 5/4, August 1998) in which he referred to 277 finalised projects affecting 33 338 households or 174 000 people and a further 452 approved projects to which grants had been allocated and which involved another 380 000 people. Both categories of projects combined represent a redistribution of 1.1 million hectares of land.

67. Kgalema Motlanthe, ANC secretary-general, quoted in Khathu Mamaila, 'ANC warns SA farmers to aid land redistribution', *The Star*, 9 May 2000.

68. In the case of the farms in Mangete, owned by the Dunn clan (coloured descendants of the nineteenth-century adventurer John Dunn, who was given land by King Cetshwayo), the livelihoods of 60 farmers are threatened by a thousand squatters led by a former Inkatha 'warlord', inkosi Khayelihle Mathaba (see Karen MacGregor, 'Whose land is it anyway?', *Times Higher Education Supplement*, 31 August 2001).

CHAPTER 5

1. Chief financial officer Roland Hunter, quoted in 'How Johannesburg was bankrupted', Centre for Development Enterprise, *Round Table*, 5, 2000, p. 21.

2. Bongani Mlangeni, 'Action needed to put Masakhane and RDP on track', *The Star*,

27 September 1995.

3. Human Sciences Research Council and the Department of Political Studies, University of the Witwatersrand, *Markdata Omnibus Survey on Local Government*, September 1995.

4. Jane Carruthers, *Sandton: The Making of a Town*, Clet Books, Rivonia, 1993.

5. 'Do you know your mayor? Not many do', *The Star*, 7 November 1996.

6. *The Star*, 5 April 1996.

7. 'Local government reforms: What's happening and who is in charge?', Centre for Development Enterprise, *Round Table*, 5, 2000, p. 19.

8. Department of Constitutional Development, 'White Paper on Local Government', *Government Gazette*, 13 March 1998.

9. Centre for Development and Enterprise, *Response to the White Paper in Local Government*, Johannesburg, June 1998.

10. For a reasoned statement of such a view, see the letter written by councillor Judith Briggs in *The Star*, 13 September 1999.

11. *The Star*, 24 October 2000.

12. KwaZulu-Natal premier Lionel Mtshali, cited in *The Star*, 27 October 1999.

13. Rob Haswell, chief executive officer of the Pietermaritzburg transitional local council, cited in 'Local government reforms: What's happening and who is in charge?', Centre for Development Enterprise, *Round Table*, 5, 2000, p. 10.

14. *The Star*, 16 March 1998.

15. *Witbank News*, 9 July 1999.

16. *Eastern Province Herald*, 17 June 1999.

17. *The Representative*, 22 January 1999 and 18 June 1999.

18. See the letter written by Jack Bloom in *The Star*, 12 December 2000, on the 'deliberate' alteration of the Parktown/Houghton boundaries in Johannesburg which amalgamated the Democratic Alliance's historical stronghold of affluent Houghton with the lower middle-class suburb of Yeoville. Another DA allegation concerning the board was that its decisions reflected a 'distinct attempt to divide suburbs that have strong and active residents associations'. For further argument in this vein, see the letter by Pat Richards, councillor for Johannesburg's Ward 88, in the *Northcliffe and Melville Times*, 22 December 2000. In Cape Town in 1999, the New National Party argued in vain for the transfer of the Helderberg sub-structure from the city so that it could help consolidate NNP domination of the neighbouring district council that would embrace the Boland towns (*Financial Mail*, 24 September 1999). For an example of an ANC politician opposing the board's decisions, see the views of mayor Isaac Mahlangu on the incorporation of Midrand into Johannesburg, which, he contended, would 'take away resources geared to stimulating growth and service delivery to the East Rand mega-city' (*The Star*, 6 October 1999). For support of the board's decision from a Midrand ANC leader, Alan Dawson, see his letter in *The Star*, 13 September 1999.

19. Philip Frankel, Stephen Louw and Simon Stacey, *Governmental Performance and Capacity: Transitional Local Authorities in Mpumalanga*, Department of Political Studies, University of the Witwatersrand, and Human Sciences Research Council External Projects Programme, April 1997, p. 241.

CHAPTER 6

1. For an illuminating account of the political and social tensions surrounding 'good governance' in Stutterheim, one of the few Eastern Cape towns to have remained financially solvent, see Patrick Bond, 'Local economic development and the municipal services crisis in post-apartheid South Africa', *Urban Forum*, 9, 2, 1998, pp. 159–96.

2. Electoral Institute of South Africa, *Local Government Elections Update*, 6, 29 November 2000, p. 2.

3. *Evening Post*, 15 June 2000.

4. *Business Day*, 11 December 2000; *The Star*, 21 November 2000.

5. *Mail & Guardian*, 14 April 2000.

6. *Daily Dispatch*, 5–6 September 2000.

7. Electoral Institute of South Africa, *Local Government Elections Update*, 5, 11 November 2000, p. 3.

8. In Pietermaritzburg, five National Party councillors withdrew their names from the list for the Democratic Alliance. In this town, the two parties' municipal caucuses continued to hold separate meetings and vote differently in council debates (see Cheryl Goodenough, in Electoral Institute of South Africa, *Local Government Elections Update*, 4, 27 October 2000).

9. *Financial Mail*, 20 October 2000.

10. *Sunday Times*, 10 December 2000.

11. *Sunday Times*, 10 December 2000.

12. *Eastern Province Herald*, 1 December 2000.

13. At several rallies and meetings Tony Leon recited a list of 25 ANC candidates who were guilty of corruption or who had criminal charges pending against them (*The Star*, 9 and 20 November 2000).

14. Several years ago, Marais was widely quoted as having boasted that he did not have a drop of African blood in his body. As a National Party leader he had more recently gained popularity and notoriety for his outspoken views about the impact of African affirmative action on coloured people.

15. DA leaflet for Marcelle Ravid, candidate for Johannesburg's Ward 73.

16. DA leaflet for Ismail Jones, candidate for Cape Town's Ward 68.

17. For an example, see the leaflets distributed in Ward 68, Steenberg and Lavender Hill, on behalf of councillor Hennie van Wyk, a municipal worker for 35 years, who was described as 'actively involved in civic organisations in the area since 1960 ... involved in his church and loves his family'.

18. *Natal Mercury*, 16 October 2000.

19. *The Star*, 20 October 2000.

20. United Democratic Movement, *Local Government Elections Manifesto*, Pretoria, 18 October 2000.

21. United Democratic Movement, *A Better Plan for the Future*, Arcadia, 2000.

22. Compare the proposals in the ACDP's manifesto (Cape Town, 2000) with the very similar vision of Christian democracy – as opposed to 'democratic centralism' – in the programme of Johannesburg's Christian Democratic Party (see *Vote Yes for the Christian Democratic Party*, Westgate, 2000).

23. The author is extremely grateful to the South African Civil Society Observer Coalition (SACSOC) and its secretary, Ashley Green Thompson, for access to the observer reports.

24. *The Star*, 25 October 2000.

25. *Business Day*, 29 November 2000.

26. Sean Jacobs, in Electoral Institute of South Africa, *Local Government Elections Update*, 4, 27 October 2000, p. 11.

27. *Business Day*, 29 November 2000.

28. *Mail & Guardian*, 13 October 2000.

29. *Sunday Times*, 1 December 2000.

30. Max Ozinsky, 'Our elections campaign in the Cape Town metro', *Umrabulo*, 10, May 2001, Department of Political Education and Training, African National Congress, Marshalltown, p. 18–19.

31. *The Star*, 24 October 2000.

32. *Die Volksblad*, 11 October 2000.

33. *Mail & Guardian*, 24 November 2000.

34. *Mail & Guardian*, 24 November 2000.

35. *Mail & Guardian*, 24 November 2000, p. 15.

36. See the remarks of the deputy director of the Independent Electoral Commission, Dr Nomsa Masuku, in *The Star*, 2 October 2000.

37. *The Star*, 9 December 2000.

38. *Sunday Independent*, 10 December 2000.

39. *The Star*, 8 December 2000.

40. 'Most municipalities are now involved in integrated development planning', *Department of Constitutional Development Decentralised Development Planning Newsletter*, 1, February 1999.

41. 'Local government survey', *The Star*, 30 January 2001.

42. Conversation with councillor Mike Moriarty, DA leader in Johannesburg, 8 November 2001.

43. Anna Cox, 'City introduces new housing policy', *The Star*, 5 November 2001.

44. Conversation with councillor Malcolm Lennox, DA chief whip, Ekurhuleni, 8 November 2001.

45. Conversation with Pieter Vorster, DA caucus leader, Masilonyane, 13 November 2001.

46. Conversation with councillor Lorraine Hatch, Emalahleni, 13 November 2001.

47. Conversation with Marianna Seyffert, DA office, Buffalo City, 13 November 2001.

48. Philip Frankel, *Local Governance and Social Transformation in Emfuleni: A Needs Analysis for Integrated Development Planning*, unpublished research report, Department of Political Studies, University of the Witwatersrand, October 2001, vol. 1 and 2, Ward Profiles. I am very grateful to my colleague, Professor Frankel, for allowing me to use the findings in this richly detailed investigation.

49. Sithole Mbanga, 'Howick can do it', *Department of Constitutional Affairs Decentralised Development Planning Newsletter*, August 1999.

50. Maj Fiil-Fynn, 'Electricity crisis in Soweto', *Municipal Services Project, Occasional Paper*, 4, Johannesburg, 2001, pp. 7–8.

51. Ray Wolder, 'ANC councillor threatens voters', DA media release, Johannesburg, 10 November 2001.

52. Lynne Altenroxel, 'Bribes scandal rocks Johannesburg', *The Star*, 23 August 2001.

53. Mike Moriarty, 'Joburg back in overdraft', DA media release, Johannesburg, 2 October 2001.

54. Michael Schmidt, 'Mayor in the hot seat over

R12 000 throne', *Sunday Times*, 11 November 2001.

55. John Matisonn, 'Marais dispute threatens to split DA', *Sunday Independent*, 14 October 2001.

56. Barry Streek, 'New scandals plague DA', *Mail & Guardian*, 7 September 2001.

57. Cheryl Goodenough, 'District municipalities' funds cut', *Mail & Guardian*, 10 August 2001.

58. Niki Moore, 'Disgraced Xulu resurfaces as municipal manager', *Mail & Guardian*, 9 November 2001.

59. David Macfarlane, 'NDA mired in controversy', *Mail & Guardian*, 24 August 2001; Sabelo Ndlangisa, 'This is what they earn', *Sunday Times Metro*, 9 December 2001.

60. 'Mokoena: Unfairly treated or out of line?', *The Enquirer*, 1 November 2001.

CHAPTER 7

1. Victor Levine, *Political Corruption: The Ghana Case*, Stanford University Press, Stanford, 1975.

2. Robert Klitgaard, *Controlling Corruption*, University of California Press, Berkeley, 1988, p. 20.

3. *The Economist*, 10 August 1996.

4. Crawford Young and Thomas Turner, *The Rise and the Decline of the Zaïrean State,* University of Wisconsin Press, Madison, 1985, pp. 401–2.

5. J S Nye, 'Corruption and political development: A cost-benefit analysis', *American Political Science Review*, 56, 1967; M Beenstock, 'Corruption and development', *World Development*, 7, 1, 1979.

6. M. McMullen, 'A theory of corruption', *Sociological Review*, 1961, p. 184.

7. Donatella Della Porta and Yves Meny (eds.), *Democracy and Corruption in Europe*, Pinter, London, 1967.

8. Anthony Minnaar, Ian Liebenberg and Charl Schutte, *The Hidden Hand: Covert Operations in South Africa*, Human Sciences Research Council, Pretoria, 1994, p. 321.

9. R. Hengeveld and J. Rodenburg, *Embargo: Apartheid's Oil Secrets Revealed*, Shipping Research Bureau, Amsterdam University Press, Amsterdam, 1995.

10. *Commission of Inquiry into the Department of Development Aid*, Republic of South Africa, Pretoria, RP 73/1992.

11. *Verslag van die Kommissie van Ondersoek na die 1980 Onluste en beweerde Wanbestuur in Kwa-Ndebele*, Republic of South Africa, Pretoria, RP 137/1993.

12. Gerhard Maré and Georgina Hamilton, *An Appetite for Power: Buthelezi's Inkatha and the Politics of 'Loyal Resistance'*, Ravan Press, Johannesburg, 1987, p. 91.

13. Themba Sepotokele, 'Claims of housing corruption', *The Star*, 31 December 1997.

14. Media and Marketing Research, *Sowetan Crime Survey: Presentation of Crime Findings*, Johannesburg, January 1996, p. 12.

15. Jovial Rantao, 'Judge's help sought in uncovering welfare scams', *The Star*, 11 March 1998.

16. Anna Cox, 'Many traffic officers are corrupt', *The Star*, 21 February 2001.

17. Jovial Rantao, 'Enormous fraud found in food programmes', *The Star*, 4 June 1998.

18. Fikile-Ntsikelelo Moya, '300 officials in corruption probe', *The Star*, 28 August 2001.

19. Stephen Mulholland, 'Mtshali must stop playing poker with the rule of the law', *Sunday Times*, 20 February 2000.

20. At least this is perceived to be so. Among the 90 countries surveyed in the 2000 Transparency International *Corruption Perception Index*, South Africa was ranked 34th. In this system the top country, Finland, obtained a rating of 10 ('highly clean') and the last country on the list, Nigeria, received a rating of 1.2. South Africa's rating was a middle-level 5. In Africa, Botswana, Namibia and Tunisia were rated less corrupt than South Africa, while Mauritius, Morocco, Malawi, Ghana, Senegal, Zambia, Burkina Faso, Zimbabwe, Tanzania, Uganda, Mozambique, Kenya, Cameroon, Angola and Nigeria received poorer ratings. South Africa's position in the 1999 index was also 34th (*Transparency International Press Release*, Berlin, 13 September 2000). In the 2001 index South Africa's ranking slipped down to 38th position with a 4.8 rating. It retained its position as the fourth least corrupt African country (see Peter Fabricius, 'SA slipping down corruption index', *The Star*, 28 June 2001).

21. 'Corruption shrinking budgets', *The Star*, 28 August 1998.

22. Susan Rose-Ackerman, *Corruption and Government: Causes, Consequences and Reform,* Cambridge University Press, Cambridge, 1999, pp. 199–223.

23. 'New frontiers in diagnosing and combating corruption', in *Poverty Reduction and Economic Management*, World Bank, Washington, 7 October 1998.

24. A. Doig, 'Good government and sustainable anti-corruption strategies: A role for independent anti-corruption agencies?', *Public Administration and Development*, 15, 1991, pp.152–65.

25. For useful comments on the public cynicism that results from commissions of inquiries which are principally 'aimed at justifying the legitimacy of new leaders and discrediting those ousted' and which, moreover, reinforce the view that corruption is merely the consequence 'of flawed personalities rather than the outcome of complex social and structural defects', see Sahr John Kpundeh's study 'Limiting administrative corruption in Sierra Leone', in *Journal of Modern African Studies*, 32, 1, 1994, p. 147, which deals with the progress of anti-corruption undertakings in Sierra Leone.

26. Jon S. T. Quah, 'Singapore's experience in curbing corruption', in Arnold Heidenheimer (ed.), *Controlling Corruption: A Source Book*, Transaction Books, New Brunswick, 1989.

27. Robert Klitgaard, 'International cooperation against corruption', *Finance and Development*, International Monetary Fund, 35, 1, March 1998, pp. 3–6.

28. *Mail & Guardian*, 13 November 1987

29. See, for example, the National Party's *Corruption Barometer, 1994–1998* (compiled by Shaun Vorster and published by the National Party's Federal Council in Cape Town), a dossier of press coverage and an analysis of the incidence of press reports. A similar project by a more politically impartial organisation is the press survey for 1997 undertaken for Transparency International South Africa by the Community Agency for Social Enquiry (*Corruption and Good Governance Profile: South Africa 1997*, Transparency International, Johannesburg, 3 September 1998).

30. Robert Mattes and Cherrel Africa, 'Corruption – the attitudinal component: tracking perceptions of official corruption in South Africa, 1995–1998', unpublished paper, Institute for Democracy in South Africa (IDASA), Cape Town, 1999, p. 6.

31. Mark Orkin, *Victims of Crime Survey*, Statistics South Africa, Pretoria, 1998.

32. *The Star*, 8 August 2000. By contrast, an international survey conducted in 1996 found that 129 South African companies reported that kickbacks, bribes or secret commissions had cost them a total exceeding R5 million (see Lala Camerer, 'South Africa – derailing the gravy train – controlling corruption', *Journal of Financial Crime*, 4, 4 June 1997, p. 365).

33. *Sunday Independent Reconstruct*, 5 November 2000.

34. *Daily Dispatch*, 25 March 1999.

35. Roshila Pillay, 'North West suspends pensions for the disabled', *Mail & Guardian*, 1 June 2000.

36. *The Star*, 5 October 1998.

37. *Sunday Independent*, 3 March 2000. Part of this expenditure was attributable to the habit of MECs and their bodyguards to stay in five-star hotels in Durban while on official business away from the provincial capital, Ulundi. Prince Gideon Zulu, MEC for welfare, took hotel rooms for 107 days at a cost of R500 000 (see Veven Bissety, 'IFP instructs leaders to save on hotel bills', *The Star*, 9 April 2001).

38. *The Star*, 22 August 1998.

39. *The Star*, 10 November 1998.

40. Nawall Deane, 'Stofile's wife in tender wrangle', *Mail & Guardian*, 23 March 2001.

41. 'Premier hits back at auditor', *The Star*, 26 September 2001.

42. Lynne Altenroxel, 'Concern over MEC's private deals', *The Star*, 12 April 2001

43. Mungo Soggot, 'Raid: Kickbacks and Armagnac for oil', *Mail & Guardian*, 16 February 2001.

44. Marvin Meintjies, 'Taxi industry offered R3 million bribe', *The Star*, 4 May 2001.

45. *The Star*, 17 April 2000.

46. *Evening Post*, 25 February 1999.

47. 'Traffic correspondent hounded out of job', *The Star*, 17 September 1999.

48. *Mail & Guardian*, 31 March 2000.

49. In 1998, the police anti-corruption unit opened 2 653 dockets involving allegations against 926 policemen. Of these, 475 were arrested. By the end of the year 128 had been convicted and 268 acquitted (*The Star*, 31 August 2000). At the beginning of 1998, however, the commander of a police anti-corruption unit in Gauteng was under investigation for receiving kickbacks from informer fees (*The Star*, 14 January 1998).

50. In 1999, the South African Revenue Service dismissed 54 customs officials for receiving bribes (*The Star*, 27 September 1999).

51. The Directorate's Division of Special Operations includes the elite 'Scorpion' investigative unit and the Office of Serious Economic Offences. These, together with the Asset Forfeiture Unit, which reports separately to the Director of Public Prosecutions, all include the eradication

of public-sector corruption in their preoccupations. There were plans within the directorate to
establish a specialised anti-corruption division,
but these foundered after officials within the
Scorpions objected to the appointment of Sipho
Ndluli, an old associate of the minister of justice,
to head corruption investigations. Ndluli was
insufficiently experienced, they maintained. For a
report on recent Scorpion anti-corruption activity
directed at Mpumalanga provincial politicians
and efforts by deputy president Jacob Zuma to
halt the Scorpion probe in favour of an ANC
internal investigation, see Justin Arenstein, 'Jacob
Zuma drawn into Mpumalanga scandal probe',
Mail & Guardian, 16 March 2001.

52. *Business Day*, 12 March 1999; *The Star*,
12 March 1999.
53. Lala Camerer and Mark Shaw, 'Countering
organised crime', *South African Institute of International Affairs Yearbook,* 1997/98.
54. *The Star*, 11 April 1999.
55. *Mail & Guardian*, 1 September 2000.
56. *Corruption and Good Governance Profile: South
Africa*, Transparency International, Community
Agency for Social Enquiry, Johannesburg,
3 September 1998.
57. Ann Crotty, 'Time to hit corruption for six',
Business Report, 11 April 2001.
58. 'Corruption is public enemy No. 1 says
Mbeki', *The Star*, 27 July 2001.
59. *The Star*, 25 March 1999.
60. *The Star*, 20 May 2000.
61. *Mpumalanga News*, 24 June 1999.
62. *The Star*, 12 February 1999.
63. *The Star*, 10 September 1999.
64. *Mail & Guardian*, 10 November 2000. The
accusation against Joe Modise originated from a
former ANC 'intelligence operative' who supplied
the information to the Coalition for Defence
Alternatives (*Mail & Guardian*, 10 November
2000). Suspicions that Modise may have received
bribes date back to 1997 when Modise as a
member of a black empowerment consortium
bought an electronic company, Conlog, allegedly
with the help of a R40 million loan from an
unknown source in Germany. A subsidiary of
Conlog in which Modise did not have a direct
interest later became one of the sub-contractors
in the arms deal (*Business Report*, 2 April 2001).
65. *Mail & Guardian*, 3 November 2000.
66. *Sunday Independent*, 4 February 2001.
67. Sam Sole and John Matisonn, 'Mbeki's
minister tries to derail probe', *Sunday Independent*,
12 November 2000.
68. *Mail & Guardian*, 2 February 2001.
69. John Matisonn, 'The straw that broke rebel
Feinstein's back', *Sunday Independent*,
2 September 2001.
70. *Sunday Times*, 25 March 2001.
71. Patrick Lawrence, 'Arms deal probe: Unanswered questions', *Helen Suzman Foundation
Focus*, 24, December 2001, p. 4.
72. Public Protector of South Africa, Auditor-
General and National Prosecuting Authority of
South Africa, *Joint Investigation Report into the
Strategic Defence Procurement Packages*, RP
184/2001, Pretoria, November 2001.
73. John Matisonn and Pamela Kimburg, 'President Mbeki brands critics of arms report racist',
Sunday Independent, 18 November 2001.
74. Mosiuoa Lekota, 'We've sailed through the
litmus test', *Sunday Times*, 18 November 2001.
75. See comments by Rocky Williams on the
'less than apparent' utility of the aircraft to be
purchased in the programme. The airforce's own
experts favoured Italian and French bids over the
proposal submitted by British Aerospace, which
won the contract on the grounds that Italian
trainers and French fighters would be cheaper to
operate (see Rocky Williams, 'How does the arms
deal measure up to our needs?', *Sunday Independent*, 27 May 2001, and 'Mirages for sale!',
Noseweek, 35, August 2001, p. 5).
76. One analysis of the political connections of
the South African beneficiaries in the arms deals
suggests that many belonged to an 'Indian cabal'
and intended to use the profits from the contracts
to mobilise support within the ANC against
Thabo Mbeki to 'resurrect the spirit of non-
racialism'. The original accusations of contractual
impropriety in the arms procurements were,
apparently, based on a report by Congress
Consultants, a company owned by a former
Umkhonto operative, Bheki Jacobs. For a time,
the company provided Thabo Mbeki with a
personal source of intelligence about his rivals in
the ANC contest for Mandela's successor ('The
spy who's out in the cold', *Noseweek*, 32, April
2001, pp. 7–9).
77. John Matisonn, 'Finance DG in bid to halt
cheque fraud', *Sunday Independent*, 13 May 2001.
78. *Eastern Province Herald*, 22 July 1999.
79. *Mail & Guardian*, 16 February 2001.
80. Jacques Modipane, former MEC for finance
in Mpumalanga, was the subject of an inconclusive police investigation in 1999/2000 as a

consequence of his involvement in the illegal use of provincial parks as collateral for offshore loans. Allan Boesak, once an MEC in the Western Cape, was charged and successfully convicted for defrauding a charity he ran with the help of his bookkeeper, but this was after his departure from government.

CHAPTER 8

1. Patrick Heller, 'Degrees of democracy: Some comparative lessons from India', *World Politics*, 52, July 2000, p. 488.

2. Richard Rose and Doh Chull Shin, 'Democratization backwards: The problem of third-wave democracies', *British Journal of Political Science*, 31, 2001, pp. 331–54.

3. For a comparative analysis of the fragility of democratic institutions in such situations, see Dietrich Rueschemeyer, Evelyne Huber Stephens and John D. Stephens, *Capitalist Development and Democracy*, Polity Press, Oxford, 1992. Rueschemeyer, Stephens and Stephens find that 'large landlords engaged in labour-repressive agriculture [are] implacable opponents of democracy [while] the working class [are] the most frequent proponent of the full extension of suffrage right', an issue on which the middle class was ambivalent (pp. 6–7).

4. Bruce Baker, 'The quality of African democracy: Why and how it should be measured', *Journal of Contemporary African Studies*, 17, 2, 1999, pp. 273–86.

5. Adam Przeworski, *Democracy and the Market: Political and Economic Reforms in Eastern Europe and Latin America*, Cambridge University Press, Cambridge, 1991, p. 23.

6. Samuel P. Huntington, *The Third Wave: Democratization in the Late Twentieth Century*, University of Oklahoma Press, Norman, 1991, pp. 266–7.

7. 'Overtures to Afrikaners scorned', *The Star*, 17 August 2001.

8. Former Eastern Cape NNP provincial chairman Manie Schoeman, quoted in John Matisonn, 'Twisting the chicken's neck and other party tricks', *Sunday Independent*, 11 November 2001.

9. For discussion of a range of opinion polls which have found that approval ratings for government have remained buoyant amongst black South Africans generally and poorer South Africans especially, see chapter 3, Tom Lodge, *Consolidating Democracy: South Africa's Second*

Popular Election, Witwatersrand University Press, Johannesburg, 1999, pp. 55–76, and chapter 6, Bert Klandermans, Marlene Roefs and Johan Olivier, *The State of the People: Citizens, Civil Society and Governance in South Africa, 1994–2000*, Human Sciences Research Council, Pretoria, 2001, pp. 137–84.

10. Parks Mankahlana, 'Angola shows us how valuable ANC–IFP unity would be to SA', *Sunday Independent*, 11 January 1998.

11. Blade Nzimande, 'ANC–Inkatha alliance far-fetched', *New Nation*, 26 July 1996.

12. Jeremy Cronin, 'Base ANC–IFP merger on honesty, not fiction', *Mail & Guardian*, 13 February 1998.

13. Ruth Rabinowitz, 'ANC and IFP not likely to merge soon', *The Star*, 18 December 1997; M J Bhengu, 'Loose talk about a national alliance is irresponsible', *Natal Mercury*, 9 December 1997.

14. The phrases are from *Speech by ANC President Thabo Mbeki to the Annual Conference of the IFP, 18 July 1998*, ANC Department of Information and Publicity, Marshalltown, 1998, p. 6.

15. Jaspreet Kindra, 'Inkatha joins "the better devil" to twist ANC arm on amakhosi', *Mail & Guardian*, 12 January 2001.

16. David Pottie, 'The electoral system and opposition parties in South Africa', in Roger Southall (ed.), *Opposition and Democracy in South Africa*, Frank Cass, London, 2001, p. 39.

17. André Koopman, 'DA beset by growing divisions', *The Star*, 24 February 2001.

18. 'When Marais goes, the entire coloured platteland and the whole of the Cape Flats will follow', according to New National Party member Anwar Ismael, cited in Jeremy Michaels, 'New poll on the cards if alliance falls apart', *The Star*, 15 October 2001.

19. After the 1999 elections, the NNP owed its bank R6.2 million. A subsequent sale of its assets raised only R1 million towards paying off this debt (see Jeremy Michaels, 'Absa explains its decision on NNP's debt', *The Star*, 26 October 2001).

20. Howard Barrell and Marianne Merten, 'Fight for the DA's soul', *Mail & Guardian*, 26 October 2001.

21. For more discussion in this vein, see Hennie Kotze, 'The Democratic Alliance and its potential constituencies', in Southall, *Opposition and Democracy*, pp. 120–4.

22. L Nijzink and S Jacobs, 'Provincial elections and government formation in the Western Cape',

Politikon, 27,1, 2000, pp. 37–49.

23. For the rhetorical sentiments that accompanied the rupture in the DA and the agreement between the ANC and the NNP, see New National Party Federal Council, *Key Facts 2001: Participatory Government – Mainstream Politics*, Cape Town, November 2001.

24. The constitutional amendment released for public comment on 12 November 2001 indicated that floor-crossing and mergers would be allowed within a period 'determined by the President'. In effect, the executive could decide on the timing of the exercise to ensure that the ruling party could derive maximum benefit from any change in party affiliation.

25. Roger Southall, 'Opposition in South Africa: Issues and problems', in Southall, *Opposition and Democracy*, p. 9.

26. Pallo Jordan, 'A tradition of internal debate', *Mail & Guardian*, 2 November 2001.

27. The ANC's 1999 annual report does suggest that since 1997 membership had doubled in the Eastern Cape, but in the Free State it had been halved and in the Western Cape it had fallen by 30 per cent. In the other provinces membership remained more or less stable. Earlier statistics include the admissions by provincial spokespeople that memberships had fallen from 120 000 in 1994 to 44 000 in Gauteng and from 33 000 in the Western Cape in 1996 to 22 000 in late 1997 (see Marco Granelli, 'ANC draws up battle plan to crush all forces', *The Star*, 30 March 1998; 'Rasool chosen to lead ANC in Western Cape', *The Star*, 20 April 1998; Farouk Chothia, 'ANC grapples with deteriorating party structures', *Business Day*, 4 July 2000).

28. ANC Protea Glen Branch, *Political Report by Branch Chairperson Desmond Mahasha*, Annual General Meeting, 21 June 1998, p. 4.

29. Hein Marais, *South Africa: Limits to Change: The Political Economy of Transition*, Zed Press, London, 2001, p. 253.

30. Hermann Giliomee, James Myburgh and Lawrence Schlemmer, 'Dominant party rule, opposition parties and minorities in South Africa', in Southall, *Opposition and Democracy*, pp. 172–3.

31. For the view that cabinet ministers as elders merit such deferential treatment by the ANC's 'national media coordinator,' see Nomfanelo Kota, 'Likening ANC to Nats is abhorrent', *The Star*, 25 August 2001.

32. Mabutho Sithole, 'Youth League's wrangles

obscure the real problems', *The Star*, 23 May 2001; Pule waga Mabe, 'Old guard backs Giqaba', *Mail & Guardian*, 12 April 2001.

33. Farouk Chothia, 'ANC grapples with deteriorating party structure', *Business Day*, 4 July 2000.

34. Jeremy Cronin, 'Pirates and admirals scupper the ideal of privatisation', *Sunday Independent*, 19 August 2001.

35. Smuts Ngonyama, quoted in 'ANC pinpoints various threats to democratic change', *The Star*, 27 March 2001.

36. Dale T McKinley, 'Democracy, power and patronage: Debate and opposition within the African National Congress and the tripartite Alliance since 1994', in Southall, *Opposition and Democracy*, pp. 187–8.

37. Jaspreet Kindra, 'Anti-Mbeki pamphlet surfaces in Mpumalanga', *Mail & Guardian*, 27 July 2001.

38. Jaspreet Kindra, 'Infighting in Gauteng ANC', *Mail & Guardian*, 24 August 2001.

39. John Mattison, 'Veterans give ANC shock warning', *Sunday Independent*, 29 July 2001.

40. Marianne Merten, 'Boesak is still able to charm the masses', *Mail & Guardian*, 25 May 2001.

41. Hermann Giliomee and Charles Simkins, 'Dominant party regimes', in Hermann Giliomee and Charles Simkins (eds.), *The Awkward Embrace: One-Party Domination and Democracy*, Tafelberg, Cape Town, 1999, pp. 41–3.

42. McKinley, 'Democracy, power and patronage', pp. 196–7.

43. Estelle Randall, 'No link with other parties – COSATU', *The Star*, 10 November 2001.

44. Mziwakhe Hlangeni, 'COSATU declares real war against the government after Radebe attack', *The Star*, 24 August 2001.

45. Kathu Mamaila, 'We could possibly assimilate the ANC', *The Star*, 25 July 2001.

46. Jaspreet Kindra, 'We would not like to burn our bridges', *Mail & Guardian*, 11 May 2001.

47. Eddie Webster, 'The Alliance under stress: Governing in a globalizing world', in Southall, *Opposition and Democracy*, p. 267.

48. Jaspreet Kindra, 'SACP, COSATU gear up for a fight', *Mail & Guardian*, 27 July 2001.

49. Thabo Mabaso, 'COSATU to take its case against privatisation to ANC branches', *The Star*, 25 August 2001.

50. 'Communists not subversive', *The Star*, 30 July 2001.

51. Howard Barrell, 'Masses desert the SACP in

droves', *Mail & Guardian*, 26 May 2001.

52. Phindile Makwakwa, 'ANC turns on union leaders', *The Mercury*, 17 October 2001; Jaspreet Kindra, 'ANC offensive against far leftists', *Mail & Guardian*, 26 October 2001; Drew Forrest, 'A tendency to displease the ANC', *Mail & Guardian*, 19 October 2001. For the SACP's response, see 'Label liberal curtails debate', *Mail & Guardian*, 9 November 2001.

53. Jaspreet Kindra, 'ANC conservatives: We will lead', *Mail & Guardian*, 7 September 2001.

54. Drew Forrest, 'No stranger to the struggle', *Mail & Guardian*, 7 September 2001.

55. A. Mazrui and G. Engholm, 'The tensions of crossing the floor', in A. Mazrui, *Violence and Thought: Essays in Social Tensions in Africa*, Heinemann, London, 1969.

56. For a report on the tensions between the committee and the minister, see David Robbins, 'Musical discord and unhealthy alliances', *The Star*, 15 February 1996.

57. Estelle Randall, 'SACP hits at Radebe for disparaging words', *Sunday Independent*, 9 September 2001.

58. Luphumzo Kebeni, 'Parliament a success story of democratic change', *The Star*, 8 March 2000. For more detail, also see the newsletter of the House of Assembly, *In Session*, and Susan de Villiers, *A People's Government: The People's Voice*, Parliamentary Support Programme, Cape Town, 2001.

59. Susan Booysen, 'Democracy and public participation in policy-making in South Africa: Trends and prospects', a paper presented at the Africa Institute Colloquium, 'South Africa since 1994: Lessons and Prospects', Pretoria, 30 May 2001, p. 12.

60. Raymond Parsons, 'A history and evaluation of social dialogue in South Africa', working paper presented at the International Jubilee Conference of the Economic Society of South Africa, Johannesburg, 14 September 2001, pp. 34–5.

61. All quotations preceding this note are taken from 'The state, property relations and social transformation', *Umrabulo*, 5, 1998, Department of Political Education and Training, African National Congress, Marshalltown, pp. 38–60.

62. Cascerino Valentino, 'Who's the boss: Buthelezi or Masetlha?', *The Enquirer*, 1 November 2001.

63. Jovial Rantao, 'ANC calls Judge de Villiers a dinosaur', *The Star*, 19 June 1998.

64. Prakash Naidoo, 'Plot to foil health reforms',

Sunday Independent, 18 October 1998.

65. See the altercation between KwaZulu-Natal judge president, Vuka Shabalala, and provincial ANC chairperson, S'bu Ndebele, in Xolasi Vapi, 'ANC slated over judicial irregularities in KwaZulu', *The Star*, 14 July 2001. Shabalala's appointment was widely criticised as politically inspired. However, he has proved to be a strong defender of judicial independence.

66. Marco Granelli, 'ANC draws up battle plan'.

67. *Political Report of the President, Nelson Mandela, to the 50th National Conference of the African National Congress, 16 December 1997*, Mathibe Printing and Publishing, Johannesburg, 1997, pp. 12–18.

68. Robert Putnam, *Making Democracy Work: Civic Traditions in Modern Italy*, Princeton University Press, Princeton, New Jersey, 1993.

69. Gumisae Mutume, 'Too few NGOs in South Africa involved in development', *The Star*, 22 October 1996.

70. Glenda Daniels, 'Foreign funding likely to dry up', *The Star*, 28 September 1994.

71. Rod Amner, 'The NGO funding drought', *The Star*, 4 September 1995.

72. R W Johnson, 'Destroying South Africa's democracy', *The National Interest*, Fall 1998, p. 25.

73. Rueschemeyer et al., *Capitalist Development*, p. 61.

74. See contributions by Themba Sono and Lawrence Schlemmer, in R W Johnson and David Welsh (eds.), *Ironic Victory. Liberalism in Post-Apartheid South Africa*, Oxford University Press, Cape Town, 1998.

75. Thabo Mabaso, 'COSATU says rumours of its demise are vastly exaggerated', *Business Report*, 23 November 2001.

76. Shaun Mackay and Malachia Mathotho, *Worker Power: The Congress of South African Trade Unions and Its Impact on Governance and Democracy*, Centre for Policy Studies, Research Report, 79, Johannesburg, 2001, pp. 11–17.

77. Martin Williams, 'The press since 1994', in Johnson and Welsh, *Ironic Victory*, p. 194.

78. Wilmot James and Moira Levy (eds.), *Pulse: Passages in Democracy-building: Assessing South Africa's Transition*, Institute for Democracy in South Africa (IDASA), Cape Town, 1998, p. 93.

79. Robert Mattes, Yul Derek Davids and Cherrel Africa, 'Views of democracy in South Africa and the region', Afrobarometer Paper, 8, Institute for Democracy in South Africa (IDASA), Cape Town, 2000, p. 6.

80. Michael Bratton and Robert Mattes, 'Support for democracy in Africa: Intrinsic or instrumental?', *British Journal of Political Science*, 31, 2001, p. 459.

81. EISA/IDASA/SABC/Markinor, *Opinion '99*, *Project Nyulo*, vol. 1, Table 25, Markinor, Johannesburg, October 1998. The 1994 figure is from R W Johnson and Lawrence Schlemmer, *Launching Democracy: The First Open Election*, April 1994, Yale University Press, New Haven, 1996, p. 261. The disparity between the two survey findings may be partly attributable to the slightly less assertive wording employed in the question posed in 1994 ('would not allow' as opposed to 'might take part in action'), although the apparent growth in tolerance does correlate with other surveys.

82. Adam Habib and Rupert Taylor, 'No real opposition on the horizon', *The Star*, 9 November 1998.

83. Mattes et al., *Views of Democracy*, pp. 66–73.

84. For a sampling, see Libby Husemeyer, *Watchdogs or Hypocrites: The Amazing Debate on South African Liberals and Liberalism*, Friedrich-Naumann-Stiftung, Johannesburg, 1997.

85. Evidence wa ka Ngobeni, 'Face to face with the tiger', *Mail & Guardian*, 7 September 2001.

86. This assessment of the scope of efforts to improve women's access to their constitutional rights is drawn from Cathi Albertyn, Beth Goldblatt, Shireen Hassim, Likhapha and Sheila Meintjes, *Engendering the Political Agenda: A South African Case Study: A Report for the United Nations International Institute for Research and Training for the Advancement of Women*, Centre for Applied Legal Studies, University of the Witwatersrand, Johannesburg, July 1999.

CHAPTER 9

1. Alex Boraine, *A Country Unmasked: Inside South Africa's Truth and Reconciliation Commission*, Oxford University Press, Cape Town, 2000, p. 12.

2. For the conference proceedings, see Alex Boraine, Janet Levy and Ronel Scheffer, *Dealing with the Past*, Institute for Democracy in South Africa (IDASA), Cape Town, 1994. For the influence of this gathering on the legislation, see Boraine, *A Country Unmasked*, p. 17.

3. Dullah Omar, 'Introduction to the Truth and Reconciliation Commission', in H Russell Botman and Robin M Petersen, *To Remember and to Heal: Theological and Psychological Reflections on Truth and Reconciliation*, Human and Rousseau, Cape Town, 1996, p. 25.

4. *Truth and Reconciliation Commission of South Africa Report*, Juta and Co., Cape Town, October 1998, vol. 1, p. 53.

5. Lyn S. Graybill, 'Pursuit of truth and reconciliation in South Africa', *Africa Today*, 45, 1, 1998, p. 104.

6. Boraine et al., *Dealing with the Past*, p. 38.

7. Boraine et al., *Dealing with the Past*, p. 11.

8. *TRC Report*, vol. 1, pp. 115–77.

9. Shaun Johnson, 'It's better to lance the boil', *The Star*, 11 October 1994.

10. Wendy Orr, *From Biko to Basson: Wendy Orr's Search for the Soul of South Africa as a Commissioner of the TRC*, Contra Press, Saxonwold, 2000, p. 31.

11. Kader Asmal, Louise Asmal and Ronald Suresh Roberts, *Reconciliation through Truth: A Reckoning of South Africa's Criminal Governance*, David Philip Publishers, Cape Town, 1996, p. 48.

12. Asmal et al., *Reconciliation through Truth*, p. 49.

13. Boraine, *A Country Unmasked*, p. 101.

14. Antjie Krog, *Country of My Skull*, Jonathan Cape, London, 1998, p. 26.

15. Desmond Tutu, *No Future without Forgiveness*, Random House, Johannesburg, 1999, p. 72.

16. *TRC Report*, vol. 1, pp. 126–7.

17. Tutu, *No Future without Forgiveness*, pp. 36, 51.

18. Boraine, *A Country Unmasked*, p. 362.

19. Robin M Petersen, 'The politics of grace and the Truth and Reconciliation Commission', in Botman and Petersen, *To Remember and to Heal*, pp. 61–2.

20. Charles Villa-Vicencio, 'On taking responsibility', in Botman and Petersen, *To Remember and to Heal*, p. 133.

21. *TRC Report*, vol. 1, p. 112.

22. Richard Wilson, *The Politics of the Truth and Reconciliation Commission in South Africa*, Cambridge University Press, Cambridge, 2001, p. 47.

23. *TRC Report*, vol. 1, p. 144.

24. Anthea Jeffery, *The Truth about the Truth Commission*, South African Institute of Race Relations, Johannesburg, 1999, p. 9.

25. Tutu, *No Future without Forgiveness*, p. 33.

26. *TRC Report*, vol. 1, p. 147.

27. For more detail on the Reparations Committee's work, see Wendy Orr, *From Biko to Basson*, pp. 340–4.

28. Conversation with Wendy Orr, Johannesburg, 16 October 2001.

29. One of the original members of the committee told Antjie Krog that it had initially expected about 200 applications (see Krog, *Country of My Skull*, p. 121).

30. Boraine, *A Country Unmasked*, p.142.

31. For first-hand accounts of the opening preliminaries in East London and Alexandra, see Krog, *Country of My Skull*, pp. 26–7, and Belinda Bozzoli, 'Public ritual and private transmission: The Truth Commission in Alexandra township, South Africa, 1996', *African Studies*, 57, 2, 1998, p. 170–1.

32. All quotations in this paragraph are from Wilson, *The Politics of Truth and Reconciliation in South Africa*, Cambridge University Press, Cambridge, 2001, pp. 111–21.

33. Tutu, *No Future without Forgiveness*, p. 219.

34. Boraine, *A Country Unmasked*, p. 122.

35. See comments by Orr, *From Biko to Basson*, p. 91.

36. For a critical discussion of the decision on the Amy Biehl killing, see Linda van de Vijver, 'The amnesty process', in Wilmot James and Linda van de Vijver (eds.), *After the TRC: Reflections on Truth and Reconciliation in South Africa*, David Philip Publishers, Cape Town, 2000, p. 137.

37. Timothy Garton Ash, 'True confessions', *New York Review of Books*, 17 July 1997, p. 34.

38. Krog, *Country of My Skull*, p. 135.

39. For reservations of the Mxenge family about Vlakplaas commander Dirk Coetzee's sincerity, see Sandile Ngidi, 'The bitter pill of amnesty', *Siyaya!*, 3, Spring 1998, p. 24. Antjie Krog was also unimpressed by Coetzee (*Country of My Skull*, p. 61) while Jacques Pauw remained uncertain about the sincerity of Eugene de Kock's declarations of repentance ('Terrifyingly normal', *Siyaya!*, 3, Spring 1998, p. 33).

40. Orr, *From Biko to Basson*, p. 198.

41. Tutu, *No Future without Forgiveness*, p. 139.

42. Dumisa Ntsebeza, 'A lot more to live for', in James and Van de Vijver, *After the TRC*, p. 105.

43. Orr, *From Biko to Basson*, p. 37.

44. David Chidester, 'Stories, fragments and monuments', in James Cochrane, John de Gruchy and Stephen Martin, *Facing the Truth: South African Faith Communities and the Truth and Reconciliation Commission*, David Philip Publishers, Cape Town, 1999, p. 139.

45. Elizabeth Stanley, 'Evaluating the Truth and Reconciliation Commission', *Journal of Modern African Studies*, 39, 3, 2001, p. 542.

46. *TRC Report*, vol. 1, pp. 168–72.

47. Orr, *From Biko to Basson*, p. 59.

48. Karin Chubb and Lutz van Dijk, *Between Anger and Hope: South Africa's Youth and the Truth and Reconciliation Commission*, Witwatersrand University Press, Johannesburg, 2001, p. 176.

49. Boraine, *A Country Unmasked*, p. 252.

50. 'Commissioners reflect on public hearings', *Truth Talk*, 3, 1, November 1997, p. 15.

51. *TRC Report*, vol. 5, pp. 362–4.

52. Wilson, *The Politics of Truth and Reconciliation*, pp. 48–9.

53. Orr, *From Biko to Basson*, pp. 123–4.

54. Wilson, *The Politics of Truth and Reconciliation*, pp. 174–82.

55. Bozzoli, 'Public ritual', p. 189.

56. A visiting journalist did note the presence of a 'smartly dressed black African psychologist' who gave tearful victims 'long, and to my ear, insufferably condescending lectures about coping with trauma' (Ash, 'True confessions', p. 33).

57. For a complete account of NGO complaints about their being under-utilised by the TRC, see Hugo van der Merwe, Polly Dewhirst and Brandon Hamber, 'Non-government organisations and the Truth and Reconciliation Commission: An impact assessment', *Politikon*, 1999, 26, 1, pp. 61–71.

58. Wilson, *The Politics of the Truth and Reconciliation Commission*, p. 108.

59. Orr, *From Biko to Basson*, pp. 237–9.

60. Heidi Grunebaum-Ralph and Oren Stier, 'The question of remains', in Cochrane et al., *Facing the Truth*, p. 150. In at least one case, unfortunately, the wrong body was given to relatives for reburial. See Jovial Rantao, 'TRC blunder opened wounds', *The Star*, 10 September 1999.

61. Bozzoli, 'Public ritual', p. 190.

62. *TRC Report*, vol. 5, p. 179.

63. Heather Robertson, 'Red tape on the long road to reparations', *Sunday Times*, 20 February 2000.

64. Khatha Mamaila, 'Victims getting little in return for reconciliation', *The Star*, 29 May 2000.

65. Orr, *From Biko to Basson*, p. 227.

66. Frederik van Zyl Slabbert, *Tough Choices: Reflections of an Afrikaner African*, Tafelberg, Cape Town, 2000, p. 146.

67. Barney Pityana, 'TRC left unfinished business', *Sunday Independent*, 25 July 1999.

68. Krog, *Country of My Skull*, p. 58.

69. Asmal et al., *Reconciliation through Truth*, p. 17.
70. Asmal et al., *Reconciliation through Truth*, pp. 118–19.
71. *TRC Report*, vol. 2, pp. 335–66 and vol. 5, pp. 240–3.
72. Boraine, *A Country Unmasked*, p. 317.
73. Mathatha Tsedu, 'Tutu used his casting vote against ANC', *Sunday Independent*, 8 November 1998.
74. Jeremy Cronin, 'Tutu's report tells the truth, but not the whole truth', *Sunday Independent*, November 1998.
75. Boraine, *A Country Unmasked*, pp. 302–4.
76. Cited in D. Posel, 'The TRC Report: What kind of history? What kind of truth?', in D. Posel and G. Simpson (eds.), *The South African Truth and Reconciliation Commission: Commissioning the Past*, Witwatersrand University Press, Johannesburg, 2001.
77. Barney Pityana, cited in 'TRC went too far to appease whites', *Eastern Province Herald*, 17 June 1999.
78. Winnie Madikizela-Mandela, cited in Eddie Jayiya, 'Parties in varied response to Winnie's allegation about the TRC', *The Star*, 22 March 1999.
79. Anthea Jeffery, *The Truth about the Truth Commission*, p. 149.
80. For a sharp critique of the *TRC Report* as analytical political history, see Posel, 'The TRC Report'.
81. In fact, less was destroyed than the commission was led to believe. The commission's findings on the destruction of sensitive state documents are detailed in the *TRC Report*, vol. 1, pp. 201–43. Recent discoveries suggest that many of the military records thought to have been destroyed in fact survived. On the concealment of files by the South African National Defence Force from the TRC, see Jeremy Gordin, 'Access to Information Act assists recovery of lost records', *Sunday Independent*, 11 November 2001.
82. Elizabeth Stanley, 'Evaluating the Truth and Reconciliation Commission', *Journal of Modern African Studies*, 39, 3, 2001, p. 529.
83. Jeremy Cronin, 'Tutu's report tells the truth, but not the whole truth', *Sunday Independent*, November 1998.
84. Anthea Jeffery, *The Truth about the Truth Commission*, see p. 16 and p. 103 in particular.
85. Reverend Ollie Mahopo, head coordinator of statement-takers in Johannesburg, quoted in Wilson, *The Politics of Truth and Reconciliation*, p. 133.
86. Evangelical and Pentecostal Protestant churches, increasingly popular in South Africa, claim to subscribe to a vision of 'restorative justice', but this they understand to require a judicial system in which the prime concern is the welfare of the victims of crime and in which severe punishment has exemplary effects. For expression of such views, see the propaganda of the African Christian Democratic Party in particular.
87. Boraine, *A Country Unmasked*, pp. 267–8.
88. For example, see Krog, *Country of My Skull*, pp. 136–7.
89. James Gibson and Amanda Gouws, 'Truth and reconciliation in South Africa: Attributions of blame and the struggle over apartheid', *American Political Science Review*, 93, 3, September 1999, pp. 501–17.
90. Colin Bundy, 'The beast of the past: History and the TRC', in James and Van de Vijver, *After the TRC*, p. 19.
91. I am grateful to Brian Culross at ACNielsen's Customised Research Division, Johannesburg, for arranging access to survey data and making copies of reports available to me. The surveys used an area-stratified probability sample of 2 503 households of adults aged over 16. In the case of white and black respondents, sampling was done down to village level, whereas amongst coloured and Indian respondents it was undertaken in the major cities. See Market Research Africa (ACNielsen), *Truth Commission*, conducted for *Business Day*, Johannesburg, 1996; Market Research Africa (ACNielsen), *The TRC Evaluation*, conducted for *Business Day*, Johannesburg, 1998.
92. Valerie Møller and Helga Dickow, *Five Years into Democracy: Elite and Rank-and-File Perspectives on South African Quality of Life and the Rainbow Nation*, Institut Français d'Afrique du Sud, Johannesburg, March 2001, pp. 64–6.
93. Krog, *Country of My Skull*, p. 195.
94. Lyn S Graybill, 'Pursuit of truth', p. 123.
95. Kaizer Nyatsumba, 'Neither dull nor tiresome', in James and Van de Vijver, *After the TRC*, p. 92.
96. Mahmood Mamdani, 'A diminished truth', *Siyaya!*, 3, Spring 1998, pp. 39–40.
97. *Reparation and Memorialisation*, Newsletter of the Institute for Justice and Reconciliation, circulated as a newspaper insertion, October 2000.
98. Cornel du Toit, 'Dealing with the past', in Botman and Petersen, *To Remember and to Heal*, p. 118.

99. Wilhelm Verwoerd and Mahlubi Chief Mabizela (eds.), *Truths Drawn in Jest: Commentary on the TRC through Cartoons*, David Philip Publishers, Cape Town, 2000, pp. 45–8.

100. *TRC Report*, vol. 4, p. 1.

101. Nicoli Nattrass, 'The Truth and Reconciliation Commission on business and apartheid: A critical reflection', *African Affairs*, 98, 1999, p. 385.

102. Carl Niehaus, 'Is religion relevant?', in Cochrane et al., *Facing the Truth*, p. 88. For a discussion of some of the reservations the DRC churchmen had about the TRC as well an expression of qualified support for the TRC by an influential Afrikaner theologian, see Etienne de Villiers, 'The challenge to Afrikaans churches', in Botman and Petersen, *To Remember and to Heal*, pp. 140–53.

103. C W du Toit, *Confession and Reconciliation: A Challenge to the Churches in South Africa*, Research Institute for Theology and Religion, University of South Africa, Pretoria, 1998, p. 48.

104. For a very useful comparative survey, see Priscilla B Hayter, 'Fifteen truth commissions – 1974–1994: A comparative study', *Human Rights Quarterly*, 16, 1994, pp. 597–655.

105. For critical discussion, see Boraine et al., *Dealing with the Past*, pp. 57–87.

106. One of Timothy Garton Ash's informants in Worcester, Amos Dyanti, told him in early 1997 that the captain who directed his torture was still posted at the local police station ('True confessions', p. 33). More recently, MP Tony Yengeni complained that at the time he was arrested and charged for fraud by the elite 'Scorpions' unit, one of the policemen who were involved in his case had also been a member of the interrogation team during his previous encounter with the law – when he was captured and tortured as an Umkhonto guerrilla fighter (see John Matisonn, 'Angry Yengeni hits out at all-white Scorpions panel', *The Star*, 6 October 2001).

107. Priscilla B Hayter, 'International guidelines for the creation and operation of truth commissions', *Law and Contemporary Problems*, 59, 4, 1996, pp. 173–81.

108. Richard J Goldstone, *For Humanity: Reflections of a War Crimes Investigator*, Witwatersrand University Press, Johannesburg, 2000, p. 71.

109. Mike Kaye, 'The role of truth commissions in the search for justice, reconciliation and democratisation: The Salvadorian and Honduran cases', *Journal of Latin American Studies*, 29, 1977, pp. 693–716; Mark Ensalaco, 'Truth commissions for Chile and El Salvador: A report and assessment', *Human Rights Quarterly*, 16, 1994, pp. 656–75.

CHAPTER 10

1. Colin Bundy, 'Survival and resistance: Township organisations and non-violent direct action in twentieth-century South Africa', in Glenn Adler and Jonny Steinberg (eds.), *From Comrades to Citizens*, Macmillan, London, 1998.

2. Kevin French, *James Mpanza and the Sofasonke Movement*, MA dissertation, Department of Political Studies, University of the Witwatersrand, 1984; A. W. Stadler, 'Birds in the cornfield: Squatter Movements in Johannesburg, 1944–1947', *Journal of Southern African Studies*, 6, 1, 1979.

3. *Mail & Guardian*, 19 September 1997.

4. Marina Ottaway, 'African democratisation and the Leninist option', *Journal of Modern African Studies*, 35, 1, 1997, p. 11.

5. SANCO, *Mission Statement*, 1994, p. 2.

6. Ben Jacobs, 'SANCO: Heading for disaster', *Work in Progress*, 86, 1992.

7. Mzwanele Mayekiso, 'Institutions that themselves need to be watched over: A review of recent writings on the civic movement', *Urban Forum*, 4, 1, 1994.

8. Moses Mayekiso, interviewed in *Reconstruct*, supplement to *Work in Progress*, June 1992.

9. Lechesa Tsenoli, interview in *Development and Democracy*, 8, 1994.

10. Adrian Hadland, 'SANCO leader warns ANC that it cannot rest on its laurels', *Sunday Independent*, 17 November 1996.

11. *Umthunywa*, no. 3, June 1995.

12. 'Why SANCO changed its tune', *New Nation*, 20 March 1997.

13. Amrit Manga, 'ANC lekgotla: Does it point the way forward?', *New Nation*, 24 January 1997.

14. Jeremy Seekings, 'SANCO: Strategic dilemmas in a democratic South Africa', *Transformation*, 34, 1997, p. 16.

15. SANCO, *Presidential Address*, Second National Conference, Johannesburg, 16–20 April 1997, p. 10.

16. David Robbins, 'SANCO's radical alternative', *The Star*, 12 July 1995.

17. SANCO, *Organisational Report*, Third National Conference, Mogale City, Johannesburg, 19–22 April 2001, p. 77.

18. Newton Kanhema, 'Row over bond freeze',

Sunday Star, 26 July 1992.

19. Kimberley Lanegran, 'South Africa's civic association movement: ANC's ally or society's watchdog?', *African Studies Review*, 38, 2, September 1995.

20. Sandi Mgidlana, 'SANCO hits back', *New Nation*, 19 July, 1996.

21. William Mervin Gumede, 'SANCO marches to a business drum', *The Star*, 28 December 1996.

22. Hadland, 'SANCO leader warns ANC'.

23. SANCO, *Presidential Address*, Second National Conference, p. 7.

24. SANCO, *Strategies and Policies for Local Economic Development in the New South Africa*, Johannesburg, March 1995.

25. *Umthunywa*, no. 3, June 1995.

26. Stefaans Brummer, 'Corruption probe into SANCO donations', *Mail & Guardian*, 1 September 1995.

27. SANCO, *Organisational Report*, 2001, p. 34.

28. William Mervin Gumede, 'SANCO's Gauteng province rallies around expelled Mayekiso', *Sunday Independent*, 24 August 1997.

29. Evidence wa ka Ngobeni, 'SANCO leaders pass the buck', *Mail & Guardian*, 20 April 2001.

30. National Interim Civic Committee, *Financial Statement*, October 1991 – June 1992.

31. SANCO, *Organisational Report*, 2001, pp. 59, 65.

32. Pule Molebeledi, 'Mayor quits to join SANCO', *New Nation*, 24 January 1997.

33. Deon Delport, 'SANCO wants people to be proud informers', *The Star*, 3 March 1997.

34. SANCO, *Organisational Report*, 2001, p. 71.

35. SANCO, *Organisational Report*, 2001, p. 71.

36. SANCO, *Organisational Report*, 2001, p. 28.

37. *Reconstruct*, supplement to *Work in Progress*, June 1992.

38. Mzwanele Mayekiso, 'SANCO and politics: Then and now', *New Nation*, 13 December 1996.

39. SANCO, *Strategy Discussion Document to Radically Reshape the Vision and Role of SANCO*, Third National Conference, Mogale City, Johannesburg, 19–22 April 2001.

40. SANCO, *Organisational Report*, 2001, p. 77.

41. William Mervin Gumede, 'ANC Alliance suffers first split as Transkei civics quit', *Sunday Independent*, 19 October 1997.

42. Farouk Chothia, 'Clash over role of traditional leaders', *Mail & Guardian*, 18 November 1994.

43. Fred Esbond, 'SANCO leaders implicated in alleged murder plot', *Mail & Guardian*, 8 June 2001.

44. Francis Fukuyama, *Trust: The Social Virtues and the Creation of Prosperity*, Penguin, Harmondsworth, 1996, p. 8.

45. 'The role of civics', *Mayibuye*, December 1990, p. 31.

46. 'SANCO branch soon from Queenstown central', *The Representative*, 19 June 1998.

47. SANCO, *Organisational Report*, 2001, p. 68.

48. See reports in the *Springs and Brakpan Advertiser* on 12 February 1999, 30 April 1999 and 8 October 1999.

49. *The Star*, 22 August 1999.

50. Solomon Makgale, 'Taxi violence leads to new boycott', *East Cape Weekend*, 27 March 1999.

51. 'War against corruption continues', *Witbank News*, 16 April 1999.

52. SANCO Wattville Branch, *Organisational Report*, March 2001.

53. The Human Sciences Research Council's Social Movement Project survey interviews were conducted in June and July 2000 with Thabang Mokoena, Xoliswa Sobekwa, Richard Maluleka, Thabiso Mphachake, Ludwig Shange and Alfred Phaweni. Copies of completed interview forms are held at the Department of Political Studies, University of the Witwatersrand. See Human Sciences Research Council, *Annual Social Movement Surveys* (principal investigators: Johan Olivier and Bert Klandermans), 1994–1998.

54. 'Decent housing is Duduza's aim', *Springs African Reporter*, 9 April 1999.

55. 'Community mandates SANCO for development project', *Mpumalanga News*, 28 January 1999.

56. Justine Lucas, 'Space, domesticity and people's power: Civic organisation in Alexandra in the 1990s', *African Studies*, 54, 1, 1995, p. 102.

57. Mcebisi Ndletyana, *Changing Role of Civic Organisations from the Apartheid to the Post-Apartheid Era: A Case Study of the Alexandra Civic Organisation*, MA dissertation, Department of Political Studies, University of the Witwatersrand, 1998, pp. 64–8.

58. Caroline White, 'Democratic societies? Voluntary association and democratic culture in a South African township', *Transformation*, 36, 1998.

59. Abbey Mokoe, 'Police probe claim that R600 000 disappeared from Soweto civic's coffers', *The Star*, 8 July 1996.

60. Philip Frankel, Steven Louw and Simon

Stacey, *Governmental Performance and Capacity: Transitional Local Authorities in Mpumalanga*, Department of Political Studies, University of the Witwatersrand and Human Sciences Research Council, April 1997, p. 257.

61. *Middelburg Observer*, 11 September 1998. The researchers from the University of the Witwatersrand suggest that action against defaulters enjoys considerable community sanction, partly because the payment boycotts of the 1980s had always been locally 'goal-oriented' and 'as a result, Middelburg's black residents' were 'educated to understand non-payment as an always temporary exception to the rule' (Frankel et al., *Governmental Performance*, p. 244). It may be the case that SANCO's following is concentrated amongst older residents of the city with experiences dating from this period, whereas the new committee may draw its support from relative newcomers to the town.

62. Isaac Makgabutlane, 'SANCO consults ratepayers body', *Springs African Reporter*, 28 August 1998.

63. Human Sciences Research Council, *Annual Social Movement Surveys* (principal investigators: Johan Olivier and Bert Klandermans), 1994–1998.

64. Data sets for the *Opinion '99* surveys are held at the Electoral Institute of South Africa (EISA), Johannesburg. *Opinion '99* was a poll conducted by the Electoral Institute of South Africa in conjunction with the Institute for Democracy in South Africa (IDASA), the South African Broadcasting Corporation (SABC) and the survey agency Markinor.

65. This research was undertaken as a contribution to the *Democracy and Social Capital in Segmented Societies Project*, a joint programme by departments of political science at Witwatersrand, Jawaharlal Nehru University, Delhi, Utkal University, Orissa, and Uppsala University, Sweden.

66. 'The role of civics', *Mayibuye*, December 1990, p. 31.

67. Paul Kirk, 'Bitter feud over priest's grave', *The Star*, 3 January 1998.

68. On the roles of personal friendship and mutual trust in *stokvel* operations, see Monica Wilson and Archie Mafeje, *Langa: A Study of Social Groups in an African Township*, Oxford University Press, Cape Town, 1963, p. 132.

69. For a *stokvel* housing initiative in Vosloorus, East Rand, see Bongiwe Mlangeni, 'Building bigger for less without the government subsidy', *The Star*, 24 March 1997. For Mhinga, Limpopo Province, and Orange Farm, near Johannesburg, see William Mervin Gumede, 'They're helping themselves to houses', *The Star*, 20 July 1996. For reference to the Tswaranang Stokvel Group, Soweto, which built 40 houses in 1996, see Bongiwe Mlangeni, 'Housing for all still a dream', *The Star*, 23 December 1996.

70. It can be argued that the authorities have made their task even more difficult by disregarding the networks represented by the existing community organisations such as branches of SANCO or the Rural Women's Movement. See Department of Water Affairs and Forestry, *Evaluation of the Community Water Supply and Sanitation Programme*, Workshop Document, Mvula Trust, Pretoria, November 1997. Women's associations are especially effective when they are engaged in water reticulation programmes, a reflection of the role assigned to women in domestic water collection within the rural household division of labour. Alexius Amtaika's doctoral research (Department of Political Studies, University of the Witwatersrand) on local government in Pietermaritzburg identified a strong example of effective management of the Imadi Water and Sanitation Project by women's groups.

71. For examples of local tensions between SANCO and the municipalities, see Zweli Dlamini, 'SANCO to hold first rally of '99', *Springs and Brakpan Advertiser*, 30 April 1999 (protest against electricity tariffs), Solomon Makgale, 'Taxi violence leads to new boycott', *East Cape Weekend*, 27 March 1999 (SANCO and ANC at odds over taxi violence); 'SANCO, COSATU plan to oppose EL casino site', *Eastern Province Herald*, 11 June 1999; 'War against corruption continues', *Witbank News*, 16 April 1999 (SANCO call for ANC councillor resignation); 'Springs CEO Stanley Khanyile anti-SANCO', *Springs Advertiser*, 12 February 1998.

72. Sports and especially football are among the most common organised leisure activities in South Africa. Kenny Hlela's fieldwork in Sweetwaters, a township outside Pietermaritzburg, suggests that two factors have contributed to the decline of the 'brotherhood' that upheld the strong local football culture in the early 1980s. One was a specific feature of communities in the KwaZulu-Natal Midlands – inter-communal political violence. The other may have a more general salience: there has been a proliferation of households that now own television sets and an increase in black youth-directed programming in television schedules. See Kenny Hlela, *The Applicability of Putnam's Social Capital Theory in the Case of Sweetwaters in Pietermaritzburg, KwaZulu-Natal*, MA dissertation, Department of Political Studies, University of the Witwatersrand, 1999.

73. Goodwill Gabriel Ditlhage, *Social Capital and its Prospects for Development in South Africa*, MA dissertation, Department of Political Studies, University of the Witwatersrand, 1998, pp. 85–6.

74. There is wide disagreement on this. For a discussion of the relationship between different South African religious affiliations and political-democratic activism, see: Jean Comaroff, *Body of Power, Spirit of Resistance: The Culture and History of a South African People*, Chicago University Press, Chicago, 1988, and David Chidester, *Shots in the Streets: Violence and Religion in South Africa*, Beacon Press, Boston, 1991.

75. *Local Election Survey*, Human Sciences Research Council Omnibus Poll, September 1995. Data held in the Department of Political Studies, University of the Witwatersrand.

76. Jennifer Widner and Alexander Mundt, 'Researching social capital in Africa', *Africa*, 1999, pp. 8–9.

77. Helen Taylor and Bob Mattes, *Political Parties and the Consolidation of Democracy in South Africa*, Institute for Democracy in South Africa (IDASA), Kutlwanong Democracy Centre, Pretoria, 29–30 September 1977; for Human Sciences Research Council survey findings, see Marlene Roefs, 'Notes on perceptions of legitimacy of national and provincial government', paper presented at the workshop 'Democracy and Social Capital in Segregated Societies', Department of Political Studies, University of the Witwatersrand, Johannesburg, 9–12 October 1997.

78. 'Reality check', supplement to *The Star*, 28 April 1999.

79. Edward N Muller and Mitchell A Seligson, 'Civic culture and democracy: The question of causal relationships', *American Political Science Review*, 88, 3, September 1994, pp. 639–42.

80. EISA/IDASA/SABC/Markinor *Opinion '99*. Fieldwork conducted in November 1998 showed that 76 per cent of the poll's African respondents (63 per cent overall) felt that the government had performed well in improving basic health services and 59 per cent of African respondents (54 per cent overall) believed that it had also managed

low-cost housing construction effectively.

81. For more discussion in this vein, see Widner and Mundt, 'Researching social capital', pp. 18–21.

CHAPTER 11

1. Nelson Mandela anticipated Thabo Mbeki in talking about such a theme in his references to the necessity of bringing about an African Renaissance in government in the light of the Rwandan genocide in his address to an Organisation of African Unity summit in June 1994. Cited in Alec Russell, *Big Men, Little People: Encounters in Africa*, Macmillan, London, 1999, p. 290.

2. *Debates of the National House of Assembly*, 10 June 1997, p. 3 654.

3. 'The deputy president's address to the Corporate Council Summit, Chantilly, Virginia, April 1997', in Konrad-Adenauer-Stiftung, *Occasional Papers: The African Renaissance*, Johannesburg, May 1998.

4. *Political Report of the President, Nelson Mandela, to the 50th National Conference of the ANC*, Mafikeng, 16–20 December 1997, Mathibe Printing and Publishing, Johannesburg, 1997, pp. 34–7.

5. Nthobi Moahloli (general manager, Corporate Affairs, Engen Limited), 'Afrikatourism – using tourism to let Africans know Africa', address to the African Renaissance Conference, Johannesburg, 28 September 1998.

6. Mondli Makhanya, 'Time to recolonise bits of Africa', *The Star*, 28 August 1998.

7. 'Africa's share of FDI pie falls to under 1 per cent', *Business Report*, 19 September 2001.

8. Francis Kornegay, 'Should SA lead a split in Africa?', *Global Dialogue*, 6, 2, July 2001, p. 2.

9. Khathu Mamaila, 'Mbeki MAPs out Africa's fresh beginning', *The Star*, 20 July 2001.

10. Jordan K Ngubane, *Ushaba: A Zulu Umlando*, Three Continents Press, Washington, 1975.

11. Jabu Sindane, *Democracy in African Societies and Ubuntu*, Human Sciences Research Council, Centre for Constitutional Analysis, Pretoria, no date, p. 8.

12. Yvonne Mokgoro, 'Ubuntu and the law in Africa', in Konrad-Adenauer-Stiftung, *Occasional Papers: The African Renaissance*, Johannesburg, May 1998, p. 52.

13. Department of Correctional Services, 'Restorative justice', Advertisement, *Sunday Times*, 9 December 2001.

14. For Museveni's thinking on the 'politics of

unity', see 'Ours is a fundamental change', in Yoweri Museveni, *What is Africa's Problem?*, NRM Publications, Kampala, 1992.

15. Frank Nxumalo, 'Asmal taps into safe water', *The Star*, 5 May 1997.

16. Constitutive Act of the African Union, July 2000, Article 4, reproduced in *African Association of Political Science Newsletter*, 6, 1, January 2001. Significantly, the Act omitted from its principles the reference to free and fair elections, which was included in article 4 of the preliminary draft treaty establishing the African Union.

17. Francis Kornegay, 'The geopolitics of redress: Reconfiguring Africa's diplomacy', *Global Insight*, 13, October 2001, p. 2.

18. Jonathan Derrick, 'Will there be an African Union?', *West Africa*, 4 259, 22 January 2001, p. 20.

19. Hans Pienaar, 'Nigeria's poor driving record may steer MAP off the unity course', *The Star*, 4 September 2001.

20. Peter Fabricius, 'SA backs off from oil deal with Sudan', *Sunday Independent*, 29 July 2001.

21. Jaspreet Kindra, 'We won't make the same mistake with Zim', *Mail & Guardian*, 2 March 2001.

22. As early as October 2000, Mbeki informed a business conference in Cape Town that he had twice informed the Zimbabwean public that land invasions would not be permitted in South Africa. The situation, he told the delegates, was 'unacceptable' (Thabo Leshilo, 'Zimbabwe land issue a grave hindrance to foreign interest', *Business Report*, 7 December 2000). By February 2001, the director-general of the Presidency was registering Thabo Mbeki's 'deep concern' at Zimbabwean events (letter to the editor, *Sunday Independent*, 4 March 2001). In March, after a ground-breaking meeting between the ANC and the Zimbabwean opposition Movement for Democratic Change, Mbeki's 'softly softly' approach was reported to be under review (Estelle Randall, 'Call to arrest Mugabe', *Sunday Independent*, 4 March 2001). At the end of the year, prompted by speculation about the fall in the value of the rand, Trevor Manuel urged investors not to confuse South Africa 'with that country to the north'.

23. For a succinct analysis of Pretoria's African policies since 1994, see Chris Landsberg, 'Promoting democracy: The Mandela–Mbeki doctrine', *Journal of Democracy*, 11, 3, July 2000. Unattributed quotations in this paragraph are

from this useful article.

24. Andrew Meldrum, 'Green light for Mugabe', *Mail & Guardian*, 14 December 2001.

25. Jonathan Moyo, *Generational Shifts in African Politics: Prospects for a New Africa*, African Association of Political Scientists, Occasional Paper, 2, 3, Harare, 1998, p. 17.

26. Michael Mortimore and Mary Tiffen, *More People, Less Erosion*, John Wiley, New York, 1994.

27. Quotations from Robert W July, *An African Voice: The Role of the Humanities in African Independence*, Duke University Press, Durham, 1987, pp. 222–3.

28. Marco Granelli, 'Afrikaners are Africans, says Mbeki in call for unity', *The Star*, 28 July 1999.

29. Mashupye Kgaphole and Sipho Seepe, 'Unleashing African intellectual energy', *Mail & Guardian*, 18 February 2001.

30. William Makgoba, 'A basis for the African Renaissance', in *African Renaissance Conference*, 28–29 September 1998 (booklet), Johannesburg.

31. Kwesi Kwaa Prah, 'Who is an African?', in *African Renaissance Conference*.

32. Cited on the letters page, *Mail & Guardian*, 11 September 1998, p. 26.

33. For a fuller discussion of Mbeki's predecessors in this field, see contributions by Eddy Maloka and Munyaradzi Morobe to Eddy Maloka and Elizabeth le Roux (eds.), *Problematising the African Renaissance*, Africa Institute, Pretoria, 2000.

34. Nnamdi Azikiwe, *Renascent Africa*, Negro University Press, New York, 1969.

35. Leonard Barnes, *African Renaissance*, Victor Gollancz, London, 1969.

36. Thoahlane Thoahlane, *Black Renaissance: Papers from the Black Renaissance Convention*, Ravan Press, Johannesburg, 1974, pp. 7–8.

37. John Battersby, 'Mbeki the philosopher soars above the turmoil of Africa', *Sunday Independent*, 16 August 1998.

38. Laleka Kaunda, 'A new pride in things African', *Evening Post*, 3 March 1999

39. Patrick Dooms, 'Why politicians go to Shembe', *Challenge*, 62, October 2000, pp. 14–15.

40. John Spira, 'Boom time for black business', *Sunday Independent*, 21 June 1998.

41. 'Public servants won't be ousted, says minister', *The Star*, 14 June 1998.

42. Pila Rulashe, 'Booming black middle class transforming insurance', *Sunday Independent*, 18 May 1998.

43. Thabo Leshile, 'Mazwai carves monument to black success', *Sunday Independent Business*, 9 November 1997.

44. 'Why Africa matters', address by H E Yoweri Kaguta Museveni (Republic of Uganda), Buenos Aires University, 1 November 1994, p. 10.

45. Statement of deputy president Thabo Mbeki, in *African Renaissance Conference,* Johannesburg, 28–29 September 1998, p. 2.

46. Joe Teffo, 'An African Renaissance – could it be realized?', *Woord en Daad*, 37, Spring 1997, p. 361.

CHAPTER 12

1. From 16 May 1999, the Johannesburg *Sunday Times* published the first of six biographical essays by Mark Gevisser, which remain the most factually detailed and the most interpretatively illuminating studies of Thabo Mbeki. This chapter is heavily indebted to the insights they contain.

2. Colin Bundy, 'Introduction', in Govan Mbeki, *Learning From Robben Island*, David Philip Publishers, Cape Town, 1991, p. ix.

3. Kaizer Nyatsumba, 'The humble Mbeki', *The Star*, 3 September 1993.

4. Shaun Johnson, 'Pipe aroma marks Thabo territory', *The Star*, 10 June 1994.

5. Charlene Smith, 'Two faces of the struggle', *Saturday Star*, 20 June 1998.

6. Thabo Mbeki, 'The historical injustice', in African National Congress, *Selected Writings on the Freedom Charter*, Sechaba Commemorative Publications, London, 1985, p. 48.

7. Mark Gevisser, 'The deal-maker', *Sunday times*, 13 June 1999.

8. John Matisonn, 'Mbeki's turbulent journey to power', *Sunday Independent*, 29 April 2001.

9. Ramaphosa succeeded in making this transition, apparently despite efforts by Mbeki to discourage his ascent in business. Lizeka Mda writes 'that the same Mbeki is reported to have summoned a prominent member of the National Empowerment Consortium in 1996 to impress upon that member that under no circumstances should Cyril Ramaphosa … be allowed to take control of Johnnic's media assets, largely represented by Times Media Limited. Today Ramaphosa is chair of both Johnnic and TML.' (Lizeka Mda, 'A short leap to dictatorship', *Mail & Guardian*, 27 March 1998).

10. Justice Malala, 'Lasting enigma of South African politics', *The Star*, 17 March 1997.

11. Andy Duffy, 'A caretaker in the cabinet', *Mail & Guardian*, 17 July 1998.

12. 'The people behind the cabinet', *Mail & Guardian*, 12 November 1999.

13. According to one apparently well-informed authority, Mbeki 'was the first of the senior leadership to discern that the model the ANC had constructed for the RDP was seriously, probably fatally flawed. He believed the RDP might lead his countrymen up a blind alley of expectations which could not be met and might therefore give the government cause for serious regret. Other counsels prevailed and Mbeki's thumbs-down prior to the tabling of the White Paper was disregarded, to his dismay.' Ingrid Uys, 'The compelling future of Thabo Mbeki', *Millennium Magazine*, May 1996, p. 34.

14. 'Mbeki's blues', *Southern African Report*, August 1998, p. 3.

15. *Sunday Times*, 7 May 1995.

16. For discussion of Mbeki's talents as negotiator and a comparison of his non-confrontational approach with Cyril Ramphosa's brinkmanship, see Mark Gevisser, 'The dealmaker', *Sunday Times*, 9 May 1999.

17. Kaizer Nyatsumba, 'Mbeki is passing the acid test', *The Star*, 11 June 1997.

18. Kaizer Nyatsumba, 'Rank and file flex their muscles', *The Star*, 19 February 1997.

19. Mondli Makhanya, 'Mbeki: Ruthless politician or inefficient successor to Mandela?', *The Star*, 27 August 1996.

20. 'Mbeki returns to his Idutywa roots to be blessed for tasks ahead', *The Star*, 24 December 2001.

21. Mark Gevisser, 'The Thabo Mbeki story: The family man', *Sunday Times*, 16 May 1999.

22. These ideas are drawn from Mbeki's speech to the ANC's National General Council meeting in Port Elizabeth in 2000. For a revealing excerpt, see 'ANC must stay true to its great ideals', *The Star*, 13 July 2000. Mbeki's commitment to his role as party president in distinction to the obligations of his government post is a source of pride amongst his official spokespeople who have noted that he devotes three days every week to party political work, so that there is often tension between the ANC headquarters and the Union Buildings about the distribution of his time. (See Parks Mankahlana, 'Mbeki is no populist', *Mail & Guardian,* 9 June 2000.)

23. These observations are derived from Helen Epstein's perceptive commentary on Mbeki's intellectual formation in 'The mystery of AIDS in South Africa', *New York Review of Books*, 20 July 2000.

24. For an indication of the prominence ANC discourses accord to Mbeki's advocacy of 'the spirit of a new cadre and volunteerism', see a letter to *The Star*, 10 January 2001, by Nomfanelo Kota, the ANC's 'media coordinator'. Kota was taking her cue from the themes of Mbeki's presidential address on the ANC's 90th anniversary, in which 2001 was declared to be 'the year of volunteerism'. For illuminating intellectual parallels with Mbeki's voluntarist idealism, see the introduction in Jerome Chen (ed.), *Mao*, Prentice-Hall, Englewood Cliffs, 1969.

25. See, for example, Mbeki's remarks to Pik Botha at the launch of an anti-apartheid history project, in John Battersby, 'Relaxed Mbeki finds a place for Pik in liberation history', *Sunday Independent*, 26 March 2001.

26. *From Resistance to Reconstruction. Tasks of the ANC in the New Epoch of the Democratic Transformation. Unmandated Reflections.* 9 August 1994, p. 18.

27. Jovial Rantao, 'Blacks must create own destiny, says Mbeki', *The Star*, 4 June 1998

28. Ray Wood, 'South Africa's leaders rate Mbeki', *Professional Management Review*, July 1966, pp. 20–1; 'Fifty one leaders rate Mbeki highly as future president', *Professional Management Review*, December 1997, pp. 8–10.

29. Kaizer Nyatsumba, 'Mbeki is passing the acid test'.

30. Jeremy Cronin, 'Mbeki sets off on long walk to the future', *Sunday Independent*, 13 December 1998.

31. Frederik van Zyl Slabbert, 'South Africa under Thabo Mbeki', in Andrew Reynolds (ed.), *Election '99 South Africa: From Mandela to Mbeki*, David Philip Publishers, Cape Town, 1999, p. 212.

32. Albert Venter, 'The executive', in Albert Venter (ed.), *Government and Politics in the New South Africa*, second edition, Van Schaik, Pretoria, 2001, p. 78.

33. Patrick Bulger, 'Mbeki ready to show his mettle', *The Star*, 3 March 1998.

34. 'SA's cabinet has a spread of backgrounds', *Business Day*, 12 August 1999.

35. Greg Mills, 'The paradox of power: South African foreign policy and southern African challenges', unpublished paper, April 2001.

36. In addition to Chris Landsberg's favourable assessment of Mbeki's foreign policy and inter-

national statesmanship cited in chapter 11, for two sharply contrasting evaluations see James Barber and Brendan Vickers, 'South Africa's foreign policy', in Venter, *Government and Politics*, and Greg Mills, *The Wired Model: South Africa, Foreign Policy and Globalisation*, Cape Town, Tafelberg, 2000.

37. James Myburgh, 'Mbeki and the total formula', *Sunday Independent*, 1 April 2001.

38. Charles Phahlane, 'Zuma denies ANC leadership challenge or rift', *The Star*, 4 April 2001.

39. Amongst Mbeki's supposed mistresses was Linda Zama, a Durban attorney and adviser to S'bu Ndebele, KwaZulu-Natal MEC for transport, as well as a mysterious beneficiary of an ANC loan.

40. Sven Lunsche, 'World needs a clear signal from Africa', *Sunday Times*, 24 May 1998.

41. For example, 'It took a visit by Mbeki himself to a hospital to unblock an intergovernmental procedure that had prevented a hot water geyser from being repaired.' Such interventions are unlikely to result in hospital staff developing the confidence to put such matters right on their own initiative, certainly not while 'intergovernmental procedures' remain in place. See Charles Phahlane, 'Listen to the people', *The Star*, 14 November 2001.

42. Kader Asmal, 'Sense of loss behind anti-Mbeki tirade', *Sunday Independent*, 8 April 2001.

43. Clive Sawyer, 'Mbeki, cabinet leave questions unanswered', *The Star*, 15 December 1999.

44. Firoz Cachalia, 'Democracy requires wisdom too', *Mail & Guardian*, 22 September 2000.

45. Jaspreet Kindra, 'Mbeki fuels Alliance tensions', *Mail & Guardian*, 1 September 2000.

46. Karen MacGregor, 'South Africa has one of the highest HIV rates in the world', *Times Higher Education Supplement*, 13 April 2001, p. 17.

47. Anso Thom, 'AIDS report paints grim picture for SA's youth', *The Star*, 17 October 2001.

48. Thabo Mbeki, 'Alien goings-on to mar Virodene fight', *Sunday Independent*, 8 March 1998; Stefaans Brummer, 'Virodene's unanswered questions', *Mail & Guardian*, 13 March 1998; Anso Thom, 'The pros and cons of Virodene', *The Star*, 20 March 1998.

49. Ann Crotty and James Lamont, 'Mandela hits a raw nerve', *Sunday Independent*, 17 September 1996.

50. 'Medical body raps Mbeki over AIDS', *The Star*, 31 January 2000.

51. Mike Robertson, 'Face to face with the president', *Sunday Times*, 6 February 2000.

52. Epstein, 'The mystery of AIDS'.

53. 'President's infiltration claim scorned by union', *The Star*, 31 January 2000.

54. Drew Forrest, 'Behind the smokescreen', *Mail & Guardian*, 26 October 2001.

55. Epstein, 'The mystery of AIDS'.

56. 'What Mbeki and Leon had to say', *Mail & Guardian*, 6 October 2000; Robert Brand, 'AZT has not been tested for use in the case of rape', *The Star*, 10 October 2000; Tony Leon, 'Brand merely panders to Mbeki', *The Star*, 17 October 2000.

57. Pat Sidley, 'Mbeki still sceptical about gravity of AIDS epidemic', *Business Day*, 10 July 2000.

58. Interview text, *Time*, 4 September 2000.

59. Howard Barrell, 'ANC concern over Mbeki fiasco', *Mail & Guardian*, 22 September 2000.

60. Zweli Mkhize, 'The HIV/AIDS debate', 28 April 2000, ANC website.

61. Estelle Randall, 'Let's start again: HIV causes AIDS', *Sunday Independent*, 24 September 2000.

62. Robert Brand, 'ANC backs Mbeki in dispute over HIV/AIDS', *The Star*, 4 October 2000.

63. Jaspreet Kindra, 'Mbeki fingers CIA in AIDS conspiracy', *Mail & Guardian*, 6 October 2000. See letter from Aziz Pahad criticising the report's accuracy, as well as the editor's reply in *Mail & Guardian*, 13 October 2000.

64. 'All the presidents' scientists: Diary of a round earther', *Mail & Guardian*, 8 September 2001; 'Presidential AIDS Panel reports', *The Star*, 4 April 2001.

65. Lynne Altenroxel, 'AIDS Panel's report reveals divergent views', *The Star*, 5 April 2001.

66. Magnus Linklater, 'Pragmatist or prophet of a dream?', *Sunday Independent*, 3 June 2001.

67. 'Thabo stirs a hornet's nest on AIDS/HIV link', *The Star*, 28 June 2001.

68. Khanyisile Nkosi, 'ANC dismisses report citing AIDS as leading killer in SA', *The Star*, 2 October 2001.

69. Howard Barrell and Jaspreet Kindra, 'Shocking AIDS report leaked', *Mail & Guardian*, 5 October 2001.

70. Drew Forrest, 'Mbeki in bizarre AIDS outburst', *Mail & Guardian*, 26 October 2001.

71. *Mail & Guardian*, 21 July 2000. For comparable contentions by Department of Health officials, see Charlene Smith, 'AZT denied and AIDS keeps killing', *Sunday Times*, 16 January 1999.

72. Belinda Beresford, '2.7 million needed to fight AIDS', *Mail & Guardian*, 21 September 2001; Lynne Altenroxel, 'UN report endorses anti-retrovirals', *The Star*, 22 June 2001.

73. *Mail & Guardian*, World AIDS Day Supplement, 30 November 2001; Jon Jeter, 'Project for rape victims loses its home base', *The Star*, 4 October 2001.

74. Kerry Cullinan, 'Govt's HIV policy faces court challenge', *The Star*, 23 November 2001.

75. Hector Sauer, 'Truth of Mbeki and AIDS and Mbeki', *The Star*, 21 September 2000.

76. Jaspreet Kindra, 'Mbeki fingers the CIA in AIDS conspiracy', *Mail & Guardian*, 6 October 2000; Howard Barrell, 'ANC concern over Mbeki fiasco', *Mail & Guardian*, 22 September 2000.

77. ANC Today Briefing Document, *HIV/AIDS in South Africa: Challenges, Obstacles and Responses*, 30 November 2001, p. 9.

78. Lynne Altenroxel, 'Gains in HIV-AIDS awareness at risk', *The Star*, 25 September 2000; Jaspreet Kindra, 'Church fray over Mbeki's AIDS message', *Mail & Guardian*, 9 November 2001; 'Mbeki's questioning set back the AIDS campaign', *Sunday Independent*, 24 September 2000.

79. A Markinor survey based on a national sample conducted for the US State Department in December 2000 showed that 79 per cent of its respondents agreed that HIV caused AIDS, though black South Africans were less likely to believe this than other groups. However, only 30 per cent of sexually active males claimed to use condoms every time they had sexual relations despite the much broader awareness of the link between AIDS and risky sexual behaviour.

80. For reports of the impact of Mbeki's ideas about AIDS on US business, see Richard Stovin Bradford, 'Hard-hitting report takes a stern view of South Africa', *Sunday Times*, 11 November 2001; Marco Granelli, 'AIDS blunders overshadow president's MAP message in the US', *Sunday Independent*, 1 July 2001.

81. For arguments that link Mbeki's views on AIDS to ANC and SACP intellectual traditions, see Chris Kenyon, 'The AIDS crisis: Mbeki, Mao and the emperor with no clothes', *Sunday Independent*, 11 November 2001; Steven Robins, 'Political interference is undermining AIDS battle', *Sunday Independent*, 23 December 2001; Paul Trewhela, 'Mbeki and AIDS in Africa: A comment', *New York Review of Books*, 19 October 2001.

82. Keith Grint, *The Arts of Leadership*, Oxford

University Press, Oxford, 2000.

83. The ambiguities of South African afrocentrism are most perceptively explored in Hein Marais, *South Africa: Limits to Change: The Political Economy of Transition*, Zed Books, London, 2001, p. 249–52.

84. Khathu Mamaila, 'The message is passing ordinary voters by', *The Star*, 19 June 2001.

85. On poll evidence, see Howard Barrell, 'Mbeki's popularity plummets', *Mail & Guardian*, 20 October 2000.

86. L Schlemmer, 'Race relations: changing priorities, *Fast Facts*, South African Institute of Race Relations, Johannesburg, September 2001.

87. Thabo Mbeki, 'Where is the black intelligentsia?', *Sunday Independent*, 13 August 2000.

88. Valerie Møller and Helga Dickow, *Five Years into Democracy: Elite and Rank and File Perspectives on the Quality of Life and the Rainbow Nation*, Institut Français d'Afrique du Sud, Johannesburg, March 2001, pp. 64–6.

89. Ronnie Kasrils, 'Nyatsumba's views on Mbeki and fate show silly season is in full swing', *The Star*, 27 December 2000.

90. Pumla Gobodo-Madikizela, 'Where did compassion go?', *Mail & Guardian*, 5 October 2001.

BIBLIOGRAPHY

DOCUMENTS

African Christian Democratic Party, *Manifesto Local Government Elections*, Cape Town, 2000.

African National Congress, *Selected Writings on the Freedom Charter*, Sechaba Commemorative Publications, London, 1985.

African National Congress, *The Reconstruction and Development Programme: A Policy Framework*, Umanyano Publications, Johannesburg, 1994.

African National Congress, *Agricultural Policy*, Westro Reproductions, Johannesburg, 1994.

African National Congress, *The State and Social Transformation*, Johannesburg, November 1996.

African National Congress, *All Power to the People: Proposed Constitutional Amendments*, ANC 50th National Conference, Marshalltown, Johannesburg, 1997.

African National Congress, *Strategy and Tactics of the African National Congress, Presidential Address*, ANC 50th National Conference, Mafikeng, December 1997.

African National Congress, *Political Report of the President, Nelson Mandela, to the 50th National Conference of the African National Congress*, 16 December 1997, Mathibe Printing and Publishing, Johannesburg, 1997.

African National Congress, Protea Glen Branch, *Political Report by Branch Chairperson Desmond Mahasha*, Annual General Meeting, 21 June 1998.

African National Congress, *Speech by ANC President Thabo Mbeki to the Annual Conference of the IFP*, 18 July 1998, Department of Information and Publicity, Marshalltown, 1998.

African National Congress, *Together: Speeding Up Change: Fighting Poverty and Creating a Better Life for All*, 10 October 2000.

African National Congress, *ANC Today Briefing Document: HIV/AIDS in South Africa: Challenges, Obstacles and Responses*, 30 November 2001.

Christian Democratic Party, *Vote Yes for the Christian Democratic Party*, Westgate, 2000.

Congress of South African Trade Unions, National Council for Trade Unions and Federation of South African Labour, *Social Equity and Job Creation: The Key to a Stable Future. Labour's Proposals on Growth, Development and Job Creation*, Johannesburg, 1 April 1996.

Democratic Alliance, Local Government Elections leaflets, 2000.

National Interim Civic Committee, *Financial Statement, October 1991 – June 1992*.

New National Party, *Corruption Barometer, 1994–1998*, NNP Federal Council, Cape Town, 1998.

New National Party, *Key Facts 2001 – Participatory Government – Mainstream Politics*, NNP Federal Council, Cape Town, November 2001.

South African Civil Society Observer Coalition, 2000 local government elections observation reports (held at the Electoral Institute of Southern Africa, Johannesburg).

South African National Civic Organisation, *Mission Statement*, Johannesburg, 1994.

South African National Civic Organisation, *Strategies and Policies for Local Economic Development in the New South Africa*, Johannesburg, March 1995.

South African National Civic Organisation, *Presidential Address*, Second National Conference, Johannesburg, 16–20 April 1997.

South African National Civic Organisation, *Organisational Report*, Wattville Branch, March 2001.

South African National Civic Organisation, *Organisational Report*, Third National Conference, Mogale City, 19–22 April 2001.

South African National Civic Organisation, *Strategy Discussion Document to Radically Reshape the Vision and Role of SANCO*, Third National Conference, Mogale City, 19–22 April 2001.

Supreme Court of South Africa, *State vs Mewa Ramgobin*, Pietermaritzburg, 1985, Trial Exhibits.

United Democratic Movement, *Local Government Elections Manifesto*, Pretoria, 18 October 2000.

United Democratic Movement, *A Better Plan for the Future*, Arcadia, 2000.

SURVEY DATA

Community Agency for Social Enquiry, *Corruption and Good Governance Profile: South Africa 1997*, Transparency International, Johannesburg, 3 September 1998.

Community Agency for Social Enquiry, *Corruption and Good Governance: A Media Profile*, Transparency South Africa, Johannesburg, December 2000.

Electoral Institute of Southern Africa, Institute for Democracy in South Africa, South African Broadcasting Corporation and Markinor, *Opinion '99* (data sets held in EISA Library).

Human Sciences Research Council, *Annual Social Movement Surveys*, principal investigators: Johan Olivier and Bert Klandermans, 1994–1998.

Human Sciences Research Council and Department of Political Studies, University of the Witwatersrand, *Markdata Omnibus Survey on Local Government*, September 1995 (data set held at Department of Political Studies, University of the Witwatersrand).

Marketing Research Africa (ACNielsen), *Truth Commission: Conducted for Business Day*, Johannesburg, 1996.

Marketing Research Africa (ACNielsen), *The TRC Evaluation: Conducted for Business Day*, Johannesburg, 1998.

Media and Marketing Research, *Sowetan Crime Survey: Presentation of Crime Findings*, Johannesburg, January 1996.

NEWSPAPERS AND NEWSLETTERS

African Communist (Johannesburg), 1997
Business Day (Johannesburg), 1998–2000
Citizen (Johannesburg), 1994–2000
Daily Dispatch (East London), 2000
Die Volksblad (Bloemfontein), 2000
East Cape Weekend (Port Elizabeth), 1999
Eastern Province Herald (Port Elizabeth), 1999–2000
Election Update (Johannesburg), 1999
Enquirer (Johannesburg), 2001
Evening Post (Port Elizabeth), 1999–2000
Financial Mail (Johannesburg), 1999–2000
Helen Suzman Foundation Focus (Johannesburg), 2001
Helen Suzman Foundation KwaZulu-Natal Briefing (Durban), 1998
Highveld Herald (Ermelo), 1999
Housing in Southern Africa (Pretoria), 1999
IDASA Provincial Whip (Cape Town), 1997–1999

Inform: Newsletter of the National Housing Forum (Johannesburg), 1997
In Session – Newsletter of the House of Assembly (Cape Town), 2001
Land and Rural Digest (Pretoria), 1999
Land Info (Pretoria), 1997–1998
Land Update (Pretoria), 1998
Local Government Elections Update (Johannesburg), 2000
Lowvelder (Nelspruit), 1998
Mail & Guardian – formerly *Weekly Mail* (Johannesburg), 1991–2002
Mayibuye (African National Congress, Johannesburg), 1990
Middelburg Observer, 1998
Mpumalanga News (Nelspruit), 1999
Natal Mercury (Durban), 1997–2000
New Nation (Johannesburg), 1988–1996
New York Newsday, 1990
New York Times, 1990
Northcliffe and Melville Times, 2000
Noseweek (Johannesburg), 2001
RDP Monitor (Johannesburg), 1995
Reparation and Memorialisation – Institute for Justice and Reconciliation (Cape Town), 2000
Round Table – Centre for Development Enterprise (Johannesburg), 2000
SASPU National (Johannesburg), 1987
South Africa Report (Johannesburg), 1997–1998
Springs African Reporter, 1999
Springs and Brakpan Advertiser, 1998–1999
Sunday Independent – also includes *Reconstruct* (Johannesburg), 1996–2002
Sunday Times (Johannesburg), 1990–2001
The Representative (Queenstown), 1999
The Star – also includes *Business Report* (Johannesburg), 1991–2002
Truth Talk – Truth and Reconciliation Commission (Johannesburg), 1997
Umrabulo (Department of Political Education and Training, African National Congress, Marshalltown), 1998–2001
Umthunya (South African National Civic Organisation, Johannesburg), 1995
Village Voice (New York), 1990
Witbank News, 1999–2000

OFFICIAL PUBLICATIONS

Constitutive Act of the African Union, July 2000, reproduced in *African Association of Political Science Newsletter*, 6, 1, January 2001.

Government of Kwa-Zulu, Bureau of Communication, Department of the Chief

Minister, *Inhlabamkhosi*, Ulundi, February 1984.

Pali Lehohla, *South Africa in Transition*, Statistics South Africa, Pretoria, 2001.

Mark Orkin, *Victims of Crime Survey*, Statistics South Africa, Pretoria, 1998.

Republic of South Africa, *Commission of Inquiry into Department of Development Aid*, Pretoria, RP 73/1992.

Republic of South Africa, *Debates of the National House of Assembly*, Cape Town, 10 June 1997.

Republic of South Africa, Department of Constitutional Development, *White Paper on Local Government*, Government Gazette, 13 March 1998.

Republic of South Africa, Department of Health, *Annual Reports*, 1998, 1999.

Republic of South Africa, Department of Land Affairs, *Annual Report*, 1997, Pretoria, RP 96/98.

Republic of South Africa, Department of Public Service and Administration, *Provincial Review Report*, Pretoria, 1997.

Republic of South Africa, Department of Water Affairs and Forestry, *Annual Report*, 1999/2000, Pretoria, RP 101/2001.

Republic of South Africa, Department of Water Affairs and Forestry, *Evaluation of the Community Water Supply and Sanitation Programme*, Workshop Document, Mvula Trust, Pretoria, November 1997.

Republic of South Africa, Office of the Executive Deputy President, *Report for the Office of the Executive Deputy President's Inter-ministerial Committee on Poverty and Inequality*, Pretoria, 13 May 1998.

Republic of South Africa, Office of the President, *White Paper on Reconstruction and Development: The Government's Strategy for Total Transformation*, Cape Town, 1994.

Republic of South Africa, South African Communication Service, *The Foundation for a Better Life Has Been Laid: The Government's Mid-term Report to the Nation*, Pretoria, February 1997.

Republic of South Africa, *Verslag van die Kommissie van Ondersoek na die 1980 Onluste en beweerde Wanbestuur in KwaNdebele*, Pretoria, RP 137/1993.

Statistics South Africa, 'Human Development Index', Press Release, Pretoria, June 2001.

The Truth and Reconciliation Commission of South Africa, *Report*, Volumes 1–5, Juta and Co., Cape Town, October 1998.

World Bank, *Development Report*, Oxford University Press, Oxford, 1997.

UNPUBLISHED RESEARCH REPORTS AND POSTGRADUATE DISSERTATIONS

Cathi Albertyn, Beth Goldblatt, Shireen Hassim, and Sheila Meintjes, *Engendering the Political Agenda: A South African Case Study: A Report for the United Nations International Institute for Research and Training for the Advancement of Women*, Centre for Applied Legal Studies, University of the Witwatersrand, Johannesburg, July 1999.

Goodwill Gabriel Ditlhage, *Social Capital and its Prospects for Development in South Africa*, MA dissertation, Department of Political Studies, University of the Witwatersrand, 1998.

Philip Frankel, *Local Governance and Social Transformation in Emfuleni: A Needs Analysis for Integrated Development Planning*, report commissioned by the Emfuleni Municipality, Department of Political Studies, University of the Witwatersrand, 2002.

Philip Frankel, Stephen Louw and Simon Stacey, *Governmental Performance and Capacity: Transitional Local Authorities in Mpumalanga*, Department of Political Studies, University of the Witwatersrand and the HSRC External Projects Programme, April 1997.

Kevin French, *James Mpanza and the Sofasonke Movement*, MA dissertation, Department of Political Studies, University of the Witwatersrand, 1984.

ARTICLES AND UNPUBLISHED PAPERS

Anon., 'From resistance to reconstruction. Tasks of the ANC in the new epoch of the democratic transformation. Unmandated reflections', 9 August 1994.

Anon., 'New frontiers in diagnosing and combating corruption', *Poverty Reduction and Economic Management*, World Bank, Washington, 7 October 1998.

Timothy Garton Ash, 'True confessions', *New York Review of Books*, 17 July 1997.

Bruce Baker, 'The quality of African democracy: Why and how it should be measured', *Journal of Contemporary African Studies*, 17, 2, 1999.

M Beenstock, 'Corruption and development', *World Development*, 7, 1, 1979.

Patrick Bond, 'Local economic development and municipal services crisis in post-apartheid South Africa', *Urban Forum*, 9, 2, 1998.

Susan Booysen, 'Democracy and public participation in policymaking in South Africa: Trends and prospects', paper presented at the Africa Institute Colloquium, 'South Africa since 1994: Lessons and Prospects', Pretoria, 30 May 2001.

Belinda Bozzoli, 'Public ritual and private transgression: The Truth Commission in Alexandra township, South Africa, 1996', *African Studies*, 57, 2, 1998.

Michael Bratton and Robert Mattes, 'Support for democracy in Africa: Intrinsic or instrumental?', *British Journal of Political Science*, 31, 2001.

Lala Camerer, 'South Africa – derailing the gravy train – controlling corruption', *Journal of Financial Crime*, 4, 4, June 1997.

Michael Cleverley, 'South Africa's obstacles: The RDP's opportunities', address by the counsellor for economic affairs, US Embassy, Pretoria, 22 June 1995.

Lionel Cliffe, 'Land reform in South Africa', *Review of African Political Economy*, 84, 2000.

Ben Cousins, 'Livestock production and common property struggles in South Africa's agrarian reform', *Journal of Peasant Studies*, 23, 2/3, April 1996.

Polly Dewhirst and Brandon Hamber, 'Non-government organisations and the Truth and Reconciliation Commission: An impact assessment', *Politikon*, 26, 1, 1999

A Doig, 'Good government and sustainable anti-corruption strategies: A role for independent anti-corruption agencies?', *Public Administration and Development*, 15, 1991.

Patrick Dooms, 'Why politicians go to Shembe', *Challenge*, 62, October 2000,

Mark Ensalaco, 'Truth commissions for Chile and El Salvador: A report and an assessment', *Human Rights Quarterly*, 16, 1994.

Helen Epstein, 'The mystery of AIDs in South Africa', *New York Review of Books*, 20 July 2000.

Chris Erasmus, 'Mandela: The options', *Inside South Africa*, September 1988.

David Fveratt and Sifiso Zulu, 'Analysing rural development programmes in South Africa 1994–2000', *Development Update*, 3, 4, 2000.

Steven Friedman and Ivor Chipkin, 'The politics of inequality in South Africa', paper presented at the Centre for Policy Studies, Johannesburg, August 2001.

James Gibson and Amanda Gouws, 'Truth and reconciliation in South Africa: Attributions of blame and the struggle over apartheid', *American Political Science Review*, 93, 3, September 1999.

Lynn S Graybill, 'Pursuit of truth and reconciliation in South Africa', *Africa Today*, 45, 1, 1998.

Adam Habib and Rupert Taylor, 'South Africa: Anti-apartheid NGOs in transition', *Voluntas: International Journal of Voluntary and Nonprofit Organisations*, 10, 1, 1999.

Gillian Hart, 'The agrarian question and industrial dispersal in South Africa: Agro-industrial linkages through Asian lenses', *Journal of Peasant Studies*, 23, 2/3, April 1996.

Priscilla B Hayter, 'Fifteen truth commissions – 1974–1994: A comparative study', *Human Rights Quarterly*, 16, 1994.

Priscilla B Hayter, 'International guidelines for the creation and operation of truth commissions', *Law and Contemporary Problems*, 59, 4, 1996.

Patrick Heller, 'Degrees of democracy: Some comparative lessons from India', *World Politics*, 52, July 2000.

Kenny Hlela, 'The applicability of Putnam's social capital theory in the case of Sweetwaters in Pietermaritzburg, Kwa-Zulu Natal', MA research essay, Department of Political Studies, University of the Witwatersrand, 1999.

André Horn, 'Land restitution: The South African programme in the African context', paper presented at the African Studies Association of South Africa biennial conference, 'Africa in a Changing World', Broederstroom, 8–10 September 1997.

Ben Jacobs, 'SANCO: Heading for disaster', *Work in Progress*, 86, 1992.

Courtney Jung and Ian Schapiro, 'South Africa's negotiated transition: Democracy, opposition and the new constitutional order', *Politics and Society*, 23, 2, September 1995.

Mike Kaye, 'The role of truth commissions in the search for justice, reconciliation and democratisation: The Salvadorian and Honduran cases', *Journal of Latin American Studies*, 29, 1977.

Robert Klitgaard, 'International cooperation against corruption?', *Finance and Development*, International Monetary Fund, 35, 1, March 1998.

Francis Kornegay, 'Should SA lead a split in Africa?', *Global Dialogue*, 6, 2, July 2001.

Francis Kornegay, 'The geopolitics of redress: Reconfiguring Africa's diplomacy', *Global Insight*, 13, October 2001.

Sahr John Kpundeh, 'Limiting administrative corruption in Sierra Leone', *Journal of Modern African Studies*, 32, 1, 1994.

Gerald Kraak, 'The South African voluntary sector in 2001', *Development Update*, 3, 4, 2001.

Chris Landsberg, 'Promoting democracy: The Mandela–Mbeki doctrine', *Journal of Democracy*, 11, 3, July 2000.

Kimberley Lanegran, 'South Africa's civic association movement: ANC's ally or society's watchdog?', *African Studies Review*, 38, 2, September 1995.

Murray Leibbrandt and Ingrid Woolard, 'The labour market and household income inequality in South Africa', *Journal of International Development*, 2001.

Richard Levin and Daniel Weiner, 'Peasants speak: The land question in Mpumalanga', *Journal of Peasant Studies*, 23, 2/3, April 1996.

Justine Lucas, 'Space, domesticity and people's power: Civic organisation in Alexandra in the 1990s', *African Studies*, 54, 1, 1995, p. 102.

William Makgoba, 'A basis for the African Renaissance', African Renaissance Conference, Johannesburg, 28–29 September 1998.

Robert Mattes and Cherrel Africa, 'Corruption – the attitudinal component: Tracking perceptions of official corruption in South Africa, 1995–1998', unpublished paper, IDASA, Cape Town, 1999.

Rober Mattes, Yul Derek Davids and Cherrel Africa, 'Views of democracy in South Africa and the region', *Afrobarometer Paper* No. 8, Institute for Democracy in South Africa, Cape Town, 2000.

Mzwanele Mayekiso, 'Institutions that themselves need to be watched over: A review of recent writings on the civic movement', *Urban Forum*, 4, 1, 1994.

M McMullen, 'A theory of corruption', *Sociological Review*, 1961.

Greg Mills, 'The paradox of power: South African foreign policy and southern African challenges', unpublished paper, April 2001.

Nthobi Moahloli, 'Afrikatourism – using tourism to let Africans know Africa', address to the African Renaissance Conference, Johannesburg, 28 September 1998.

Edward N Muller and Mitchell A Seligson, 'Civic culture and democracy: The question of causal relationships', *American Political Science Review*, 88, 3, September 1994.

Colin Murray, 'Land reform in eastern Free State: Policy dilemmas and political conflicts', *Journal of Peasant Studies*, 23, 2/3, 1996.

Colin Murray, 'Changing livelihoods in the Free State: 1990s', *African Studies*, 59, 1, 2000.

Andrew Nash, 'Mandela's democracy', *Monthly Review*, April 1999.

Nicoli Nattrass, 'Politics and economics in ANC policy', *African Affairs*, 93, 372, July 1994.

Nicoli Nattrass, 'The Truth and Reconciliation Commission on business and apartheid: A critical reflection', *African Affairs*, 98, 1999.

Nicoli Nattrass and Jeremy Seekings, 'Democracy and distribution in highly unequal economies: The case of South Africa', *Journal of Modern African Studies*, 39, 3, 2001.

Sandile Ngidi, 'The bitter pill of amnesty', *Siyaya!*, 3, Spring 1998.

L Nijzink and S Jacobs, 'Provincial elections and government formation in the Western Cape', *Politikon*, 27, 1, 2000.

Joseph S Nye, 'Corruption and political development: A cost benefit analysis', *American Political Science Review*, 56, 1967.

Sophie Oldfield, 'The centrality of community capacity in state low-income housing provision in Cape Town, South Africa', *International Journal of Urban and Regional Research*, 24, 4, December 2000.

Johan Olivier and Rose Ngwane, 'Marching to a different tune', *Indicator South Africa*, 1996.

Marina Ottaway, 'African democratisation and the Leninist option', *Journal of Modern African Studies*, 35, 1, 1997.

Raymond Parsons, 'A history and evaluation of social dialogue in South Africa', working paper presented to the International Jubilee Conference of the Economic Society of South Africa, Johannesburg, 14 September 2001.

Jacques Pauw, 'Terrifyingly normal', *Siyaya!*, Spring 1998.

David Pottie, 'Housing the nation: The politics of low-cost housing in South Africa since 1994', paper presented to the South African Political Science Association, Durban, 2001.

Kwesi Kwaa Prah, 'Who is an African?', African Renaissance Conference, Johannesburg, 28–29 September, 1998.

Marlene Roefs, 'Notes on perceptions of legitimacy of national and provincial government in the Western and Eastern Cape, KwaZulu-Natal and Gauteng', paper presented at the workshop on 'Democracy and Social Capital in Segmented Societies', Department of Political Studies, University of the Witwatersrand, Johannesburg, 9–12 October 1997.

Richard Rose and Doh Chull Shin, 'Democratization backwards: The problem with third wave democracies', British Journal of Political Science, 31, 2001.

Stefan Schirmer, 'Policy visions and historical realities: Land reform in the context of recent agricultural developments', African Studies, 59, 1, 2000.

Lawrence Schlemmer, R W Johnson, and Craig Charney, 'South Africa: Findings of a survey of political and social attitudes in post-election South Africa', Centre for Policy Studies, Johannesburg, December 1994.

Jeremy Seekings, 'SANCO: Strategic dilemmas in a democratic South Africa', Transformation, 34, 1997.

John Sender, 'Rural poverty and land redistribution: Some macro-economic issues', paper presented at the Land and Agricultural Policy Centre's Redistribution Options Workshop, 13 September 1993.

Sheona Shackleton, Carlie Shackleton and Ben Cousins, 'Re-valuing the communal lands of Southern Africa: New understandings of rural livelihoods', Natural Resource Perspectives, Overseas Development Institute, 62, November 2000.

A W Stadler, 'Birds in the cornfield: Squatter movements in Johannesburg, 1944–1947', Journal of Southern African Studies, 6, 1, 1979.

Elizabeth Stanley, 'Evaluating the Truth and Reconciliation Commission', Journal of Modern African Studies, 39, 3, 2001.

Richard Stengel, 'The Mandela I came to know', The Spectator, 19 November 1994.

Helen Taylor and Bob Mattes, 'Political parties and the consolidation of democracy in South Africa', IDASA, Kutlwanong Democracy Centre, Pretoria, 29–30 September 1997.

Joe Teffo, 'An African Renaissance – could it be realized?', Woord en Daad, 37, 361, Spring 1997.

Lechesa Tsenoli, 'Interview', Development and Democracy, 8, 1994.

Ingrid Uys, 'The compelling future of Thabo Mbeki', Millennium Magazine, May 1996.

Stanley Uys, 'The ANC generation gap that haunts Mandela', Guardian Weekly, 23 April 1993.

Caroline White, 'Democratic societies? Voluntary association and democratic culture in a South African township', Transformation, 36, 1998.

Jennifer Widner and Alexander Mundt, 'Researching social capital in Africa', Africa: Journal of the International Africa Institute, 1999.

Gavin Williams, 'Options for land reform and rural restructuring in South Africa', paper presented to the Land and Agriculture Centre's Land Redistribution Options Conference, Johannesburg, 12–15 October 1993.

Gavin Williams, 'Setting the agenda: A critique of the World Bank's rural restructuring programme for South Africa', Journal of Southern African Studies, 22, 1, March 1996.

Ray Wood, 'South Africa's leaders rate Mbeki', Professional Management Review, July 1996.

BOOKS

Richard Abel, Politics by Other Means: Law in the Struggle Against Apartheid, Routledge, London, 1995.

Konrad-Adenhauer-Stiftung, Occasional Papers: The African Renaissance, Johannesburg, May 1998.

Glenn Adler and Jonny Steinberg (eds.), From Comrades to Citizens, Macmillan, London, 1998.

David Apter, Ghana in Transition, Princeton University Press, New Jersey, 1972.

Kader Asmal, Louise Asmal and Ronald Suresh Roberts, Reconciliation through Truth: A Reckoning of South Africa's Criminal Governance, David Philip, Cape Town, 1996.

Nnamdi Azikiwe, Renascent Africa, Negro University Press, New York, 1969.

Leonard Barnes, African Renaissance, Victor Gollancz, London, 1969.

Mary Benson, Nelson Mandela, Panaf Great Lives, London, 1980.

Mary Benson, Nelson Mandela, Penguin Books, Harmondsworth, 1986.

Ann Bernstein, Policy-making in a New Democracy, Centre for Development Enterprise, Johannesburg, 1999.

Alex Boraine, A Country Unmasked: Inside South Africa's Truth and Reconciliation Commission, Oxford University Press, Cape Town, 2000.

Alex Boraine, Janet Levy and Ronel Scheffer, Dealing with the Past, IDASA, Cape Town, 1994.

H Russell Botman and Robin M Petersen, To Remember and to Heal: Theological and Psychological Reflections on Truth and Reconciliation, Human and Rousseau, Cape Town, 1996.

Edward Breslin and Bethuel Netshswinzhe, *Strengthening Sustainability Initiative: Results of the Mvula Trust AusAid Evaluations*, Mvula Trust, Johannesburg, 15 February 2000.

Colin Bundy, *The Rise and Fall of the South African Peasantry*, Heinemann, London, 1979.

Jane Carruthers, *Sandton; The Making of a Town*, Clet Books, Rivonia, 1993.

Centre for Development Enterprise, *Response to the White Paper on Local Government*, Johannesburg, June 1998.

Jerome Chen (ed.), *Mao*, Prentice-Hall, Englewood Cliffs, 1969.

David Chidester, *Shots in the Street: Violence and Religion in South Africa*, Beacon Press, Boston, 1991.

Karin Chubb and Lutz van Dijk, *Between Anger and Hope: South Africa's Youth and the Truth and Reconciliation Commission*, Witwatersrand University Press, Johannesburg, 2001.

James Cochrane, John de Gruchy and Stephen Martin, *Facing the Truth: South African Faith Communities and the Truth and Reconciliation Commission*, David Philip, Cape Town, 1999.

Jean Comaroff, *Body of Power, Spirit of Resistance: The Culture and History of a South African People*, Chicago University Press, Chicago, 1998.

Consolidated Business Movement, *Building a Winning Nation*, Ravan Press, Johannesburg, 1994.

Steve Davis, *Apartheid's Rebels: Inside South Africa's Hidden War*, Yale University Press, New Haven, 1987.

Donatella Della Porta and Yves Meny (eds.), *Democracy and Corruption in Europe*, Pinter, London, 1967.

Jacques Derrida and Mustapha Tlili (eds.), *For Nelson Mandela*, Seaver Books, New York, 1987.

Susan de Villiers, *A People's Government: The People's Voice*, Parliamentary Support Programme, Cape Town, 2001.

C W du Toit, *Confession and Reconciliation: A Challenge to the Churches in South Africa*, Research Institute for Theology and Religion, University of South Africa, Pretoria, 1998.

Pieter Esterhuysen, *Africa A–Z: Continental and Country Profiles*, Africa Institute, Pretoria, 1998.

Maj Fiil-Fynn, *Electricity Crisis in Soweto*, Municipal Services Project Occasional Paper No. 4, Johannesburg 2001.

Francis Fukuyama, *Trust: The Social Virtues and the Creation of Prosperity*, Penguin, Harmondsworth, 1996.

Hermann Giliomee and Charles Simkins (eds.),

The Awkward Embrace: One-Party Domination and Democracy, Tafelberg, Cape Town, 1999.

Richard J Goldstone, *For Humanity: Reflections of a War Crimes Investigator*, Witwatersrand University Press, Johannesburg, 2000.

James Gregory, *Goodbye Bafana: Nelson Mandela, My Prisoner, My Friend*, Headline Book Publishing, London, 1995.

Keith Grint, *The Arts of Leadership*, Oxford University Press, Oxford, 2000.

Adrian Hadland and Jovial Rantao, *The Life and Times of Thabo Mbeki*, Zebra Press, Rivonia, 1999.

Albrecht Hagemann, *Nelson Mandela*, Fontein Books, Johannesburg, 1996.

Robin Hamilton, *South African Institute of Race Relations Social and Economic Update: Special Issue on AIDS*, Johannesburg, May 1991.

Nancy Harrison, *Winnie Mandela: Mother of a Nation*, Victor Gollancz, London, 1985.

Ronald Harwood, *Mandela*, Channel 4 Books, London, 1987.

R Hengeveld and Jo Rodenburg, *Embargo: Apartheid's Oil Secrets Revealed*, Shipping Research Bureau, Amsterdam University Press, Amsterdam, 1995.

Samuel P Huntington, *The Third Wave: Democratization in the Late Twentieth Century*, University of Oklahoma Press, Norman, 1991.

Libby Husemeyer, *Watchdogs or Hypocrites: The Amazing Debate on South African Liberals and Liberalism*, Friedrich-Naumann-Stiftung, Johannesburg, 1997.

Rupert Isaacson, *The Healing Land: A Kalahari Journey*, Fourth Estate, London, 2001.

Wilmot James and Moira Levy (eds.), *Pulse: Passages in Democracy-building: Assessing South Africa's Transition*, IDASA, Cape Town, 1998.

Wilmot James and Linda van de Vijver (eds.), *After the TRC: Reflections on Truth and Reconciliation in South Africa*, David Philip, Cape Town, 2000.

Anthea Jeffery, *The Truth about the Truth Commission*, South African Institute of Race Relations, Johannesburg, 1999.

Sheridan Johns and R Hunt Davis, *Mandela, Tambo and the African National Congress,* Oxford University Press, New York, 1991.

R W Johnson and Lawrence Schlemmer, *Launching Democracy in South Africa: The First Open Election*, Yale University Press, New Haven, 1996.

R W Johnson and David Welsh, *Ironic Victory:*

Liberalism in Post-Apartheid South Africa, Oxford University Press, Cape Town, 1998.

Robert W July, *An African Voice: The Role of the Humanities in African Independence*, Duke University Press, Durham, 1987.

John Kane-Berman, *Soweto: Black Revolt, White Reaction*, Ravan Press, Johannesburg, 1978.

Alf Khumalo and Es'kia Mphahlele, *Mandela: Echoes of an Era*, Penguin Books, Harmondsworth, 1990.

Bert Klandermans, Marlene Roefs and Johan Olivier, *The State of the People: Citizens, Civil Society and Governance in South Africa, 1994–2000*, Human Sciences Research Council, Pretoria, 2001.

Robert Klitgaard, *Controlling Corruption*, University of California Press, Berkeley, 1988.

Antjie Krog, *Country of My Skull*, Jonathan Cape, London, 1998.

Victor Levine, *Political Corruption: The Ghana Case*, Stanford University Press, Stanford, 1975.

Tom Lodge, *Consolidating Democracy: South Africa's Second Popular Election*, Witwatersrand University Press, Johannesburg, 1999.

Shaun Mackay and Malachia Mathotho, *Worker Power: The Congress of South African Trade Unions and its Impact on Governance and Democracy*, Centre for Policy Studies, Research report 79, Johannesburg, 2001.

Ernest Maganya and Rachel Houghton (eds.), *Transformation in South Africa? Policy Debates in the 1990s*, Institute for African Alternatives, Johannesburg, 1992.

Eddy Maloka and Elizabeth le Roux (eds.), *Problematising the African Renaissance*, Africa Institute, Pretoria, 2000.

Nelson Mandela, *No Easy Walk to Freedom*, Heinemann, London, 1973.

Nelson Mandela, *Long Walk to Freedom*, Abacus, London, 1995.

Hein Marais, *South Africa: Limits to Change: The Political Economy of Transition*, Zed Books, London, 2001.

Gerhard Maré and Georgina Hamilton, *An Appetite for Power: Buthelezi's Inkatha and the Politics of 'Loyal Resistance'*, Ravan Press, Johannesburg, 1987.

Malachia Mathoho and Tobias Schmitz, *Poverty, Civil Society and Patronage: A Study of Two Farmers' Associations in the Northern Province*, Centre for Policy Studies, Research report no. 80, Johannesburg, 2001.

Ali Mazrui (ed.), *Violence and Thought: Essays in Social Tensions in Africa*, Heinemann, London, 1969.

Govan Mbeki, *Learning from Robben Island*, David Philip, Cape Town, 1991.

Dale T McKinley, *The ANC and the Liberation Struggle*, Pluto Press, London, 1997.

Fatima Meer, *Higher than Hope: Rolihlahla We Love You*, Skotaville Publishers, Johannesburg, 1988.

Fatima Meer, *Higher than Hope: The Authorised Biography of Nelson Mandela*, Harper and Row, New York, 1990.

Jonathan Michie and Vishnu Padayachee, *The Political Economy of South Africa's Transition*, The Dryden Press, London, 1997.

Greg Mills, *The Wired Model: South Africa, Foreign Policy and Globalisation*, Tafelberg, Cape Town, 2000.

Anthony Minnaar, Ian Liebenberg and Charl Schutte, *The Hidden Hand: Covert Operations in South Africa*, HSRC, Pretoria, 1994.

Valerie Møller and Helga Dickow, *Five Years into Democracy: Elite and Rank and File Perspectives on the Quality of Life and the Rainbow Nation*, Institut Français d'Afrique du Sud, Johannesburg, 2001.

T Dunbar Moodie, *The Rise of Afrikanerdom: Power, Apartheid, and the Afrikaner Civil Religion*, University of California Press, Berkeley, 1975.

Jonathan Moyo, *Generational Shifts in African Politics. Prospects for a New Africa*, African Association of Political Scientists, Occasional Paper, 2 3, Harare, 1998.

Yoweri Museveni, *What is Africa's Problem?*, NRM Publications, Kampala, 1992.

Credo Mutwa, *Let Not My Country Die*, United Publishers International, Pretoria, 1986.

Jordan Ngubane, *Ushaba: A Zulu Umlando*, Three Continents Press, Washington, 1975.

Mark Orkin, *The Struggle and the Future: What Black South Africans Really Think*, Ravan Press, Johannesburg, 1986.

Rob Nixon, *Homelands, Harlem and Hollywood: South African Culture and the World Beyond*, Routledge, London, 1994

Deborah Posel and Graham Simpson (eds.), *The South African Truth and Reconciliation Commission: Commissioning the Past*, Witwatersrand University Press, Johannesburg, 2001.

Adam Przeworski, *Democracy and the Market: Political and Economic Reforms in Eastern Europe and Latin America*, Cambridge University Press, Cambridge, 1991.

Robert Putnam, *Making Democracy Work: Civic Traditions in Modern Italy*, Princeton University Press, Princeton 1993.

E S Reddy, *Nelson Mandela: Symbol of Resistance and Hope for a Free South Africa*, Sterling Publishers, New Delhi, 1990.

Andrew Reynolds, *Electoral Systems and Democratization in Southern Africa*, Oxford University Press, New York, 1999.

Andrew Reynolds (ed.), *Election '99 South Africa: From Mandela to Mbeki*, David Philip, Cape Town, 1999.

Susan Rose-Ackerman, *Corruption and Government: Causes, Consequences and Reform*, Cambridge University Press, Cambridge, 1999.

Dietrich Rueschemeyer, Evelyne Huber Stephens and John D Stephens, *Capitalist Development and Democracy*, Polity Press, Oxford, 1992.

Alec Russell, *Big Men, Little People: Encounters in Africa*, Macmillan, London, 1999.

Isaac Saki Shabangu, *Madiba, The Folk Hero*, Lingua Franca Publishers, Giyani, 1995.

Lawrence Schlemmer, *The Buthelezi Commission*, Vol. 1, H and H Publications, Durban, 1982.

Jabu Sindane, *Democracy in African Societies and Ubuntu*, HSRC, Centre for Constitutional Analysis, Pretoria, n.d.

Theda Skocpol, *States and Social Revolutions*, Cambridge University Press, Cambridge, 1979.

Roger Southall (ed.), *Opposition and Democracy in South Africa*, Frank Cass, London, 2001.

Allister Sparks, *Tomorrow is Another Country*, Heinemann, London, 1995.

Raymond Suttner and Jeremy Cronin, *30 Years of the Freedom Charter*, Ravan Press, Johannesburg, 1986.

Thoahlane Thoahlane, *Black Renaissance: Papers from the Black Renaissance Convention*, Ravan Press, Johannesburg, 1974.

Desmond Tutu, *No Future without Forgiveness*, Random House, Johannesburg, 1999.

F Van Zyl Slabbert, *Tough Choices: Reflections of an Afrikaner African*, Tafelberg, Cape Town, 2000.

Albert Venter (ed.), *Government and Politics in the New South Africa*, second edition, Van Schaik, Pretoria, 2001.

Wilhelm Verwoerd and Mahlubi Chief Mabizela (eds.), *Truths Drawn in Jest: Commentary on the TRC through Cartoons*, David Philip, Cape Town, 2000.

Shaun Vorster, *Land Reform in Southern Africa: Conference Report*, Democratic Union of Africa, Cape Town, 2001.

Monica Wilson and Archie Mafeje, *Langa: A Study of Social Groups in an African Township*, Oxford University Press, Cape Town, 1963.

Richard Wilson, *The Politics of the Truth and Reconciliation Commission in South Africa*, Cambridge University Press, Cambridge, 2001.

Erik Olin Wright, *Class Counts*, Cambridge University Press, Cambridge, 1997.

Crawford Young and Thomas Turner, *The Rise and the Decline of the Zaïrean State*, University of Wisconsin Press, Madison, 1985.

David Yudelman, *The Emergence of Modern South Africa*, David Philip, Cape Town, 1983.

INDEX